Novell®
Open Enterprise Server
Administrator's Handbook
SUSE® LINUX® Edition

MIKE LATIMER
JEFFREY HARRIS

Novell
PRESS™
Novell.

Published by Pearson Education, Inc.
800 East 96th Street, Indianapolis, Indiana 46240 USA

Novell® Open Enterprise Server Administrator's Handbook, SUSE LINUX Edition

International Standard Book Number: 0-6723-2749-X

Library of Congress Catalog Card Number: 2004114198

Printed in the United States of America

First Printing: June 2005

08   07   06   4   3   2

Trademarks

Warning and Disclaimer

About Novell Press

Novell Press is the exclusive publisher of trade computer technology books that have been authorized by Novell, Inc. Novell Press books are written and reviewed by the world's leading authorities on Novell and related technologies, and are edited, produced, and distributed by the Que/Sams Publishing group of Pearson Education, the worldwide leader in integrated education and computer technology publishing. For more information on Novell Press and Novell Press books, please go to **www.novellpress.com**.

Special and Bulk Sales

Pearson offers excellent discounts on this book when ordered in quantity for bulk purchases or special sales. For more information, please contact

U.S. Corporate and Government Sales
1-800-382-3419
corpsales@pearsontechgroup.com

For sales outside of the U.S., please contact

International Sales
international@pearsoned.com

Program Manager
Darrin Vandenbos

Acquisitions Editor
Jenny Watson

Development Editor
Emmett Dulaney

Managing Editor
Charlotte Clapp

Senior Project Editor
Matthew Purcell

Copy Editor
Margaret Berson

Indexer
John Sleeva

Proofreader
Elizabeth Scott

Technical Editor
Dave Muhlestein

Publishing Coordinator
Vanessa Evans

Book Designer
Gary Adair

Page Layout
Brad Chinn

Table of Contents

About the Author

Mike Latimer has worked at Novell's support organization for ten years, including expert third-level support on GroupWise and eDirectory. Mike is one of the founding members of Novell's SUSE LINUX Server support team, and provides advanced Linux training within the Novell organization, including Linux Professional Institute (LPI) courses and Guru training for Novell's technical staff.

Jeffrey L. Harris, a ten-year veteran of Novell, has worked throughout the Novell organization, including stints in Novell Technical Services, Major Market Sales Operations, Technical/Product Marketing, and Contract Management. Mr. Harris has written books, articles, marketing collateral, and technical white papers on several products and technologies, including directories, network and Internet security, network protocols, and proxy caching. Mr. Harris has a B.S. in Computer Science and a Masters of Business Administration (MBA).

Dedication

For my family—Amy, Carly, Trace and Matthew—who I hope will still recognize me after all the hours spent apart.   —ML

For my family—Susan, Tyler, Rylee, Austin, and Joshua— without whom none of this would matter.   —JH

Acknowledgments

I must first thank Jeff Harris for asking me to participate in this collaboration project. Without his foundation work, this book would not have been possible.

I would also like to thank my co-workers on the Worldwide Support Linux team for their advice and support on this project. In particular, Dave Muhlestein, Ken Johnson, Scott Ivie, and Dell Harris all offered invaluable advice on this project.

—Mike Latimer

As is usually the case, this book wouldn't have been possible without the willing collaboration of many who provided information, support, and encouragement. My support group includes the following folks who lent their talent and resources along the way:

Ryan Taylor, Ron Warren, Scott Rhoades, Tim Boisvert, Eric Michelson, Denise Jewkes, Matt Ryan, and Jeff Fischer.

I would like to give a special thanks to my team of editors, who made this project much more enjoyable through their hard work.

—Jeff Harris

We Want to Hear from You!

As the reader of this book, *you* are our most important critic and commentator. We value your opinion and want to know what we're doing right, what we could do better, what topics you'd like to see us cover, and any other words of wisdom you're willing to pass our way.

You can email or write me directly to let me know what you did or didn't like about this book—as well as what we can do to make our books better.

Please note that I cannot help you with technical problems related to the topic of this book and that due to the high volume of mail I receive I may not be able to reply to every message.

When you write, please be sure to include this book's title and author as well as your name and email address or phone number. I will carefully review your comments and share them with the author and editors who worked on the book.

Email: feedback@novellpress.com

Mail: Mark Taber
Associate Publisher
Novell Press/Pearson Education
800 East 96th Street
Indianapolis, IN 46240 USA

Reader Services

For more information about this book or others from Novell Press, visit our Web site at www.novellpress.com. Type the ISBN or the title of a book in the Search field to find the page you're looking for.

Open Enterprise Server Overview

## CHAPTER 1

Introduction to Open Enterprise Server

Instant Access

Open Enterprise Server (OES) incorporates the best of both open source and enterprise network operating systems: NetWare 6.5, and SUSE Linux Enterprise Server 9 (SLES), with a common set of services, applications, and management tools. Not only does this provide value to customers, but it keeps them from being locked into a single-technology foundation.

Why Open Enterprise Server?

Novell's Open Enterprise Server (OES) is a secure, highly available information platform that provides powerful networking, communication, collaboration, and application services in an open environment. As network operating systems have become increasingly commoditized, Novell has recognized that the way to provide value to its customers is not to lock them into a single-technology foundation. To that end, OES incorporates the best of both open-source and enterprise network operating systems: NetWare 6.5, and SUSE Linux Enterprise Server 9 (SLES), with a common set of services, applications, and management tools.

With the release of OES, organizations can choose NetWare, SUSE Linux, or a combination of both platforms, as dictated by real business needs. Moreover, common management, directory, and upgrade utilities allow organizations to manage both platforms with a single set of tools, simplifying daily administration.

With OES, Novell demonstrates its commitment to its traditional NetWare customers while embracing the power and new opportunity represented by Linux and the Open Source movement.

What Is Open Enterprise Server?

OES lets you deploy any combination of NetWare-based and Linux-based technologies. Core OES components include

- The NetWare 6.5 Service Pack 3 operating system, and all related NetWare 6.5 services
- The SLES9 operating system, based on the Linux v2.6 kernel, and all SLES9–related services
- The latest Novell Nterprise Linux Services
- Common management tools that allow seamless coexistence and management of the two operating systems

Given that NetWare and Linux are very different operating systems, it's not surprising to find a certain amount of variation between the services available between the platforms. Novell, however, has done an admirable job of providing a common set of core services across both platforms, but there are still specific differences as to some of the services offered on each platform. Table 1.1 lists the major OES services and the platform on which they are offered. As you can see, the majority of services are available on both platforms, so organizations can pick their services and implement them on the platform that makes the most sense in their specific environment. This table also includes references to the part of this book in which each service is discussed.

TABLE 1.1
Platform Support for OES Services

OES SERVICE	OFFERED ON	COMMENTS
PART I: OPEN ENTERPRISE SERVER OVERVIEW		
iManager	Both	Web-based OES administration console.
Novell Remote Manager	Both	Web-based NetWare and Linux operating-system management console.
iMonitor	Both	Web-based eDirectory monitoring and maintenance console.
Novell Client	Both	Client utility used to access NetWare and Linux NCP services.

OES SERVICE	OFFERED ON	COMMENTS
PART I: OPEN ENTERPRISE SERVER OVERVIEW		
NetIdentity	Both	Provides transparent eDirectory authentication.
NetDrive Client	Both	File redirector used to map local drives without the full Novell Client.
NICI Client	Both	Novell International Cryptographic Infrastructure. Provides access to robust cryptographic and security features in eDirectory.
NMAS Client	Both	Novell Modular Authentication Service. Provides desktop support for a robust set of authentication and security methods.
Package Management	Linux	OES components managed via YaST.
ConsoleOne	NetWare	Java-based NetWare management console. Linux version is available for download.
Native File Access	NetWare	Provides connectivity to NetWare server resources for Windows, Apple, and UNIX clients. Linux provides this service through NFS and Samba.
PART II: OPEN ENTERPRISE SERVER INFRASTRUCTURE		
Novell eDirectory	Both	Comprehensive, LDAP-enabled directory services.
DNS/DHCP services	Both	Suite of IP address management utilities.
Nsure Identity Manager	Both	User provisioning services.
Novell Storage Services (NSS)	Both	Robust, journaling filesystem format.
Cluster support	Both	High availability and manageability of critical network resources.
Multiprocessor support	Both	Takes advantage of multiprocessor hardware with a threaded architecture that allows processes to run on multiple processors simultaneously.

TABLE 1.1
Continued

OES SERVICE	OFFERED ON	COMMENTS
PART II: OPEN ENTERPRISE SERVER INFRASTRUCTURE		
Console utilities	Both	Granular configuration and management options on both the NetWare and Linux consoles.
NICI	Both	Novell International Cryptographic Infrastructure. Foundation for robust cryptographic and security features in eDirectory.
NMAS	Both	Novell Modular Authentication Service. Provides desktop support for a robust set of authentication and security methods.
Open WBEM CIMOM	Linux	Web-based Linux management infrastructure.
Linux User Management	Linux	eDirectory-enabled Linux user management.
NCP Server	Linux	NetWare Core Protocol services available on Linux. Core component of NetWare.
Nsure Audit	NetWare	Centralized, cross-platform auditing service.
PART III: OPEN ENTERPRISE SERVER USER ACCESS		
iPrint	Both	Internet Printing Protocol (IPP) based printer management.
iFolder	Both	Individual, server-based file storage and synchronization service.
Storage Management Services (SMS)	Both	Advanced backup, restore, and data migration services.
iSCSI support	Both	IP-based SCSI storage network.
FTP Server	Both	File Transfer Protocol. Traditional method for accessing files on the Net.
NetStorage	Both	Secure file storage and Internet-based access.
Samba	Linux	Open source implementation of Microsoft SMB/CIFS protocol. NetWare provides this service via the Native File Access component.

OES SERVICE	OFFERED ON	COMMENTS
PART III: OPEN ENTERPRISE SERVER USER ACCESS		
DFS	NetWare	Distributed File System. eDirectory-based access to distributed NetWare file structure.
Nterprise Branch Office	NetWare	Secure, productivity-enhancing server offering centralized control of remote offices. Linux-based version is under development.
PART IV: OPEN ENTERPRISE SERVER WEB SERVICES		
Apache Web Server	Both	Extremely powerful and popular open source web server.
Tomcat Servlet Engine	Both	Web Application container used to provide Java Servlet and Java Server Page support in Apache Web Server.
Java Virtual Machine (JVM)	Both	Java interpreter used by OES web-based management consoles.
eGuide	Both	Web-based eDirectory query tool, typically used for directory-based white pages.
Virtual Office	Both	Web-based workgroup collaboration environment.
Quickfinder	Both	Website indexing server.
MySQL Database	Both	Open-source, structured query language (SQL) database.
OpenSSH	Both	Secure Shell server used for remote server access.
Perl and PHP	Both	Powerful scripting languages.

The remainder of this book will discuss each of the Linux-supported services noted in Table 1.1. Common administrative information for each service is provided, including installation, configuration, and ongoing maintenance and troubleshooting.

## CHAPTER 2

Installing OES for Linux

Instant Access

Preparing to Install

- Ensure that your server hardware meets the minimum requirements of OES Linux:

  - Server-class computer with Pentium II or AMD K7 450MHz processor (Pentium III, Pentium 4, AMD K8, or higher recommended)

  - 512MB of RAM (1GB recommended)

  - 2GB of available, unpartitioned hard disk space (10GB recommended; additional space may be required depending on OES component implementation)

  - 4X CD-ROM drive (48X recommended)

- Plan out the layout of your OES Linux filesystem, eDirectory tree, and network configuration prior to creating a new OES Linux environment.

- Prior to implementing OES for Linux on an existing SLES9 server, ensure that you have a full backup and verify that you can recover the data from it.

Configure Installation Source

- Use netInstall.sh to configure a network-based installation source. This script is available from the following URL:

http://www.novell.com/documentation/oes/script/netInstall.sh

- Export your installation source directory using a network protocol such as NFS, HTTP, or FTP.

Installing OES Linux

- To install a new SLES9 server with OES, insert the OES CD1 CD-ROM into your server's CD-ROM drive and reboot the server. Follow the subsequent installation prompts.

Upgrading SLES9 to OES

- Ensure that Linux authentication is set to use local files for authentication—rather than OpenLDAP-based LDAP authentication.

- Ensure that a static IP address and valid hostname and domain name (resolvable in DNS) are configured on the server.

- Begin the installation by inserting the OES CD1 CD-ROM into your server's CD-ROM drive, and then use YaST to begin the OES installation.

The OES Linux installation is a very straightforward process. Nevertheless, investing some time in planning will help ensure the installation will be as smooth as possible, and reduce the chances of repeating the process due to misunderstood requirements, such as network or eDirectory layout. This chapter will discuss these important preparation steps, which should be taken prior to the installation of OES Linux.

This chapter will also describe how to configure a network installation source to reduce the complexity of multiple installations, and increase the speed of the installation process. Finally, the installation process of OES Linux and the upgrade process of a SLES9 server to OES Linux are discussed.

Getting Ready for OES Linux

Whether you are building a new network with OES Linux or installing it into an existing network, there are certain preparations you should make so that the installation goes as smoothly as possible.

For those rare few of you creating a new network from the ground up, you have the opportunity to do all the little things that will make that network easier to manage down the road. Carefully consider your choices of cabling, addressing, naming schemes, access methods, and so forth. As the technical foundation of your network, these are very difficult to change midstream. Consider business factors such as potential company growth, mergers or acquisitions, reorganizations, and all the other business considerations of the twenty-first century. If you don't, your network might lack the flexibility necessary to adapt to strategic and structural changes in your organization.

Unfortunately, the results of all this planning will then have to be weighed against the realities of your budget. There will be inevitable compromises, but this type of advanced planning will make sure those compromises don't come back to haunt you when the network is running.

Server Hardware Planning

Consider the following as you prepare your server hardware for the OES Linux installation:

- *Processor speed*—The server must have an Intel Pentium II or AMD K7 processor or higher. Novell recommends Pentium III 700MHz or higher processors for multiprocessor servers.

- *CD-ROM drive*—The server must have an ISO9660-compatible CD-ROM drive. Novell also recommends using a bootable CD-ROM drive compatible with the El Torito specification for booting directly from the CD.

- *Server memory*—An OES Linux server must have a minimum of 512MB of system memory (RAM).

- *Types of storage adapters and devices*—The OES Linux installation routine will properly detect most storage adapters and devices, but you should be familiar with the brand and type of your server's storage controllers (SCSI board, IDE controller, and so on), as well as the brand, type, capacity, and other specifications of the storage devices (such as hard disks, CD-ROM/DVD drives, tape drives) attached to those controllers.

- *Size of hard disks*—OES Linux requires 2GB of unpartitioned space for a basic installation. Odds are that this disk space will seem awfully low if you plan on fully implementing OES Linux. Review your planned installation and ensure that the local disks or shared storage devices are sufficient.

- *Network adapters*—Know the type of network adapters installed in the server. This should not be necessary, but if the installation routine has trouble identifying your adapters, having this information handy can help resolve the problem quickly. Keep in mind that drivers for unsupported hardware may only be available directly from your third-party vendor. To locate certified hardware, go to http://www.novell.com/partnerguide/.

- *Display and input devices*—An SVGA or better video adapter and monitor along with a standard keyboard and mouse for direct console operation are recommended for use with OES Linux. However, with the powerful web-based administrative tools available with OES, it is possible to operate a "headless" server without any direct input or output devices.

- *Server name*—If you haven't already done so, you should define a naming convention for your network resources, and determine an appropriate name for this server within those conventions.

Remember that installing a new network operating system is a significant undertaking. All hardware configurations should be tested in a lab environment before introducing them to your production network.

Partition Planning

By default, the OES Linux installation will create two partitions on your local disks—one for the root filesystem and one for the swap partition. Depending on your configuration plans, you may want to customize this partitioning scheme.

If you decide to modify your OES Linux server's main filesystem partitioning, consider the following commonly partitioned directories:

- **/ (root) *directory*—**The / directory is the storage location for all core SUSE Linux system files and products. As such, it is absolutely critical that the filesystem holding your / directory not run out of space. You should plan a minimum of 2GB for the partition used for /. In order to have room for the many additional products and services available with OES Linux, you may want to increase this to as much as 10GB.

- **/var *directory*—**The /var directory is the storage location for variable length files, such as log file and databases—including eDirectory. By default, this directory is not partitioned out. However, if your system will be under a heavy load, or you expect a large eDirectory database, it may be a good idea to partition out /var. To help performance and isolate disk activity, you can also use a separate disk for this partition.

- **/opt *directory*—**The /opt directory is the primary storage location for OES component files. This directory structure does not normally consume a large amount of space, but third-party applications also often rely on this directory. If you are planning on adding additional products to your server, you may want to consider creating a partition for this directory.

- **/home *directory*—**The /home directory is the default storage location for all local users' home directories. If you are planning on using the Linux User Management (LUM) component, and allowing local logins to the OES Linux server, be sure to partition this directory out with enough space to meet your users' needs.

- *Swap partition*—The swap partition is a critical component of any Linux server. With OES Linux, the default size of your swap partition will be based on a percentage of the amount of RAM in your server. If the server will be under a heavy load, this default size may not be sufficient. Unfortunately, it is very difficult to determine exactly how much swap file space you might need. The general rule of thumb for swap file space is approximately twice the amount of RAM in the server. If you find this number insufficient, additional swap partitions or swap files can be created after installation.

- *Additional partitions and NSS volumes*—You will likely want to create additional storage locations beyond the default created during installation. These can either be Linux partitions or NSS volumes on local or remote disks. Each type of storage location can be mounted into the root filesystem and used for either network applications or data storage. NSS offers unique capabilities in this regard as NSS disk pools can span physical drives, and multiple volumes can reside inside each disk pool. To take advantage of these features, NSS pools and volumes must be created after the main OES Linux installation. Additional native Linux partitions can be created during the installation using the expert mode of the Disk Partitioner.

Remember that the root filesystem, mounted to /, should be reserved exclusively for system files and "nonvolatile" files that won't be changing a lot or growing significantly over time. Create as many other partitions or NSS pools and volumes as you need to support your applications and data, and avoid mixing it into your root filesystem.

eDirectory Planning

You have to supply some basic pieces of eDirectory information in order to complete the OES Linux installation:

NOTE

eDirectory design concepts are presented in Chapter 7, "Novell eDirectory Management." Additional eDirectory reference material is available in Appendix B, "eDirectory Reference Materials."

- *Tree name*—You need to know the name of the eDirectory tree into which the OES Linux server will be installed.

- *Server location within the eDirectory tree*—Prior to installing the server, make sure you are familiar with the organization of your eDirectory tree.

You need to specify the context within which the server will reside. This consists of the name of the Organization or Organizational Unit to which this server will belong.

- *Administrator name and password*—If you are installing the first server in a new tree, an Admin account will be created and you will specify the Admin password. If you are installing the server into an existing eDirectory tree, you will need to provide the name, including context, and password of the existing Admin user.

- *Server's time zone*—You need to specify the server's time zone and whether that time zone supports daylight savings time.

- *Time synchronization*—OES Linux relies on the Network Time Protocol (NTP) daemon to provide time synchronization services. If you are adding OES Linux to an existing Novell network, be sure all servers are configured properly for synchronization using the same NTP source, or through a time synchronization structure that ensures NTP synchronization to the OES Linux server. Time synchronization across all servers in your environment is crucial for proper operation of eDirectory.

OES Linux includes Novell eDirectory v8.7.3. In order to support this version of eDirectory in your existing network, make sure you apply the latest eDirectory Service Packs on your existing servers. You can get the latest eDirectory service packs from Novell at http://support.novell.com.

Network Preparation

Before you install OES Linux into an existing Novell NetWare network, there are a few things you should do to make sure the network is ready for the introduction of OES Linux. Novell includes Deployment Manager with NetWare to help identify and automate these tasks. Although this tool was designed for use with NetWare, the tasks performed through Deployment Manager are applicable to OES Linux.

Deployment Manager can be found as NWDEPLOY.EXE on the root of your NetWare or OES NetWare Operating System CDs. For information on using Deployment Manager, see the online OES NetWare documentation.

Installing OES Linux

Installing OES Linux is a straightforward process, but you should be familiar with several aspects of the installation prior to beginning the process. When you know what to expect, you can begin the process of installing a new server or upgrading an existing server to OES.

The following topics are contained in this section:

- Preparing to install OES Linux
- Installing a new OES Linux server
- Upgrading SLES9 to OES Linux

Preparing to Install OES Linux

Before beginning the OES Linux installation, it is a good idea to double-check the installation prerequisites. This section contains the official prerequisites of an OES Linux server.

It is also important to understand the OES Linux installation patterns. These patterns determine what OES components are installed by default. If necessary, each pattern can be customized to address specific needs.

Finally, creating a network-based installation source is an efficient way to perform multiple installations, or just maintain the installation without relying on the CD media.

When you fully understand these topics, you'll be ready to begin the actual OES Linux installation.

INSTALLATION PREREQUISITES

Before attempting to install OES for Linux, review the following minimum hardware prerequisites list to ensure that your server meets these requirements:

- Server-class computer with Pentium II or AMD K7 450MHz processor (Pentium III, Pentium 4, AMD K8 or higher recommended)
- 512MB of RAM (1GB recommended)
- 2GB of available, unpartitioned hard disk space (10GB recommended; additional space may be required depending on OES component implementation)
- 4X CD-ROM drive (48X recommended)

Keep in mind that these requirements are specifically referring to the minimum hardware requirements and may not be sufficient for your needs. It is obviously a good idea to use the best hardware available to you, and plan for increased server use in the future.

INSTALLATION PATTERNS

New installations of OES allow you to perform the installation based on one of several different patterns. The installation screen providing these choices is seen

15

in Figure 2.1. Depending on the pattern you choose, one or more of the pre-configured OES Linux software categories are installed. After you select a pattern, additional software can be installed through a Detailed Selection option.

FIGURE 2.1
OES Linux installation patterns.

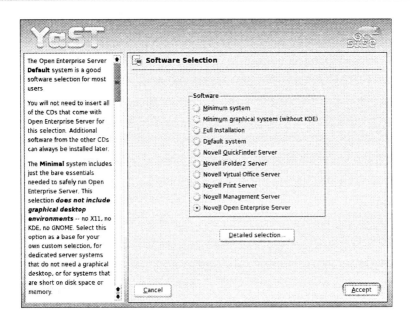

The patterns available for installation, and their description, are as follows:

- *Minimum System*—Installs the bare minimum required for a SLES9 server. With this pattern, the following software categories are installed:
  - Basis Runtime System
  - YaST
- *Minimum Graphical System (without KDE)*—This performs the same type of installation as a Minimum System, but also adds the X server and FVWM graphical environment. With this pattern, the following software categories are installed:
  - Basis Runtime System
  - YaST
  - Graphical Base System

- *Full Installation*—This performs a complete installation of SLES9 and includes all standard software categories. This pattern does not install any Novell OES components, but all non-OES categories of software are installed.

- *Default System*—This performs a default installation of SLES9. This pattern does not install any Novell OES Components. The following software categories are installed:

  - Basis Runtime System

  - Basis Sound Libraries and Tools

  - Graphical Base System

  - KDE Desktop Environment

  - YaST

  - Linux Tools

  - Authentication Server (NIS, LDAP, Kerberos)

  - Print Server (CUPS)

  - Help & Support Documentation

- *Novell QuickFinder Server*—This performs an installation of a dedicated QuickFinder server. The following software categories are installed:

  - Basis Runtime System

  - YaST

  - Novell QuickFinder

- *Novell iFolder2 Server*—This performs an installation of a dedicated iFolder server. The following software categories are installed:

  - Basis Runtime System

  - YaST

  - Novell iFolder 2.x

- *Novell Virtual Office Server*—This installs a server configured to provide access to Virtual Office. The following software categories are installed:

  - Basis Runtime System

  - YaST

  - Novell eDirectory

  - Novell eGuide

  - Novell Linux User Management

  - Novell iPrint

- Novell iManager
- Novell QuickFinder
- Novell Virtual Office
- Novell NetStorage
- *Novell Print Server*—This installs a server configured for offering iPrint services. With this pattern, the following software categories are installed:
  - Basis Runtime System
  - YaST
  - Novell eDirectory
  - Novell Linux User Management
  - Novell iPrint
  - Novell iManager
- *Novell Management Server*—This installs a server with the primary management tool for OES—iManager. No graphical environment is installed with this pattern, so management must be performed from a browser running on a local workstation. The following software categories are installed with this pattern:
  - Basis Runtime System
  - YaST
  - Novell iManager
- *Novell Open Enterprise Server*—This installs a default Open Enterprise Server. This does not install every OES component. The following software categories are installed:
  - Basis Runtime System
  - Basis Sound Libraries and Tools
  - Graphical Base System
  - KDE Desktop Environment
  - YaST
  - Linux Tools
  - Authentication Server (NIS, LDAP, Kerberos)
  - Help & Support Documentation
  - Novell eDirectory
  - Novell eGuide

- Novell Linux User Management
- Novell iPrint
- Novell iManager
- Novell QuickFinder
- Novell Virtual Office
- Novell Samba Configuration
- Novell Health Monitoring
- Novell Backup Services (SMS)

CONFIGURING INSTALLATION SOURCES

Although it is possible to install OES Linux directly from the CD media, there are many reasons why you might want to consider creating a network-based installation source. For example, you might want to install multiple OES Linux servers, or you may just want to perform an installation without having to watch the install and swap CDs occasionally. Regardless of the reason, creating a network-based installation source is easy and definitely recommended for ease of installation.

Creating a network-based installation source only requires a SUSE Linux server and enough disk space to hold the contents of the OES Linux CDs. If you meet these requirements, complete the following steps to create your installation source:

1. Download the `netInstall.sh` script from the Novell documentation site at the following URL:

   http://www.novell.com/documentation/oes/script/netInstall.sh

2. From your SUSE Linux machine, execute `netInstall.sh` and provide the following information:

   - *Installation Directory*—This is the directory you would like the installation source to be created in. There should be sufficient space at this location to hold the contents of all the OES Linux CDs.

   - *ISO Image Location*—This is the directory in which ISO images for OES Linux can be located.

   At the conclusion of the `netInstall.sh` script, your installation source should be complete. At this point, the server needs to be configured to make the installation source available over NFS.

NOTE

You can also provide an installation source over FTP and HTTP. For information on this configuration, see the online OES documentation.

3. On your installation server, edit `/etc/exports` using a text editor and add an entry for your installation source directory as follows:

   `<Full_Path_To_Install_Source>    *(ro,root_squash,sync)`

4. Restart your NFS server using `/etc/rcnfsserver restart`.

If you only have ISO images of OES Linux, be sure to burn a copy of CD1. This CD will be used to boot the new OES Linux server and initiate access to the network-based installation source.

Installing a New OES Linux Server

After you have gathered all the information you need and made the necessary decisions with regard to installation and configuration, you are ready to perform the OES Linux installation.

This section explains how to install a new server. If you are adding OES to an existing SLES9 server, skip to "Upgrading SLES9 to OES Linux" later in this chapter.

There are three main steps to the OES Linux installation:

- Configure primary installation options
- Create filesystem and copy files
- Configure OES components

The first step is required to configure the entire server installation process. It is this step that allows the disk partitions to be created, software selection to be made, and general installation options to be configured.

The second step is an automated step that actually installs the requested software. If this is a CD-based installation, you will be required to swap disks when prompted. Network-based installations do not require any type of administration during this phase.

The final step takes place after the software has been installed and the server is rebooted. Upon startup, the installation process will resume and prompt for information such as the root user's password, network configuration, and final hardware configuration. This stage also performs your OES component configuration. At the conclusion of this step, your OES Linux server is ready for use!

After you have gathered all the information you need and made the necessary decisions with regards to installation and configuration, you are ready to perform the OES Linux installation.

CONFIGURE PRIMARY INSTALLATION OPTIONS

To begin the installation, you will use the bootable, OES Linux CD1 to boot your new OES Linux server. To begin the installation process, follow these steps:

1. Boot the server with the OES Linux installation CD (CD 1).

2. After the CD has booted, you will be presented with a GRand Unified Bootloader (GRUB) prompt (shown in Figure 2.2).

FIGURE 2.2
GRUB boot menu.

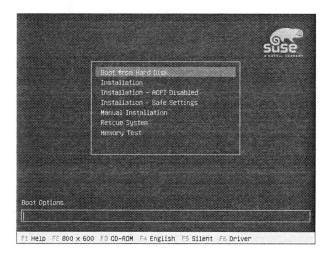

The GRUB menu provides the following startup options:

- *Boot from Hard Disk*—This option will exit the GRUB menu and attempt to boot from the first hard disk.

- *Installation*—This will begin the installation process.

- *Installation - ACPI Disabled*—If necessary, this option can be used to begin the installation process with Advanced Configuration and Power Interface (ACPI) disabled. This is useful if the normal installation option is failing due to ACPI settings on your server.

- *Installation - Safe Settings*—If necessary, this option can be used to begin the installation process using safe settings. Safe settings disables DMA mode for the CD-ROM device, and power management functions.

- *Manual Installation*—This option can be used to begin a manual installation process. This may be necessary to customize the device drivers being loaded, or provide advanced settings to the installation routine.

- *Rescue System*—If you are unable to boot your OES Linux server, this option will invoke a rescue mode version of Linux running off the installation CD-ROM. After bootup, you are presented with a command shell where manual repairs to the installed system can be performed. Automated repairs are available through the normal installation routine.

- *Memory Test*—This option automatically loads Memtest-86 and performs memory read and write procedures in a continuous loop. This is used to locate defective RAM. If you suspect defective RAM, run this routine for several hours. If no problems are detected, your RAM is most likely intact.

In addition to the standard menu selections, there are a number of additional options that can be used to begin a network-based installation, configure a remote VNC-based installation, or configure specific installation parameters. For information on these options, refer to the following description of each main GRUB option:

- *Boot Options*—This field is used to enter options that are passed to the Linux kernel used during the installation process. One way this field is commonly used is to enable a remote installation over VNC. To enable this type of installation, enter the following options in this field:

  `vnc=1 vncpassword=<PASSWORD>`

This causes a VNC server to be spawned during the installation process. When the server is running, a message is displayed on the server console containing instructions on accessing the installation over VNC.

NOTE

If you are performing a remote installation over VNC, also use the `ipaddress=X` `netmask=X` and `gateway=X` parameters to enable your static network from the beginning. This is necessary to configure OES components later in the installation.

In addition to VNC configuration, many other Linux kernel options can be passed using this field. For information on these options, see the online OES Linux or SLES documentation.

- *F1 Help*—This invokes the GRUB help screen. Use this option immediately after selecting one of the other function-key options for help on that specific topic.

- *F2 800×600*—If you are encountering graphical problems during the OES Linux installation, use this option to select an appropriate screen resolution.

- *F3 CD-ROM*—This option is used to select between a CD-ROM-based installation and one of several alternate installation methods. Depending on the option selected, you will be prompted to provide the information required to perform that type of installation. Possible installation options are

  CD-ROM

  SLP

  FTP

  HTTP

  NFS

  SMB

  Hard Disk

- *F4 English*—This option can be used to change the language used on the GRUB screen.

- *F5 Silent*—This option is used to adjust the log level during the startup of the installation program. If problems are encountered starting the installation, set this option to Native.

- *F6 Driver*—If you are using hardware that requires drivers that do not ship with OES Linux, use this option to load those drivers prior to beginning the installation process.

After configuring any installation options, parameters or installation sources, select Installation and press Enter.

3. Read through the license agreement. (The English agreement can be found near the bottom of the page.) When finished, select I Agree to begin the installation.

4. Select the appropriate language for the installation and click Accept.

5. Select the type of installation being performed from the following list. After deciding on an installation type, click OK to continue.

■ *New Installation*—This will begin a new installation of OES Linux using default settings that will overwrite any existing operating system already on the disk.

■ *Update an Existing System*—This option can be used to update an installed version of Linux to OES Linux. This will attempt to preserve configuration settings from the installation of Linux being upgraded.

■ *Repair Installed System*—This option can be used to repair a damaged OES Linux installation.

■ *Boot Installed System*—This option will attempt to boot the Linux distribution that is currently installed on the local hard disk. This is useful if the Master Boot Record (MBR) or Bootloader has been damaged, and the installation will not boot automatically.

■ *Abort Installation*—This option can be used to abandon the installation process without writing data to the hard disk.

6. The Installation Settings page, shown in Figure 2.3, is now displayed. This is the main configuration page, which allows you to determine general options for the OES Linux install process.

FIGURE 2.3
Installation Settings page.

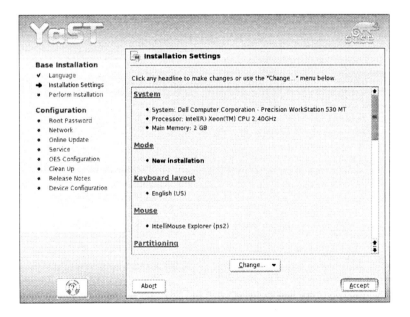

- *System*—This option invokes the hardware detection process, which scans for all devices attached to the server. At the conclusion of the scan, you have the option to review the scan results, and save those results to a file.

- *Mode*—This provides access to the initial list of possible installation types: New Installation, Update an Existing Installation, Repair Installation, and Boot Installed System.

- *Keyboard Layout*—This option is used to select and test an appropriate keyboard layout.

- *Mouse*—This option is used to select and test the mouse configuration to ensure that the correct driver is in use.

- *Partitioning*—This option invokes the YaST Partitioner, which is used to create and modify your disk partitioning scheme. The default partition configuration is based largely on the type of installation you are performing (New Install or Update). The default partitioning can be used as a base for further customizing, or the default recommendations can be ignored and partitioning can be manually defined.

- *Software*—This option is used to configure which SLES and OES Linux components will be installed on the new server. Upon selecting this option, you are presented with the Software Selection window, which is used to select an installation pattern for the server. Possible installation patterns were explained earlier in this chapter.

Although there are a wide variety of installation patterns available, it is possible that one matching your requirements does not exist. In this case, select the Detailed Selection option to customize your installation. The Detailed Selection option invokes the YaST Install and Remove Software module, as shown in Figure 2.4.

From this module, it is possible to select OES Linux components, such as Novell Virtual Office, or individual software packages, such as NOVLice, or `findutils-locate`. To select OES components, ensure that the Filter drop-down box is set to Selections. To locate specific software packages, change the Filter to Search and use the resulting dialog to locate the desired software.

After customizing your installation, select Accept to finalize the installation choices. Prior to accepting the changes, software dependencies are checked. If additional software must be installed in addition to your selections, an informational dialog is displayed. Click Continue to accept the automatic changes, and return to the main Installation Settings page.

FIGURE 2.4

Detailed Software Selection—YaST Add and Remove Software.

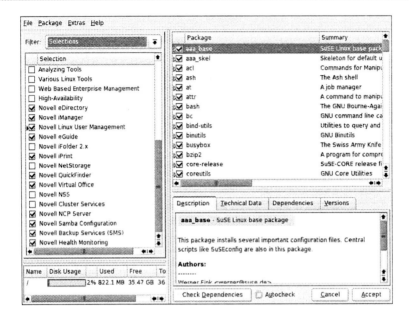

- *Booting*—This option is used to adjust the default configuration of the GRUB bootloader.

- *Time Zone*—This option is used to select the current time zone in which the server is located. The server's clock can also be adjusted and designated as using GMT or local time.

- *Language*—This option is used to adjust the default language of the OES Linux installation.

- *Default Runlevel*—This option is used to adjust the default runlevel of the server. Possible runlevel settings are

  2 Multiuser mode with limited network support

  3 Multiuser mode with full network support.

  5 Graphical, multiuser mode with full network support

  For more information on runlevels, see Chapter 6, "SUSE Linux Enterprise Server Management."

7. When satisfied with the configuration of your installation, click Accept.

8. Prior to beginning the installation, the YaST installation process will warn you that the installation process is about to begin. When prompted with this warning, select Yes, Install to begin the installation process.

At this point, the configuration of the installation process is complete, and the second stage of the install is begun. The second stage of install is responsible for performing the tasks configured in stage one.

CREATE FILESYSTEM AND COPY FILES

The second stage of the installation process requires no manual user intervention for network-based installations. Installations being performed via CD-ROM will require you to swap disks when prompted.

The following processes are completed during this phase:

1. The disk partitions are formatted with the filesystem you selected during the installation configuration.

2. When the filesystems exist, the file copy process can begin. This process will display a progress bar and estimated usage time remaining on the current installation disk. If you are performing an installation using CD-ROM media, this phase will require you to swap the CDs.

3. At the end of the file copy process, the GRUB bootloader configuration is written to the disk. When this is complete, the system is rebooted to begin the final configuration phase.

At the conclusion of phase two, the final phase of installation is the configuration phase. This phase is used to customize the components that were installed on the server during phase two.

CONFIGURE OES COMPONENTS

After the server has performed the first reboot, the operating system is loaded off the root filesystem, and the final phase of the installation is automatically started. Among other things, this phase configures the OES components, so pay careful attention.

A number of steps need to be completed in the final phase of installation. First, on the root password configuration page, enter the password for the root, administrative user. After entering the password twice, click Next to continue.

Next, the Network Configuration page is used to adjust network settings, including the server's IP address, hostname, default gateway, and DNS information. OES Linux requires a static IP address that can be configured through these steps:

1. Select the Network Interfaces link.

2. If your device was automatically configured, select Change to adjust the networking parameters. If the device was not automatically configured, select your device in the available devices list and click Configure.

3. In the Network Cards Configuration Overview, select the appropriate device and click Edit. If no device is listed, select Add to manually add your card.

4. In the Network Address Setup page, shown in Figure 2.5, complete the following configuration options:

FIGURE 2.5
Network Address Setup options.

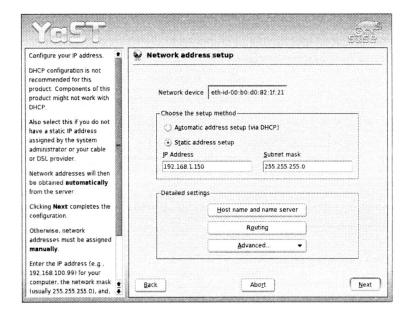

- *Setup Method*—In the Setup Method box, ensure that the Static Address Setup radio button is selected. After selecting this option, enter the IP Address and Subnet Mask for your OES Linux server.

- *Host Name and Name Server*—This option is used to configure the host name and domain name of your OES Linux server. Name resolution (local DNS client) is also configured through this option.

- *Routing*—Use this option to configure a default route on your OES Linux server.

5. When finished, click Next to save your network configuration.

When prompted to test your Internet connection and download the latest product updates, select No. This option can be performed after installation using Red-Carpet. Click Next to continue.

Complete the installation by following these steps:

1. At the Service Configuration screen, you have the option to configure your Certificate Authority (CA) and your OpenLDAP server. The CA password is defaulted to match the password specified for the root user. If you would like a higher level of security, it is recommended that you change this at this time. The OpenLDAP server should be left as disabled.

2. At the main Open Enterprise Server Configuration screen, you have the option of configuring the components now or later. It is typically best to configure the components now. If you are performing an installation over VNC, and did not specify a static IP address configuration, select to configure later and skip to step 9. Click Next to continue.

3. Select New Tree to install your OES Linux server into a new eDirectory tree. Select Existing Tree if you are adding this server to an existing eDirectory tree. Enter either the new or existing eDirectory tree name in the appropriate field and click Next.

4. If you selected to install a new eDirectory tree, enter the new, fully distinguished name of the admin user and a password for the user. If you are installing into an existing eDirectory tree, enter the current admin name and password, as well as the IP address of a server in the existing tree. Click Next to continue.

5. Enter the eDirectory context in which the new server will be installed. Also make any necessary changes to port assignments and click Next.

6. Enter the IP address of the Network Time Protocol (NTP) server you are using for time synchronization. This should be the time source used to synchronize both NetWare and Linux servers if in a mixed environment.

   SLP is also configured on this screen. SLP is required for eDirectory trees consisting of more than three servers. If you are unsure of how to configure SLP, see the online OES documentation.

7. The eDirectory configuration is written to the disk and the eDirectory daemon is started; this step may take some time.

8. When the eDirectory daemon has started, you are presented with a list of all OES components selected for installation (shown in Figure 2.6).

FIGURE 2.6

OES component configuration settings.

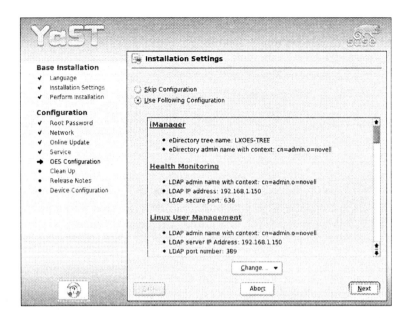

From this main OES Component screen, each OES component can be configured. To configure an OES component, select the desired component name. This will invoke a dialog box specific to the component and similar to the one shown in Figure 2.7.

Each OES component has a specific list of requirements that may need to be configured. Table 2.1 shows the requirements for each component.

TABLE 2.1

OES Component Configuration Options

OES COMPONENT	CONFIGURATION OPTIONS	NOTES
iManager	eDirectory Tree Admin name with Context	These parameters should be configured automatically and do not normally need adjustment.
Health Monitoring	Directory Server Address Admin name with Context Admin Password	This component requires an LDAP connection to a local or remote eDirectory tree.

OES COMPONENT	CONFIGURATION OPTIONS	NOTES
		The default configuration uses an LDAP connection to the eDirectory tree on the local server.

Linux User Management	Directory Server Address Admin name with Context Admin Password Linux/Unix Config Object LUM Workstation Context (Optional) Proxy user name with context (Optional) Proxy user password PAM-enabled services to integrate with eDirectory	This component requires an LDAP connection to a local or remote eDirectory tree. The default configuration uses an LDAP connection to the eDirectory tree on the local server. In addition to the LDAP configuration, a LUM configuration object, and location for users must be configured. The following PAM-enabled services can be configured for use with LUM:
		
		`login` `rlogin`
		`ftp` `passwd`
		`sshd` `xdm`
		`su` `openwbem`
		`rsh`

eGuide	Directory Server Address Admin name with Context Admin Password	This component requires an LDAP connection to a local or remote eDirectory tree. The default configuration uses an LDAP connection to the eDirectory tree on the local server.
Novell Samba	Directory Server Address Admin name with Context Admin Password LDAP server Host IP address Base Context for Samba Users eDirectory Tree name Proxy user name with context Proxy user password	This component requires an LDAP connection to a local or remote eDirectory tree. The default configuration uses an LDAP connection to the eDirectory tree on the local server. Samba also requires additional information such as the LDAP server used for client authentication, and the location of Samba users in the eDirectory tree.

TABLE 2.1
Continued

OES COMPONENT	CONFIGURATION OPTIONS	NOTES
iPrint	Directory Server Address Admin name with Context Admin Password iPrint eDirectory Tree Name	This component requires an LDAP connection to a local or remote eDirectory tree. The default configuration uses an LDAP connection to the eDirectory tree on the local server. iPrint also requires the name of the eDirectory tree.
Novell Storage Services (NSS)	Directory Server Address Admin name with Context Admin Password NSS Unique Admin Object	This component requires an LDAP connection to a local or remote eDirectory tree. The default configuration uses an LDAP connection to the eDirectory tree on the local server. The NSS Unique Admin Object is a user in eDirectory who should have administrative rights to NSS.
NetStorage	Directory Server Address Admin name with Context Admin Password (Optional) iFolder 2 Server Address Authentication Domain Host Proxy user name with context Proxy user password User context	This component requires an LDAP connection to a local or remote eDirectory tree. The default configuration uses an LDAP connection to the eDirectory tree on the local server. If NetStorage is to be integrated with iFolder, enter the iFolder 2 server address. The authentication domain host, proxy user name and password, and location in eDirectory for your NetStorage users are also required.
QuickFinder	LUM Enable Admin User QuickFinder Admin name QuickFinder Admin Password	You have the option of using a LUM-enabled user or local user account for administering QuickFinder.

OES COMPONENT	CONFIGURATION OPTIONS	NOTES
	Add nov1www user to shadow group Admin name with Context Admin Password	If local user accounts will also be used with QuickFinder, you must select to add the nov1www user to the shadow group. The eDirectory admin name and password are also required for this component.
Virtual Office	Directory Server Address Admin name with Context Admin Password Virtual Office server address or DNS Hostname User Context	This component requires an LDAP connection to a local or remote eDirectory tree. The default configuration uses an LDAP connection to the eDirectory tree on the local server. The Virtual Office server address and context in eDirectory for Virtual Office users are also required.
Novell Cluster Services (NCS)	Directory Server Address Admin name with Context Admin Password Cluster fully distinguished name Cluster IP Address (Optional) Device for SBD partition	This component requires an LDAP connection to a local or remote eDirectory tree. The default configuration uses an LDAP connection to the eDirectory tree on the local server. NCS can be configured at a later date (after configuring hardware components such as a SAN). If you choose to configure NCS now, you can connect the server to an existing cluster or create a new cluster. New clusters require the name of the cluster and an IP address for the cluster. The device for the SBD partition is optional, but should be specified when creating new clusters.

TABLE 2.1
Continued

OES COMPONENT	CONFIGURATION OPTIONS	NOTES
NCP Server	Admin name with Context Admin Password	The NCP Server is a component of eDirectory and does not normally require modification.
Storage Management Services (SMS)	Directory Server Address Admin name with Context Admin Password	This component requires an LDAP connection to a local or remote eDirectory tree. The default configuration uses an LDAP connection to the eDirectory tree on the local server.
iFolder 2.x	Directory Server Address Admin name with Context Admin Password iFolder 2.x Server IP Address iFolder 2.x Server Netmask iFolder 2.x Server DNS Hostname iFolder 2.x user data path iFolder 2.x admin users	This component requires an LDAP connection to a local or remote eDirectory tree. The default configuration uses an LDAP connection to the eDirectory tree on the local server. If iFolder will be the only web application on the server, specify the path to the user data. If iFolder will be running alongside other web applications, iFolder must have a dedicated IP address. Specify the dedicated IP address, netmask, and DNS hostname in addition to the path to user data.

9. After the configuration of your OES components, the SuSEconfig process is used to update local configuration files.

10. Following SuSEconfig, Novell Open Enterprise Server Release Notes are displayed. Be sure to review this document for last-minute notices regarding OES. After installation, the release notes can be found in the /usr/share/doc/release-notes directory. When finished, click Next to continue.

FIGURE 2.7
Health Monitoring LDAP configuration.

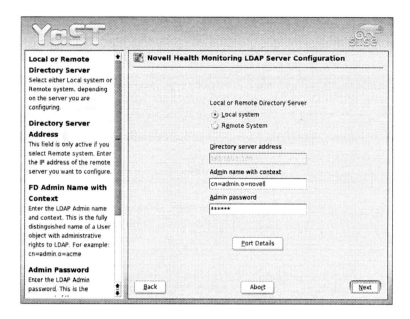

11. At the Hardware Configuration screen you have the option to configure video and sound. If you are performing a VNC-based installation, video can only be configured after installation using **sax2** at the server console. Make any necessary changes on this screen, and then click Next.

12. The Installation Completed page provides basic information about getting started with OES. After reviewing this page, click Finish to exit the installation program.

Your OES Linux server is now fully installed and ready for use. To begin further customizing of OES, access the OES Linux home page at the following URL:

http://<Server_IP_Address_or_DNS_Name>

Upgrading SLES9 to OES Linux

In addition to installing a new OES Linux server, it is possible to upgrade an existing SLES9 server to OES. In order to upgrade a SLES9 server, that server must first meet the following requirements:

- The server must be configured with a static IP address.
- The server name must be properly registered in DNS.
- A server certificate must exist for this server, and this certificate must be exported as a "common server certificate."
- No LDAP daemons can be running on the server. These daemons will conflict with eDirectory and must be disabled.

If the SLES9 server meets these prerequisites, review the "Getting Ready for OES Linux" section earlier in this chapter, and then perform the upgrade to OES by following these steps:

1. Insert the Open Enterprise Server CD1 in the server's CD-ROM drive and restart the server.

2. Begin the OES installation by selecting an installation method as documented in step 2 of the "Installing a New OES Linux Server" section earlier in this chapter.

3. Read through the license agreement. (The English agreement can be found near the bottom of the page.) When finished, select I Agree to begin the installation.

4. Select the appropriate language for the installation and click Accept.

5. Select Update an Existing System as the type of installation, and then click OK to continue.

6. Select the Update Options category to customize the upgrade process to OES Linux.

7. Select the radio option labeled "Update with Installation of New Software and Features Based on the Selection."

8. At this point, you have the option of selecting one of the previously described OES installation patterns. Select the desired pattern, such as Novell Open Enterprise Server, then click Accept.

9. If prompted for confirmation to reset your detailed selection, select Yes.

10. Click Accept to begin the upgrade process.

11. Click Yes, Update to acknowledge the warning and begin the file copy process. If you are performing a network-based installation, no intervention is required during the file copy. If you are installing from CD, you will be required to swap CDs when prompted.

12. At the conclusion of the file copy process, the server will reboot. When the server restarts, the YaST installation process will resume.

13. Select No to skip the network connectivity test, and then click Next.

14. After the `SuSEconfig` process has completed writing the system configuration, click Next after reviewing the release notes and then Finish to exit the upgrade process. After the server has switched to the configured run-level, OES component customization can be performed through YaST.

Common Post-Installation Tasks for OES Linux

After the installation of OES Linux has been completed, there are a number of tasks you are likely anxious to perform. The majority of these tasks are documented in the relevant chapters of this book. However, there are a few basic tasks that are appropriate to mention here.

The following topics are contained in this section:

- Verifying your OES Linux installation
- Post-install OES component configuration
- Updating OES Linux components using Red-Carpet

Verifying Your OES Linux Installation

Depending on the OES components you selected for installation, there are a number of methods you can use to confirm that the installation was successful. The easiest way to confirm that your OES components are properly configured and started is by accessing the OES Linux Welcome pages.

To access the Welcome pages, use a browser to access the following URL:

http://<OES_Linux_Server_IP_Address_Or_DNS_Name>

If your OES installation was successful, you should see the Welcome pages as shown in Figure 2.8.

At this point, you can follow the iManager 2.5.x link to begin customizing your eDirectory environment.

For further confirmation that your OES components have been successfully installed, use the Add and Remove Software module of YaST to ensure that the OES components are marked as being installed.

FIGURE 2.8

OES component Welcome pages.

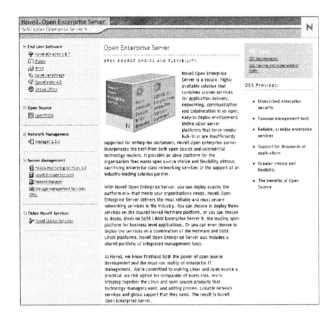

Post-Install OES Component Configuration

During the installation of OES, the configuration of each individual OES component can be modified. It is also possible to access those same component configuration pages after installation. These pages are available through component-specific modules in YaST.

YaST can be accessed from a terminal or from within the graphical environment. To access YaST from a terminal, execute **yast**. To access YaST from a graphical environment, execute **yast2** or use the YaST launcher from the application menu.

YaST is divided into the following seven general categories:

- Software
- Hardware
- System
- Network Devices

- Network Services
- Security and Users
- Misc

Beneath each category there are modules used to configure specific components of OES Linux. Many of these modules are used to configure traditional SLES components, such as the system language and date and time. However, OES-specific component administration can also be performed through YaST. Table 2.2 lists the location of these OES-specific modules.

TABLE 2.2
OES COMPONENT MODULES IN YAST

YAST CATEGORY	OES COMPONENT
System	Novell Storage Services (NSS)
	Novell Cluster Services (NCS)
	Storage Management Services (SMS)
Network Services	NCP Server
	NetStorage
	Novell Health Monitoring
	Novell QuickFinder
	Novell Samba
	Virtual Office
	eDirectory
	eGuide
	iFolder 2.x
	iManager
	iPrint
Security and Users	Linux User Management

For more information on using these modules, check the Table of Contents in this book, or refer to the online OES documentation.

Updating OES Linux Components Using Red-Carpet

After completing the installation of OES Linux, it is a good idea to check for OES updates using the OES online update tool—Red-Carpet.

Red-Carpet, or the companion terminal-based **rug**, can be accessed from the Software category of YaST. From within this category, the Online Update module can be used to begin the update process. If this is the first time you have performed an online update, you will be required to register your server using your Novell ID and Password, which you should have received when you purchased this product.

After activation, you should be able to easily select available OES patches and apply those to your new server. For a more detailed explanation of this process, please see the "Updating OES Linux" section of Chapter 6.

## CHAPTER 3

Working with SUSE Linux Enterprise Server 9

Instant Access

Working with SUSE Linux Enterprise Server (SLES) requires an understanding of the login process, including local account files, system accounts, and managing identities.

Using a console shell or the graphical environment are two possible methods of working on a SLES machine.

Finding your way around a SLES installation requires an in-depth knowledge of the filesystem layout. Essential filesystem components are documented and explained in this chapter. Basic filesystem permissions are also described.

The SLES help system includes the use of both man and info pages.

Editing text files from a console session is normally done with the vi editor. Modes of vi are explained and tables of common commands used with vi are provided.

Although a complete guide to using SUSE Linux Enterprise Server (SLES) is beyond the scope of this book, an understanding of Linux and basic Linux functionality is necessary for successful deployment of OES Linux.

This chapter will discuss essential Linux concepts, such as understanding the login process, using the command-line and graphical environments, finding your way around the filesystem, using the available help systems, and understanding text-editing tools. Linux-proficient administrators may want to skip to Chapter 6, "SUSE Linux Enterprise Server Management," for more in-depth SLES information, but breezing through this chapter for an introduction to SUSE-specific utilities and environments might be helpful. If you are new to Linux, this chapter should get you started, but this is not intended to be a comprehensive or beginner's Linux guide.

If you'd like a more thorough investigation into Linux fundamentals or SLES administration, Novell Education's Certified Linux Professional (CLP) and Certified Linux Engineer (CLE) programs are well worth looking into. For more information on Novell's SUSE Linux certification options, see Appendix A, "CLE Certification Options."

Logging in to Linux

After installing and booting a SLES server, you should be presented with either a text or graphical login prompt. Entering an appropriate username and password will give you access to the server. For an administrator, it is important to understand how access is granted and how local SLES user accounts are configured. It is also important to have this knowledge prior to implementing OES components such as Linux User Management (LUM). The following section will briefly discuss local user accounts and how the local authentication process works.

Local Account Files

On a SLES9 server, local user accounts are defined in the /etc/passwd file as shown in Figure 3.1. Every user defined in this file must have certain attributes that are used by the server for determining such things as user permissions and login name. The format of /etc/passwd is one user account entry per line.

Each line within the passwd file is made up of five fields, separated by colons. These fields provide the necessary attributes for user accounts to be considered valid by the operating system. The purpose of each field is documented in Table 3.1 for the entry jdoe:x:1000:100:John Doe:/home/jdoe:/bin/bash.

FIGURE 3.1
An example of the /etc/passwd file.

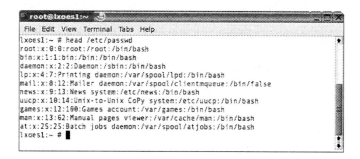

TABLE 3.1
Explanation of /etc/passwd Entry

FIELD ENTRY	DESCRIPTION
jdoe	User login name.
x	Password field. If an "x" is in this field, shadow passwords are enabled. A "*" in this field prevents most types of local logins.
1000	Numeric User ID (UID) of this account.
100	Numeric primary Group ID (GID) of this account.
John Doe	General Electric Comprehensive Operating System (GECOS) field. Commonly used for the user's full name or description.
/home/jdoe	User's home directory.
/bin/bash	User's default shell.

If the second field in the /etc/passwd file is an "x", shadow passwords are enabled. This is the default configuration for SLES. Shadow passwords provide for a more secure environment, and allow for additional password aging options.

When you use shadow passwords, an additional configuration file is used for storing encrypted user passwords. This file is the /etc/shadow file. Table 3.2 explains the fields of this file for the entry jdoe:AztgeYU5TrGn.:12702:0:38:7:3:::.

TABLE 3.2
Explanation of /etc/shadow Entry

FIELD ENTRY	DESCRIPTION
jdoe	User login name.
AztgeYU5TrGn.	Encrypted password.
12702	Date password was last changed. This value is the number of days between January 1, 1970 and the day the password was last changed.
0	Days before password may be changed.
38	Days after which password must be changed.
7	Days before password expires that user is warned to change the password.
3	Days after password expires that account is disabled.
<blank>	Date account is to be disabled. This value is the number of days between January 1, 1970 and the day the account will be disabled.

Within the /etc/passwd file, the fourth field contains the GID of the primary group of the specified user. When users create files and directories, the new filesystem objects receive a user owner and a group owner. The user owner is the UID of the user who created the filesystem entry. The group owner is the GID of the user's primary group at the time of object creation. (Both the UID and GID numbers are converted to user and group names when viewing file listings.) Local groups are defined in the /etc/group file. Table 3.3 shows the fields and their definitions for the entry users:x:100:tjohnson,mblack.

TABLE 3.3
Explanation of the /etc/group File

FIELD ENTRY	DESCRIPTION
users	Group name.
x	Encrypted password. An "x" in this field indicates that shadow group files are in use.
100	Numeric Group ID (GID).
tjohnson,mblack	Secondary members of the current group.

NOTE

A user's primary group designation is performed within the /etc/passwd file. Any additional or secondary groups the user belongs to are defined using the last field of the /etc/group file.

Creating and modifying local user accounts and groups can be done with several utilities. Within SLES, the YaST utility can be used to easily create these accounts. (Information on YaST can be found in Chapter 6.) Users and groups can also be added to the system using several command-line utilities. A few of these utilities are listed in Table 3.4.

TABLE 3.4
Local User and Group Utilities

UTILITY	DESCRIPTION
useradd	Create a new local user account
userdel	Delete local user account
passwd	Set or change user password
usermod	Modify a local user account (including password expiration intervals)
grpadd	Add a local group
grpdel	Delete local group
pwconv	Convert to secure shadow accounts
pwunconv	Convert from shadow accounts to normal password accounts

The Root Administrator Account

Within Linux, the superuser or administrator account is known as root. This account has all rights over everything found on a Linux server. It is important to realize that these rights cannot be locked out or restricted in any way. Given the vast amount of power root has, a secure and confidential password must be used for this account.

It is also important to avoid using the root account just for the sake of accessibility. When you are logged in as root, malicious scripts or programs can potentially be deadly to your Linux environment if they are run accidentally. Be sure to avoid these issues by logging in as a regular user and only using root privileges when necessary. (See the "Switching Identities" section later in this chapter for more information on that topic.)

The UID for root is always 0 (zero). This is hard-coded into many aspects of Linux and should not be manually adjusted. Also, when integrating local Linux accounts into OES through LUM, the root account should not be included. Local user account access to the server as the root user is critical for many troubleshooting steps.

NOTE

The UID for root is always 0. UID numbers from 1 to 999 are reserved for special daemon or system user accounts. Normal SLES user account UID numbers begin at 1000.

The Login Process

There are actually many methods by which a user can authenticate or log in to a Linux server. The tables in the preceding section describe how local user accounts are stored in the system, but having a local user account is only one step in the login process.

Local logins are not the only method of authentication to a Linux server. Logins can be initiated through several methods, including remote graphical sessions, remote shell sessions, and service-specific type of authentications, such as occur when authenticating to a Samba server.

Although these types of authentications normally rely on the local user account files, most can also be configured to authenticate using a remote user account store. These stores can be many different types, but authentication back to an LDAP-enabled directory, such as eDirectory, is an extremely common method of providing account management. OES provides for this functionality in the Linux User Management (LUM) component. LUM is covered in detail in Chapter 8, "Users and Network Security." LUM is actually quite complex, and understanding the authentication process of a local login should help you get prepared for implementing LUM.

In SLES, Pluggable-Authentication Modules (PAM) are used to provide user authentication to all PAM-enabled services. PAM-enabled services include local logins, secure shell access, and most other services requiring authentication. PAM configuration of these services is performed using service-specific configuration files found in /etc/pam.d. In this directory, each service relying on PAM to enforce authentication has a configuration file. The default login configuration file used for local logins is shown in Figure 3.2.

PAM configuration divides the authentication process across four distinct module types. The explanations for these module types can be found in Table 3.5.

FIGURE 3.2

Contents of /etc/pam.d/login.

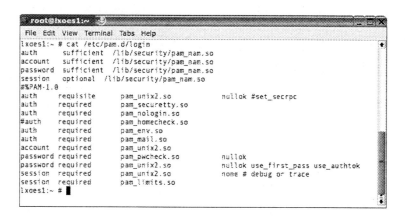

TABLE 3.5

PAM Module Types

MODULE TYPE	DESCRIPTION
Auth	Used to establish the user's validity through checking passwords or other credentials.
Account	Used to ensure a valid user account exists and is allowed access. This stage will not allow expired, disabled, or otherwise invalid accounts to proceed.
Password	Used to set the authentication token (password) of the user.
Session	Used to create a session for the authenticated user.

Each module type takes one of four control flags as a parameter used to indicate how that specific module is to be handled. These control flags are explained in Table 3.6.

TABLE 3.6

PAM Control Flags

CONTROL FLAG	DESCRIPTION
Required	All module checks are required to complete successfully. If a module fails, all other modules are processed. All failures are then returned to the authentication process.
Requisite	Similar to required, but with a requisite control flag, execution halts at the first failure. The corresponding error code is immediately returned to the authentication process.

TABLE 3.6
Continued

CONTROL FLAG	DESCRIPTION
Sufficient	After a sufficient module is successfully processed, the module type is considered to have been successfully processed and execution skips to the next module type.
Optional	Optional modules are not required to be successfully completed in order for the login to be successful.

The last two fields of the PAM configuration file for any service are used to denote external authentication modules and any parameters those modules may require. Many different modules can be used for each portion of the authentication stages. These modules range from providing LDAP lookup for user accounts to checking passwords for certain security requirements.

In the case of a login process based on the configuration file in Figure 3.2, the authentication process would have to successfully pass all requirements for each specified module in order to generate a fully authenticated connection. In other words, the pam_unix2.so module would ensure that the user's account exists and is allowed access. The pam_securetty.so module then determines if the user is allowed to log in from the current terminal. The pam_nologin.so module is used to check for the existence of an /etc/nologin file, which would prevent non-root users from logging in. This process continues until all modules have been processed. If the PAM modules are successfully processed, the user is authenticated and provided with a shell prompt. Otherwise, the user is denied access.

NOTE

For more information on PAM configuration, including possible authentication modules and their options, please refer to the PAM documentation found in /usr/share/doc/packages/pam.

Switching Identities

When you have logged in to a Linux environment using your local account, you may find that you have insufficient privileges to accomplish a specific task. In order to execute certain commands, or have rights to view specific files, it is sometimes required to change your identity to that of the root user. To do this, you must use the **su** command.

The **su** or "substitute user" command is used to temporarily substitute your identity with that of another user. When run as a normal user and executed with no parameters, the **su** command will prompt for root's password. After the password has been entered, the current session will be given root-level access. (To return to your normal permissions, use **exit**.) The **su** command can also be used to switch to the identity of another, non-root user. To perform this action, specify the desired user name as a parameter to **su**, as shown in Figure 3.3.

FIGURE 3.3

An example of using the su command.

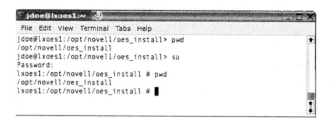

It is important to realize that the **su** command does not otherwise modify the current environment. In other words, executing **su** will not change the current directory, or the currently configured environment variables. When switching to another user's identity, it is often desirable to also assume that user's environment. This requires switching identities and also executing a normal login process for the new user. In order to temporarily switch users and complete a login cycle as that user, the **su** command must be executed using a "-" command-line parameter, as shown in Figure 3.4.

FIGURE 3.4

Example of the su - command.

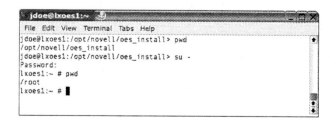

The Shell and the GUI

You can interact with SLES by using one of two methods. The first method is the use of a shell or console, and the second method is a Graphical User Interface (GUI). This section will explain and discuss both environments and provide tips for using these two components of SLES.

The Shell

The heart of the SLES operating system is the Linux kernel. The kernel's primary responsibility is to manage running processes and their interaction with the various hardware components of a computer. This includes management of memory (RAM), processors (CPU), hard disks, and other hardware components. Left on its own the kernel manages these components quite well. However, without the guidance of a user or administrator, the kernel certainly will not accomplish much!

For an administrator, the ability to interact with the Linux kernel can be more important than the kernel itself. One important way to facilitate interaction with the kernel is through the use of a "shell."

A *shell* is a program designed to accept user input, validate that input based on certain criteria (such as syntax and permissions), and then pass instructions off to the kernel for processing. This shell functionality is very similar to the familiar DOS shells under Microsoft Windows environments. Linux shells, however, are much more powerful than traditional non-Unix shells and therefore can be more complex and difficult to master.

One reason for this complexity is the fact that several shells are available for use in Linux environments. Although the purpose of these shells is essentially the same across all variations, the implementations can differ dramatically. These differences are typically manifest in syntax and feature-set capabilities, but each shell can also be substantially different from a usability perspective as well.

Table 3.7 offers a list of some of the shells commonly found in Linux environments.

TABLE 3.7
Common Linux Shells

SHELL	BINARY PROGRAM	COMMENTS
Bourne Shell (SH)	/bin/sh	The standard command interpreter. On Linux, sh is often a symbolic link to /bin/bash.

SHELL	BINARY PROGRAM	COMMENTS
GNU Bourne-Again SHell (BASH)	/bin/bash	An improved version of the Bourne Shell. Supports some advanced features of the C and Korn Shells. Excellent shell for new Linux users.
Public Domain Korn Shell	/bin/ksh	An open source version of the Korn Shell. Among other things, supports advanced floating-point arithmetic features.
C Shell	/bin/tcsh	Enhanced version of the Berkley Unix C shell. Features a C programming type of command-line syntax support.
The Z Shell	/bin/zsh	An enhancement of the ksh shell. Features such capabilities as command-line editing and spell checking.

Each shell has its own specific features and advantages. If you already use one of these shells, or some other shell, feel free to continue to use that shell. If you are new to the Linux environment, the BASH shell is usually the default shell and is an excellent shell for new users. Throughout this book, all shell command syntax will be issued with BASH in mind, although other shells nearly always understand this syntax as well. The remainder of this section will introduce you to concepts and features of the BASH shell.

INVOKING THE SHELL

Although invoking the shell may seem like a rather straightforward topic, there are a few important aspects of this topic that should be pointed out.

If no graphical environment was installed with SLES, after server startup a login prompt should be presented. Simply logging in as a valid user will invoke that user's default shell. This behavior will also be encountered if the graphical environment is installed, but not configured for automatic startup. In either case, following the login prompts will lead you to a shell environment.

From within a graphical environment on Linux, there are a number of terminal programs that will invoke a shell. Common graphical shells are listed in Table 3.8.

TABLE 3.8
Common Graphical Terminal Programs

GRAPHICAL SHELL PROGRAM	PRIMARY GRAPHICAL ENVIRONMENT	COMMENTS
Console	KDE	Full-featured graphical shell including tab support for multiple windows, and customizable view profiles. Based on the Qt toolkit.
gnome-terminal	GNOME	Full-featured graphical shell including tab support for multiple windows and customizable view profiles. Based on the GTK+ toolkit.
Xterm	All	Minimalist graphical terminal window.

NOTE

When using graphical shells, be aware that the type of shell invoked (BASH, ZSH, and so on) may be configured within the graphical application itself. If so, this setting may override your user's default shell environment.

Launching a graphical shell is a simple task of locating the corresponding shell icon and clicking on it, or entering the application command name in a "run command" type of dialog. This will typically start the shell using the credentials of the currently logged-in user. A commonly found graphical shell is the KDE-based Konsole, which is shown in Figure 3.5.

In addition to graphical terminals, another method used to gain shell access is using the "Virtual Terminals" available in Linux environments.

Virtual Terminals are terminal sessions bound to a specialized device on Linux. Rather than being attached to a physical hardware device, such as the connection of a serial cable to a COM port, connections to Virtual Terminals are accomplished through bindings represented by the keyboard function keys. Typically, the first six function keys (F1–F6) are bound to full-screen terminal sessions using the `mingetty` program. Function key F7 is normally bound to the first graphical environment running on the Linux computer. It is also possible to have a second graphical environment running and bound to the F8 function key.

FIGURE 3.5
Konsole terminal utility.

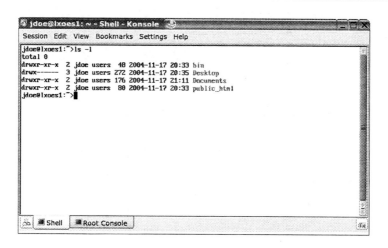

You can access these Virtual Terminals by pressing a combination of control keys. In graphical environments such as KDE, this keystroke combination is Ctrl+Alt+F*n* (where F*n* is substituted for the desired terminal). When you have accessed a Virtual Terminal, you must enter valid user credentials prior to invoking a usable shell.

NOTE

Switching between Virtual Terminals can be accomplished using either Alt+F*n* (where F*n* is one of the other Virtual Terminals), or Ctrl+Alt+F*n*.

From within the graphical environment, Virtual Terminal access is only possible using the three-keystroke combination of Ctrl+Alt+F*n*.

NOTE

Pressing Ctrl+Alt+F7 from within a Virtual Terminal will return you to the graphical environment.

Another common way of invoking a command shell is through remote shell access via another computer. The basic method of invoking this access is through a telnet session. Telnet connections can be made from nearly every operating environment to a Linux server. However, telnet uses an insecure protocol and therefore telnet connections are not normally allowed to Linux servers. By default, SLES does not allow telnet connections. To alleviate security risks inherent with telnet, a Secure SHell (SSH) session can be used for encrypted remote access.

Secure shell support on Linux servers is provided by the OpenSSH software program. On SLES, OpenSSH is configured by default and is the recommended method of remote access. Connecting to the OpenSSH server is possible from other Linux machines using the **ssh** program. Basic usage of **ssh** is as follows:

```
#ssh johndoe@192.168.1.56
```

NOTE

If the username (johndoe@ in the preceding example) is not specified, the user login will be attempted using the current username on the local Linux system.

After issuing the **ssh** command, the user is prompted for a password for the SSH session. Upon successfully entering the password, the default shell of the designated user is invoked.

The only potential drawback to SSH is the fact that SSH client programs are not commonly available on non-Linux workstations. Table 3.9 lists a few commonly used programs that provide SSH client support in Windows environments.

TABLE 3.9
SSH Clients for Windows

SSH CLIENT PROGRAM	HOME PAGE	COMMENTS
SecureShell for Windows	http://www.ssh.com/	Full-featured SSH client
PuTTY	http://www.chiark.greenend.org.uk/~sgtatham/putty/	Free Telnet/SSH Client
SSHWindows	http://sshwindows.sourceforge.net/	SSH Server and Client implementation for Windows

Given the benefits of SSH remote shells, using one of these or other secure shell clients on non-Linux workstations is well worth the investment.

USING THE SHELL

After you've invoked a shell, you can perform any number of actions. Command execution is the primary reason for invoking a shell, and for that execution to be successful, there are a few rules you need to be aware of:

- External commands (standalone programs, not built-in shell functions or aliases) can only be executed if they are found within directories specified by your **PATH** environment variable. All other external commands can only be executed if the command is referenced using a valid path to the program.

NOTE

The current directory is not normally in your path. To execute a script or program found in the current directory, it is typically necessary to invoke the command using the full path as follows:

```
./script
```

The "./" indicates the current directory.

- The permissions on a file determine whether or not that file is executable. Most standalone applications and utilities should already have a correct set of rights assigned to them. However, if you are working with shell scripts, be sure to assign the execute (x) flag to the script prior to attempting to execute the script.

- Linux shells are case sensitive. This means that all filenames, commands, and command parameters are case sensitive. Often, command-line parameters differ dramatically based on the case used. Be sure to double-check all parameters before executing critical commands!

- Know the difference between relative and absolute paths. Many commands in Linux reference source or destination directories and files. When using these commands, it is critical that you distinguish between a relative and an absolute path.

  Any path or filename reference beginning with a slash (/) is referring to the absolute path to that file—from the root of the drive. Relative path and filenames typically start with no path or with a single period followed by a slash (./) indicating the current directory. The parent directory can be referenced using a double period followed by a slash (../).

  If relative and absolute paths are used incorrectly, files can be inadvertently written to locations off the root of the drive, rather than the intended location.

Before you begin following these rules, there are a number of shell features you should know about that make working in a Linux shell a much more effective practice. A few important features are explained in this list:

- *Tab completion*—Tab completion allows users to press the Tab key while working at a shell prompt and have BASH attempt to autocomplete the filename or path. If a beep is heard, multiple matches have been found. Pressing Tab a second time will display all matching items.

- *History*—The BASH shell automatically tracks commands entered by each user. These commands can be accessed by pressing the Up and Down arrow keys. The `history` command can also be used to display the entire known history of the current user.

  You can then issue commands stored in your history using an exclamation point (!) followed by the history number entry, or an exclamation point followed by the first few characters of the desired command. When using the first few characters of a command, the most recent entry that matches those characters is executed.

- *File globbing*—File globbing is the process of the shell interpreting wildcard characters rather than the utility being called. When a command-line utility is executed, the shell itself searches and satisfies any wildcard characters and then executes the command using the matching parameters. For example, if the command `ls /etc/is*` was executed, the BASH shell would actually determine all matches for `/etc/is*` and actually execute `ls /etc/issue /etc/issue.net`.

  File globbing can be beneficial if used properly and quite harmful if used incorrectly. If you would like to prevent file globbing, be sure to escape any wildcard characters by using a backslash or by enclosing the parameter containing the wildcard in quotation marks.

- *I/O redirection*—Linux uses built-in file descriptors to denote the standard input, standard output, and standard error channels. These descriptors are numbered 0, 1, and 2 respectively. Redirecting input or output to and from a command can be done using the > and < metacharacters.

  The less-than (<) metacharacter is used exclusively for redirecting input into a command from a file. The greater-than (>) metacharacter is used for redirecting either or both standard output and standard error channels to a file. To execute a command and log the output into a text file, the following syntax would be used:

  ```
  ls /etc/* > etc.dir
  ```

  When redirecting both standard output and standard error to a file, the following syntax is used:

  ```
  cat /etc/passwd /etc/passwd.bad > ok.txt 2> err.txt
  ```

To write both standard error and standard output to the same file, the following syntax is used:

```
cat /etc/passwd /etc/passwd.bad > ok.txt 2>&1
```

WARNING

When you redirect output using the ">" metacharacter, output will be written to the specified destination file whether or not the file exists. Existing files will be overwritten. To append data to existing files rather than overwriting those files, use double greater-than signs (>>).

- *Command chaining*—Command chaining allows the standard output of one command to be redirected into the standard input channel of a second command. To perform this function, the two commands are separated on the same command line using the pipe (|) metacharacter. The following example shows the output of the **cat** command being redirected and used as input for the **sort** command:

```
cat /etc/passwd | sort
```

Command chaining can be used to chain a virtually unlimited number of commands together. The BASH shell processes these commands one at a time. After completing each command, the output of that command is then passed as input to the next command.

With the preceding framework of required rules and shell tips, you are now ready to interact with files, run commands, and navigate the filesystem. Unfortunately, providing a list of all BASH commands you might need would require another complete book! However, some essential command-line tools are described in the "Finding Your Way" section of this chapter. A more complete list of the most essential commands used in Linux has also been compiled in Appendix B, "The Most Essential Linux Commands."

The SLES Graphical Environment

The SLES graphical environment is similar to most Linux-based workstations, such as the Novell Linux Desktop (NLD). These graphical environments tend to be rather complex and a complete understanding of each graphical component is necessary to thoroughly troubleshoot any issues that might arise. The following section provides an overview of these components.

XFREE86

To provide a graphical environment, SLES uses the XFree86 implementation of the X Window System. This same graphical, or X, server is used on Linux workstations and is not always installed in server environments, but SLES, by default, does install the graphical environment.

Your server may be configured to automatically start the graphical environment and provide for a graphical login, or it may start and prompt for a text-based login. To reduce operating overhead in a server environment, many configurations provide for text-based logins, but do allow the graphical environment on demand. To start the graphical server from a text-based login, execute the startx command after logging in.

A complete graphical environment on SLES consists of several layers of graphical components. These components and a brief description of them can be found in Table 3.10.

TABLE 3.10
Components of the SLES Graphical Environment

COMPONENT	DESCRIPTION
Video hardware	The video card, monitor, and physical connections to these components.
X Server	The XFree86 X Server is responsible for passing graphical instructions from client applications to the video card hardware.
Display Manager	The Display Manager is responsible for providing a graphical login to users in runlevel 5. Graphical environments starting from runlevel 3 do not use a Display Manager. SLES uses the K Display Manager (KDM) by default. The GNOME Display Manager (GDM) is also provided with SLES.
Window Manager	A Window Manager is responsible for providing window functionality to X clients. This functionality includes the minimize/maximize functionality, title bars, window resizing, and so on. SLES uses the K Window Manager (KWin) by default. The Metacity Window Manager is used with GNOME desktop environments. (If the minimal graphical environment is selected during installation, the FVWM window manager is installed to provide basic graphical functionality. No desktop environment is installed in this situation.)

COMPONENT	DESCRIPTION
Desktop Environment	A desktop environment's primary purpose is to provide all X clients with a common look and feel. They accomplish this task through border enhancement, color coordination, and context-sensitive menus. Desktop environments also commonly provide taskbars and launcher menus used to facilitate access to installed programs. SLES provides the K Desktop Environment (KDE) by default. The GNOME desktop can also be selected as part of the SLES installation.
X Client Applications	Applications that rely on graphical libraries for displaying their interface, dialogs, menus, and so on. Examples of X clients include such things as OpenOffice, KCalc, and KMail.

Each component of the X Window System plays an important role in the over-all goal of providing users with a complete graphical environment. Although some components are optional, all components rely on the base X server for graphical functionality by interacting with the video card and monitor.

The X server configuration is performed using the sax2 utility. This utility is automatically launched during the SLES installation if a graphical environment is selected for installation. After installation, sax2 can be run from either the command line or the graphical environment to adjust graphical settings. Additional hardware configuration changes, such as selecting an appropriate mouse, can be performed from within the Hardware section of YaST.

NOTE

The main configuration file for the X server is /etc/X11/XF86Config. This file is generated by the sax2 utility and should never be manually edited.

However, prior to making changes with sax2, the current copy of XF86Config is saved as XF86Config.saxsave. If necessary, this backup can be manually renamed to revert to the previous graphical settings.

DESKTOP ENVIRONMENTS

When installing SLES, you have the option of installing a KDE, GNOME, or minimal graphical environment. The minimal graphical environment is a bare-bones environment designed to provide an X server for graphical applications. On the other hand, KDE and GNOME are both desktop environments and offer a full graphical environment complete with taskbars, application launchers, unified menus, screensavers, and many other components common to workstation environments.

K DESKTOP ENVIRONMENT (KDE)

The K Desktop Environment (KDE) is the default desktop for SLES 9. A typical desktop view is shown in Figure 3.6. KDE is based on the Qt graphical toolkit and therefore most applications used under KDE are also based on this toolkit. As long as required libraries are available, applications based on other graphical toolkits can still run under a KDE environment (such as running GNOME apps under KDE).

FIGURE 3.6

The K Desktop Environment (KDE) workspace.

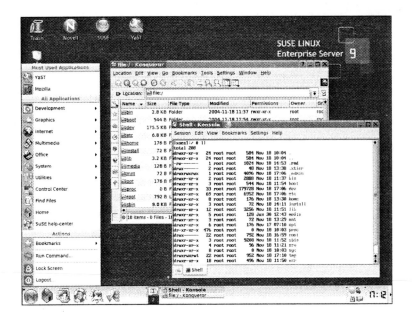

KDE offers a complete desktop environment that includes the following components:

- *The Desktop*—The desktop consists of the background and one or more icons used to access common programs or utilities. Launching applications from the desktop is done using a single mouse click on the appropriate icon.

- *The KDE Control Panel or Kicker*—The Kicker is known as a taskbar in other graphical environments. In KDE, the Kicker is used to provide immediate access to commonly used programs, a task manager for running programs, virtual desktops, and environment-specific applets (such as the clock). You can configure the Kicker by right-clicking on the main panel and selecting Configure Panel.

- *The KDE menu*—The KDE menu is accessed using the green button with a red "N" on the left side of the Kicker. The KDE menu provides easy access to graphical programs installed on the local server. Right-clicking on the KDE menu provides a link to a tool for menu editing. This tool can be used to adjust or add icons to the menu easily.

- *Virtual Desktops*—KDE includes support for up to 16 virtual desktops. By default, only two virtual desktops are configured. You can access each desktop by using the center section of the Kicker panel. To configure the virtual desktop, right-click on the desktop and choose Configure Desktop, Multiple Desktops.

Central to KDE is the Konqueror utility. Konqueror is an integrated file manager and web browser. In addition to performing those two tasks, Konqueror also offers extensive features such as accessing information through several different network protocols, interacting with local hardware devices, and providing the KDE help system.

Konqueror is the default web browser with KDE, but Mozilla and Firefox can both be installed as part of the SLES installation, and used in place of Konqueror. OES officially supports both the Mozilla and Konqueror browsers.

GNOME

During the SLES installation, the GNOME desktop can be installed either in addition to KDE or as a replacement for KDE. GNOME is based on the GTK+ graphical toolkit. As with KDE, as long as the required graphical libraries are available, all graphical applications can be used under GNOME. Figure 3.7 shows a GNOME desktop with common GNOME-based utilities.

GNOME offers a complete desktop environment that consists of the following components:

- *The Desktop*—The desktop consists of the background and one or more icons used to access common programs or utilities. Unlike KDE, launching applications from the GNOME desktop is done using a double mouse click on the appropriate icon.

- *The Top Panel*—The Top Panel is used to provide easy access to available applications. This panel is fully configurable and can be customized with additional links to applications. By default, this panel includes links to the Nautilus file manager, a terminal emulation window, and applets for the clock and volume control.

- *The Bottom Panel*—The Bottom Panel is used to provide access to current-ly running programs through a task manager interface in the middle of this panel. The Bottom Panel also displays an icon for closing all open windows and revealing the desktop. Accessing virtual workspaces is also accomplished using this panel.

- *The Applications Menu*—The Applications menu is accessed using the Top Panel. This menu contains links for currently installed graphical applications.

- *Virtual Workspaces*—GNOME includes support for up to 36 virtual work-spaces (called virtual desktops in KDE). By default, only 4 virtual work-spaces are configured. You can access each workspace by using the right section of the Bottom Panel. Right-click on the Virtual Workspaces applet to configure the virtual workspace.

FIGURE 3.7
The GNOME Desktop workspace.

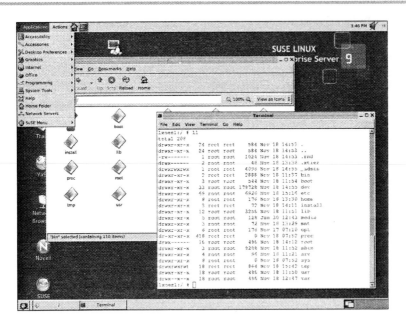

GNOME utilizes Nautilus as the main tool for file management and Epiphany as the default web browser. The Epiphany web browser is also supported for OES web-based utilities. As in KDE environments, both Mozilla and Firefox can be installed and used in place of Epiphany.

FVWM

In addition to the two desktop environments of KDE and GNOME, the SLES installation also allows for the installation of a minimal graphical environment. This environment is based on the Feeble Virtual Windows Manager (FVWM) window maker (**fvwm2**). As shown in Figure 3.8, this Desktop Environment certainly offers fewer features than KDE and GNOME.

FIGURE 3.8
The FVWM Desktop workspace.

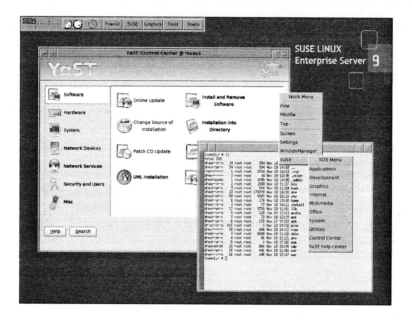

FVWM is a powerful, yet minimalist window environment. Rather than employing large, memory-consuming menus and advanced window features, FVWM focuses on providing an efficient and powerful graphical environment. Due to this focus, new users may find FVWM a difficult environment to master. Other users appreciate the low-resource footprint when using FVWM—particularly in a server environment.

Features of FVWM include the following:

- *The Desktop*—The desktop of FVWM consists of just a background graphic. Unlike KDE and GNOME, there are no desktop icons in FVWM. Clicking on the desktop with the left mouse button will invoke the "Work Menu" pop-up. Clicking the right mouse button will invoke the "KDE Menu" pop-up.

- *FvwmButtons*—FvwmButtons create a group of buttons on the root desktop screen. The grouping of buttons includes such things as a clock, and links to SUSE and FVWM utilities. Links to shells and other utilities can also be found in the button grouping.

- *KDE Menu*—Accessed by clicking the right mouse button on the desktop, the KDE menu contains links to applications configured in the KDE environment. Applications visible in this menu are determined by what is installed on the server.

- *Work Menu*—Accessed by clicking the left mouse button on the desktop, the Work menu provides a menu containing links to commonly used applications such as the Pine editor, Mozilla browser, and other configuration utilities.

NOTE

Regardless of the graphical environment chosen, working within the GUI is a straightforward process of launching applications using icons or command lines, and interacting with the environment using menu items. GNOME and KDE both have built-in help systems to provide assistance if you really get lost. FVWM has no such integrated help system.

CREDENTIALS AND THE X SERVER

When you're logged into the graphical environment as a normal user, a common operation is to open a terminal and launch graphical X client applications directly from the shell prompt. If your shell credentials are the same as your credentials in the graphical environment, these commands can be executed without issue. However, if you switch identities to that of the root user (or any other user), access to the X server will be denied, and you will be unable to launch graphical programs.

When starting the X server, your credentials are provided to the X server. For security purposes, SLES configures X to only allow access to the local X server from trusted sources. By default, this is only the logged-in user. To allow graphical access while switching users, SLES provides the **sux** utility.

The **sux** utility automatically configures the new user's environment to support access to the local X server. The **sux** utility replaces the functionality of the **su** utility, which is used to switch identities within normal shells. The syntax of **sux** is identical to that of **su**.

TUNNELING X

In addition to providing graphical access to switched identities, it is also possible to redirect the display of graphical clients running on the SLES server to a remote X server running on the local workstation. This is useful when you want to run a graphical program on the SLES server, but do not want to start the X server. Running programs in this manner is best accomplished by forwarding the X connection through an SSH tunnel.

SSH tunnels can be established to the SLES server from a Linux workstation using the **ssh** command. Through the use of the **-X** startup option, X11 forwarding can be enabled via that same SSH tunnel. When you are connected in this manner, you can launch graphical programs on the SLES server and display them using the local X server.

NOTE

Because tunneling X over SSH requires a local X server for display, the local workstation must be either a Linux-based workstation or a Windows machine running an X server. One popular X server for Windows is Cygwin. Information on Cygwin can be found at http://x.cygwin.com/.

REMOTE GRAPHICAL SESSIONS

Using Virtual Network Computing (VNC), a graphical desktop session can be started on the local server while physically using a Linux, Windows, or Apple MacOS-based workstation. During the SLES 9 installation, remote administration through VNC can be set to "enabled." Otherwise, remote administration will be disabled and must be enabled using the YaST – Network Services – Remote Administration module.

When remote administration has been enabled, VNC connections can be made to the server using one of three methods:

- *VNC client-based connections*—Using a VNC client, a connection using the VNC protocol can be made to the server on port 5901. VNC clients include **krdc** for Linux, and RealVNC for Windows (www.realvnc.com). VNC clients are also available for several other platforms.

- *VNC connection in Konqueror*—Using a Linux workstation, the Konqueror browser can be used to provide a VNC connection to the SLES 9 server. This connection is a true VNC connection and connects to the same port (5901) that the standalone VNC client would connect to. The full URL for this type of connection within Konqueror is vnc://<serverDNSorIP>:5901.

- *Brower-based connections*—Using a Java-capable web browser, an HTTP connection to the server on port 5801 (http://<serverDNSorIP>:5801) will invoke the Java-based VNC client.

TIP

The VNC configuration file is /etc/xinetd.d/vnc. This file can be manually edited to modify screen resolution, color depth, and port assignments.

Although remote administration through VNC is convenient, the VNC protocol is not as secure as a full secure shell (SSH) session. For this reason, establishing a full SLES login through VNC is not recommended outside of secure LAN environments.

Finding Your Way

Now that you are familiar with the graphical and console working environments in SLES, you might still find yourself somewhat lost within the environment itself. This section provides an introduction to the filesystem layout and offers an insight into filesystem permissions and potential navigation pitfalls.

System Filesystem

During the system startup process, the Linux kernel loads modules required to access the hard disks into memory. With these modules, physical connections to the hard disk partitions can be established.

Under Microsoft Windows and other operating systems, the filesystem is accessed through drive letters assigned to each individual partition. Linux, on the other hand, provides access to all partitions through a single, virtual directory structure. Accessing separate partitions is a matter of navigating to the correct directory.

The process of associating a partition to a directory within the filesystem is known as "mounting." During system initialization, the partition containing the core operating-system files is mounted to the root (/) of the directory tree. This partition is known as the system or "root" partition.

After root has been successfully mounted, remaining partitions are then mounted to specific directories within the root directory structure. The /etc/fstab file is used as a configuration file, which determines where each partition will be mounted. Directories used for mounting filesystems are known as "mount points."

NOTE

When mounting partitions, the destination mount point must exist within the original directory tree. This directory does not have to be empty. Contents of directories used as mount points are inaccessible for the duration of the partition being mounted. Directory contents will again be accessible when the partition using the mount point is unmounted.

Table 3.11 lists the main directories found after a SLES installation and briefly describes their purposes.

TABLE 3.11
Root Filesystem Components

DIRECTORY	CONTENTS AND PURPOSE
/bin	Commands used by all users.
/boot	Boot-specific files, including the Linux kernel and GRUB configuration files.
/dev	Device files representing possible hardware components.
/etc	Host-specific configuration files.
/home	Home directory for local user accounts.
/lib	Shared library and kernel module directory.
/media	Default mount directory structure for removable media such as CD-ROMs.
/mnt	Default mount point for temporarily mounted network file-systems.
/opt	Optional directory for use by additional software packages. Novell OES components can be found in this directory structure.
/proc	Virtual filesystem used for querying the Linux kernel.
/root	Home directory of the root user.
/sbin	System binaries typically used only by root.
/srv	Data directories used by such things as web and FTP servers.
/sys	Virtual filesystem of Linux system structure—new version of the /proc filesystem.
/tmp	System-wide temporary directory.
/usr	Shareable, read-only data.
/var	Variable-length files such as log files, databases, printer spools, and so on.

NOTE

For more information on the filesystem layout in SLES, refer to the Filesystem Hierarchy Standard (FHS) at http://www.pathname.com/fhs/.

Upon opening a shell terminal, you are normally presented with a command prompt while residing within your user's home directory. This can be confirmed by using the Print Working Directory (**pwd**) command, as shown in Figure 3.9.

FIGURE 3.9
Displaying the current path using pwd.

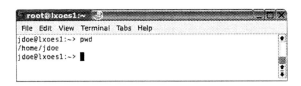

Navigation through the filesystem is similar to other operating systems. There are a few shortcuts you should be aware of. Table 3.12 describes these useful shortcuts and provides examples for using them.

TABLE 3.12
Navigation Shortcuts

SHORTCUT	DESCRIPTION
.	Represents the current directory. An example of using this character would be when copying files to the current directory: # cp /etc/passwd .
..	Represents the parent directory. Examples of this include changing to the parent or a sibling directory: # cd .. # cd ../sibling_directory
.<filename>	Filenames beginning with a period are hidden files and should not be confused with representing the current directory. To execute a script in the current directory, the current directory is explicitly identified as follows: # ./test_script

SHORTCUT	DESCRIPTION

~
~jdoe
	Represents the current user's home directory. Using the tilde (~) metacharacter, you can change to the current user's home directory using the following syntax:
	`# cd ~`
	A valid user name can also be appended to the ~ character to represent a specific user's home directory.
	`# cp /etc/passwd ~jdoe/passwd.old`

-	Represents the last working directory. You can easily change to the last valid working directory using the following command: `# cd -`

In addition to knowing the shortcuts, knowing basic navigation tools is also important to successfully navigate the filesystem. Although Table 3.13 is not a comprehensive list of commands, it identifies the major navigation-related commands used in Linux.

TABLE 3.13
Basic Navigation Commands

COMMAND	DESCRIPTION
pwd	Prints the current working directory.
cd	Used to change the current working directory to another directory within the filesystem. When changing directories, the absolute path to the new directory (beginning with a leading slash—/) or a relative path can be used.
ls	List directory contents.
ll	Actually a command alias to the ls command. This command provides a long listing of directory contents—including the filesize, ownership, and permission information.
mkdir	Used to create a new directory.
rmdir	Used to remove empty directories.
cp	Used to copy files from one location to another.
mv	Used to move or rename files.
rm	Used to remove or delete files from the filesystem.

NOTE

A compiled list of essential Linux commands, including command-line utilities, can be found in Appendix B.

Filesystem Permissions

With knowledge of the filesystem layout and the commands required to navigate that filesystem, there is only one thing that could possibly stop you— permissions.

Permissions on files and directories in Linux can be viewed using a long file listing (1s -1). The output of this command will look similar to Figure 3.10.

FIGURE 3.10
Output of 1s -1.

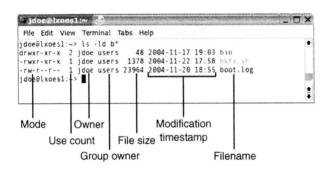

Mode
Owner
Use count
Group owner
File size
Modification timestamp
Filename

Long file listings display the permissions on a file or directory on the far left side of each entry. This field is known as the "mode" of the file and consists of ten specific bits. The first bit is used to indicate the type of file being viewed. Possible file type values are listed in Table 3.14.

TABLE 3.14
Possible File Types

TYPE DESIGNATION	DESCRIPTION
–	Normal file
d	Directory
l	Symbolic link

TYPE DESIGNATION	DESCRIPTION
c	Character device
b	Block device
p	Named pipe
s	Socket

The remaining nine bits represent the permissions on the specified file, as shown in Figure 3.11. These bits are logically divided into three groups of three bits each. The first set of three bits represents the permissions that the owner of the file has. (The owner is displayed as the third field in a long directory listing with ls.)

FIGURE 3.11
Layout of file mode.

The second set of three bits represents the permissions assigned to the group owner of the specified file. (The group owner is displayed as the fourth field in a long directory listing with ls.) All members of the specified group receive the designated rights to the file.

The final set of three bits represents permissions that all other users receive to the specified file.

NOTE

Permissions on Linux are not cumulative. File owners receive just the permissions assigned to the owner—even if the owner is also a member of the group designated as the group owner. Likewise, members of the group owner receive only those rights—even if the "other" rights are more permissive.

Each of these sets of three bits all represent the same set of three rights—read, write, and execute. These permissions behave differently based on whether they are set on a file or a directory. Table 3.15 describes the difference in these permissions.

TABLE 3.15
Permission Differences Between Files and Directories

PERMISSION	MEANING ON FILES	MEANING ON DIRECTORIES
r (read)	The ability to read or view the specified file.	The ability to view contents within a directory. This ability requires the execute permission to be set as well.
w (write)	The ability to modify or write to the specified file.	The ability to create and delete files within a directory. This ability requires the execute permission to be set as well.
x (execute)	The ability to execute the file (required for script and binary program execution).	The ability to work within a specified directory.

SETTING PERMISSIONS AND OWNERSHIP

The chown utility can be used to change the owner and group owner of files and directories. When using chown, specify the new user and group owners followed by the file or directory. The user and group names are separated with a period. Here's an example of this:

```
chown jdoe.users /tmp/tmpfile
```

In order to change permissions on a file or directory, you must use the chmod utility. The chmod utility can be used to change permissions using two different methods. The first method is through using a symbolic representation of permission assignments. This requires identifying which set of permissions you are changing; what permissions you are assigning; and an operator that determines whether rights are being added or subtracted. Table 3.16 lists possible values for these three fields.

TABLE 3.16
Common Symbolic Parameters for chmod

CATEGORY	OPERATOR	PERMISSIONS
u (user)	+ (add permissions)	r (read)
g (group)	- (subtract permissions)	w (write)
o (other)	= (set permissions equal to designated values)	x (execute)
a (all)		

Using the symbolic method, multiple permissions can be set by separating each setting with a comma. The following example demonstrates this:

```
chown u+a,o+r /tmp/tmpfile
```

The second method of changing permissions with chmod is through using an octal number representation of the desired permissions. This is routinely seen and important to understand.

In an octal interpretation of permissions, each right is assigned a number. The read permission is assigned a value of 4, write is assigned a value of 2, and execute is assigned a value of 1. These numeric assignments are used for all three sets of permissions as shown in Figure 3.12.

FIGURE 3.12
Octal representation of file mode.

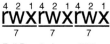

Full Permissions = 777

To assign permissions using the octal method, add up the value of each set permission bit in each category (user, group, and other). Each category will range from 0 to 7. After each category has been calculated, use chmod as follows:

```
chmod 750 /tmp/testfs.sh
```

In the preceding example, all permissions (rwx) are assigned to the user category, read and execute (r-x) are assigned to the group, and no permissions (---) are assigned to the other category.

NOTE

Using octal notation, every category must be explicitly entered. Entered values are right-justified, with missing values filled with zeros.

SPECIAL PERMISSIONS

In addition to the normal permissions, there are three special permissions that you might encounter. These permissions are as follows:

- *Set User ID (SUID)*—The SUID bit is used on executables to modify the permissions allowed to the running process. When an executable with the SUID bit is executed, the running process inherits the permissions of the owner of the executable—rather than the permissions of the user who launched the program. This is useful when a running process should have more rights than a normal user is typically provided.

- *Set Group ID (SGID)*—The SGID bit performs two functions. The first is similar to the SUID bit. An executable with the SGID bit set inherits the permissions of the group owner when running—rather than the group permissions of the user who started the process.

  The second function the SGID bit performs is only valid on directories. With the SGID bit set on a directory, all newly created files within that directory automatically receive the same group owner as the group owner of the directory. This overrides the default assignment of each file receiving a group owner set to the individual user's primary group.

- *Sticky Bit*—The Sticky Bit is only valid on directories. When the Sticky Bit is set on a directory, users are only allowed to delete files that they own. Without this setting, users are allowed to delete files owned by other users as long as they have the write (**w**) permission on the directory.

Special permissions are stored as part of the regular mode of the file, but there is no room for three more permission bits for these permissions. Because of this, special permissions are actually included within the execute (**x**) bit of user, group, and other permissions. Figures 3.13 and 3.14 demonstrate how these permissions are displayed when the corresponding execute bit is set and not set, respectively.

FIGURE 3.13
Special permissions that appear when the execute bit is set.

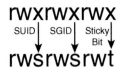

FIGURE 3.14
Special permissions that appear when the execute bit is not set.

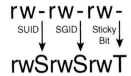

Even though special permissions are displayed as part of the normal mode of the file, setting special permissions is done through the use of one more permissions category with the octal mode of chmod. With this category, SUID is assigned a value of 4, SGID a value of 2, and the Sticky Bit a value of 1. You can set these permissions as follows:

```
chmod 3775 /data/sales
```

NOTE

For more information on permissions and the chmod command, see man 1 chmod.

Getting Help

SUSE Linux provides literally thousands of possible commands that can be used to perform various tasks on a server. Having firsthand knowledge of each utility and all parameters that utility may take is a very challenging task! Thankfully, through the use of utility manuals and application documentation, help is never too far away.

Console-Based Help

Working on the command line is the most common method of interacting with SLES. Providing easy access to application and utility usage information from this environment is essential to effectively working on the command line. Thankfully, a help system has been designed around just this need. This system consists of three distinct types of documentation: manual or man pages; info pages; and system and third-party documentation.

man **PAGES**

man pages on Linux are syntax-level documentation of utilities and applications, stored in an easily retrievable, command-line-friendly format. man pages are physically stored in the /usr/share/man directory and divided into the nine sections shown in Table 3.17.

TABLE 3.17
man Page Sections

man SECTION	SECTION PURPOSE
1	Executable programs and commands all users can access
2	System calls
3	Functions and library routines
4	Special device files (/dev/*)
5	Configuration file formats and conventions
6	Games
7	Macro commands and packages
8	System administration programs and commands used by the root user
9	Kernel routines

All programs utilizing the **man** system should store their **man** pages within the correct section. In order to view **man** pages for a specific command, the following basic syntax must be used:

```
man [section] command
```

NOTE

When accessing man pages, specifying the desired section is optional, but the man command satisfies the man page request by performing a search. If a matching man page is located in an earlier section, that entry will be returned rather than the desired entry. Specifying the section avoids this issue.

Upon entering the **man** command, you are presented with syntax-level documentation for the specified command or utility. The pages presented typically contain information divided into the following sections:

- *Name*—This is a one-line summary of the application in question. This field is displayed individually when using the **whatis** command.

- *Synopsis*—This section contains a summary of the command line for the application in question. Optional parameters are enclosed in square brackets [], and required parameters are listed normally.

- *Description*—This section documents the possible parameters the application in question can receive. Some **man** pages also include specific usage examples in this section.

- *Author*—The author's name and contact information are typically noted in this section.

- *Reporting Bugs*—Information on where to report bugs for the specific utility is normally noted in this section.

- *Copyright*—The utility's copyright information is normally displayed in this section.

- *See Also*—This section identifies additional locations for information on the utility in question. Quite often this section will identify related utilities, man pages, and info pages for the specific utility. Checking all specified resources is recommended for advanced usage techniques including troubleshooting of the utility.

Most man pages are only a few pages in length, but some man pages can be quite detailed with many, many pages of information. (See man bash for one such example!) Navigation through larger man pages can be greatly simplified with details on a few valid keystrokes. Table 3.18 lists a small number of important navigation commands within man.

TABLE 3.18
Internal man Keystrokes

KEYSTROKE	DESCRIPTION
PageDown	Scroll down one page at a time.
PageUp	Scroll up one page at a time.
Enter	Scroll down a single line at a time.
Space	Scroll down one full window at a time.
/pattern	Invokes the search dialog for the specified pattern. When you press Enter, the next instance of the desired term will be located. Navigating to the next hit is done by pressing "n". Moving to the previous instance of the search term is done using "N".
?pattern	Invokes the search-backward dialog for the specified pattern. When you press Enter, the first instance (in the backward direction) of the desired term will be located. You can navigate to the previous hit by pressing "n". You can move to the next instance of the search term using "N".
q	Quit the man page system.

TIP

By default, the man system utilizes the less paging utility. If you prefer another paging utility, the PAGER environment variable can be modified manually. For more information on navigation within man using the less pager, see the man page for less (man less).

It is also common to want to search through man pages for a specific type of utility. Although searching through the contents of all man pages is possible, it is more likely that you just need to locate a command that performs a specific action. Searching just the "Name" section of all man pages is the best way to accomplish this. The apropos or man -k commands can be used for this purpose. For example, to find all commands related to cron, you would use the following command:

```
# man -k cron
```

The output of this man command would be a listing of all commands containing the word "cron" anywhere in the Name field. After the utility has been identified, the man page for the desired command can then be directly accessed for more information.

info **PAGES**

In addition to the man system, information regarding programs and commands can also be found using the info system. Due to the syntax-documentation-only focus of man pages, background information, tutorials, and detailed information on using the program in question are sometimes lacking in man pages. The info system was created to directly resolve that issue.

info pages are detailed usage instructions and program or command guides. This documentation is accessed via an emacs-type interface that supports hypertext links, and advanced navigation features not found in the man system. The following command is an example of using the info system to locate documentation on the Concurrent Versions System (CVS):

```
info cvs
```

Within the info system, multiple individual pages of information make up the entire set of info pages for each specific application. These pages of information are referred to as *nodes*. You can page through nodes one at a time, or you can jump to specific pages through the use of hypertext links. For new users, this navigation can be challenging.

To help node navigation, info pages all display a header across the top of the page. This header includes information such as the current node, next and previous nodes, and information regarding the parent node. Although this helps to visualize your location in the info system, you still need to know basic navigation commands before you'll feel entirely at home. Table 3.19 describes some of these important navigation keys.

TABLE 3.19
Internal info Keystrokes

KEYSTROKE	DESCRIPTION
n	Next node.
p	Previous node.
u	Parent node.
Space	Scroll down one page at a time.
Del	Scroll up one page at a time.
b	Return to the beginning of the current node.
Tab	Select next hypertext link.
m *<link text>*	Performs a direct jump to the specified subnode. Pressing Tab displays all available subnodes. When entering a subnode name, enter enough characters to ensure the subnode name is not ambiguous.
Enter	Follow current hypertext link. Hypertext links are designated by an asterisk (*) at the beginning of the link, and a double colon (::) at the end of the link.
q	Quit the info system.

TIP

For a great introduction to the info system, use the built-in user's tutorial by executing info info. When you're in the info system, press **h** to begin the tutorial.

SYSTEM AND THIRD-PARTY DOCUMENTATION

The final common forms of documentation found on SLES are system- and application-specific documentation. This documentation can be in HTML, PDF, plain text, or many other formats. All application-specific documentation can be found in application-specific directories beneath /usr/share/doc/packages. SLES-specific documentation, release notes, and a collection of HOWTO guides can also be found beneath specific directories in /usr/share/doc.

Graphical Help Systems

KDE and GNOME both have an integrated help system. This makes accessing help from a graphical environment a much simpler task than from the command line. The graphical help systems normally provide help for the graphical environments, but they also provide access to the existing man and info pages as well.

KDE HELP

In KDE, the KDE Help Center is the interface into the SUSE help system. To access the SUSE help system, single-click on the "SUSE Help Center" icon (the image of a gecko in the middle of a life preserver) from the KDE Kicker. When you're in the Help Center, SUSE documentation and application-specific documentation can easily be accessed.

Using KDE, info pages and man pages can also be easily viewed. To access these systems, launch Konqueror and enter a specific URL for man or info pages. The syntax for accessing man pages is man:<desired_pages>. For example, man:ls would be used to view the man pages for the ls command from within Konqueror. To access info pages, substitute info: for man:, for example, info:cvs to view the info pages for CVS.

TIP

man and info help URLs can also be entered into a run dialog (Alt+F2) and Konqueror will be automatically launched with the appropriate page.

GNOME HELP

As with KDE, GNOME also provides a graphical help system. This help system is based on the yelp utility.

From within GNOME, the help system is accessed from the Applications program menu. Within this menu, click on the Help icon (life preserver) to launch yelp at the home page for GNOME help. If complete GNOME documentation is installed, links to GNOME-specific help will be displayed on the yelp home page. (SLES does not provide GNOME Desktop documentation.) Links to additional documentation (man and info pages) are also displayed on the yelp home page.

TIP

As with KDE, man and info URLs can also be entered into a run dialog (Alt+F2) under GNOME. In this case, yelp will be automatically launched with the appropriate page.

Editing Text Files

A chapter on working with SLES would not be complete without a discussion on one more important topic—editing text files. Although editing text files may not sound like a difficult subject, common tools used when editing text files under Linux tend to be rather cryptic. Devoting some space in this chapter to help clear up confusion in this area should make first-time administrators much more comfortable and effective with any task involving text editing.

The vi Utility

It is possible to use graphical text-editing tools under SLES. Many such tools are easily available in both the KDE and GNOME graphical environments. However, a reliance on graphical editors (such as Kate or Gedit) also produces a dependence on a graphical environment. This graphical environment is often not running on a SLES machine. Also, when using a remote shell for SLES administration, graphical tools require tunneling X over SSH. Rather than enabling this tunneling or always using a graphical session on the server, learning and using a command-line editor is more effective and a better solution for the long term.

As in the graphical environment, several command-line text editors are available. Among the choices for command-line editors are pico, emacs, and vi. Pico and emacs are both powerful text-editing utilities that offer several appealing qualities. However, these utilities are not always available on SLES installations. The vi utility is the only text-editing utility that is nearly guaranteed to be available with any Linux installation.

NOTE

The vi utility on SLES is actually the Vi IMproved, or vim utility. As vim is designed to be compatible to vi, it is still commonly referred to as vi.

The vi utility is an extremely powerful text-editing utility. Unfortunately, the almost limitless capabilities of vi have also caused its usage to become fairly cryptic and challenging for new users. The most important vi concept to understand is that vi operates in a bimodal fashion. *Bimodal* means that when using vi, you can be in one of two possible modes—command mode or insert mode.

The command-mode environment is used for such tasks as performing file operations, copying and pasting text, performing global search-and-replace operations, and working with macros. The insert mode of vi is used for normal text-editing operations. Probably more important than the two modes themselves is the ability to determine what mode vi is currently in!

When vi is initially launched, the interface is left in command mode. It is important to understand that direct file editing is not possible in command mode. Text can be copied and pasted, and various actions such as deleting text can still be accomplished, but adding additional text to the file by typing is not possible. In order to add text to the document, you must first switch to insert mode.

Insert mode is entered by pressing "i" or one of a few other insert text keys. When you are in insert mode, the bottom of the vi window will display the text "— INSERT –". Prior to adding text to the file, be sure you are in the correct mode by looking at the bottom of the window for that text. When you're in insert mode, you can switch back to command mode by pressing the ESC key. Table 3.20 lists some of the commands that can be used with insert mode.

TABLE 3.20
Commands Used to Enter Insert Mode

KEYSTROKE	DESCRIPTION
i	Change to insert mode and place the active cursor before the current character.
I	Change to insert mode and place the active cursor at the beginning of the current line.
a	Change to insert mode and place the active cursor after the current character.
A	Change to insert mode and place the active cursor at the end of the current line.
o	Change to insert mode and insert a new blank line after the current line. Place the active cursor at the beginning of the new line.
O	Change to insert mode and insert a new blank line before the current line. Place the active cursor at the beginning of the new line.
[ESC]	Exit insert mode and return to command mode.

As previously mentioned, the command mode is used to perform file operations, global text operations, and several other possible actions. These operations are either entered via one of several keystroke combinations, or through a special ":" prompt within vi. A few of the possible commands issued via the : prompt are documented in Table 3.21.

TABLE 3.21

Common Prompt Commands Used in Command Mode

COMMAND	DESCRIPTION
:q	Quit vi.
:q!	Quit without saving.
:w	Write (save) file.
:w filename	Write file as new filename.
:wq	Write file and quit vi.
:!date	Invoke command shell and run specified command. In this case, date is executed.
:r!date	Invoke command shell, run specified command, and retrieve output into current file. In this case, date is executed and the output is added to the file at the current cursor location.
:1,$ s/Bill/Bob/g	Starting from the first line and continuing until the end of the file, search and replace every instance of "Bill" with "Bob".

Table 3.22 lists keystroke combinations that can be used when in the command mode of vi.

TABLE 3.22

Common Keystroke Combinations Used in Command Mode

KEYSTROKE	DESCRIPTION
h,j,k,l (or arrow keys)	Move cursor position left, down, up, and right.
w,b	Move cursor forward and back one word at a time.
G	Move to last line of file.
*<linenum>*G	Move to specified line number. Use 1G to move to the first line of the file.
^	Move cursor to beginning of current line.
$	Move cursor to end of current line.
x, DEL	Delete current character.
5x	Delete five characters beginning at the current cursor position.
dw	Delete current word.

TABLE 3.22
Continued

KEYSTROKE	DESCRIPTION
d5w	Delete five words beginning with the word the cursor is currently on.
d$	Delete contents of current line, from current cursor position to end of line.
d^	Delete contents of current line, from current cursor position to beginning of line.
yw	Copy current word to buffer.
y5w	Copy five words to buffer beginning with the word the cursor is currently on.
yy	Copy current line to buffer.
y3y	Copy next three lines to buffer.
dd	Delete current line (stores line in buffer).
d3d	Delete next three lines (stores lines in buffer).
p	Paste contents of buffer underneath current line.
P	Paste contents of buffer above current line.
^	Move cursor to beginning of current line.
$	Move cursor to end of current line.
u	Undo previous operation.
.	Repeat previous operation.
/pattern	Search in the forward direction for specified pattern.
?pattern	Search in the reverse direction for specified pattern.
n,N	Find next and previous instance of search criteria.

TIP

For a great introduction to vi, execute **vimtutor** from a command prompt and follow the instructions. Upon completion of the tutorial, most important vi commands should at least be a little more familiar when you need to execute them again!

These three tables of vi commands have just barely scratched the surface of what vi is capable of. Although it may seem challenging, the most effective way to learn vi is by using it. When you are proficient with the commands outlined here, enter **:help** from the command mode of vi for more usage information.

## CHAPTER 4

OES Linux Clients

Instant Access

The Novell Client and OES Linux

- The Novell Client provides NetWare Core Protocol (NCP) services to client workstations. Used in conjunction with the NCP Server component of OES Linux, the Novell Client allows workstations to log in to eDirectory, map local drives to OES Linux NCP volumes, and seamlessly authenticate to OES services.

- The Novell Client provides a single method of accessing files in mixed NetWare and OES Linux environments.

- The Novell Client is an optional component that is not required for administration of OES Linux.

Installing/Upgrading the Novell Client

- Two Novell Clients are currently available: one for Windows 9x and one for Windows XP/2000. The Novell Client for Linux is expected to become available shortly after OES ships. Novell Client files may be downloaded from http://download.novell.com and installed directly, or copied to any convenient location, such as a network server, for installation by any client with existing network access.

- Use the Novell Client Upgrade Agent to periodically check for updated client files. When updated files are found, the Upgrade Agent will automatically start the client upgrade routine.

- If you are upgrading multiple existing Novell or Microsoft clients for OES, you can use the Automatic Client Upgrade (ACU) feature to automate this process. Place ACU commands in a profile or container login script to detect whether the client software needs to be installed, and then the ACU updates the workstation automatically, if necessary, when the user logs in.

- To install the Novell Client from a web server, copy the client files to the web server and use the WriteIP utility to create a SETUPIP executable that will download the Novell Client install files from the web server and launches the client install routine.

Configuring the Novell Client

- After installing the Novell Client, you can configure it by using the Novell Client property pages. Right-click on the red "N" icon in the system tray and select Novell Client Properties.

- To configure the login for a Novell client user, create a login script. Login scripts can be associated with Container, Profile, and User objects. A login script can control what happens when a user logs into your Novell network. For information and syntax on login scripts, see Appendix B, "The Most Essential Linux Commands."

The NICI Client

- NICI Client v2.2 ships with OES NetWare. The NICI client (Novell International Cryptographic Infrastructure) provides cryptographic services to all client-side applications and services, including Deployment Manager, Native File Access, Novell Modular Authentication Service (NMAS), and Certificate Server.

Integrating the NMAS Client

- Novell Modular Authentication Services (NMAS) allow you to supplement or replace the traditional Novell password authentication mechanism with alternative mechanisms such as SmartCards, Tokens, and Biometrics.

- The NMAS client provides a framework within which authentication methods can be configured and integrated with Novell eDirectory to provide a flexible and seamless authentication process.

- The NMAS client can be installed from the Novell Clients CD-ROM.

Mapping Drives to Servers with NetDrive Client

- With NetDrive, you can access your files on any server and modify them through standard Windows utilities such as Windows Explorer.
- The NetDrive client can be installed from the Novell Clients CD-ROM.

Accessing Files Through Native Linux Methods

- OES Linux servers natively support remote file access through Network File System (NFS) and Samba.
- The YaST administrative tool is used to enable and configure native file access methods.

Getting the Latest Client Software

- Novell frequently updates its client software.
- Check on Novell's support website's software download page at http://download.novell.com/ for the latest versions of the NetWare clients.

On a NetWare network, workstations traditionally use special Novell client software to access NetWare servers. (Workstations are often called *clients* because they request services from the network.) With the inclusion of the NCP Server with OES Linux, these same traditional Novell clients can now access the SLES filesystem as easily as a NetWare volume!

The Novell Client software enables workstations to communicate with the network. However, the majority of OES Linux components do not rely on a specific client. Rather, OES components provide clientless services and small service-specific clients. Web-based management, iFolder, and iPrint are a few such services that OES Linux provides to ensure that your network is not bound by client requirements.

In a pure OES Linux environment, the Novell Client is not required to make use of most OES resources. The NCP Server component of OES is the only feature that can only be accessed via the Novell Client. However, NCP file access is not the only reason to deploy the Novell Client. Workstations running the Novell Client can also receive the benefit of single sign-on authentication, the flexibility of modular authentication, and the power of an eDirectory-based user environment.

When combining OES Linux with OES or traditional NetWare, workstations using the Novell Client also have the ability to access data on either platform using a single, familiar method. This capability greatly decreases the complexity for such multiplatform environments.

NOTE

At the time of this writing, Novell only offers the Novell Client for Windows-based environments. A Novell Client for Linux is under development, and should be released shortly after OES. Unfortunately, this client was not available in time for inclusion in this book.

Because of this, the focus of this chapter is on Windows-based clients accessing OES Linux resources. Depending on the section focus, path and filenames may be displayed using either a Linux or Windows notation.

This chapter explains how to install and configure the traditional Novell client software. It also describes how to use the Automatic Client Upgrade (ACU) feature to simplify the process of upgrading numerous workstations to the latest Novell client software. It also explains how to remove the client software, should that become necessary.

In addition to the traditional Novell client software, Novell offers other modular client pieces with OES. These include the NICI client, the NMAS client, the NetDrive client, and the NetIdentity client. This chapter presents overviews and installation procedures for these client pieces. This chapter also discusses other file access options for OES Linux that can eliminate the need for the traditional Novell client for some network users.

The Traditional Novell Client

The Novell Client installation program automatically copies all necessary client files to the workstation and edits any configuration files that require modification. Although the Novell Client is required for OES NetWare and mixed environments, OES Linux does not require the Novell Client for full administrative capabilities.

You can choose one of three methods for installing the Novell Client on your workstation:

- Download and install the Novell Client from http://download.novell.com. Periodically, Novell releases updated clients with new features, so the client files on the Internet may be newer than those versions described here. It's a good idea to check this location occasionally for updates.

- Install the Novell Client from a web server.
- Upgrade existing workstations with the Novell Client Update Agent.

Novell offers a Novell Client for Windows XP/2000 (currently v4.91) and for Windows 9x (currently v3.4). The installation procedure for both versions is identical, so you can use the installation, configuration, and removal instructions regardless of the version of Windows you are running.

Novell is also nearing completion of development on a Novell Linux client for Linux workstations. Although complete details were not available at the time of writing, this new client is expected to bring many of the client features so important to Windows users to the Linux platform as well. Release of the Linux client is expected to be shortly after the shipping of OES.

For either Windows platform, if you are installing a new client, you should have an Internet connection to access the Novell client install files. If you're upgrading an existing workstation that already has a connection to the network, you can run the installation program from a network directory instead.

Installing the Client Software

To install the Novell client software on a Windows workstation from an OES Linux server, download the latest client from http://download.novell.com and complete the following steps:

NOTE

You can use the following procedure whether you're installing a new network workstation or upgrading an existing one. If you are upgrading an existing workstation, the installation program will detect existing settings (such as the protocol used, the network card, and optional features) and use those same settings as the default settings for the upgraded workstation.

1. (Conditional) If necessary, install a network card in the workstation according to the manufacturer's documentation and connect the workstation to the network. It's a good idea to record the card's configuration settings, such as its interrupt and port address.

2. (*Optional*) If you are planning to upgrade a workstation and want to run the installation program from the network, create a directory called CLIENT under SYS:PUBLIC, and extract the contents of the Novell Client ZIP file to the newly created network directory.

NOTE

With OES Linux, the NCP Server component is required for hosting a client upgrade directory for workstations. This directory must exist beneath the NCP exported SYS volume. On an OES Linux server, the full path to the SYS volume is /usr/novell/sys. The CLIENT directory must have Read and Execute rights to the directory so that users can locate the installation files. For more information on file system rights, see Chapter 11, "OES Linux File Storage and Management."

3. Run SETUPNW.EXE (Windows XP/2000) or SETUP.EXE (Windows 9x).

4. Specify either Typical or Custom installation and click Install. If you select Custom, continue with step 8. If you choose Typical installation, skip to step 13. The Typical installation configures the Novell client as follows:

   ■ The Typical installs only the Novell client files, the NICI client, and the NMAS client. If you want to install optional components such as NDPS, Novell Workstation Manager, and ZENworks Application Launcher, use the Custom installation.

   ■ Both IP and IPX protocols.

   ■ Directory-based authentication (eDirectory).

5. Select the client components you want to install and click Next. If the installation program detects that any of these options are already installed on this workstation, those options will be checked.

6. Select the additional products you want to install, and click Next:

   ■ *Novell Modular Authentication Services (NMAS)*—The NMAS client provides advanced authentication options to the standard Novell Client. The NMAS client is discussed later in this chapter.

   ■ *NetIdentity Agent*—The NetIdentity agent automates authentication to popular Novell services. NetIdentity is discussed later in this chapter.

7. Choose the network protocol(s) to support and click Next:

   ■ *IP only*—Installs only the IP protocol. The workstation will be able to communicate only with IP servers, and will not be able to communicate with IPX servers.

   ■ *IP with IPX Compatibility*—Installs the IP protocol, but allows the workstation to communicate with IPX networks if the servers have IPX compatibility mode and a migration agent installed.

   ■ *IP and IPX*—Installs both protocols, allowing the workstation to communicate with either type of server.

- *IPX*—Installs only the IPX protocol, allowing the workstation to communicate with IPX servers, but not directly with IP servers.

8. Choose NDS and click Next. Choose a Bindery connection only if NetWare 3 is the primary server environment.

9. (Conditional) If you selected Workstation Manager as a component to install, enter the eDirectory tree to be used by Workstation Manager, and click Next.

10. Click Finish to complete the installation. The installation program will automatically detect and load most LAN drivers for common network adapters. If it cannot detect your network card, it will prompt you to select one. You will need to specify the location of the driver your network adapter requires.

11. At the Installation Complete screen, click Reboot to restart the workstation and load the Novell client.

When the workstation reboots, it will automatically connect to the network and present you with a login screen.

Removing the Client Software

To remove the Novell client software from a Windows workstation, use the Network control panel. The Novell Client uninstall will remove all client components from the workstation, but will leave behind a minimal footprint in the Windows Registry. That way, if you reinstall the client at a later time, the installation program can automatically load the same settings that were used previously.

To remove the Novell client from Windows XP/2000, complete the following steps:

1. Open the Network control panel by right-clicking My Network Places and selecting Properties.

2. Right-click Local Area Connection and then select Properties.

3. Select the Novell Client for Windows entry from the list of installed network services and click Uninstall.

4. Click Yes to confirm your decision.

5. Reboot the workstation to complete the client removal.

To remove the Novell client from Windows 9x, complete the following steps:

1. Open the Network Control Panel applet by selecting Start, Settings, Control Panel and then selecting Network. Alternatively, you can access this utility by right-clicking Network Neighborhood.

2. Select Novell NetWare Client from the list of installed network services and click Remove.

3. Click Yes to confirm your decision.

4. Reboot the workstation to complete the client removal.

NOTE

You can also remove the client from the Control Panel by selecting the Add/Remove Programs option, selecting Novell Client for Windows, and then clicking Remove. You will still have to reboot to complete the removal of the client software.

To remove the Novell client from Windows 9x, complete the following steps:

1. Open the Network Control Panel applet by selecting Start, Settings, Control Panel and then selecting Network. Alternatively, you can access this utility by right-clicking Network Neighborhood.

2. Select Novell NetWare Client from the list of installed network services and click Remove.

3. Click Yes to confirm your decision.

4. Reboot the workstation to complete the client removal.

When the workstation has rebooted, the removal of the Novell client is complete.

Installing from a Web Server

You can now set up a Novell client installation from any web server by completing the following steps:

1. Copy the complete \WINNT or \WIN95 directory structure to the desired location on the web server. This structure is created when you extract the Novell Client files from the ZIP file downloaded from http://download.novell.com. You can place the files on up to five web servers in order to provide faster access.

2. From a Windows workstation, run `WRITEIP.EXE`. Using the WriteIP utility, you can create a small executable called `SETUPIP` that downloads the Novell client install files from a web server IP address and launches the Novell client install routine. There are versions for both Windows 9x and Windows XP/2000, and for all supported Novell Client languages:

- Windows XP/2000—`WRITEIP.EXE` is located in `\WINNT\i386\admin`.

- Windows 9x—`WRITEIP.EXE` is located in `\WIN95\IBM_<lan>\ADMIN\` where `<lan>` is one of the languages supported by the Novell Client.

3. In the WriteIP utility (see Figure 4.1), provide the necessary information and click OK.

FIGURE 4.1
The WriteIP utility is used for creating a setup application for installing the Novell Client from a web server.

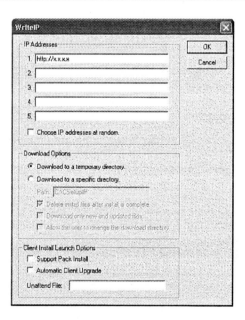

- Specify the IP address(es) or DNS name(s) of the web server(s) that host the Novell client files, and the full path to the client files, for example, http://www.quills.com/nwclient. Web servers will be checked in the order listed until a connection is made.

- Select Choose IP Addresses at Random to help balance the load of the Novell client downloads across all participating web servers.

- Specify download options for the client installation. Files can be downloaded to a temporary or a specific directory.

  Unchecking Delete Install Files After Install Is Complete will leave the Novell Client installation files on the workstation after the installation is complete.

  Allow User to Change the Download Directory lets the user specify the copy location of the Novell client files and change the default location.

- Specify the client install options. The Service Pack Install option lets you add service pack files to the web installation as Novell releases them. Both the new client software and any service pack software are downloaded and will be installed if needed.

  Automatic Client Upgrade permits the client install to run only if the Novell Client software being installed is a later version than the one currently installed on the workstation.

- Specify an unattended configuration file in order to fully automate the installation routine. For more information on creating this file, see the section on Novell Client Install Manager (NCIMan) later in this chapter.

SETUPIP.EXE will be created based on the options you have selected. You can then distribute SETUPIP.EXE from a corporate website, through email, or by whatever method is most convenient.

When a user launches SETUPIP.EXE, the Novell Client software will be downloaded from the specified web server, and the client installation routine will run.

Upgrading the Novell Client

There are a couple of options for upgrading workstations with existing Novell Client installations. You have the option of automatically checking for updates, and running fully or partially automated upgrade routines for your users, depending on their needs.

Novell Client Install Manager

The Novell Client platform-specific installation utilities each read a configuration file in order to properly install and configure the various properties of the client. This file is stored in the same folder as the installation utility, and provides information such as where to copy drivers during installation and the most recent version number. This configuration file is configurable through the Novell Client Install Manager (NCIMan).

NOTE

For Windows 9x workstations, options that were previously stored in NWSETUP.INI or were made available from the command line in previous versions of Novell Client are now configured through NCIMan.

To create or modify a configuration file with NCIMan, complete the following steps:

1. Copy the complete \WINNT or \WIN95 directory structure to the server from which users will access the client files. This structure is created when you extract the Novell Client files from the ZIP file downloaded from http://download.novell.com.

2. Launch Novell Client Install Manager (see Figure 4.2):

   - Windows XP/2000—NCIMAN.EXE is located in \WINNT\i386\admin.

   - Windows 9x—NCIMAN.EXE is located in \WIN95\IBM_<lan>\ADMIN\ where <lan> is one of the languages supported by the Novell client.

FIGURE 4.2
NCIMan utility from the Novell Client.

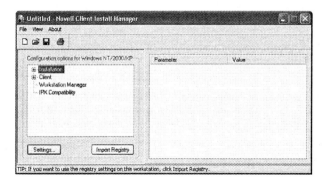

3. Click the New button.

4. Specify the platform for which you are creating a configuration file and click OK.

5. Double-click Installation in the left pane. Make your installation option choices and click OK. Each of the installation pages contains a list of the configurable parameters for the various Novell Client components (see Figure 4.3).

FIGURE 4.3
NCIMan installation pages are used to configure a Novell Client installation.

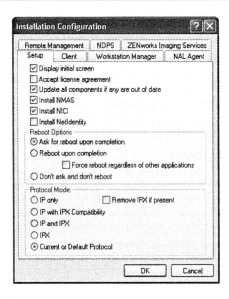

Any installation options different than the default selections will be listed in the right pane of NCIMan.

6. Double-click Client in the left pane to open the Client tab in the Novell Client Configuration page (see Figure 4.4). From this page you can configure how, or if, each client component will be installed.

NOTE

If you have previously installed the Novell Client with all the installation and client property options you want, NCIMan can read that information from the Windows Registry if you select Import Registry from the main NCIMan screen.

7. When you have selected all the installation and configuration options you want, click the Save button. You can save the configuration file with any name you want. Make sure you save the file in the same directory as the

SETUP.EXE (Windows 9x) or SETUPNW.EXE (Windows XP/2000) file that will run to install the client:

- Windows 9x—win95\ibm_language
- Windows NT/XP/2000—winnt\i386

FIGURE 4.4
NClMan client pages are used to configure default Novell client properties.

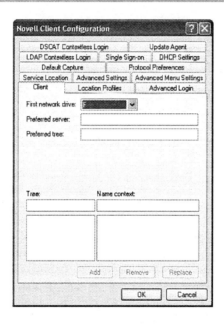

When the configuration file has been saved, it can be used as the Unattend file for performing an unattended client installation or upgrade. This option can be used with web server installations, the Novell Client Upgrade Agent, and Automatic Client Upgrades, all discussed earlier in this chapter.

Novell Client Upgrade Agent

The Novell Client Upgrade Agent simplifies client upgrades by allowing you to schedule periodic checks for updated client software. The Upgrade Agent will query a specified location for a newer Novell client. If one is found, the install routine will start automatically.

To configure the Novell Client Upgrade Agent, complete the following steps:

1. Create an unattended configuration file with the Novell Client Install Manager (NCIMan), as discussed earlier in this chapter.

2. To configure the Upgrade Agent, right-click the Novell N icon in the system tray and select Novell Client Properties.

3. Select the Update Agent tab (see Figure 4.5).

FIGURE 4.5
Novell Client Update Agent configuration options—available from Novell Client Properties.

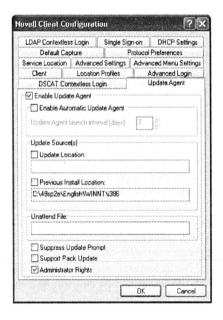

4. Configure the Update Agent and click OK when you're finished:

   ■ Select Enable Automatic Update Agent, and specify the launch interval, which defines how often, in days, the Update Agent will check for updated client files.

   ■ Specify the source location for the Novell client upgrade files. You can use the previously defined location, specify a new file location, or specify a web page for the client download if you have created one (see the section "Installing from a Web Server," earlier in this chapter).

- Specify the location and name of the Unattend file if one has been created. For more information on unattended configuration files, see the section "Novell Client Install Manager," earlier in this chapter.

- (Conditional) Select Suppress Update Prompt to perform the update without prompting the users.

- (Conditional) Select Support Pack Update to have the Update Agent check for client support packs in addition to full software updates.

- (Conditional) Select Administrator Rights to grant the client install administrator rights, which are required to install the client, even if the user who is logged in is not an administrator on the workstation. This option is checked by default.

When these steps are completed, you can use the Novell Client Update Agent to automatically query for and update Novell Client software on your workstations. When enabled, Update Agent can also be run manually by right-clicking the Novell N icon in the Windows system tray and selecting Update Novell Client.

Automatic Client Upgrade

Although the Client Upgrade Agent has largely replaced this functionality, Novell still offers the Automatic Client Upgrade (ACU) feature to automate the upgrade of multiple existing workstations to the latest Novell client. With the ACU, you place ACU commands in a container login script to detect whether the client software needs to be installed, and then the ACU updates the workstation automatically, if necessary, when the user logs in. For more information on login scripts, see Appendix B.

The ACU feature works best in situations when your workstations have similar configurations because you define a common set of instructions for updating all the workstations in the same way.

To use the ACU process to upgrade a workstation to the Novell client, complete the following steps:

1. Copy the complete WINNT or WIN95 directory structure to the server from which users will access the client files. This structure is created when you extract the Novell Client files from the ZIP file downloaded from http://download.novell.com.

NOTE

With OES Linux, the NCP Server component is required for hosting a client upgrade directory for workstations. This directory must exist beneath the NCP exported SYS volume. On an OES Linux server, the full path to the SYS volume is /usr/novell/sys. The CLIENT directory must have read and execute rights to the directory so that users can locate the installation files. For more information on file system rights, see Chapter 10, "Identity Manager Bundle Edition."

2. *(Conditional)* If you want to create an install routine that doesn't require any user input, use NCIMan to create an UNATTEND.TXT file, as discussed earlier in this chapter. Save the UNATTEND.TXT file in the same directory from which users will run SETUP.EXE or SETUPNW.EXE to install the new Novell client. If you use a platform-specific configuration file to configure the Novell client and you are using ACU.EXE, you must change the [UNATTENDFILE] option to Yes in the ACU.INI file.

3. Use iManager to add the following to the container login script for those users whom you want to receive the updated client. These commands support both Windows 9x and Windows XP/2000 clients.

```
IF OS = "WINNT" THEN
    @\\SERVERNAME\VOLNAME\...\SETUPNW.EXE /ACU /u:UNATTEND.TXT
END

IF OS = "WIN95" THEN
    @\\SERVERNAME\VOLNAME\...\SETUP.EXE /ACU /u:UNATTEND.TXT
END
```

TIP

For Windows 9x workstations only, you can back up the old client configuration instead of just replacing it with the new client software. To do this, add the option /RB (for *rollback*) to the end of this command. This option will copy the current software configuration to NOVELL\CLIENT32\NWBACKUP.

4. When the login script executes during a user login, the appropriate setup program will check the Windows Registry on the destination workstation to see exactly which version of the client is currently running. The setup routine will run only if the workstation's Registry indicates a Novell client version older than the version to be installed.

TIP

If you need to reinstall the same client version on a workstation, you can use NCIMan to modify the Major or Minor INTERNAL version of the client so that it looks to the setup routine as if the client is newer than that previously installed. The version setting is stored in the UNATTEND.TXT file.

The next time the users in the group log in, their workstations will be upgraded automatically to the new Novell client. For more information on ACU options, see the Novell online documentation.

The Client Login

When the Novell client has been installed, you can view and set login options from the Novell Login by clicking the Advanced button, as shown in Figure 4.6.

FIGURE 4.6
Novell client login screen showing the Advanced options.

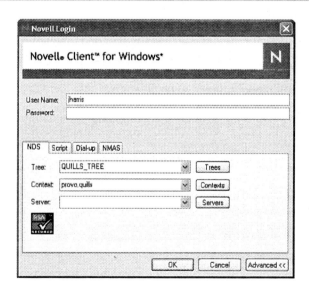

NOTE

The Windows tab, not shown in Figure 4.6, is only available prior to logging in to Windows. From this tab, you can specify the Windows username and workstation name that will be used by the Novell Client to transparently log you in to the workstation as part of the Novell login process.

NDS Tab

The NDS tab, as shown in Figure 4.6, allows you to specify the eDirectory tree, name context, and server to use during login. All users should specify their eDirectory tree and name context. A server needs to be specified only when connection to a NetWare 3 server is needed or when you are trying to log in to a specific server. When logging into a specific Linux server, that server must be running OES. In order to map drives to that Linux server, the NCP Server OES component must also be installed.

Script Tab

The Script tab (see Figure 4.7) is used to manage the execution of login scripts. It allows you to specify whether or not to run scripts; whether or not to display the login results window (and close it automatically); and which profile and user login scripts to execute. The Variables button allows you to specify values for any script variables that might be included in the login scripts.

Dial-up Tab

The Dial-up tab (see Figure 4.8) is used only when a user is connecting to the network via a modem connection. It allows you to configure a client to automatically dial in to the network whenever a user attempts to log in. The Dial-up tab taps into the Windows Dial-Up Networking information. You can select a dialing entry from the Windows phone book and a Windows dialing location profile. This option is used only rarely.

NMAS Tab

The NMAS tab (see Figure 4.9) is used to configure a couple of the authentication-related features of Novell Modular Authentication Services (NMAS). NMAS consists of a number of components and is covered in greater detail in Chapter 8, "Users and Network Security."

FIGURE 4.7
Novell Client Script tab.

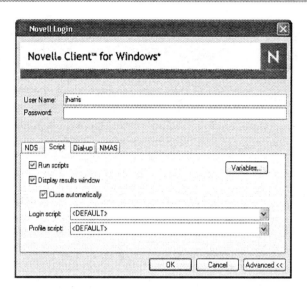

FIGURE 4.8
Novell Client Dial-up tab.

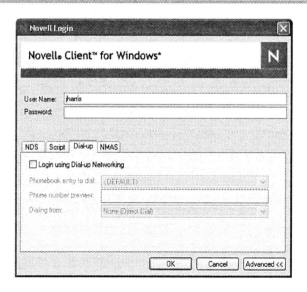

FIGURE 4.9
Novell Client NMAS tab.

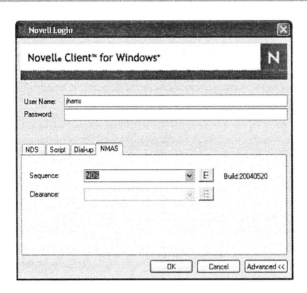

Configuring the Client

After you have installed the Novell client software, you can configure the client software by modifying its properties. The client properties enable you to specify information such as login preferences, protocol settings, default capture settings, and so on. To open the client property pages, right-click the red N icon in the system tray and click Novell Client Properties, which will open the Novell Client Configuration options (see Figure 4.10).

Several configuration pages are available in Novell Client properties. For detailed information on Novell Client property pages, see the online OES documentation.

- *Client*—The Client page lets you define basic login preferences, similar to the NDS tab in the Novell Login screen.

- *Location Profiles*—Location profiles allow you to save a specific login configuration so that users don't have to enter login information manually. Location profiles are especially powerful for users who log in from multiple locations (such as the office, home, laptop, and so on).

- *Advanced Login*—Advanced Login options let you hide certain aspects of the Novell Login screen to prevent users from making changes.

FIGURE 4.10
Configuration options for the Novell Client.

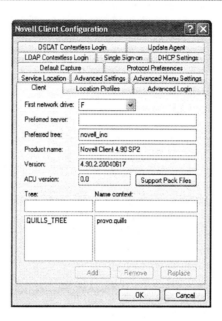

- *Service Location*—The Service Location page is used to configure the client for the use of Service Location Protocol (SLP). You can specify where and how the client will request network services. For more information on SLP, see the OES NetWare documentation.

- *Advanced Settings*—Advanced Settings allow you to configure a host of network communications details. For more information on the Advanced settings options, see Appendix A, "CLE Certification Options."

- *Advanced Menu Settings*—Advanced Menu Settings give you full control over the client network environment, including which network resources are available, and how they are offered to the network user.

- *Default Capture*—This page lets you configure a user's NetWare print jobs.

- *Protocol Preferences*—Protocol Preferences let you define the usage order for network protocols and name resolution protocols. The listed protocols are used in the order specified.

- *LDAP Contextless Login*—Allows contextless login without requiring the support of a catalog on the back end. When a user authenticates, LDAP is used to search the entire eDirectory tree, or trees, for the specified username. If a username is found, the login process will continue based on the tree and context information associated with that user. If the same username exists in multiple contexts, the user is prompted to select the correct user.

- *(Conditional) Single Sign-on*—Novell client for Windows XP/2000 adds the Single Sign-on tab. This allows you to store the workstation-specific password in eDirectory so that it can be automatically presented as part of an NMAS or single sign-on authentication, if available.

- *(Conditional) DHCP Settings*—Novell client for Windows XP/2000 adds the DHCP settings to configure the client DHCP environment.

- *DSCAT Contextless Login*—Specify the use of an eDirectory catalog for login. This allows users to authenticate using their common name only, rather than having to remember their entire name context. LDAP contextless login is recommended over this option.

- *Update Agent*—Configure Novell Client Upgrade Agent options, as discussed earlier in this chapter.

With these client pages you have very granular control over the operation of the Novell Client.

NetIdentity

The NetIdentity agent leverages what is known as the XTier framework used with NetStorage, Apache, and Tomcat services to provide single sign-on across all Novell services that use eDirectory authentication. The only caveat to this is that the first service with which a user authenticates must be NetIdentity-enabled. The list of NetIdentity-enabled services includes the following:

- Novell Client (v3.4x for Windows 9x and v4.9x for Windows XP/2000)
- iFolder 2.x
- iPrint
- NetStorage
- Novell Portal Services

When you have authenticated with one of these services, accessing any other service, such as iManager, that uses eDirectory authentication will prompt a transparent, background authentication so that you aren't required to re-enter your authentication information.

To enable NetIdentity-based single sign-on to Novell services, complete the following tasks:

- Make sure that the XTier framework is installed on all OES NetWare servers to which users will authenticate.
- Install the NetIdentity Agent on the workstation where you want NetIdentity services enabled.

The XTier framework is installed automatically when you install NetStorage, Apache, and Tomcat services. It cannot be selected and installed separately, so if you want to use NetIdentity, install one or more of these services on your OES Linux server prior to continuing. If you are unsure if XTier is installed on a given server, point your browser to the following URL:

`http://<server IP or DNS name>/oneNet/xtier-login`

If XTier is installed you will see an authentication dialog box, indicating that the server can recognize credentials passed by NetIdentity.

To install the NetIdentity Agent, complete the following steps:

1. Locate the `\netidentity` folder created when the Novell Client files are extracted from the ZIP file downloaded from http://download.novell.com. For example, for Novell client for Windows XP/2000, the NetIdentity folder is located in `\WINNT\i386\`.
2. Run `SETUP.EXE` located in the `\netidentity` folder.
3. Select the Installation language and click OK.
4. At the InstallShield welcome screen, click Next, and then click Install to start the installation routine.
5. When the installation completes, click Finish.

When NetIdentity has been installed, it will provide single sign-on to all Novell services that authenticate through eDirectory.

Other Novell Clients

In addition to the traditional Novell client, there are three other clients compatible with OES Linux. They are as follows:

- NICI client
- NMAS client
- NetDrive client

In addition to these three feature-specific clients, there are a few others that are installed automatically with their respective product software. Each of these clients will be discussed as part of its product overview in other chapters throughout this book.

NICI Client

The Novell International Cryptographic Infrastructure (NICI) is the modular foundation for all crypto-services offered in Novell products and services. NICI client provides cryptographic services to client-side applications and services. NICI client has received FIPS 140-1 (Level 1) certification, which is as good as it gets for client-based cryptographic services.

The NICI client is included with the Novell Client download, available from http://download.novell.com. In an OES NetWare environment, the NICI client is required for several components, including Deployment Manager, Novell Nsure Audit, and Native File Access. With OES Linux, the only components that require the NICI client are the Novell Modular Authentication Service and ConsoleOne (when downloaded and installed on a local Windows workstation).

The NICI client is installed automatically as part of the Novell Client installation process, discussed earlier. It can also be installed separately by completing the following steps:

1. Locate the \nici folder created when the Novell Client files are extracted from the ZIP file downloaded from http://download.novell.com. For example, for Novell client for Windows XP/2000, the NICI folder is located in \WINNT\i386\.
2. Launch WCNICIU0.EXE from the \nici folder.
3. At the NICI client Welcome screen, click Next.
4. At the License Agreement screen, click Yes.
5. At the Setup Complete screen, click Finish.

This completes the installation of the NICI client.

NMAS Client

Novell Modular Authentication Services (NMAS) allow you to supplement or replace the traditional Novell password authentication mechanism with alternative mechanisms such as SmartCards, tokens, and biometrics. OES Linux includes the NMAS Starter Pack, which offers two alternative authentication methods. NMAS Enterprise Edition, which is sold as an add-on product, adds support for many third-party authentication methods, multifactor authentication, and graded authentication.

The NMAS client provides a framework within which authentication methods can be configured and integrated with Novell eDirectory to provide a flexible and seamless authentication process. For more information on NMAS, see Chapter 8.

To install the NMAS client, complete the following steps:

1. The latest version of the Novell client and the NICI client are required for installation of the NMAS client. Make sure they are installed prior to installing the NMAS client.

2. Locate the \nmasclient folder created when the Novell Client files are extracted from the ZIP file downloaded from http://download.novell.com. For example, for Novell client for Windows XP/2000, the NICI folder is located in \WINNT\i386\.

3. Launch CLIENTSETUP.EXE from the \nmasclient folder.

4. At the NMAS Client Welcome screen, click Next. The installation routine will review the versions of the Novell client and NICI client to make sure that all prerequisites have been met.

5. At the License Agreement screen, click Yes.

6. At the Setup Complete screen, click Finish.

7. Click OK to finish the installation. Note that you will have to restart the workstation for the NMAS client installation to be complete.

When the workstation reboots, you will see the new NMAS login screen. For more information on configuring and using NMAS login methods, see Chapter 8.

NetDrive Client

Novell NetDrive lets you map a drive to any server without using the traditional Novell client. This means that with NetDrive, you can access your files on any server and modify them through standard Windows utilities such as Windows Explorer. For more information on using NetDrive, see Chapter 12, "OES Linux File Access."

The NetDrive client is available online at http://support.novell.com/filefinder. The current version as of this writing is NDRV41862.EXE. To install the NetDrive client, complete the following steps:

1. Create a folder off the root of your C:\ drive for the NetDrive client files and download NDRV41862.EXE into the newly created folder.

2. Launch NDRV41862.EXE to extract the NetDrive installation files to the folder you created in step 1.

3. Launch NDINT.EXE to install the NetDrive client.

4. Select the language for the client installation and click OK.

5. At the Welcome screen, click Next.

6. At the License Agreement screen, click Yes.

7. At the Destination Location screen, browse to the location where the NetDrive client should be installed and click Next.

When all files have copied, the installation of the NetDrive client is complete. With NetDrive installed, you can then easily access your OES server resources through mapped drives using any standard internet connection. For more information, see Chapter 12.

Accessing OES Through Native Linux Methods

In addition to accessing files through the OES NCP Server, clients can easily access the OES Linux filesystem through several native Linux methods. The two most common options for remote file access are the Network File System and Samba.

Network File System (NFS)

The Network File System (NFS) was originally created to provide for seamless disk access across a network. Through the use of an NFS server, local disk contents are exported to NFS client machines. NFS clients then access the NFS directories as though they were physically on the local disk.

SLES includes both client and server components of NFS. Although providing NFS access to the local disks is not required when using the NCP Server, it is sometimes useful or necessary to provide NFS access to clients. The following section will briefly describe the server configuration and client access methods required by NFS.

CONFIGURING NFS ACCESS

Configuring NFS file access on SLES is performed using the YaST management utility. YaST is discussed in detail in Chapter 6, "SUSE Linux Enterprise Server Management." To configure NFS, the "NFS Server" module within YaST's Networking Services section must be used.

The NFS Server module first prompts for enabling or disabling the server. If the server is enabled, the next screen allows for configuration of local directories for NFS export. To export a directory properly, the following components must be filled out:

- *Directory*—Absolute path of a local directory must be entered for proper functioning on the NFS server.

- *Hosts Wildcard*—Representation of clients that are allowed to connect to the current exported directory. A valid hosts list can consist of a set of asterisks (*) to indicate all clients or a specific IP address to represent a single client. Ranges of IP addresses and DNS names are also valid entries.

- *Options*—The options list of an NFS export is used to configure the permissions of that export. Common options include ro for read-only access, root_squash for disabling root access to the export, and sync for enabling synchronize file access.

NOTE

For more information on host wildcards and export options, see man 5 exports.

Upon completing the NFS Server configuration module, the NFS server is started automatically and clients can begin accessing NFS exports.

MOUNTING AN NFS EXPORTED DIRECTORY

When a SLES directory has been exported for NFS clients, it is imported into a remote filesystem for access. Linux systems use the mount command to accomplish this. To mount an exported directory on a Linux system, complete the following steps:

1. Use the mkdir command to create a directory that will hold the OES Linux NFS export, for example: mkdir /OESFiles.

2. Use the mount command to link the new directory to the OES Linux export, for example: mount *<server identifier>*:/data/linux /OESFiles.

WARNING

The server identifier is the IP address or DNS name of the OES Linux server on which you created the NFS Export. Make sure to use both the colon and forward slash between the server identifier and the path. The mount target directory must be an absolute path from the root and is separated from the source path by a space.

For more information on the Linux mount command, refer to your system's man pages.

Samba

Samba is a suite of programs that were created to improve interoperability between Windows and Unix-based operating systems. One major goal of Samba was to provide file and print services to Windows workstations as though the Samba server were another Windows server.

SLES includes both client and server components of Samba. Although providing Samba access to clients is purely optional, and may be alleviated by using the NCP Server, it is an extremely common requirement for Linux installations. One major problem with Samba installations is the complication of Samba normally storing valid users outside of the local Linux account structure. This essentially produces an environment where users have separate usernames and passwords just for accessing Samba resources. OES Linux resolves this problem through the use of the Linux User Management Component.

Linux User Management (LUM) acts as a middle layer between Samba and Samba users. Rather than relying on Samba-specific user accounts, LUM allows eDirectory to be used as an LDAP directory of Samba users. The configuration behind LUM is discussed in detail in Chapter 8. Configuring Samba services for users is then discussed in detail in Chapter 12.

Given the goal of Samba acting as another Windows server, configuration changes to a Windows workstation are not required. It may be desirable to configure a Windows workstation to join a specific Samba domain, but this is optional and not necessary for basic Samba implementations.

NOTE

Samba is a very complex suite of programs. For advanced configuration, including replacing Windows domains, please see the official Samba documentation at http://www.samba.org.

After enabling Samba on the SLES server, you can do file access testing using the Windows-based networking utilities or via a DOS shell. To map a drive to a Samba share from a DOS shell, use the following command:

```
C:\> net use f: \\<SLES_DNS_OR_IP_ADDRESS>\<SAMBA_SHARE>
```

To access Samba printers, the normal Windows printer configuration utilities can be used to configure a network printer, or the local printer port can be captured to a Samba printer using the following command:

```
C:\> net use lpt1: \\<SLES_DNS_OR_IP_ADDRESS>\<PRINTER>
```

In a Linux workstation environment, NFS is normally preferred over Samba. However, in mixed environments, Samba is often used for all client access. The easiest way to set up access to Samba resources from a SUSE Linux workstation is through using YaST. To access a Samba share through YaST, complete the following steps:

1. Launch the Samba Client module under YaST | Network Services.

2. Enter the name of the Windows Domain or Workgroup you want to join. Click Finish to complete the client configuration.

3. Use Konqueror to browse the entire network, or access a specific Samba share using the following URL format:

   ```
   smb://<SLES_DNS_OR_IP_ADDRESS>/<SHARE>
   ```

Samba resources can also be accessed directly from a Linux shell. The smbclient and smbmount utilities are normally used for this. The smbclient utility is used to browse Samba services on a Samba server, and the smbmount utility is used to map a Samba share to a local directory (as with NFS).

NOTE

Refer to the man pages for smbclient and smbmount for more information and on accessing Samba services from a Linux workstation.

OES Management Tools

Instant Access

Welcome Pages

- OES Linux Welcome Pages provide an introduction to OES components and links to administrative and user-level tools. You can access these Welcome Pages using a web browser to connect to the IP address or DNS name of the OES Linux server. For example:

  http://www.quills.com

  or

  http://192.168.1.100

ConsoleOne

- ConsoleOne is a Java-based tool for managing your network and its resources. Although not shipped as part of OES Linux, ConsoleOne for Linux, and several other platforms, it can be downloaded from http://support.novell.com.

- ConsoleOne is not capable of managing all components of OES Linux. However, some administrative tasks (such as eDirectory administration) can still be performed via ConsoleOne.

iManager

- iManager provides role-based management of your OES Linux network, together with a nearly comprehensive set of administrative tools. When you've loaded iManager, you will use it to perform most of the day-to-day administrative tasks in your OES environment, including management of most services that are available with OES Linux.

- You can access the iManager web page by appending the iManager path (`/nps/iManager.html`) to the IP address or DNS name of the server running iManager. For example:

  https://www.quills.com/nps/iManager.html

  or

  https://192.168.1.100/nps/iManager.html

- To force iManager into Simple mode to support Federal accessibility guidelines, use the Simple mode path (`/nps/Simple.html`). For example:

  https://www.quills.com/nps/Simple.html

  or

  https://192.168.1.100/nps/Simple.html

- You will be prompted to authenticate using a valid eDirectory username. Users can access only the iManager features for which they have been assigned rights.

Novell Remote Manager

- Novell Remote Manager (NRM) is used for remote management of OES Linux servers.

- NRM is launched directly by accessing the OES Linux server's domain name or IP address via secure HTTP, followed by a colon and the port number (default is **8009**). For example:

  https://www.quills.com:8009

  or

  https://192.168.1.100:8009

- You will be prompted to authenticate. For access to all NRM features, the user should authenticate as the root user on the local SLES machine.

iMonitor

- iMonitor is used for web-based management and maintenance of Novell eDirectory in your OES Linux network.

- Launch iMonitor from iManager by selecting "Repair via iMonitor" under the eDirectory Maintenance group. Alternatively, you can go straight to iMonitor using the following URL:

  https://www.quills.com:8030/nds

  or

  https://192.168.1.100:8030/nds

Throughout Novell's history, several management tools have been employed to provide various aspects of network administration. Some of these tools, such as ConsoleOne, are in widespread use today and still have a purpose in enterprise networks.

With the introduction of OES Linux, Novell has focused its efforts toward enhancing a central management tool originally found on NetWare. This tool is known as iManager. iManager is a web-based management portal into administration of all OES components. iManager offers a true platform-independent management interface that can be used from any workstation at any location to perform network management and maintenance of any kind.

iManager v2.5, which ships with OES, provides a complete set of tools for managing OES Linux. However, some additional advanced administration and maintenance utilities do exist outside of iManager. This chapter provides an introduction to each of these core Novell management utilities. Requirements and installation information for each utility, as well as an overview of features and capabilities of each utility, will be discussed.

Because multiple web-based utilities are available with OES Linux, the central access point for all utilities—the OES Linux Welcome Pages—will be explained first. These pages should be the starting point into OES Linux component management.

Next, the chapter mentions ConsoleOne, and describes why this utility is not necessary for OES Linux. (ConsoleOne can still be used for eDirectory-specific management functions.)

Finally, OES Linux's web-based management tools are presented, including iManager, Novell Remote Manager (NRM), and iMonitor. These browser-based utilities collectively provide complete OES component administration, and offer substantial flexibility for network administrators looking to get their jobs done from any place at any time.

Welcome Pages.

Prior to discussing the various administrative tools themselves, there is one important OES Linux tool to point out—the OES Linux Welcome Pages. These pages, shown in Figure 5.1, are a collection of introduction pages for each OES Linux web-based utility. These utilities are both administrative utilities, such as iManager and NRM, and user-level utilities, such as Virtual Office and NetStorage.

FIGURE 5.1
The OES Linux Welcome Pages.

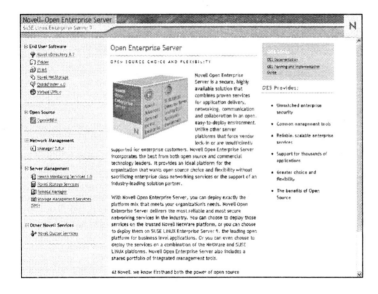

To view the OES Linux Welcome Pages, use a web browser to access your OES Linux server's IP address or DNS. For example:

http://www.quills.com

or

http://192.168.1.100

The Welcome Pages are made up of two frames. The left-hand frame is the navigation frame and contains links to all Welcome Pages divided into five categories. Beneath each category are links to introduction pages for specific utilities. Selecting one of these utilities opens the appropriate introductory page in the right-hand frame of the Welcome Pages.

Welcome Page categories and introductory pages found within each category are described in the following list:

- *End User Software*—This category contains introductory pages that end users may be interested in, including iFolder, iPrint, NetStorage, QuickFinder, and Virtual Office. Also included in this category is an introductory page for Novell eDirectory.

- *Open Source*—This category contains an introductory page for OpenWBEM, which forms a foundation of OES Health Monitoring.

- *Network Management*—This category contains an introductory page for iManager. This is the central administrative tool for OES Linux.

- *Server Management*—This category contains introductory pages that help manage the local OES server. Introductory pages include such things as Health Monitoring, Novell Storage Services (NSS), Remote Manager (NRM), and Storage Management Services (SMS).

- *Other Novell Services*—This category contains an introductory page for Novell Cluster Services (NCS).

Each OES component introductory page includes links to utilities, and documentation specific to the component in the upper-right corner of the introductory page. From an administrative perspective, the two most important categories are Network Management and Server Management. On the introductory pages beneath these categories, links to iManager, NRM and several other important utilities can be found.

ConsoleOne

ConsoleOne is a Java-based tool used for managing your eDirectory-based network and resources. ConsoleOne has been an important tool for the last several versions of NetWare, and has also been provided for standalone versions of eDirectory on Linux.

Natively, ConsoleOne provides support for basic management of eDirectory and core eDirectory objects (such as users, groups, and servers). As additional products are added to an eDirectory network, the eDirectory schema is extended to provide support for new object classes and attributes. In order for ConsoleOne to recognize these new objects, a corresponding product-specific snap-in is required.

OES Linux provides a number of new components that do not have a corresponding ConsoleOne snap-in. Because of this, OES Linux does not include

ConsoleOne. However, for basic eDirectory administration, ConsoleOne v1.3.6c can be downloaded from http://support.novell.com. Downloadable versions are available for Linux, Windows, NetWare, and Solaris. ConsoleOne running on any of these platforms may connect to and manage eDirectory objects on OES Linux.

It is important to remember that ConsoleOne cannot be used to manage every component of OES Linux. Existing infrastructures employing eDirectory can continue to use ConsoleOne for eDirectory administration, but comprehensive OES Linux management is only available through iManager. Additional information regarding ConsoleOne is available through the online OES documentation.

iManager

OES Linux includes iManager 2.5, a web-based tool for administering, managing, and configuring OES components, services, and eDirectory objects. iManager allows Role Based Services (RBS) to give you a way to focus the user on a specified set of tasks and objects as determined by the user's role(s). What users see when they access iManager is based on their role assignments in eDirectory.

iManager has been architected to leverage Novell's exteNd web services platform, and is in effect a management portal for Novell's products and services. It runs on Apache Web Server. For more information on Apache Web Server, see Chapter 14, "OES Web Foundations."

Although other management tools, such as ConsoleOne, can be used to administer specific components of OES Linux, nearly all management tasks can be done through iManager. Among other things, you can define management roles to administer Linux User Management (LUM), iPrint, iFolder, IP address management, and perform eDirectory object management. iManager is the preferred management platform for OES Linux.

Installing iManager

In some OES Linux installations and patterns, iManager will not be installed automatically. If you did not select to install iManager during the server installation, it can be manually reinstalled through YaST, or the command line. To install iManager via YaST, complete the following steps:

1. Access YaST from a terminal using **yast**, or from a graphical environment using **yast2** or the YaST launcher from the application menu.

2. Select the Network Services category in YaST. From within this category, locate and select the iManager module. This module will detect that the RPMs for iManager are missing and ask if you want to install them. Select Continue to install the necessary packages.

3. At the conclusion of the software installation, SuSEconfig is executed to update the system configuration. When this completes, the configuration of the iManager will begin automatically.

4. At the iManager Configuration screen, enter the following information and click Next:

   ■ *eDirectory Tree*—Enter the name of the eDirectory tree iManager will be servicing.

   ■ *FDN Admin Name with Context*—Enter the eDirectory administrators credentials using fully qualified dot notation, for example, cn=admin.o=novell.

5. The iManager configuration is now saved, and necessary iManager plug-ins are automatically installed. Depending on the OES components installed, this step can take some time.

6. In order for iManager to be active, select to restart Apache and Tomcat when prompted.

When you've installed iManager, you can open it from its URL, using either HTTP or HTTPS, at *<server IP address>*/nps/iManager.html. You will be required to authenticate in order to access iManager, and will have access to only those features to which you have rights. For full access to all iManager features, authenticate as a user with Supervisory rights to the eDirectory tree (see Figure 5.2).

You can also open iManager in Simple mode, suitable for compliance with Federal accessibility guidelines. It provides the same functionality as Regular mode, but with an interface optimized for accessibility by those with disabilities (for example, expanded menus for blind users who rely upon spoken commands). To use Simple mode, replace iManager.html with Simple.html in the iManager URL. For example:

https://www.quills.com/nps/Simple.html

or

https://192.168.1.100/nps/Simple.html

FIGURE 5.2

The iManager 2.5 home page.

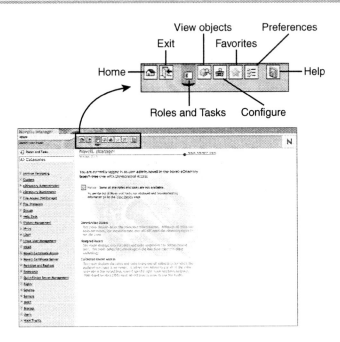

Using either interface, you will have access to only those features to which you have rights. For full access to all iManager features, authenticate as a user with Supervisory rights to the eDirectory tree.

iManager Basics

As shown in Figure 5.2, iManager is organized into three main sections, or frames:

- *Header frame*—The Header frame is located at the top of the screen. Its buttons provide access to the various "views," or content categories, available through iManager, as well as an Exit link to close the browser window.

- *Navigation frame*—The Navigation frame is located on the left side of the screen. It allows you to navigate among the various management tasks associated with the selected iManager view. What you see is further constrained by the rights of your authenticated identity.

- *Content frame*—The Content frame occupies the middle-right part of the screen. When you select a link in the Header or Navigation frames, the appropriate information is displayed in the Content frame.

TIP

If you see the Looking Glass icon next to a field in iManager, you can use it to browse or search the tree for specific objects to use in creating, defining, and assigning roles.

Role-Based Management with iManager

Role-Based Services (RBS) allow administrators to assign users a management role. A *role* is a specific set of functions, or tasks, that the user is authorized to perform. After users have been given a role, or roles, what they see and have access to in iManager is based on their role assignments. Only the tasks assigned to the authenticated user are displayed.

Compared to older iManager versions on NetWare or Linux, RBS has been significantly expanded in iManager 2.5. RBS now offers very robust configuration and assignment of network management responsibilities. RBS is configured through iManager, and all RBS-related information is maintained in a set of RBS objects in eDirectory. These object types include the following:

- *RBS Collection*—A container object that holds a set of RBS modules that will be assigned to a given portion of your eDirectory tree.

- *RBS Module*—A container inside the RBS collection that organizes available RBS Tasks and Books into functional groups. RBS modules let you assign users responsibility for specific functionality within a product or service.

- *RBS Role*—Specifies the tasks that users (members) are authorized to perform. Defining a role includes creating an RBS Role object and linking it to the tasks that the role can perform. RBS roles can be created only in an RBS Collection container.

- *RBS Task*—Represents a specific function, such as resetting login passwords. RBS Task objects are located only in RBS Module containers.

- *RBS Book*—Represents written materials associated with a given module, such as manuals, instructions, and so on. RBS books are located only in RBS Module containers.

- *RBS Scope*—Represents the context in the tree where a role will be performed, and is associated with RBS Role objects. This object is dynamically created when needed, and automatically deleted when no longer needed.

WARNING

Never change the configuration of an RBS Scope object. Doing so can have very serious consequences and could potentially break the system.

CONFIGURING ROLE-BASED SERVICES

During the iManager installation, the schema of your eDirectory tree was extended to support the RBS object types specified previously. To set up RBS for the first time, complete the following steps in iManager:

1. In the Header frame, select the Configure button.

2. In the Navigation frame, open the Role Based Services group and select RBS Configuration.

3. Select Configure iManager in the Content frame.

4. Finish applying RBS schema extensions by selecting Next.

5. Specify the name and location for the RBS Collection and click Next.

6. In the RBS Modules page, make your desired selections and click Start:

   - Specify the RBS Modules that you want installed in this RBS Collection. Each module provides a different set of management tasks that can be assigned as a group.

   - Specify a scope for the RBS Modules you have selected. The scope specifies the container in which those assigned this management role will be able to perform those management tasks. Select Inheritable if you want the management tasks to be applicable to all subcontainers of the Scope you specify.

7. When the installation of iManager modules completes, click Close.

Based on your selections, this will create all the appropriate RBS objects in your eDirectory tree. When you have configured your RBS Collection, selecting RBS Configuration in the Navigation frame will open the RBS Configuration task, as shown in Figure 5.3.

FIGURE 5.3
RBS Configuration page in iManager 2.5.

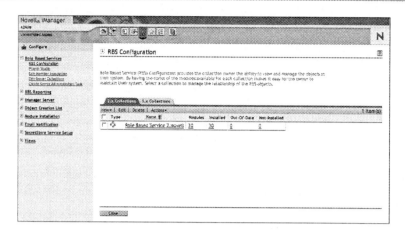

CONFIGURING RBS

From RBS Configuration you have full control over the structure of your role-based management system, including creating new Collections, adding/deleting Modules within Collections, and creating/assigning Roles to users.

When you install RBS, iManager creates specific relationships between Tasks, Modules, and Roles. However, you can modify task assignments, create customized Roles, or do most anything else you might need in order to align the RBS system to the realities of your network. For example, to assign a Role object to a specific user, complete the following steps in iManager:

1. In the Header frame, select the Configure button.

2. In the Navigation frame, open the Role Based Services group and select RBS Configuration.

3. Select the Collection in which you want to work by clicking its name in the Content frame.

4. From the Roles tab, select the Role you want to assign and click Actions, Member Associations.

5. In the Member Associations screen, provide the requested information and click Add. You can repeat this process for as many users as you want.

   ▪ Browse to, or specify, the User object you want to assign to this Role.

- Specify the scope for which the specified user should have access to the Role. The scope specifies the directory context under which the User can perform the management tasks associated with this Role. By default, the scope will be inheritable, meaning that the Role will be active from that point down in the eDirectory tree for this user.

6. When finished assigning users to this Role, click OK.

After being assigned to Roles, users will have access to the iManager pages associated with the assigned Role.

RBS is a powerful framework for configuring and managing administrative access to your network. Consider your assignments carefully and you can greatly increase the security of your environment by giving only the level of access necessary for a user to perform his or her job.

Novell Remote Manager

Another essential management tool with OES Linux is the traditional NetWare utility Novell Remote Manager (NRM). In a NetWare environment, NRM combines the functionality of the console Monitor utility, together with functionality from several other console utilities, and NRM makes it available from a web browser. With OES Linux, NRM brings this same ease of web-based server administration to Linux!

You can use NRM to monitor your server's health, change the configuration of your server, and perform diagnostic and debugging tasks. The following list outlines some of the major tasks you can perform with NRM:

- *Manage server health*—Monitoring the health status of one or more servers, building groups of servers to monitor—including servers not running OES

- *Configure server environment*—Viewing information about kernel modules, hardware resources, disk partitions, and processor(s); viewing and managing running processes; monitoring server memory and swap statistics; accessing and uploading files on local partitions; managing, installing, and removing software packages; and shutting down, restarting, or resetting a server

- *Troubleshoot server problems by*—Finding CPU hogs, finding high memory users, locating server process hogs, finding disk space hogs

Primary features of NRM include the following:

- *Logging in*—When you point your browser at NRM, you will be prompted to authenticate before seeing any pages.

- *Health Monitoring Notification*—Health aspects of the server, including memory, swap, and disk partition statistics, can easily be monitored. Thresholds for warning notifications can then be set to ensure that action is taken for critical situations.

- *Software package management*—Software packages can be managed, removed, and installed directly from the NRM interface.

- *Process management*—All running processes, and memory and CPU resources they are consuming, can be quickly viewed and sorted in several manners. Rogue processes can be killed from this same interface.

NRM is a very robust management utility that promises extremely flexible operation for OES administrators.

Accessing NRM

With most installations and patterns for OES Linux, NRM is installed automatically. After the installation, use a web browser from a client computer in your network to access the NRM interface. In order to access NRM from an Internet connection outside your firewall, you will need to make sure that TCP port 8009 is opened through the firewall to the IP address of your web server. Port 8009 is the default port through which you will access the NRM interface. If you like, this port can be changed as long as it doesn't conflict with any other service on the OES server.

To use NRM, you must use a web browser such as Konqueror or Mozilla on a Linux workstation, or Internet Explorer or Netscape Communicator on a Windows workstation. Make sure that Java or JavaScript is enabled on your web browser.

To access NRM, open your web browser and enter your OES server's domain name or IP address, followed by a colon and the port number. The default port for HTTP is 8008, and HTTPS is 8009. For example:

https://www.quills.com:8009

or

https://192.168.1.100:8009

You might be prompted to accept an unknown certificate. At the Authentication dialog, enter the SLES **root** username and password, or valid eDirectory administrator name and password, and then select OK. After authentication, the Novell Remote Manager home page will be displayed (see Figure 5.4).

FIGURE 5.4
The Novell Remote Manager home page.

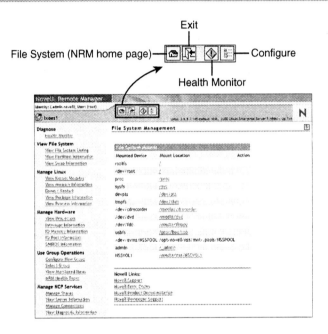

NOTE

If you don't log in as a user with administrative rights to the server, you will not have access to all pages necessary to manage your server remotely. You will see only pages that display the volumes, directories, and files for which you have trustee rights. In this case, you can view files (where you have read access), and upload files into directories where you have write access. You will not have access to any other management functions.

After you log in, your NRM session remains open until you close all your browser windows at that workstation. To log out of NRM, close all the browser windows at the workstation from which you logged in.

NRM Basics

Similar to iManager, NRM's user interface is organized into three main sections, or frames:

- *Header frame*—The Header frame is located at the top of the screen. It provides a semaphore (Green, Yellow, Red) assessment of the server's health, in addition to links to the File System Management and Health Monitor pages in NRM. There is also an icon used to allow editing of NRM configuration files. Clicking the Novell Remote Manager title in the header will also take you to the NRM configuration page. Selecting the semaphore icon next to your server name will take you to the Health Monitor page. By default, the File System Management page is always displayed when NRM first starts.

- *Navigation frame*—The Navigation frame is located on the left side of the screen. It lists different management tasks, organized into groups that you can perform with NRM. Each link takes you to the specific page(s) for performing that task. The list of available tasks in the Navigation frame can change based on the services configured on the server.

- *Content frame*—The Content frame occupies the middle-right part of the screen. When you select a link in the Header or Navigation frames, the appropriate information will be displayed in the Content frame. If an Information icon appears in the upper-right corner of the page, you can view help for the page that is displayed in the main content frame.

In the navigation frame of NRM, the main capabilities of NRM can be accessed using links found beneath six different general categories. These categories, and their general purpose, are described in the following list:

- *Diagnose*—This category contains a link to the OES Linux Health Monitor. Health Monitor is used to track and manage specific server statistics, such as CPU utilization, memory, and LAN statistics.

- *View File System*—This category provides access to the server file system. Options found here can be used to view, download, and upload file to the file system. General information regarding file system usage can also be found in this category.

- *Manage Linux*—This category is used to manage installed packages, kernel modules, and running processes. The server can also be shut down or restarted directly from NRM using options found here.

- *Manage Hardware*—This category can be used to retrieve information regarding server hardware. Specifically, processor information, interrupt configuration, IO memory and port information, and SMBIOS information are all available.

- *Use Group Operations*—This category is used to create Health Monitoring groups. These groups can include multiple servers (both OES and non-OES servers) for basic or complete health monitoring. Monitored servers can be arranged on maps to represent each server's physical location.

- *Manage NCP Services*—This category can be used to create, delete, and adjust NCP shares. Additional information regarding NCP services, such as connections and diagnostic information, is also available here.

Each of the options found in these categories can potentially play an important role in administering your OES Linux server. Be sure to drill down on every option and explore the many features found within NRM. Additional information on all aspects of NRM can be found in the online OES Linux documentation.

CONFIGURING NRM

You can access NRM configuration options by selecting the Configure button in the header (see Figure 5.5). To access the configuration options you must be logged in as a user with supervisor rights to the server from which NRM is being run.

FIGURE 5.5

NRM configuration interface to httpstkd.conf.

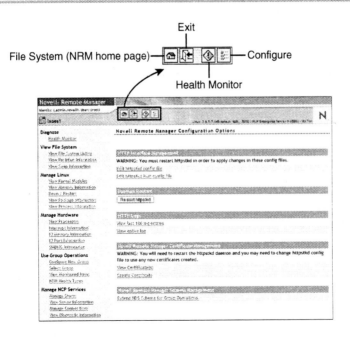

The NRM configuration settings are organized into five groups:

- *HTTP Interface Management*—This section allows you to configure NRM's basic environment, including TCP and SSL ports, default login contexts, startup parameters, and restricting NRM access through PAM configuration. After you've made any changes to these files, the daemon must be restarted using `rcnovell-httpstkd restart`.

- *Daemon Restart*—In addition to restarting the `httpstkd` daemon from the command line, a button in this section can be used to restart the daemon if configuration changes have been made.

- *HTTP Logs*—This section provides quick access to the `httpstkd` logs. These log entries are useful for troubleshooting any NRM issues. The `httpstkd` daemon uses `syslog` for the logging process. This allows these logs to be located outside NRM through `/var/log/messages`.

- *Novell Remote Manager Certificate Management*—This section provides the ability to create a new certificate for use with NRM. This is normally not required and should only be performed by someone with experience creating and implementing OpenSSL certificates.

- *Novell Remote Manager Schema Management*—This section provides an interface into the `ndssch` schema extension utility. The only schema extension that can be performed using this option is to extend the schema for use with NRM Group Operations, used with Health Monitoring.

NOTE

By clicking the word Novell in the upper-right portion of the header frame, you can access the Novell Support Connection at http://support.novell.com/. From this site, you can get current updates, locate troubleshooting information, or open an online support incident.

After making any necessary configuration changes, you can use NRM as a powerful web-based tool for managing your network servers. For more information on NRM, see the online OES Linux documentation.

iMonitor

OES Linux ships with iMonitor v2.3. The goal of iMonitor is to provide a web-based alternative, and eventual replacement, for many of the traditional eDirectory management and troubleshooting tools such as DSBrowse, DSTrace, DSDiag, and much of DSRepair.

iMonitor is capable of gathering information not only from OES servers, but from most any version of eDirectory, including NDS version 4.11 or higher, and NDS or eDirectory running on any supported platform (NetWare, Windows NT/2000, Solaris, Linux, and Tru64).

Although iMonitor does provide tree-wide management, it is designed to get "down in the weeds" just like the console-based tools that you may have used in the past. It keeps track of the activities of the DSAgent running on each eDirectory server, so you can get an accurate picture of what is happening at any given time.

The following list identifies some of the major features offered by iMonitor in OES:

- *General eDirectory tasks*—This category of features includes search for eDirectory object(s), status of DirXML in your environment (if applicable), both preconfigured and customizable eDirectory reports, and detailed eDirectory error code and troubleshooting references.

- *Monitor eDirectory agent health*—This includes synchronization status, detailed synchronization information, known eDirectory servers, and partition and replica status for this server.

- *Browse eDirectory agent*—This feature lets you view eDirectory objects and attributes from the perspective of the server as well as viewing eDirectory schema on the server.

- *Configuring eDirectory agent*—Configure partition lists, replication filters, background processes, agent triggers, login settings, schema and partition synchronization, and database cache settings.

- *Server-centric tasks*—This includes web-based versions of DSTrace, simplified DSRepair, and a background process scheduler. These services are available only for the server from which iMonitor is running.

As you can see, much of what was previously accomplished by console-based tools is now available via the web-based interface of iMonitor.

Installing iMonitor

iMonitor is installed automatically during the installation of OES Linux. Because it shares resources with NRM, the `httpstkd` daemon must be loaded on the server in order to access iMonitor. The `novell-httpstkd` daemon is started in runlevels 2 through 5 to accomplish this.

After the installation, use a web browser from a client computer in your network or from the server itself to access iMonitor. To access iMonitor from an Internet connection outside your firewall, you will need to make sure that TCP port **8030** is opened through the firewall to the IP address of your web server. Port **8030** is the default port through which you will access the Web Manager interface. If you like, you can change this port as long as it doesn't conflict with any other service on the OES NetWare server.

To use iMonitor, you must use a web browser such as Konqueror or Mozilla on a Linux workstation, or Internet Explorer or Netscape Communicator on a Windows workstation. Make sure that Java or JavaScript is enabled on your web browser.

Access iMonitor directly by opening your web browser and entering your web server's domain name or IP address, the iMonitor port number (**8009**), and the iMonitor path (**/nds**). For example:

https://www.quills.com:8030/nds

or

https://192.168.1.100:8030/nds

You might be prompted to accept a certificate. At the Authentication dialog box, enter the full username, with a leading dot, and password of an eDirectory user with administrative rights to this server, and then select OK to display the screen shown in Figure 5.6.

FIGURE 5.6
The iMonitor home page showing a summary of DSAgent information.

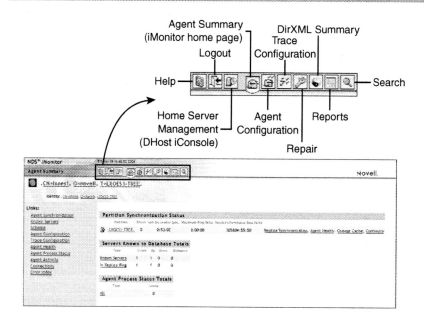

As with NRM, your iMonitor session remains open until all browser windows at your workstation are closed.

iMonitor Basics

iMonitor adheres to a page layout similar to that of NRM and iManager. There are four possible frames to an iMonitor page:

- *Header frame*—The Header frame is located at the top of the screen. It provides a semaphore (Green, Yellow, Red) assessment of the eDirectory tree's health, in addition to access to other iMonitor tools and the iMonitor configuration. Clicking the NDS iMonitor title in the header will take you to an About iMonitor description of iMonitor software components. By default, the Agent Summary page is always displayed when iMonitor first starts.

- *Navigation frame*—The Navigation frame is located on the left side of the screen. It lists different management tasks, organized into groups, which you can perform with iMonitor. Each link takes you to the specific page(s) for performing that task.

- *Content frame*—The Content frame occupies the middle-right part of the screen. When you select a link in the Header or Navigation frames, the appropriate information will be displayed in the Content frame.

- *(Conditional) Replica frame*—When needed, the Replica frame will appear in the lower-left corner of iMonitor. This will happen when another replica of the requested data exists, or when another replica has a different view of the information being presented in the Main Content frame. From the Replica frame you can change the replica that you are using to view the requested data.

The amount and type of information that you see in iMonitor is dependent on your current eDirectory identity and the version of the DSAgent with which you are currently working. As new versions of eDirectory are released, they will be updated to provide more information to iMonitor. Therefore, older versions of eDirectory or NDS, although still accessible via iMonitor, will not provide the same level of detail offered by current versions of eDirectory provided with OES.

MODES OF OPERATION

iMonitor can function in one of two possible modes. You don't need to do anything to select between the two modes; iMonitor handles it automatically. However, it is important to understand them in order to properly interpret iMonitor data and navigate the eDirectory tree.

- *Direct mode*—Direct mode is used when iMonitor is gathering information or executing an operation on the same server from which iMonitor is running. The server-centric iMonitor features mentioned previously, which include DSTrace, DSRepair, and Background Scheduler, are available only from Direct mode. Direct mode gives you full access to all iMonitor features and is faster than Proxy mode.

- *Proxy mode*—Proxy mode is used when iMonitor is gathering information or executing an operation on a server other than that from which iMonitor is running. Proxy mode makes it possible to gather information and statistics from older versions of eDirectory or NDS. Proxy mode is the default method of operation for iMonitor, meaning that after iMonitor is opened, it will continue to run from the specified server until explicitly told to switch to an instance of iMonitor on a different server.

iMonitor chooses the mode based on the URL request submitted from your browser. If the URL contains a server query, iMonitor will use Proxy mode. If no server query is present, iMonitor will run the query against the local DSAgent using Direct mode.

CONFIGURING IMONITOR

The default configuration of iMonitor is suitable for most environments. However, iMonitor offers a configuration file, /etc/ndsimon.conf, that allows you to customize iMonitor. It allows you to change both the general execution of iMonitor, as well as customize specific iMonitor features. For more information on iMonitor, see the OES online documentation.

PART II

Open Enterprise Server Infrastructure

## CHAPTER 6

SUSE Linux Enterprise Server Management

Instant Access

- Effective management of a SLES environment requires a working knowledge of the SLES startup process, including an understanding of the GRUB bootloader configuration and all boot-related files.

- Processes can be administered through the use of signals and process-related commands.

- Kernel and kernel module management involves understanding the contents of the /boot directory and configuration files found in the /etc directory.

- SLES administration is centrally located in the YaST command-line or graphical utility. All major SLES components can be managed via this interface.

- Although command-line editing of configuration files can often be used to accomplish administrative tasks, SuSEconfig may overwrite changes unless those changes are performed via YaST.

- System updates must be installed via the Red-Carpet software management system after installing OES. Using the YaST Online Update module can result in an inoperable server!

- Effective troubleshooting of SLES should involve the use of log files found within the /var/log directory. If additional investigation is required, Rescue Mode and a large number of additional investigative tools are available.

SLES administration is a broad and complex topic. This chapter will discuss core server administration tasks and important OES component administration concepts. Specifically, this chapter will cover the system startup process, process management, system logging facilities, and kernel management concepts. SLES and OES component administration through the YaST utility, and software installation options will also be discussed.

In addition to the administration concepts mentioned here, there are many other Linux topics you may be interested in exploring. Novell Education has several Linux-specific programs that will provide a more comprehensive insight into Linux administration. For more information on Novell's SUSE Linux certification options, please see the Novell Education website at http://www.novell.com/education.

SLES Startup Procedures

After you power on your SLES server, the operating system is initialized and background services (including OES daemons) are started prior to the server providing a login prompt. As an administrator, it is important for you to understand the process your SLES server follows to bring the server up to this usable state.

Bootloader Configuration

By default, a SLES9 installation uses the GRand Unified Bootloader (GRUB) to load the Linux kernel into memory. GRUB performs this task by writing a loader program to the Master Boot Record (MBR) of the first hard disk in the computer system. Following the computer's Power-On Self Test (POST) process, GRUB will be initialized and able to load the appropriate Linux kernel into memory.

GRUB employs a dual-stage loader process in which the configuration of GRUB itself is stored on the local filesystem under the /boot/grub directory. This directory is known as the GRUB Root Partition and contains the configuration files used by the GRUB bootloader. With a SLES installation, the file containing the GRUB menu configuration options is called menu.lst and resides within this GRUB Root Partition. An example of menu.lst is shown in Figure 6.1.

The menu.lst file contains a listing of possible boot configurations for the computer. These configurations typically include at least a normal bootup configuration and a failsafe configuration. All possible bootup configurations are listed in menu.lst and identified using the title directive. Each of these configuration entries includes a reference to the kernel being used and any number of possible kernel parameters, which are used during the initialization process. These kernel parameters are required for proper hardware initialization and can be customized to meet specific requirements of the SLES server. Table 6.1 shows common kernel parameters.

FIGURE 6.1

A sample SLES9 menu.1st configuration file.

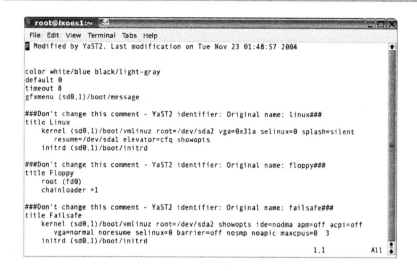

TABLE 6.1

Common Kernel Parameters

PARAMETER	DESCRIPTION
acpi=off acpi=oldboot	When this parameter is set to off, the Advanced Configuration and Power Interface (ACPI) system is completely disabled. Setting this to oldboot disables most ACPI components, but leaves boot-related components intact.
apm=off	Disables Advanced Power Management.
ide=nodma	Disables DMA mode for all IDE controllers.
noapic	This parameter instructs the kernel not to use the computer's Advanced Programmable Interrupt Controller (APIC).
nosmp	Disables multiprocessing capabilities of an SMP-aware kernel.

TABLE 6.1
Continued

PARAMETER	DESCRIPTION
splash=silent splash=verbose splash=native	Causes boot messages to be hidden behind the SLES splash screen. Setting this to verbose enables messages written on a colored splash screen. A setting of native enables a simple black console screen with boot messages.
vga=normal	This parameter causes the console resolution to be set to the default video resolution.
0-6	Specifying a number as an option forces the system to boot to the specified runlevel.

NOTE

For more information on possible kernel parameters, refer to the kernel-parameters.txt document found in /usr/src/linux/Documentation.

After you select a bootup configuration, GRUB loads the appropriate Linux kernel (as designated by the kernel directive in the configuration entry) into memory. The kernel itself is normally found in the /boot directory and called vmlinuz-<version number>.

In addition to the kernel, GRUB also loads a file called initrd-<version number> into memory. The initrd file is actually a compressed filesystem that contains all hardware modules required to access the root filesystem. The contents of initrd can be modified by editing the /etc/sysconfig/kernel file and making the appropriate changes to the INITRD_MODULES directive. Following modifications to this file, the mkinitrd command is used to generate a new initrd image. This is normally not required, but hardware changes after installation may require some manual intervention.

Daemon Initialization

After the root filesystem has been mounted, the process of bringing the server up to a usable state can continue. To accomplish this task, the Linux kernel loads the initialization (or init) daemon into memory. The init daemon is responsible for the final "look and feel" of a Linux server. It does this by referencing a configuration file, and then parsing a number of startup directories.

NOTE

A *daemon* is simply a system process that runs in the background to provide specific services. Daemons do not typically have a user interface.

The configuration file for the init daemon is /etc/inittab. This file is used to do such things as trap the Ctrl+Alt+Del keystroke, set up UPS monitoring services, enable the virtual terminals, and determine the default initialize level of the server. In Linux, any number of background daemons can be started or stopped at any point in time. However, the server itself can be considered to be running in one of a small set of possible configurations. These possible configurations are called *runlevels*. A server's runlevel is used to describe what state the server is in and what background daemons are started. Table 6.2 lists standard runlevels used in SLES9.

TABLE 6.2
Runlevels in SLES9

RUNLEVEL	DESCRIPTION
0	System halt (power down)
1 or S	Single-user mode (troubleshooting mode)
2	Local multiuser mode with no remote networking support (such as NFS)
3	Full multiuser mode with networking services
4	Not used
5	Full multiuser mode with networking and graphic environment
6	System reboot

After the init daemon is started, the inittab file is checked for the default initialization level. This value is one of the possible runlevels listed in Table 6.2 (although using a default runlevel of 0 or 6 doesn't make much sense). After the runlevel has been determined, the init daemon executes the /etc/init.d/boot script to control the bootup process, and must then process startup scripts for daemons allowed in the specified runlevel. This process is very important to understand and worth a little looking into.

To start daemons required in a certain runlevel, the init daemon executes the Master Resource Control script, /etc/init.d/rc, with a parameter indicating the desired runlevel. The rc script then uses the information found in the /etc/init.d directory and its subdirectories to finish the runlevel initialization.

The /etc/init.d directory contains startup scripts for all daemons installed on the local server. Some examples of commonly installed daemons include sshd, postfix, and nfsserver. Each of these daemons should have a startup script located in the /etc/init.d directory, shown in Figure 6.2.

FIGURE 6.2
Contents of the /etc/init.d directory.

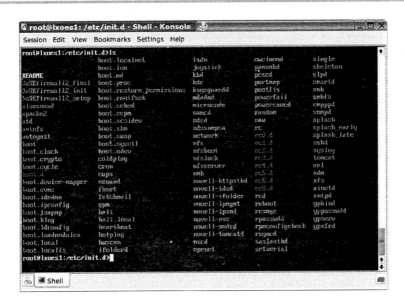

These scripts accept command-line parameters that indicate whether the corresponding daemon is to be started or stopped (among other possible parameters). For an administrator, using these startup scripts is the correct method of invoking background daemons. (For example, the command /etc/init.d/sshd start would be used to start the sshd daemon.) During system initialization, the rc script must also use these daemon initialization scripts.

TIP

In addition to starting services by directly calling the /etc/init.d startup scripts, SLES also creates symbolic links to these startup scripts under /sbin. These symbolic links all start with "rc". Because the /sbin directory is in the root user's PATH, these links can be used to start and stop services quickly. For example, to start sshd using one of these links, you would use the rcsshd start command.

Under the /etc/init.d directory, subdirectories are used to represent all possible runlevels. These subdirectories are named rc*.d (where * represents 0 through 6 or every possible runlevel). Within each rc*.d directory, there are symbolic links back to daemon initialization scripts found in /etc/init.d, shown in Figure 6.3. The naming of these links is quite important. These links can use either a "K" or an "S" as the first character in the naming of the link.

FIGURE 6.3
Contents of the /etc/init.d/rc3.d directory.

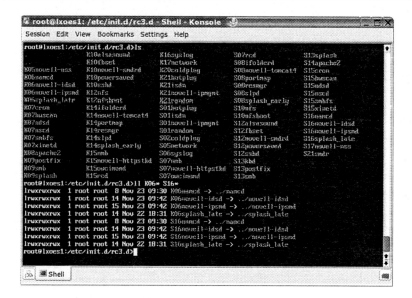

When the rc script attempts to initialize a certain runlevel, the symbolic links in that runlevel's directory are analyzed. During the initial boot cycle, this is a straightforward process in which all links that begin with an "S" are executed using a **start** command-line parameter.

When switching from one runlevel to another, links that begin with a "K" are scripts for services that should be stopped in the new runlevel. These scripts are executed with a **stop** command-line parameter. Scripts starting with an "S" are then executed using a **start** command-line parameter.

The second and third characters in the link filenames should be numeric. These are used in ordering the startup and shutdown of system daemons. Symbolic links to daemon startup scripts are simply executed with a **start** or **stop** parameter in numeric order, based on these second and third characters.

NOTE

The rc script in SLES9 does have a large amount of logic built in. When changing runlevels, the rc script will check the current runlevel and compare its configuration to the new runlevel. Services running in both runlevels are not unnecessarily stopped and then restarted.

Managing the system services enabled in each runlevel can be easily done on a SLES server via the graphical YaST tool or via command-line tools such as insserv and chkconfig. More information on YaST can be found later in this chapter.

Summary of the SLES Startup Process

Table 6.3 and the diagram in Figure 6.4 summarize the key aspects of the startup process of a SLES9 server.

FIGURE 6.4
Overview of the SLES9 boot process.

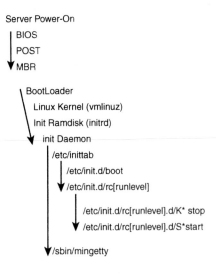

TABLE 6.3
Summary of SLES9 Boot-Related Files and Commands

FILE OR COMMAND	DESCRIPTION
/boot/grub	GRUB root partition containing bootloader configuration files.

FILE OR COMMAND	DESCRIPTION
/boot/grub/menu.lst	Main configuration file for GRUB.
/boot/vmlinuz-<version>	The Linux kernel.
/boot/initrd-<version>	Ramdisk image used to provide hardware modules to the kernel during the boot process.
/etc/sysconfig/kernel	Configuration file used when building initrd image.
/etc/inittab	Configuration file for init daemon.
/etc/init.d	Directory containing startup scripts for system daemons.
/etc/init.d/boot	First script used during the initialization process. This script configures system-wide variables and is responsible for control of the startup process.
/etc/init.d/rc*.d	Configuration directory for specific runlevels.
mkinitrd	Used to build new initrd image.
runlevel	Used to display previous and current runlevel. "N" indicates that the runlevel has not changed since startup.
init N	Used to switch to a new runlevel.

Interacting with Processes

All running processes within Linux are assigned a Process ID (PID). This PID can be used to manage and interact with each process. To locate the PID of a running process, you can use the **ps** command, as shown in Figure 6.5.

By default, the **ps** command produces a listing of all running processes in the current shell session. Using command-line switches, processes running in other sessions and background daemons can also be viewed. The information displayed for each process includes such things as the user who initiated the process, the Process ID (PID), and the Parent Process ID (PPID).

The first process started on a Linux server is the init process. All other processes are either spawned by init or spawned by a process already started by init. This produces a hierarchical structure for running process. Using the PPID and the PID, the path back to the init daemon can be tracked and is often useful when tracking down rogue or problematic processes.

FIGURE 6.5

The output of the ps command.

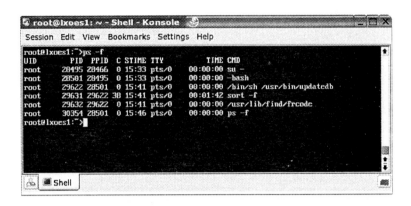

Another command useful for tracking down troublesome processes is **top**, shown in Figure 6.6. The **top** utility can be used to view running processes and also has the advantage of viewing processes based on statistics such as CPU utilization, memory usage, or many other parameters.

FIGURE 6.6

The output of the top command.

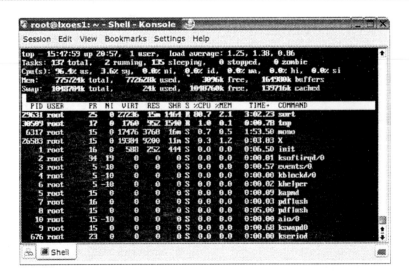

Using **top**, programs consuming an unusual amount of memory, CPU utilization, or other resources can be quickly identified. When these processes have been identified, several preventative or administrative actions can be taken to resolve potential problems. Normal actions include such things as shutting down and restarting services, but these actions can also include passing a signal directly to the running program.

Signals are an important part of running processes. If a critical event occurs, the kernel communicates that event to the respective process using a signal specific to the event. Using the **kill** command, these same signals can be manually passed to running programs. The use of signals is similar to passing control characters, such as Ctrl+C, directly to a running process. The syntax for the **kill** utility is as follows:

```
kill [Signal Number or Name] [pid]
```

Table 6.4 lists signals commonly used against running processes.

TABLE 6.4
Common Kill Signals

SIGNAL NUMBER	SIGNAL NAME	DESCRIPTION
1	SIGHUP	Sends a hang-up signal to the specified process. This action causes the process to reinitialize itself thereby reloading its configuration.
2	SIGINT	Sends a keyboard interrupt to the specified process.
9	SIGKILL	Sends a kill signal to the process instructing the kernel to destroy the specified process.
15	SIGTERM	Sends a terminate signal to the process instructing it to shut down or exit.
18	SIGCONT	Sends a continue signal to a process that has been stopped using SIGSTOP.
19	SIGSTOP	Sends a stop signal to the process.

NOTE

For a complete listing of all Linux signals, please use man 7 signal.

The **kill** command requires the PID of a process in order to function. If you would like to use the name of the process rather than the PID, you can use the killall command. The killall process sends the specified signal to all processes with the specified process name. This is useful when working with several processes, but can also cause signals to be sent to processes unintentionally. Because of this, care should be taken with the killall process.

Introduction to Linux Kernel Management

At the heart of the SLES operating system is the Linux kernel. As mentioned in the "SLES Startup Procedures" section of this chapter, the Linux kernel is found in the /boot directory and is typically named vmlinuz-<kernel version>. The default kernel with an OES Linux installation is version 2.6.5-7.112-default. The kernel version number can actually be divided into the following three important numbers:

- *Major Number*—This number represents the current major version number of the Linux kernel. The Linux kernel is currently at a major number of 2.

- *Minor Number*—This number represents the minor version number of the Linux kernel. Modern distributions are based on either minor number 4 or 6 of the Linux kernel. SLES9 uses a kernel with a minor number of 6. This kernel is commonly referred to as the 2.6 kernel.

  The minor number can also be used to represent the status of the kernel version. If the minor number is an odd number (such as in kernel version 2.5), that version of the kernel is a non-stable or developmental release of the kernel. Minor numbers using an even number (such as 2.6) are known as production or stable versions of the kernel.

- *Revision Number*—The final number of the Linux kernel version is the revision number of the kernel. SUSE also adds some information to this field to indicate the build of the kernel, as well as the specific environment the kernel was intended for. In the OES kernel version number 2.6.5-7.112-default, the revision number is 5-7 and the SUSE build number and environment designations are 112-default.

NOTE

The uname -r command can be used to display the version of the currently running kernel.

The most common administrative task relating to the kernel is most likely applying kernel updates to resolve security issues. Applying kernel updates through the YaST Online Update or Red-Carpet tools is a very straightforward process, but if problems are encountered, you may need to know more details regarding the layout of the kernel-related files.

Table 6.5 outlines the important kernel-related files found within the /boot directory.

TABLE 6.5
Important Kernel-Related Files in /boot

FILE	DESCRIPTION
vmlinuz-2.6.5-7.112-default	The 2.6.5-7.112-default version of the Linux kernel.
vmlinuz	A symbolic link that points to the current version of the Linux kernel. The /boot/grub/menu.1st file typically configures GRUB to reference this vmlinuz file rather than the actual vmlinuz-<*version number*> file.
initrd-2.6.5-7.112-default	Initialization RAM Disk used by the startup routine to provide required hardware drivers to the initialized kernel. This is used prior to the root filesystem being mounted.
initrd	Symbolic link that points to the current version of the initrd file. The /boot/grub/menu.1st file typically configures GRUB to reference this initrd file rather than the actual initrd-<*version number*> file.
config-2.6.5-7.112-default	Configuration file used for the compiling of the current kernel.
kerntypes-2.6.5-7.112-default	File containing information about data structures within the Linux kernel—used by the Linux Kernel Crash Dump facility for debugging purposes.
system.map-2.6.5-7.112-default	Map file containing address of symbols for the current kernel.

NOTE

As mentioned in Table 6.5, the GRUB bootloader is typically configured to load both the kernel and the `initrd` image using the symbolic links rather than the actual filenames. This is normally a good thing, but if a kernel patch fails to properly configure these links, the bootloader process will be unable to locate these important files and the boot process will fail.

Kernel Sources

Compiling your own Linux kernel is not necessarily a difficult process, but because of the potential for misuse and catastrophic side effects, Novell does not support compiling your own kernel. As a matter of fact, if you do require support by Novell and you're running a custom kernel, the first question you will likely hear is "Does this problem occur when using the default kernel?"

Even though compiling a custom kernel is not a good idea for a production server, there are a number of reasons why you might want to install the kernel source code. One example might be that a custom program you need to compile requires the kernel source to be installed. An even better example is the potential ability to look through the kernel source code to help track down error messages and their causes.

Using the **grep** command to search for a specific error message within the kernel source code tree can often lead to the exact error message. When you find the code surrounding the error message, you can analyze it and the root cause of your problem may be apparent.

In order to use kernel sources in this manner, the kernel-source package must be installed. This package is not typically selected for installation using the default configurations, but can be easily installed after the initial installation. When installed, the Linux kernel source code is located in the `/usr/src/linux` directory structure.

Working with Kernel Modules

When the Linux kernel is built, it must be built in such a way as to support as much third-party hardware as possible. There are essentially two ways to accomplish this. The first is to compile the kernel with specific drivers for all third-party hardware as part of the kernel itself. Although this type of kernel does work, it is generally not considered an efficient method of building the kernel as any one server really only needs a somewhat limited number of third-party drivers loaded.

The second and more common method of building the kernel is compiling a kernel with internal support for common hardware components (such as PCI support) and providing third-party hardware support through the use of external modules. This type of modular kernel is what is available with SLES.

When using external modules, the system must be configured to load the appropriate hardware modules upon system startup. During the installation of SLES, the installation routine will scan and detect hardware devices and build the `initrd` image with the required modules. However, when adding hardware after the installation or when installing proprietary drivers for unsupported hardware, it may be necessary to configure the server manually.

Table 6.6 lists commands used to manage kernel modules.

TABLE 6.6
Commands and Files Used with Kernel Modules

COMMAND OR FILE	DESCRIPTION
lsmod	Lists all currently loaded kernel modules.
rmmod	Removes the specified kernel module from memory.
insmod	Inserts a specific kernel module into the running kernel.
modprobe	Inserts a specific kernel module into the running kernel. If the specified module is dependent on other kernel modules, additional required modules will be dynamically loaded.
/etc/modprobe.conf	Configuration file used to load and alias kernel modules at system initialization. Additions to this file should be placed in /etc/modprobe. conf.local.
/etc/sysconfig/kernel	Configuration file used by the kernel during system initialization. The MODULES_LOADED_ON_BOOT directive can be edited to load specific modules at system startup.

After you have used the utilities listed in Table 6.6 to load and test a required hardware module, you must configure your server to automatically load the module upon server restart. This can be accomplished by adding the module to the MODULES_LOADED_ON_BOOT directive of the /etc/sysconfig/kernel file, or the module can be added to the /etc/modprobe.conf.local file.

NOTE

If you have a complex loading requirement, such as the specific ordering of more than one module, the /etc/modprobe.conf.local file is much more flexible than /etc/sysconfig. For more information on the syntax of this file, please see the man page for modprobe.conf(5).

Managing SLES with YaST

The Yet another Setup Tool (YaST) utility is the central management console of a SLES installation. YaST is available in a graphical version (**yast2**), shown in Figure 6.7, and a command-line version (**yast**). Each of these utilities relies on the same modular system for managing installed components of SLES. Although the look and feel of these modules may change between the graphical and console-based utilities, the functionality of these modules is identical across either version.

FIGURE 6.7
The Yet another Setup Tool (YaST) utility.

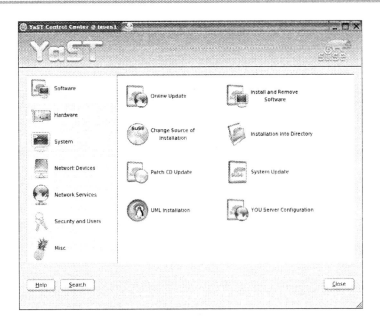

YaST management modules are divided into seven categories—Software, Hardware, System, Network Devices, Network Services, Security and Users, and Miscellaneous. Modules found within each category can be selected from within the YaST utility itself or initiated directly from the command line. To specifically execute a particular module upon starting YaST, the following command line should be used:

`yast <module name>`

TIP

To retrieve a list of all available YaST modules, use `yast -l`.

Modules used for initial configuration of many of the Novell OES components are also found in YaST. These components are all represented in the graphical environment with an icon containing a red "N" for Novell. Although many of these modules are found in the Network Services category, the actual category where each module is found depends on the module in question.

WARNING

The functionality of the OES modules is mainly the installation and basic setup of each service. Most services require additional setup within a management utility such as iManager. Using YaST modules to configure OES services will often revert the component back to the newly installed state!

Detailed setup and configuration instructions within iManager, or other component-specific utilities, are covered in service-specific sections throughout this book.

The following section will briefly describe each management module available through YaST.

Software

The Software category of YaST contains modules used to update and install code onto the SLES server. The following list describes each module found in this section.

- *Online Update*—The Online Update utility can be used to launch the Red-Carpet OES update service. This service connects to the Novell update server which provides patches and updates to SLES and OES components. More information on Red-Carpet is available later in this chapter.

- *Install and Remove Software*—This module is used to perform package maintenance. Software packages can be installed or removed individually or through package groups. Although packages can be installed manually outside of YaST, package dependencies are resolved automatically when using this module.

- *Change Source of Installation*—Through the use of this module, additional installation sources can be configured. This allows for easily changing the installation from CD media-based to a network-based installation source. This module can also be used to add additional software for different versions of SUSE Linux—such as SUSE Linux Professional.

WARNING

Use extreme care when adding non-SLES products as additional installation sources. Installing small utilities or programs is usually not harmful, but updating critical system components, such as glibc, can have catastrophic effects! In particular, performing a system update with the non-SLES source configured will almost certainly result in an unusable server. To avoid these types of problems, be sure to disable the non-SLES source immediately after installing the required program.

- *Installation into Directory*—This module is used to install SLES9 into a specified directory.

- *Patch CD Update*—This module is used to apply service update patch CDs onto the current SLES9 installation.

- *System Update*—Using this module, a SLES installation can be updated to a newer version. This is typically used for an update from SLES8 to SLES9.

- *UML Installation*—User Mode Linux is a virtual Linux machine installation that can be run within the current Linux session. This module provides for the installation of SLES9 in a virtual machine.

- *YOU Server Configuration*—The YaST Online Update patch server can be run locally for distributing patches across the local area network. This module allows for the configuration of a local YOU server.

Hardware

The Hardware category of YaST is used to manage hardware devices physically attached to the server. If new hardware is detected during initialization, these modules may be launched for configuration of the new hardware. These modules can also be used to manually change the configuration of existing hardware, and add hardware not automatically detected.

- *CD-ROM Drives*—CD-ROM and DVD-ROM drives are assigned to Linux devices using this module.

- *Disk Controllers*—Modules required for using installed disk controllers are configured using this module. Specific kernel modules and startup parameters are also configured within this utility.

- *Graphics Card and Monitor*—This module is used to configure the graphic card and monitor for the graphical environment. The `sax2` utility will be launched by this module to perform changes.

- *Hardware Information*—This module can be used to query the hardware components recognized on the server. The details of these components can then be saved to a file for later review.

- *IDE DMA Mode*—This module is used to enable DMA mode for IDE devices. DMA mode may increase performance, but may also be incompatible with some IDE devices.

- *Joystick*—This module is used for configuring a joystick input device.

- *Printer*—This module is used to configure printers for use by the local server. These printers can be local printers, remote printers via CUPS, or one of several less common printer configurations. If you are using CUPS for print support, accessing the CUPS web administration interface is another option for printer management. This interface can be accessed via a web browser and the http://localhost:631 address.

- *Select Mouse Model*—This module is used to modify the mouse configuration for the graphical environment.

- *Sound*—This module is used to configure a sound card for the current installation.

System

The System category of YaST contains modules used to adjust the configuration of the SLES installation itself.

- */etc/sysconfig Editor*—The `/etc/sysconfig` directory contains local configuration files for many different components of a SLES server. This module can be used to adjust various parameters for those components. These same adjustments can be made by manually editing configuration files found in `/etc/sysconfig`.

- *Boot Loader Configuration*—This module is used to modify the configuration of the GRand Unified Bootloader (GRUB). One common purpose for adjusting this is to pass additional parameters to the kernel when starting SLES.

- *Choose Language*—This module is used to select the active language for the SLES server.

- *Create a Boot, Rescue, or Module Floppy*—This module can be used to create one of several different types of floppy disk configurations. One common use is to create a Rescue Floppy Disk that can be used to boot the server for emergency troubleshooting purposes.

- *Date and Time*—This module is used to adjust the date, time, and time zone information of the SLES installation.

- *High Availability*—This module is used to enable a heartbeat server, which is used to ensure high availability of the SLES server.

- *LVM*—The Logic Volume Manager module is used to create logical volume groups, and volumes within those groups.

- *NSS*—This OES module is used to install the Novell Storage Services kernel modules and software, and to configure the NSS Admin object in eDirectory.

- *Novell Cluster Services (NCS)*—This OES module is used to install NCS software and to configure a new or existing cluster. When the cluster is configured, the current server is added as a node in the cluster.

- *Partitioner*—This module is a graphical interface to the `fdisk` partition management utility. It is also used to enable RAID, LVM, and create encrypted `CRYPT` files.

- *Power Management*—This module is used to modify ACPI settings and power-saving configurations of the SLES installation. For server installations, the power settings should be left on the Performance setting.

- *Powertweak Configuration*—This module is used to adjust low-level Linux settings to increase performance. Manually adjusting these parameters can cause extensive damage to the SLES installation and should only be performed by experts familiar with each specific setting.

- *Profile Manager*—This module is intended to be used in environments where Linux is started in multiple physical configurations such as when running on a laptop. Each configuration can be stored as a profile and managed through this module. Profile management is typically not used on a server.

- *Restore System*—This module is used to restore system files from a back-up archive created through the "System Backup" YaST module.

- *Runlevel Editor*—This module is used to determine which system daemons are running during each runlevel. In expert mode, this utility can also adjust the system default runlevel, and interact with each daemon process.

- *SMS*—This OES module is used to install and configure Novell Storage Management Services.

- *Select Keyboard Layout*—This module can be used to adjust the keyboard layout to match the layout of an international keyboard or some other custom layout.

- *System Backup*—The System Backup module can be used to automate basic system backup functionality. This utility can perform various types of backups based on customized backup profiles. These backups can then be restored using the "Restore System" YaST module. For advanced backup features, such as incremental backups, third-party backup utilities are required.

Network Devices

The Network Devices category of YaST is used to adjust network device settings such as network interface cards and modems.

- *DSL*—This module is used to configure DSL devices connected to the server.

- *Fax*—This module is used to configure an ISDN Fax device connected to the server. Multiple users can use this fax system, provided they all have unique fax numbers.

- *ISDN*—This module is used to configure ISDN devices connected to the server.

- *Modem*—This module is used to configure internal or external modems connected to the server.

- *Network Card*—This module is used to configure network interface cards (NICs) connected to the server. Among other things, this module can be used to configure a NIC for DHCP or static IP address assignment, set a default route for the NIC, and to configure the machine's host and domain name information.

NOTE

OES requires a static IP address for the SLES server. If adding OES to an existing server, ensure a static IP address is in place (rather than DHCP) using this module prior to installing OES.

- *Phone Answering Machine*—This module is used to configure a phone answering-machine system for one or more users on the SLES server.

Network Services

The Network Services category of YaST is used to adjust advanced networking services that may be in use on the SLES machine. These networking services are not required for operation of SLES, but may be in use depending on your configuration. Also, some of these services can be replaced through the installation of OES.

- *DHCP Server*—This module is used to configure the DHCP server that is available with SLES.

- *DNS Server*—This module is used to configure the DNS server that is available with SLES.

- *DNS and Host Name*—This module is used to modify the local configuration of DNS name servers and specify the value for the local host and domain names.

NOTE

OES requires a properly registered DNS and Host Name for the local SLES server. Ensure this configuration is in place using this module, or another server providing DNS services, prior to configuring OES components.

- *HTTP Server*—This module is used to modify the configuration of the Apache 2 web server. Apache is used extensively with various OES components, and care must be given when adjusting its default configuration.

- *Host Names*—This module provides an interface into the `/etc/hosts` file where known hosts can be configured.

- *Kerberos Client*—This module is used to enable Kerberos authentication for local accounts through PAM.

- *LDAP Client*—This module is used to enable LDAP authentication for local user accounts. The LUM component of OES provides this functionality. When using LUM, manual adjustment of LDAP authentication should not be performed.

- *LDAP Server*—This module is used to configure the OpenLDAP server. When using OES, OpenLDAP is not normally used as LDAP functionality is provided by eDirectory.

- *Mail Transfer Agent*—This module is used to configure PostFix for sending and receiving mail.

- *NCP Server*—This OES module is used to install the NCP Server libraries and configure default NCP volumes.

- *NFS Client*—This module is used to manage remote NFS mounts which are added to `/etc/fstab`.

- *NFS Server*—This module is used to start and configure the local NFS server. This module also provides an interface into editing the local `/etc/exports` file.

- *NIS Client*—This module is used for enabling NIS lookup of local user accounts. When using the LUM component of OES, this option should not be enabled.

- *NIS Server*—This module is used to configure the local SLES machine to be a server in an NIS domain.

- *NTP Client*—This module is used to configure Network Time Protocol (NTP) services for the local machine. NTP synchronizes the local clock with a network time server. Many components of OES rely on an accurate system clock. As such, NTP is required with OES. For more information on NTP, see the online OES documentation.

- *NetStorage*—This OES module is used to install NetStorage and configure its integration with iFolder 2.x.

- *Network Services* (`inetd`)—This module provides an interface into managing network services protected by the eXtended InterNET services Daemon (`xinetd`).

- *Novell Health Monitoring*—This OES module is used to install and configure Health Monitoring Services on the local server.

- *Novell QuickFinder*—This OES module is used to install QuickFinder, and add the QuickFinder user to the shadow user group. This is necessary to allow users to authenticate to the QuickFinder server with specific user rights.

- *Novell Samba*—This OES module is used to configure LDAP authentication for Samba users to eDirectory.

- *Proxy*—This module is used to configure an HTTP or FTP proxy that might be required for Internet access.

- *Remote Administration*—This module enables remote VNC connections to the local X server for remote graphical administration of SLES.

- *Routing*—This module provides an interface into the local routing tables. Using this interface, the default route can be modified, additional routes can be added, and IP forwarding can be enabled.

- *SLP Browser*—This module provides a browser interface into the SLP services advertised by the local SLP daemon.

- *Samba Client*—This module is used to configure the local machine as a Samba client to another Samba server. After installing OES, this module should not be used.

- *Samba Server*—This module is used to manage local services that are shared to SMB/CIFS clients.

- *TFTP Server*—This module is used to enable the Trivial FTP server. The TFTP server is protected behind **xinetd** by default. Using this module, the root directory used by TFTP can be modified.

- *Virtual Office*—This OES module is used to install Virtual Office and configure Virtual Office[nd]specific objects within eDirectory.

- *WOL*—The Wake-On-LAN module allows for remotely waking up another computer on demand.

- *eDirectory*—This OES module is used to configure or reinitialize the eDirectory database.

- *eGuide*—This OES module is used to install and configure the eGuide application.

- *iFolder 2.x*—This OES module is used to configure the iFolder 2.x service. Configuration parameters include the server IP address, DNS name, and directory for iFolder data. iFolder administration users are also added in this module.

- *iManager*—This OES module is used to install and configure the iManager server and install iManager plug-ins.

- *iPrint*—This OES module is used to install iPrint and configure iPrint server settings.

Security and Users

The Security and Users category of YaST is used to configure local users and groups, and essential security settings of the SLES installation. If the LUM component of OES is installed, user management should be performed via iManager.

- *CA Management*—This module is used to manage the certificate authority on SLES.

- *Edit and Create Groups*—This module is used to create local user groups. After you install OES, if the LUM component is in use, you should do group administration via iManager.

- *Edit and Create Users*—This module is used to create local user accounts. After installing OES, if the LUM component is in use, user account administration should be done via iManager.

- *Firewall*—This module is used to provide a graphical interface into the `iptables` firewall configuration. Use caution when you manipulate the firewall, as incorrect settings can lock users out of SLES and OES services.

- *Import Common Server Certificate*—This module is used for importing a common server certificate that is used by various YaST modules. Certificates can be imported from a floppy disk or directly from the hard disk.

- *Linux User Management*—This OES module is used to configure Linux User Management. `Linuxconfig` and workstation contexts, as well as LDAP proxy settings, are configured using this module. PAM-aware services can also be LUM-enabled or disabled using this module.

- *Security Settings*—This module is used to enforce password security settings for local accounts. These settings include such things as password encryption method, password length, and password expiration intervals.

- *VPN*—This module is used to configure IPSec-based Virtual Private Networking (VPN). This module utilizes the FreeS/WAN package to provide this functionality.

Misc

The Misc category of YaST contains a number of modules that do not fit in the other, well-defined categories of YaST.

- *AutoInstallation*—This module is used to create an automatic installation profile that can be used for subsequent SLES installations. Automatic installations are highly configurable and are commonly used to facilitate the installation of a large amount of SLES servers.

- *CD Creator*—This module is used to create installation directories or CD ISO images of a customized version of SLES.

- *Installation Server*—This module is used to provide network installation sources for versions of SUSE Linux. Using this module, network installation sources can be configured and advertised over SLP. Client installations can then be performed from those sources rather than the CD media.

- *Load Vendor Driver CD*—This module is used to install drivers provided by a third-party.

- *Post a Support Query*—This module is used to send a support query to the SUSE Support Portal. Support can also be accessed by visiting http://support.novell.com.

- *View Start-up Log*—This module is used to view the **/var/log/boot.msg** startup log.

- *View System Log*—This module is used to view the **/var/log/messages** system log file. Several other log files under **/var/log** and various files found in the **/proc** directory structure can also be viewed using this module.

SuSEconfig

When using YaST to perform administrative tasks such as package management or network service configuration, changes made within YaST are either written directly to the appropriate configuration files or to files in the **/etc/sysconfig** directory.

Files within the **/etc/sysconfig** directory contain variables used to configure the behavior of many SLES services. These variables are sometimes used directly from these files, but often must be used to adjust configuration files specific to the respective service. To synchronize application configuration files with the information contained in **/etc/sysconfig**, the **SuSEconfig** utility is launched every time YaST operations have been completed.

SuSEconfig acts as an intermediate layer between YaST and several application-specific configuration files. When run, **SuSEconfig** parses all variables defined in **/etc/sysconfig** and modifies the appropriate application-specific configuration files. This action takes place after every YaST operation to ensure that these two sets of configuration files remain in sync.

WARNING

If application configuration files are manually edited outside of YaST, subsequent YaST operations will launch **SuSEconfig** and manually edited changes can be lost. To avoid this problem, use YaST whenever adjusting installed applications and services.

Manual edits of files within /etc/sysconfig also may not change the behavior of applications or services. Depending on the application, the configuration changes may need to be synchronized with additional configuration files. To avoid this situation, manually run the SuSEconfig program after adjusting files in /etc/sysconfig.

Updating OES Linux

YaST provides several modules for installing and updating software on a normal SLES server. However, after installing OES, only the Red-Carpet software management system should be used. This is true when installing updates to both OES components and the core operating system.

NOTE

To prevent SLES updates, which may not be aware of OES components, the normal YaST Online Update (YOU) utility is disabled during the OES installation. It is still possible to manually execute the terminal-based YOU. This can potentially cause server corruption and should be avoided.

The Red-Carpet software management system is made up of the following two basic components:

- *Red-Carpet daemon (rcd)*—This daemon receives commands from the Red-Carpet client and follows those instructions to perform tasks such as updating installed software components. If necessary, the startup script /etc/init.d/rcd can be used to stop or restart the rcd daemon.

- *Red-Carpet client*—The client portion of Red-Carpet is the interface administrators use to subscribe to software update services, and to determine which updates will be applied to the local server.

  Two Red-Carpet clients ship with OES:

  - rug—Terminal-based client, which is installed by default with OES.

  - red-carpet—Graphical client, which is an optional component during an OES installation.

WARNING

In the shipping version of OES, the graphical red-carpet utility was not working as expected. Novell recommends that you use the command-line rug utility to update OES until the fix for red-carpet is made available. When the patch is available, the rug utility will apply it and the red-carpet graphical client can then be used safely.

For the Red-Carpet process to work, a ZENworks Linux Management (ZLM) server must be added as a known service to the rcd configuration. After a successful installation of OES, your server should already have a known service for the Novell Update Server (https://update.novell.com/data). This can be confirmed using the command-line **rug** utility as in the following example:

```
# rug service-list
```

This command should display an entry for the Novell Update Service. If no entries are displayed, the Novell Update Service can be manually added to your Red-Carpet configuration using the following command:

```
# rug service-add https://update.novell.com/data
```

The graphical **red-carpet** utility can also be used to check for, and, if necessary, add the Novell Update Service. These options are found under the Edit, Services menu item of the **red-carpet** utility.

Before using Red-Carpet, your OES server must be activated. Activating an OES server requires an activation code you should have received when the product was purchased. The following sections describe activating the Red-Carpet service, and basic usage of both the terminal and graphical Red-Carpet utilities.

Activating and Using red-carpet (Graphical)

The following steps describe the activation process using the graphical Red-Carpet utility **red-carpet**. Basic usage of **red-carpet** is also explained.

1. Launch **red-carpet** through YaST by accessing the Online Update module found within the Software category of YaST. The **red-carpet** program can also be started directly from a terminal authorized to write to the local X server or from a run command dialog.

2. Ensure that the Novell Update Service is registered as a valid update source by accessing Edit, Services. If necessary, add https://update.novell.com/data as a new service.

3. If your OES server has not already been activated, activate the server by accessing File, Activate. In the activation dialog, enter your email address and the activation code you received with your OES purchase. Click Activate when finished.

4. Click the Channels button to list available update channels. Locate the OES channel and select the check box in the Subscribed column to subscribe to this channel.

NOTE

If no channels are listed, no patches are currently available for OES.

5. Click the Patches tab. Both core SLES and OES component updates are available on this tab. Select the patches you want to install by highlighting the patch and clicking Mark for Installation.

WARNING

Only install software from the Patches tab! Software updates installed from the Updates tab will not execute required post-install scripts associated with some patches. Failing to execute these scripts can corrupt your server!

6. Click Run Now to install the selected patches.

Activating and Using rug (Terminal)

The following steps describe the activation process using the command-line Red-Carpet utility **rug**. Basic usage of **rug** is also described.

1. Ensure that the Novell Update Service is registered as a valid update source using the following command:

```
# rug service-list
```

If necessary, add the Novell Update Services using the following command:

```
# rug service-add https://update.novell.com/data
```

2. If your OES server has not already been activated, activate the server using the following command:

```
# rug activate -s 1 <activation_code> <email_address>
```

3. Subscribe to the OES update channel using the following command:

```
# rug subscribe oes
```

NOTE

If the message Warning: Invalid channel: 'oes' is displayed, this means no patches are currently available for OES.

4. List available patches using the following command:

```
# rug patch-list
```

If necessary, additional information regarding each patch can be obtained using the following command:

```
# rug patch-info <patch_name>
```

5. Install individual patches using the following command:

```
# rug patch-install <patch_name>
```

To install all available patches, use:

```
# rug patch-install *
```

After patches have been applied to your OES server, you may have to restart services, or the server itself, to activate those patches. If this is required, an appropriate message dialog should be displayed during the patch installation. Be sure to follow any instructions displayed in those messages.

NOTE

For more information on updating your server through the Red-Carpet software management system, see the man pages for rcd(8) and rug(1).

Monitoring SLES with Health Monitoring Services

An important aspect of managing SLES is simply being aware of how your server is performing. OES Linux reduces the complexity of this task through leveraging the capabilities of Web-Based Enterprise Management (WBEM). WBEM is a standard, Internet-based technology designed to consolidate the various tasks of enterprise server management. Through WBEM, Health Monitoring Services (HMS) can be used to easily monitor many important server health-related factors—including CPU utilization, system memory, running processes, and network utilization.

OES Linux uses the Common Information Model Object Manager (CIMOM) daemon, from the OpenWBEM project, to manage the health monitoring environment. The CIMOM daemon performs this function by accessing one or more Providers that conform to WBEM standards. These Providers facilitate the gathering of SLES and OES statistics used by HMS. For administrative use, this information is then gathered and consolidated for display in iManager—so you can easily keep tabs on your server health while performing day-to-day administrative routines.

One of the great things about HMS is its potential for future capabilities. This is the first release of HMS and is geared primarily at monitoring essential health-related information. In future releases, system alerts and robust analysis should further enhance the capabilities of HMS and make this one of the most important server monitoring tools in your arsenal.

Installing HMS

Health Monitoring Services can be installed as an optional component during the OES Linux installation. HMS can also be installed later through YaST.

NOTE

Basic server health is available for any server throughout your organization, but for complete health monitoring, Health Monitoring Services must be installed on all your OES Linux servers.

To install Health Monitoring Services using YaST, complete the following steps:

1. Access YaST from a terminal using yast, or from a graphical environment using yast2 or the YaST launcher from the application menu.

2. Select the Network Services category in YaST. From within this category, locate and select the Novell Health Monitoring module. This module will detect that the RPMs for HMS are missing and ask if you want to install them. Select Continue to install the necessary packages.

3. At the conclusion of the software installation, SuSEconfig is executed to update the system configuration. When this completes, the configuration of the OES component will begin automatically.

4. At the Novell Health Monitoring LDAP Server Configuration screen, enter the following information and click Next to complete the installation:

   - *Local or Remote Directory Server*—Select the radio button that indicates whether eDirectory is running on the local server or a remote server.

- *Directory Server Address*—If a remote eDirectory server is in use, enter the IP address for this server.

- *Admin Name with Context*—Enter the eDirectory administrator's credentials using fully qualified dot notation, for example, cn=admin.o=novell.

- *Admin Password*—Enter the password for the administrator user.

- *Port Details*—If necessary, select this button to change the configured ports for the eDirectory server you specified earlier. The default LDAP port for unencrypted communications is 389 and port 636 is used for SSL-encrypted communications.

After installing HMS, the OpenWBEM CIMOM daemon can be manually started, stopped, or restarted using the main daemon startup script /etc/init.d/owcimomd. To start the CIMOM daemon, execute the following command:

```
# /etc/init.d/owcimomd start
```

Configuring HMS

Configuring and accessing HMS is performed through iManager. All HMS-related capabilities can be found under the Monitor Servers link, in the Servers category of the left navigation frame.

The first time this page is accessed, you must select a container where your HMS configuration will be stored. Although not required, it is normally a good idea to select the container in which your OES Linux server exists for this purpose. After the HMS objects have been created in eDirectory, you are then able to configure a list of servers to monitor.

The first server you should add to your server list is your OES Linux server. To add your server to this list, select Add, and then provide the required information (server name and IP address or DNS name). You are also given a choice of the type of monitoring you would like to perform. The two options you have are as follows:

- *Robust Health*—If the server you are monitoring has OpenWBEM installed, Robust Health will provide the monitoring capabilities for the following categories:

  Memory

  Operating System

  Process/Threads

Network

CPU

- *Simple Server Status*—If OpenWBEM is not available on the specified server, this option can be used to provide a simple UP/DOWN status of the server.

After a server has been added to your server watch list, the Monitor Servers page will be refreshed with an overview of the server's health, as shown in Figure 6.8.

FIGURE 6.8
The Monitor Servers overview page in iManager.

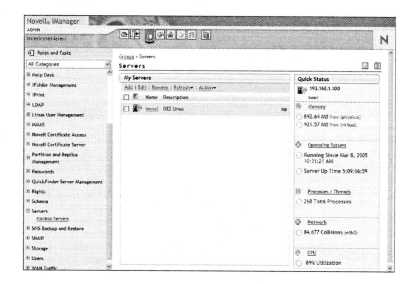

To display the Quick Status of a server's health, click on the server icon in the server watch list. For detailed information on server statistics, click the server name itself. You can then drill down on each monitored category further for complete diagnostic of your server.

NOTE

For additional information on Health Monitoring Services, see the online OES documentation.

Troubleshooting

Troubleshooting SLES can be a complex process. The following section contains important log files, procedures, and tools used during the troubleshooting process.

System Log Files

SLES uses the System Logger (syslog) utility to track events from all running processes. These events are written to log files that can be used for troubleshooting and system analysis. When you're troubleshooting nearly any type of problem on SLES, these log files are the best place to begin. Table 6.7 identifies key log files found on SLES.

TABLE 6.7
Important Log Files Found on SLES

LOG FILE	PURPOSE
/var/log/messages	The majority of syslog messages are stored in this file.
/var/log/boot.msg	All boot-related messages are written to this file upon system startup.
/var/log/YaST2	This directory contains log files for the operation of YaST and YaST modules.
/var/log/cups	CUPS-related log files can be found in this directory.
/var/log/mail	Log file for mail-related messages.
/var/log/XFree86.0.log	Log file containing messages relating to the XFree86 server.
yast2 view_anymsg -or- yast view_anymsg	Command used to launch YaST into the system log monitoring module. (yast2 is the graphical utility, and yast is the command-line version.)

NOTE

Log files for OES components can normally be located in /var/opt/novell/log.

/proc **and** /sys **Filesystems**

When you're troubleshooting hardware-related problems, it is often important to determine exactly what view the kernel has of all hardware devices attached to the server. The /proc filesystem is a virtual filesystem that allows an insight into the running kernel. Many kernel configuration values can be analyzed by viewing the appropriate file within the /proc directory structure.

Beginning with the 2.6 kernel, the sysfs filesystem has been added for accessing additional information regarding kernel data structures and attributes. This filesystem is mounted at the /sys directory and can be used to query specific settings of hardware devices recognized by the current kernel. As not all devices have interfaces within the sysfs filesystem, both the /proc and /sys filesystems must be used for low-level device management.

Table 6.8 identifies a few important files found in the /proc and /sys filesystems.

TABLE 6.8
Important Files Found Within /proc and /sys

FILE	PURPOSE
/proc/cpuinfo	Contains information regarding all identified CPUs.
/proc/interrupts	Contains information regarding allocated interrupts.
/proc/ioports	Contains information regarding configured I/O ports.
/proc/scsi/	Directory containing information regarding the SCSI subsystem. Adapter- and device-specific information can usually be located in adapter-specific directories beneath /proc/scsi.
/proc/modules	Contains information regarding currently loaded modules.
/sys/devices	Directory structure containing a view of all devices recognized by the running kernel.
/sys/bus	Directory structure containing a view of all bus-specific devices recognized by the running kernel.

Rescue Mode

Rescue mode is a method of running Linux from the installation media rather than a damaged SLES installation. This mode is useful for advanced troubleshooting and disaster recovery when the installed operating environment is failing to start up properly. Rescue mode is accessed by following these steps:

1. Boot from the installation media and select Rescue System from the GRUB menu.

2. When prompted, select an appropriate keyboard map.

3. At the Rescue Login prompt, enter **root**. After pressing Enter, you will be provided with a BASH prompt.

   At this point, SLES is actually running off the CD rather than the hard disk. The real root filesystem must now be located and mounted.

   Use `fdisk <root hard disk device>` (the hard disk device might be /dev/sda, for example), and then press **p** to view the partition table of the selected disk. The root filesystem device will have an ID of 83 and a System of "Linux". When you've located it, record the device name of the root filesystem. If you are unsure of the entry that contains the root filesystem, record all possible matches. These potential matches can be checked one at a time.

4. Mount the root filesystem that was located in the previous step using the following command:

   `mount -t reiserfs <root device (e.g. /dev/sda1)> /mnt`

   (If your filesystem type is not `reiserfs`, be sure to modify the command line accordingly.)

5. Change the current directory to /mnt and ensure that the root filesystem is correctly mounted. If it is, the original root directory structure should be visible. If this directory is not visible, unmount the /mnt directory (using `umount /mnt`) and then go back to step 3 to try locating the root filesystem device again.

6. Change your root directory from the CD-based SLES to your installed operating system using the `chroot` command as follows:

   `chroot /mnt`

At this point, a new BASH shell has been opened within the filesystem of your SLES installation. Additional troubleshooting (reviewing log files, changing passwords, disabling services, and so on) can all be performed prior to rebooting in normal mode.

Troubleshooting Utilities

Troubleshooting Linux-related problems sometimes involves in-depth investigation of the disk, running processes, networking configuration, and countless other topics. Table 6.9 outlines a small list of utilities often used in the troubleshooting process.

TABLE 6.9
Common Troubleshooting Utilities

UTILITY	PURPOSE
df	Reports total, used, and available disk space across all mounted filesystems
du	Estimates disk space usage by directories
free	Displays total, used, and free memory statistics; also reports information on memory buffers and swap space
hwinfo	Reports detailed information on known hardware
iostat	Reports input/output statistics for block devices
KDE System Guard (ksysguard)	Graphical utility used to monitor system load performance
lsof	Lists currently open files
ltrace	Traces library calls made by a process
netstat	Reports network statistics and route information
sitar	Comprehensive reporting tool used to generate a report documenting the entire running environment
strace	Traces system calls and signals made by a process
tcpdump	Used to capture network traffic for later review using a utility such as Ethereal
top	Displays running process and various statistics regarding each process (CPU utilization, memory, and so on)
vmstat	Reports virtual memory statistics
xosview	Graphical utility used to report system statistics such as CPU usage, load average memory usage, and several other parameters

Using these troubleshooting utilities to track down and resolve issues can be a daunting task. For help with this process, or any technical issue you may face, contact Novell Technical Support (http://www.novell.com/support). For more information on these utilities, see Appendix A, "The Most Essential Linux Commands," or the man page for the respective utility.

## CHAPTER 7

Novell eDirectory Management

Instant Access

Managing eDirectory Objects

- To create and manage eDirectory objects, you should use iManager. If available through an existing infrastructure or specifically downloaded, ConsoleOne can also be used for some tasks.

Managing Replicas and Partitions

- To manage replicas and partitions, use iManager.
- To manage the eDirectory schema, use iManager.

Using Indexes

- eDirectory manages most popular indexes automatically, with no intervention on your part.
- You can view the list of default indexes using the Index Management module (under eDirectory Maintenance) of iManager. You can also create custom indexes from this module.

Merging eDirectory Trees

- Use iManager to merge eDirectory trees by selecting the Merge Tree option under eDirectory Maintenance. You can also use the terminal-based `ndsmerge` utility.

Using Additional Services with eDirectory

- LDAP services for eDirectory provide robust eDirectory access to LDAP clients. Using ConsoleOne or iManager, configure LDAP through the LDAP Server and LDAP Group objects in eDirectory.

Troubleshooting

- To monitor eDirectory messages, use Trace from iMonitor or the `ndstrace` utilities from a shell console.

- Use iMonitor to repair an eDirectory tree (click the Repair icon in the header frame). You can also use the eDirectory option in iManager. Some repair operations will also require the use of the terminal-based `ndsrepair` utility.

What Is eDirectory?

In order to understand Novell eDirectory, you must first invert the standard view of network architecture. Many people assume that because the directory requires a Network Operating System (NOS) on which to run that it is part of the NOS. In reality, it is just the opposite. The directory defines the "world" of your network. As such, network servers are part of the directory, not vice versa. This is a critical shift in thinking if you are going to work effectively with directories in today's complex computing environments.

In the simplest of terms, eDirectory is a distributed and replicated database of network information that provides your network with four key services:

- *Discovery*—eDirectory makes it possible to browse, search, and retrieve information about the network. You can search for objects such as users, printers, and applications, or for specific properties of objects such as names, phone numbers, and configurations.

- *Security*—eDirectory provides a central point for authentication and access control across your entire network. You can grant specific rights to users or groups of users, control the flow of data across the network, and protect sensitive or personal information through the use of cryptographic technologies. Most importantly, eDirectory provides the foundation for managing security across networks, so you can safely and efficiently communicate with partners, suppliers, and customers without having to create a separate infrastructure to do so.

- *Storage*—eDirectory is at its heart a database. As such, it includes the capabilities to safely and securely store network data and protect it from corruption. It also provides a way to classify different data types, so you can manage the type of data in eDirectory and determine how it can be used. Finally, eDirectory allows you to split the database into discrete pieces and distribute those pieces across multiple servers to provide fault tolerance and improved performance for network users.

- *Relationship*—eDirectory allows you to model relationships between objects on the network. This allows you to move configuration information away from specific devices and make it global. Practically, this means that users can receive their profiles, privileges, and services regardless of location, connection device, or network access point. This is the foundation for providing a relatively new set of services known as Secure Identity Management (SIM), none of which is possible without a robust directory at its core.

Novell released its first version of eDirectory, then known as NetWare Directory Services (NDS), in 1993 with NetWare 4. It has been in constant improvement since that time, making it the most advanced and widely used directory in the world. The name was changed to Novell Directory Services with the release of NetWare 5 in 1998. In 2000, Novell's directory was rechristened Novell eDirectory, and was modularized so that it can be installed on platforms other than NetWare—including Linux, Windows 2000/XP, and various flavors of Unix. The following sections provide you with an overview of eDirectory architecture, design considerations, and common administrative tasks and the tools for doing them.

eDirectory Architecture

The eDirectory architecture has three main aspects:

- Physical database
- Rules governing data
- Organization of data

Each of these is addressed individually in the sections that follow.

Physical Database

At its lowest physical level, eDirectory is a database. A typical database consists of a dataset together with methods of searching and retrieving specific data from the dataset. eDirectory is an object-oriented, hierarchical database. A hierarchical database maintains data (objects) in a logical tree structure. Specific objects are located by traversing (walking) the tree. Each object in the eDirectory database is uniquely identifiable by a combination of the object name, or Common Name (CN), together with information describing the location of that object within the tree, or Context. Figure 7.1 shows a possible tree structure and the relationship between object name and logical position within the directory. The combination of Common Name and Context is known as the *Distinguished Name*.

FIGURE 7.1

A sample eDirectory tree structure showing how location determines name.

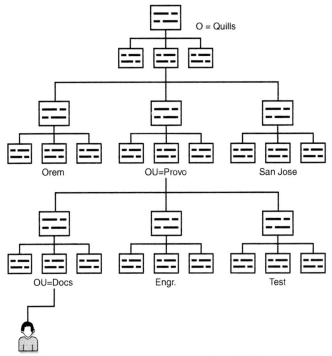

(CN=DNelson.OU=Docs.OU=Pr) Tx 1 25 Tk (o) Tx 1 10 Tk (v) Tx 1 20 Tk (o) Tx 1 30 Tk (.O=Quills)

The underlying eDirectory database is organized as a *b-tree*, which those of you with a programming background will recognize as a well-known type of data structure. B-trees are ordered, or sorted, trees in which the root node always stores values at the midpoint of the sorted value set. As new elements are added, the tree automatically reorders itself. The eDirectory b-tree nodes contain multiple elements, each of which is a directory object.

The result of these two characteristics is a data structure in which a huge number of elements can be stored, and elements that are stored can be located very quickly.

The eDirectory database also makes extensive use of indexing. Data is sorted in a variety of ways in order to decrease the time required to locate a given piece of data even more. Each index is a smaller b-tree structure that is automatically updated whenever any relevant piece of the database is added, changed, or deleted. When a query is received by eDirectory, internal logic determines what index, if any, should be used to most efficiently respond to the query. Figure 7.2 shows you some of the default indexes created by eDirectory. You can also add custom indexes by completing the following steps:

FIGURE 7.2
Default eDirectory indexes.

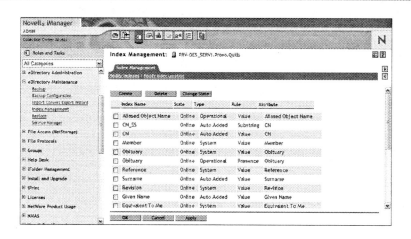

1. Launch iManager.

2. In the Navigation frame, open the eDirectory Maintenance group and click Index Management.

3. In the Content frame, select the server for which you want to manage indexes.

4. Click Create. Provide the required information and click OK.

   - *Name*—Specify a name for the new index.

   - *Attribute*—Select the attribute on which the new index should be sorted.

   - *Rule*—Select the type of index you want created from the drop-down list. Select Presence to create an index based on whether the specified attribute has a value. Select Value to create an index based on values of the specified attribute.

eDirectory will automatically create the index based on your configuration choices.

Rules Governing Data

Rules defining valid object types, where they can be stored, and what can be done with each of the object types are maintained within the eDirectory schema. The schema provides the structure to the eDirectory tree. The schema is composed of a set of object classes. Object classes describe the types of objects that can be created in eDirectory. Each object class contains a set of attributes that specifies the type(s) of data that can be stored within each object. In this way, the schema creates the logical view of the eDirectory data that network administrators and users make use of every day.

Novell provides a base set of object classes in eDirectory but has recognized that it cannot account for every possible use of the directory. To address this, the eDirectory schema is extensible/extendable, meaning that third parties are free to define new object classes and attributes in order to extend eDirectory capabilities.

Organization of Data

eDirectory organization has two aspects: the physical organization and the logical organization. Physical organization of data in eDirectory revolves around its distributed nature and the need to provide fault tolerance for the eDirectory database. Each piece of the total eDirectory database is known as a *partition*.

In order to make the data contained in a given partition more secure and accessible, multiple copies of that partition can be stored across the network. This process of creating and maintaining multiple partition copies is known as *replication*, as shown in Figure 7.3. Replication is an extremely powerful capability, and Novell has designed eDirectory with a complex set of checks and balances in order to maintain the integrity of directory data across the distributed environment.

FIGURE 7.3

eDirectory partitions and replicas.

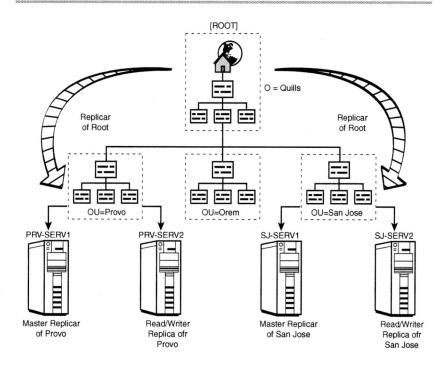

The logical organization of data in eDirectory determines how data will be presented to users and administrators. The logical organization is what you see when you look at eDirectory. The schema controls this logical eDirectory organization. The schema essentially defines the types of data that can be stored in eDirectory and the acceptable set of operations that can be performed on that data.

The eDirectory schema defines a class of objects that can store other objects. These are known as *Container objects*, or simply as *Containers*. Containers are the building blocks used to create the structure of the eDirectory tree. Objects that cannot hold other objects are known as *Leaf* objects. Leaf objects define the actual network resources available in the eDirectory tree.

Each class of Leaf objects contains a unique set of attributes that describe the data and functionality associated with that object. Leaf objects can include users, printers, network routers, applications, or even other databases. Because the eDirectory schema is fully extensible, new object classes can be defined and created within eDirectory by anyone who might need them.

eDirectory Tree Design

A key purpose of implementing a network directory is to make the operation of the network more efficient and easy to use. Unfortunately, this means that the directory cannot be rolled out without any consideration for the environment into which it is being installed. There are a few basic rules that should be followed when designing an eDirectory tree:

- The top of the tree reflects the physical layout.
- The bottom of the tree reflects the organizational structure.
- Organize objects to facilitate access and administration.
- Partition and replicate for scalability and fault tolerance.

Each of these issues is addressed in the sections that follow.

Top of the Tree Reflects Physical Layout

The top one or two levels of an eDirectory tree form the foundation for everything that comes later. If these levels are not configured properly, the whole tree suffers. Similar to the construction of a house, the eDirectory tree foundation needs to be stable and not prone to changes in structure.

The stable part of an organization tends to be its capital assets (buildings and equipment). Organizational structure might change and merge, but it still generally uses the same physical facilities. Make use of this stability by designing the foundation of the eDirectory tree around physical locations.

There are four main points to address when designing the top levels of the eDirectory tree:

- Name the tree [Root].
- Determine use of Country and Locality objects.
- Define the Organization object.
- Define location-based Organizational Unit objects.

When you name your eDirectory tree, you are naming the [Root] object. Make the name descriptive and unique. It should also be different from other Container objects. Many use the following tree name convention: Organization Name_TREE.

Next you have to decide how to create the first level in your eDirectory tree. This involves determining whether you are going to incorporate the use of a Country \ or a Locality (L) object into your eDirectory tree design, as shown in Figure 7.4.

FIGURE 7.4
eDirectory Country and Locality objects.

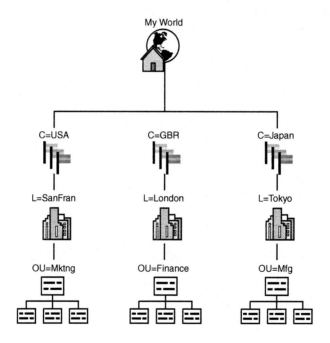

Country and Locality object use is optional and may not make sense depending on your directory structure. However, if it is important to comply with X.500 naming syntax in order to interact with external X.500 directories, these objects can be used. Other than that, it is probably easier to start with the Organization (O) object and define geographical regions under the organization as Organizational Unit (OU) objects, as shown in Figure 7.5.

FIGURE 7.5
Sample eDirectory tree.

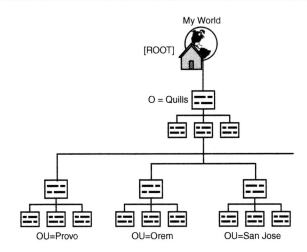

Next you must determine the name of your Organization object. Every eDirectory tree must have at least one Organization container. Normally, this is the first level of the tree, so using the organization name is a good way to go.

Finally, define subsequent levels of the tree around the physical network infrastructure currently employed (or planned) by the organization. Regional sites are usually defined as level 2 organizational units. A third level may also be appropriate for larger organizations to designate branch offices. Usually, three levels dedicated to the geographical structure of the organization will accommodate even the largest organizations.

The opposite is true for smaller companies. In some cases where the company is located at a single site, the physical levels can be eliminated altogether, if desired. However, this strategy is not recommended if there is any chance the company will grow into multiple sites in the future because the lack of containers based on physical sites will make it more difficult to expand the eDirectory structure as the organization grows.

Bottom of the Tree Reflects Organizational Structure

The bottom portion of the tree is where all the action is. Unlike the top of the tree, we fully expect adaptation and evolution to occur over time at the lower levels of the tree. This means we need to design flexibility into the system.

For this reason, the lower levels of the eDirectory tree will grow based not on physical locations, but on organizational structure, as shown in Figure 7.6. The best way to visualize the eDirectory tree at this point is to look at a current copy of your company's organizational chart. You will need to understand the divisions and/or departments that operate at each physical site in order to create the lower levels of the eDirectory tree.

FIGURE 7.6

The lower levels of an eDirectory tree mirror the organizational structure.

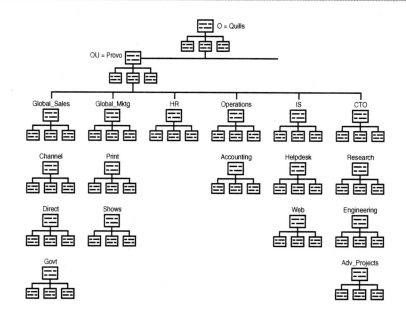

The reason that Organizational Unit containers are so useful at this level is that they allow you to group resources together. You can put the users in the Marketing department together with their printers, servers, and applications. Then those users and resources can be managed together. As you will see in the next section, this grouping also allows you to minimize the overhead associated with maintaining replica integrity and currency.

Organize Objects to Facilitate Access and Administration

Now that you have the general tree design and containers created, the next point to consider becomes how to organize the Leaf objects that will populate the eDirectory tree. The two primary considerations for this are

- Make it as easy as possible for users to access the resources they need.
- Make it as easy as possible to centrally control and administer network resources.

In most cases, you will be able to place resources such as servers, printers, and departmental applications in the same container with the users who will need access to those resources. However, if users in multiple containers will share resources, place those resources one level above the user containers. This makes the resource much easier to locate.

Furthermore, if you group users based on common needs, you can manage things like access controls, login scripts, and policies from the container level, rather than managing each user individually. Only the exceptions to the general container rules need to be specifically managed. Management by exception is tremendously powerful as a tool for reducing complexity and increasing efficiency.

Partition and Replicate for Scalability and Fault Tolerance

As a distributed database, eDirectory requires a mechanism for dividing the entire database into discrete chunks that can be installed on different servers across the organization. This is done through a process of partitioning and replicating the database.

PARTITIONS

eDirectory allows the creation of partitions in order to distribute the directory database across the network. A copy of a given eDirectory partition is known as a *replica*. By creating multiple replicas of a given partition, you build fault tolerance into the directory architecture. If a server holding a partition replica fails, the partition is still available from other replica servers.

Locating those portions of the eDirectory database close to those users who make use of them dramatically increases eDirectory performance. It also greatly reduces network traffic associated with directory queries. This is particularly important when multiple sites are connected by costly WAN links. The last thing you want to do is use a WAN link bandwidth for background operations like searching for a server or printer.

When the first eDirectory server is installed, a [Root] partition is automatically created and a replica of that partition is stored on the eDirectory server. When [Root] exists, the rest of the directory can be built by adding the necessary Container and Leaf objects.

As other eDirectory servers are installed, replicas of [Root] should be created to provide fault tolerance. If you maintain a small network at a single site, the [Root] partition might be all you need. Replicate it to two or three servers for fault tolerance and you are done. However, if your network environment is more complex, more work should be done to create an efficient eDirectory environment.

Planning your eDirectory partition strategy is similar to planning the top levels of the eDirectory tree. Partition creation should follow the physical network infrastructure. WAN links should always be considered boundaries between partitions. This eliminates the need for eDirectory to pass background traffic across these links. Refer to Figure 7.3 for a view of partitioning along geographical lines.

Each child partition should then be replicated to multiple servers at the site that partition is serving. When partitions have been created based on the physical boundaries, it is not usually necessary to partition the bottom layers of a tree. However, there are two possible exceptions to this:

- A child partition might also be further partitioned in order to limit the number of partition replicas that exist across the network. A large number of replicas for any given partition will increase the background traffic required for synchronization. It also complicates partition repair operations that may be necessary. A good rule of thumb is to try to limit the total number of replicas of a given partition to 10 or fewer.

- If you are using Filtered replicas to create specific views of eDirectory information, it is entirely acceptable to further divide a child partition.

The goal of your partitioning strategy should be a small [Root] partition and a child partition for every physical site in the network. The [Root] partition should end up containing only [Root] and the Organization object. The reason for this is explained in the next section.

REPLICAS

A *replica* is a physical copy of an eDirectory partition. By default, the first replica created is designated as the Master replica. Each partition will have one, and only one, Master replica. Other replicas will be designated as Read/Write, Read-Only, and Subordinate references. There are five types of eDirectory replicas:

- *Master replica*—The Master replica contains all object information for the partition. Objects and attributes maintained in the partition can be modified from the Master replica. These changes are then propagated to other servers holding replicas of this partition. Furthermore, all changes to the partition itself, such as creating other replicas or creating a child partition, must be performed from the perspective of the server that holds the Master replica.

- *Read/Write replica*—A Read/Write replica contains the same information as the Master replica. Objects and attributes maintained in the partition can be modified from the Read/Write replica. These changes are then propagated to other servers holding replicas of this partition. Any number of Read/Write replicas can be created. However, for the sake of overall directory performance, it is recommended that the total number of partition replicas not exceed 10. This type of replica cannot initiate partition operations.

- *Read-Only replica*—A Read-Only replica contains all the same information as the Master and Read/Write replicas. Users can read, but not modify, the information contained in these replicas. The replica is updated with changes made to the Master and Read/Write replicas. In practice, Read-Only replicas are seldom used because they are unable to support login operations. The login process requires updating some directory information. Because a Read-Only replica does not support directory updates, it cannot provide login services. One potential use is maintaining a backup copy of a partition. The Read-Only replica will receive all partition updates but will not participate in the update process in any way.

- *Filtered replica*—A Filtered replica can be either a Read-Only or a Read/Write replica. They are designed to provide specific services or applications, including other directories, with only the eDirectory information they need. Creating replicas that contain only certain types of objects and/or specific subsets of object attributes accomplishes this goal. For example, a Filtered replica might hold only User objects with their associated names, phone numbers, and email addresses for a corporate directory application.

NOTE

These replica types exist primarily to eliminate the single point of failure in an eDirectory environment. A recommended design goal is three replicas—one Master and a combination of Read/Write and/or Read-Only replicas. As stated previously, the Read-Only replica is seldom used, so most eDirectory implementations will focus on Master and Read/Write replicas in their production environments.

■ *Subordinate references*—Subordinate references are special replica types that provide connectivity between the various partitions that exist in an eDirectory environment. Subordinate references are internal replicas and are not visible to users or configurable by administrators. A Subordinate reference contains a list of all servers that hold replicas of a child partition. eDirectory uses this list to locate the nearest replica of a child partition so that it can walk down the tree when searching for an object. Figure 7.7 shows how Subordinate references are distributed across servers.

A partition's Subordinate reference is stored on all servers that hold a replica of that partition's parent. Subordinate references effectively point to child partition(s) that are not stored on that particular server. The distributed nature of eDirectory allows servers to hold replicas of the parent partition but not all of the corresponding child partitions.

FIGURE 7.7
eDirectory Subordinate references.

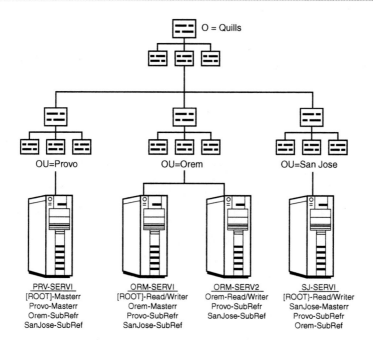

The eDirectory replication strategy is a balancing act between the need to provide consistency across the directory and the limitations of network hardware and bandwidth. You should follow three rules when creating your replication strategy:

- *Don't replicate across WAN links.* WAN links represent one of the most costly network resources. To clutter up these links with unnecessary eDirectory traffic would be a terrible mistake. To avoid this, all copies of a given partition should be maintained locally. The one situation where this rule might not apply (there's always at least one exception, isn't there?) is the case of a small satellite office with only one server. In that case, it is more important to protect the eDirectory database by placing a replica across a WAN link than it is to preserve the WAN link bandwidth itself. Fortunately, a partition that contains only one server will not usually generate a lot of eDirectory traffic.

- *Replicate to limit subordinate references.* Even though Subordinate references don't participate in the normal eDirectory replica update process, it's still a good idea to limit the number of Subordinate references to reduce complexity. There are two ways to do this:

  - Limit the number of child partitions that are created. This is only partially controllable because you always want to define WAN links as partition boundaries. However, this does argue for limiting the number of additional partitions that are created within a single site.

  - Store both parent and child partition replicas on the same server wherever possible. If multiple partitions are going to exist at a single site, try to distribute replicas such that parent and child partition replicas are stored together.

- *Replicate to improve eDirectory performance.* The final reason to replicate is to provide the best possible performance for network users. If the partition and replication guidelines in this chapter are followed, a user will find most of his or her resources within the local partition. Occasionally it may be necessary to access a resource on the other side of the world. These situations require eDirectory to traverse, or walk, the tree to locate the requested resource. As previously noted, these searches start at [Root] and proceed down the tree until the requested object is located. Placing replicas of [Root] at strategic locations, such as communications hubs, can facilitate these searches. In order to do this without significantly increasing the overall replication burden, the [Root] partition must be small (only the [Root] object and the Organization object) and the number of [Root] replicas should not exceed three or four.

TIP

Novell now offers some advanced services that are helping to redefine directory design and usage in today's modern networks. For example, Nterprise Branch Office helps greatly reduce the cost and complexity of eDirectory replication at satellite offices. Identity Manager is redefining eDirectory as a world-leading meta-directory that allows data to be transparently synchronized across many potential repositories. More information on Identity Manager is available in Chapter 10, "Identity Manager Bundle Edition." For information regarding a Linux-based Nterprise Branch office, watch Novell's website!

Managing eDirectory

When you have an understanding of the basics of eDirectory architecture and design, it is important to understand the activities and tools necessary to maintain eDirectory on a day-to-day basis.

As with the rest of OES Linux, eDirectory management is performed through web-based utilities. Specifically, comprehensive eDirectory management is available through iManager and iMonitor. For information on installing and configuring both iMonitor and iManager, see Chapter 5, "OES Management Tools."

iManager provides comprehensive role-based management capabilities for the entire OES Linux environment. iMonitor consolidates the monitoring and data-gathering aspects of several terminal-based tools, including `ndstrace` and `ndsrepair`. It also includes the object viewing and reporting functionality of the NetWare-only utilities, DSBrowse and DSDiag. The iMonitor interface is shown in Figure 7.8.

iManager provides a complete set of eDirectory management tools and functions for object, partition, and replica operations. Much of this functionality is also available from the Partition and Replica view in ConsoleOne. As mentioned in Chapter 5, although ConsoleOne is not provided with OES Linux, this utility can still be used in existing infrastructures or specifically downloaded from download.novell.com. You can also use SSH for remote access to a server terminal, from which you can run several eDirectory-specific terminal-based utilities.

This section gives you an overview of common eDirectory tasks and the tools used to perform them. eDirectory management tasks can be organized into six main categories:

- Partition operations
- Replica operations
- Tree operations
- eDirectory repair
- Monitoring eDirectory
- Managing synchronization

FIGURE 7.8
The iMonitor user interface.

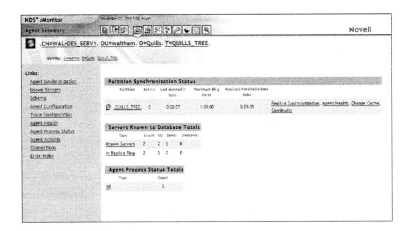

NOTE

Managing specific eDirectory objects is covered in the appropriate chapter on that topic. For example, User and Group object management is covered in Chapter 8, "Users and Network Security," whereas Printer object management is covered in Chapter 13, "OES Printing Services."

Partition Operations

You will be required to make three primary partition operations:

- Create a partition
- Merge a partition
- Move a partition

WARNING

eDirectory does a great deal of work when performing partition operations. In larger eDirectory environments, each of the operations described in the following sections can take a significant amount of time to process completely. Furthermore, each operation has to complete before the next can begin. Make sure you take this into account when planning these tasks.

CREATE A PARTITION

The first operation we want to look at is creating a partition. As mentioned earlier, partitioning the tree serves to break up the eDirectory database into chunks that can be distributed across multiple servers for fault tolerance and increased performance.

If you want to create a new partition, complete the following steps in iManager:

1. In the Navigation frame, open the Partition and Replicas group and select Create Partition.

2. In the Content frame, browse to and select the container that will be the root of the child partition, and then click OK.

3. Select Close at the message that eDirectory is processing your request.

By default, the Master replica of the new partition is created on the server that maintains the Master replica of the parent partition. Read/Write replicas are stored on servers that maintain Read/Write replicas of the parent partition. You can move or change replica placement after the partition has been created, if desired.

MERGE A PARTITION

Sometimes you want to consolidate partitions, such as when moving from an older NDS environment to a much more scalable eDirectory tree. To merge a partition with its parent, complete the following steps in iManager:

1. In the Navigation frame, open the Partition and Replicas group and select Merge Partition.

2. Browse to and select the container that is the root of the child partition, and then click OK.

3. Select Close at the message that eDirectory is processing your request.

When merged, all replicas of the child partition are removed and the child partition data will be replicated to the existing parent partition replicas.

MOVE A PARTITION

The partition move operation is commonly known as a *prune and graft*. It involves moving a partition and all its associated containers and objects from one location in the tree to another (pruning a branch from one part of the tree and grafting it in somewhere else). This is the most complex of the partition operations, so note the following qualifications before attempting a partition move:

- You cannot move a container unless it is a partition root. If you want to move a container that is not a partition, you first need to define it as a partition. Then you can move the container to its new location and merge it with its new parent partition.

- This operation is available only to partitions that do not have any subordinate (child) partitions. If you want to move a partition with subordinates, you will have to merge the subordinates into the parent partition first.

- When you move a partition, you must follow eDirectory containment rules that define what type of objects can be placed in each type of eDirectory container object. For example, you cannot move an organizational unit directly under the root of the tree because the containment rules for [Root] allow only Locality, Country, Organization, and Security objects, and not Organizational Unit objects.

If you want to prune and graft a partition, complete the following steps in iManager:

1. In the Navigation frame, open the Partition and Replicas group and select Move Partition.

2. Provide the required information and click OK.

   - In the Object Name dialog box, browse to and select the container you want to move.

   - In the Move To dialog box, browse to and select the new location for the partition. This will be the container within which the new partition will be placed.

   - Check Create an Alias in Place of Move Object if you want users to be able to continue accessing those objects from their original directory context. This is usually a good idea at least until all users have been notified of the location change.

3. At the Move summary, click Move to perform the prune and graft.

The summary screen lists all servers involved in the Move operation so that you can make sure everything is in good shape before attempting the move.

Replica Operations

Now that you have eDirectory partitions created and situated within the tree, you might notice that the default placement for the replicas is less than perfect. After all, you probably don't want all Master replicas on one server, and you want to avoid replicating across expensive WAN links, as discussed previously. Replica operations, similar to partition operations, are accomplished from iManager in Partition and Replica Management. There are four primary replica operations:

- Add a replica
- Change the replica type
- Delete a replica
- Create a Filtered replica

Selecting Replica View in iManager shows you all servers that hold replicas of the selected partition. These servers form the *replica ring*.

NOTE

You will likely see Subordinate reference replicas listed in the iManager Replica View. However, Subordinate references are not manageable in iManager, so their placement is purely informational.

ADD A REPLICA

If you want to place a partition replica on a server that does not currently have a copy of that partition, complete the following steps in iManager:

1. In the Navigation frame, open the Partition and Replicas group and select Replica View.

2. Browse to and select the partition for which you want a new replica and click Add Replica.

3. Specify the server on which you want to create the replica, select the type of replica you are going to create, and then click OK.

4. Click Done to exit the Replica View.

When created, the new partition will participate in all replication processes for that partition. Too many replicas can slow down partition operations significantly, so try to limit the number of replicas to three.

CHANGE THE REPLICA TYPE

Sometimes it is useful to be able to change the type of an existing replica. For example, if a Master replica is stored on a server and it is going down for a hardware upgrade, you can change an existing Read/Write replica to be the Master so that eDirectory partition operations can continue normally.

NOTE

You cannot change the type of a Master replica because a Master replica must exist for every partition. If you want to change a Master replica, change an existing Read/Write replica to be the new Master, and the existing Master will automatically be converted to a Read/Write.

If you want to change the type of a replica, complete the following steps in iManager:

1. In the Navigation frame, open the Partition and Replicas group and select Replica View.

2. Browse to and select the partition for which you want to change a replica type, and then click OK.

3. In the Type column, select the replica that you want to change.

4. Specify the type of replica to which you want to change the replica and click OK.

5. Click Done to exit the Replica View.

The replica will immediately start behaving as the new replica type you have selected.

NOTE

You cannot create a Master replica from a Filtered replica.

DELETE A REPLICA

Sometimes, when partitions have been merged or moved, a given replica is no longer necessary. To delete an existing replica from a server, complete the following steps in iManager:

1. In the Navigation frame, open the Partition and Replicas group and select Replica View.

2. Browse to and select the partition for which you want to delete a replica, and click OK.

3. Click the red X next to the replica name that you want to delete, and click OK in the Delete Replica window.

4. Click Done to exit the Replica View.

The replica is removed from the server on which it was stored, and all future partition operations will include only the remaining replicas.

CREATE A FILTERED REPLICA

If you are using Filtered replicas in your network, you can configure them with the Replica Wizard option in iManager. To create a Filtered replica, complete the following steps in iManager:

1. In the Navigation frame, open the Partition and Replicas group and select Filtered Replica Wizard.

2. Browse to and select the server on which the Filtered replica will reside, and then click Next.

3. Click Define the Filter Set to specify the object classes and attributes to include in this Filtered replica. Only one filter can be configured per server, meaning that you can only have Filtered replicas of one type on any given server.

4. Click The Filter Is Empty, select the eDirectory objects and classes that you want included in the Filtered replica, and then click OK. Alternatively, you can select Copy Filter From to specify an existing server with the type of Filtered replica you need, and it will be copied to the new server.

5. (Optional) Click Next to continue. You can click Define Partition Scope to add partitions for which you want to create Filtered replicas on this server. This opens the Replica View so that you can add replicas to the server.

6. Click Finish to create the Filtered replicas as defined.

Filtered replicas are often used when eDirectory is sharing data with an external system, such as another directory or database, but only a subset of eDirectory information is shared.

Tree Operations

There are a few operations that you can perform on an entire eDirectory tree, and these are available from iManager as well. Each of these operations is available under eDirectory Maintenance:

- Rename a tree
- Merge two trees
- Graft one tree into another

NOTE

Tree operations are complex operations that are *not* recommended for those who are not experienced eDirectory administrators. You can easily damage trees with these operations, so be very careful and perform these types of tree operations only when it is absolutely necessary.

RENAME A TREE

Once in a while it might become necessary to rename an eDirectory tree. Perhaps an organizational name change has occurred, or you are moving to match your directory-naming scheme to that being used on the Web. Whatever the reason, you can rename your tree by completing the following steps in iManager:

1. In the Navigation frame, open the eDirectory Maintenance group and select Rename Tree.

2. Specify the name of the server that will perform the rename operation and click Next. You can specify the server by eDirectory server name, DNS name, or IP address.

3. Specify suitable authentication information for the tree and click Next. Make sure you authenticate as a user with Supervisor rights to the tree.

4. Provide the necessary information and click Start. Specify the new tree name, the Admin username (with context), and the Admin password. Remember that the tree name can be up to 32 alphanumeric characters (dashes and underscores are also allowed).

5. Click Yes to rename the tree.

The utility will first perform a check on the tree to be sure that it can be renamed successfully. When the rename is complete, you will be prompted to log out and log back in to the "new" tree.

The terminal-based **ndsmerge** utility can also be used to rename a tree. To perform this operation with this utility, open up a terminal and execute the following command:

```
ndsmerge -r <target-tree> <source-admin>
```

MERGE TWO TREES

iManager and the terminal-based **ndsmerge** utility both have the capability to perform a tree merge. During a tree merge, a source tree is inserted into a target tree such that the tree branches at the Organization level, with each branch corresponding to the contents of one of the formerly distinct trees. To perform a tree merge from iManager, complete the following steps:

1. Under eDirectory Maintenance in the navigation frame of iManager, select Merge Tree.

2. Specify the name of the server that will perform the merge operation for the trees and click Next. You can specify the server by eDirectory server name, DNS name, or IP address.

3. Provide suitable authentication information for both the source and the target eDirectory trees and click Next. Make sure you authenticate as a user with Supervisor rights to the tree.

4. Provide the necessary information and click Start.

   - *Source Tree*—The source tree is the tree to which you are currently authenticated. It will be merged into the target tree. Specify the name and password of the Admin user for this tree.

   - *Target Tree*—The target tree is the tree that will remain after the merge. The source tree information will become part of this tree. Specify the name and password of the Admin user for this tree.

5. Click Yes to rename the tree.

The utility will first perform a check on both trees to be sure that they can be successfully merged. If you encounter an error during this check process, follow the instructions to resolve the conflict and try the merge again.

To perform a tree merge using the **ndsmerge** terminal utility, the source and destination trees, along with administrative credentials must be specified on the command line as in the following example:

```
ndsmerge -m <target-tree> <target-admin> <source-admin>
```

GRAFT ONE TREE INTO ANOTHER

A graft is a subset of a merge, in which you can choose the insertion point for the source tree objects. During a tree graft, a source tree is inserted into the specified location of a target tree. The source tree is then converted into a Domain object and it and all of its contents become part of the target tree. To graft one tree into another, complete the following steps:

1. Under eDirectory Maintenance in the navigation frame of iManager, select Graft Tree.

2. Specify the name of the server that will perform the graft operation and click Next. You can specify the server by eDirectory server name, DNS name, or IP address.

3. Specify suitable authentication information for the tree and click Next. Make sure you authenticate as a user with Supervisor rights to the tree.

4. Provide the necessary information and click Start.

   - *Source Tree*—The source tree is the tree to which you are currently authenticated. It will be grafted into the target tree. Specify the name and password of the Admin user for this tree.

   - *Target Tree*—The target tree will receive the source tree information as a Domain object after the graft. The source tree information will become part of this tree. Specify the name and password of the Admin user for the target tree. Specify the point at which you want the source tree inserted in the Container field.

5. Click Yes to perform the graft operation.

The utility will first perform a check on both trees to be sure that they can be successfully merged. If you encounter an error during this check process, follow the instructions to resolve the conflict and try the merge again.

To perform a tree graft using the **ndsmerge** terminal utility, the source and destination trees, target container, and administrative credentials, must all be specified on the command line as in the following example:

```
ndsmerge -m <target-tree> <target-admin> <source-admin>
<target-container>
```

NOTE

For more information on ndsmerge, please see ndsmerge -help.

Monitoring and Maintaining eDirectory

This section identifies some common administrative tasks that will help you effectively monitor the operation of eDirectory in your network and make little repairs as they are found. After all, the one thing more impressive than resolving a serious network problem is preventing it from occurring in the first place. Although this is not always possible, a program of active monitoring and proactive maintenance will go a long way toward getting you home on time at night. For more information on Novell management tools, see Chapter 5.

The following tasks are a starting point for maintaining your eDirectory environment. By monitoring eDirectory process execution, you can see every type of communication activity and determine whether any errors are being reported. The best way to keep track of the activities of eDirectory processes is through iMonitor (see Figure 7.9). iMonitor provides comprehensive trace capabilities for eDirectory. More detailed information on DSTrace capabilities in iMonitor is available in Appendix C, "eDirectory Reference Materials."

FIGURE 7.9
The eDirectory process monitoring configuration in iMonitor.

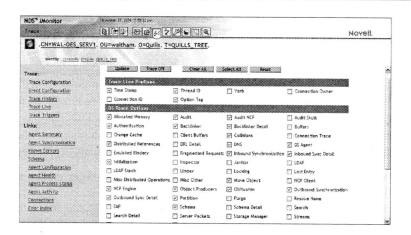

To access the iMonitor Trace page, use a browser to connect to iMonitor and click the Trace Configuration icon in iMonitor's Header frame. iMonitor can be accessed from the Novell eDirectory 8.7 Welcome page found on the OES home page, or can be accessed directly using the iMonitor URL. The iMonitor URL is

http://www.quills.com:8028/nds/summary

iMonitor Trace gives you web-based access to monitor all eDirectory processes. Tracing eDirectory activity involves the following tasks:

- From the Trace Configuration page, check the eDirectory processes that you want to monitor and click Trace On. Note that Trace preselects some of the more common processes. For more information on the individual options listed here, see Appendix C.

- To see a live view of the trace, select Trace History in the left side of the navigation frame, and click the View icon next to the current trace session.

- To stop a trace, click Trace Off in the Trace Configuration screen. Because of the added overhead and the size to which log files can grow, you usually want to run DSTrace for only enough time to gather the information for which you are looking.

eDirectory traces provide a powerful tool to track eDirectory processes and monitor operations when troubleshooting directory issues.

NOTE

There is also a terminal-based trace utility called ndstrace. The ndstrace utility can be used directly on an OES Linux terminal to view eDirectory activity. For information on using ndstrace, enter **help ndstrace** after starting the ndstrace utility.

VERIFY THE VERSION OF EDIRECTORY

Even if you don't apply updates immediately, it's a good idea to be aware of what updates exist and, more importantly, what issues they are intended to resolve. Keep track of the versions that you have installed on your servers so that as you review Novell support documents, you can keep an eye out for any problems that might relate to your environment.

NOTE

With the release of eDirectory in NetWare 6, Novell implemented a new versioning scheme in an attempt to eliminate inconsistencies in the previous model. Although still known as eDirectory v8.6 or 8.7 to provide eDirectory customers with a version context they are familiar with, the build version takes a considerably different format. For example, the build version of eDirectory 8.7 that ships with OES Linux is 10551.46.

You can check the version of eDirectory that you are currently running on any server in the following ways:

- iMonitor—Select Known Servers. The DS revision for all known eDirectory servers is listed.

- ndsrepair—Use the -E startup option to report eDirectory synchronization status. eDirectory and ndsrepair versions are displayed in the header.

- ndsmerge—Use the –c startup option to report all servers in the current tree, as well as their running status and eDirectory versions.

- ndsstat—This utility reports the tree and server name as well as the eDirectory binary and product versions.

NOTE

Review Novell's support website, http://support.novell.com, on at least a quarterly basis for updates to eDirectory files and utilities.

VERIFY THAT TIME IS SYNCHRONIZED

Check the time sync status for each partition in the tree every couple of weeks. Keep an eye out for synthetic time messages that might keep background processes from completing properly.

You can check the status of time synchronization between eDirectory servers in the following ways:

- ndsrepair—Use a -T startup option to show you the time synchronization status of all servers known by the server from which you run ndsrepair.

- ndsmerge—Use a -T startup option to show you the time synchronization status of all servers.

NOTE

The ntpq utility can be used to check time synchronization status of the local NTP client daemon. Although being synchronized to an NTP time source is important, it is technically more important that servers with eDirectory are in time sync with each other. The ndsrepair and ndsmerge utilities are used to check time synchronization between servers in the same eDirectory tree. If time sync problems are located, they are often resolved by properly configuring the local NTP client. More information on configuring NTP is available in Chapter 2, "Installing OES Linux."

If time is not synchronizing properly, you can run into problems with the time-stamps that are maintained on eDirectory objects. Timestamps indicate when the object was last synchronized.

Probably the best-known eDirectory timestamp issue is *synthetic time*. Synthetic time occurs when an eDirectory object has a modification timestamp ahead of current network time. If the period between current time and synthetic time is small, this problem will correct itself. However, if the period is large, it is possible to resolve the problem manually by reviewing the eDirectory communications processes to be sure that all replicas are communicating properly. From iMonitor, review the status of the Master replica from Agent Summary. You can drill down on the Master to review current state and a detailed set of statistics. Make sure the Master does not contain any errors, and that it is receiving current updates properly.

Timestamps can be repaired in two ways:

- Use `ndsrepair` to repair timestamps and declare a new epoch. To use this option, load `ndsrepair` with the `-P -Ad` parameters. Enter the desired partition number, and select the Repair Timestamps and Declare a New Epoch option.

- Identify the replica(s) with the synthetic timestamps and rebuild those replicas using the Receive All Objects operation:

  - *iManager*—In the Navigation frame, open the eDirectory Maintenance group and select Replica Ring Repair. Specify the server that you want to receive correct replica information from the Master replica. Select the Receive All Objects option.

  - *ConsoleOne*—Open the Partition and Replica view in ConsoleOne. Browse to and select the container on which you are going to work and select the Partition Continuity button from the toolbar. In the Partition Continuity table, highlight the replica you need to repair and select Receive Updates.

  - `ndsrepair`—Use the `-P` startup options to invoke Replica and Partition Operations. Enter the desired partition number to work with and select the View Replica Ring operation. Select the replica number to be repaired and choose Receive All Objects from the Master to This Replica.

WARNING

This operation generates a large amount of eDirectory-related traffic as time-stamps for all replicas are reset.

VERIFY REPLICA SYNCHRONIZATION

You can view synchronization status from several perspectives. However, making sure that all replicas of a given partition are synchronizing properly is probably one of the best ways to keep track of things. Check this every couple of weeks.

You can check the sync status of a replica ring in the following ways:

- *iMonitor*—From the Agent Summary, select the Continuity link next to the Partition for which you want to check synchronization status (see Figure 7.10). This will show you the status of the replica ring in general as well as the status of each replica in the ring.

- `ndsrepair`—Use the -E startup option to view synchronization status for all partitions. To select a specific partition, use the -P startup option and then select the desired partition and choose Report Synchronization Status of all Servers.

FIGURE 7.10
The Agent Synchronization summary page in iMonitor.

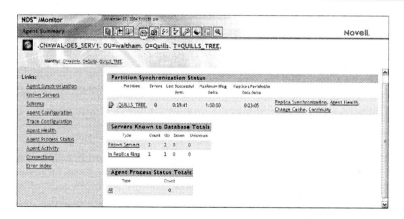

If you begin to notice inconsistencies in replica rings, you can use the following general steps to diagnose and resolve the problems:

1. Identify all servers that host replicas of this partition and the type of replica on each server.

   - *iMonitor*—Select Agent Synchronization, and then select the Replica Synchronization link beside the partition with which you need to work.

   - `ndsrepair`—Use the -P startup option to begin Replica and Partition Operations. Select the partition to work with and select View Replica Ring.

2. Examine the server hosting the Master replica because it functions as the authoritative source for partition information. If the Master replica is the source of the problem, designate one of the Read/Write replicas as a new Master:

   - *iManager*—Follow instructions outlined in the earlier section on replica operations.

   - `ndsrepair`—From the server that you want to host the new Master replica, start `ndsrepair` with the -P -Ad parameters. Select the partition with which to work, and choose Designate This Server as the New Master Replica.

3. When a healthy Master replica exists, you can receive updates on the server that is having synchronization problems to eliminate any inconsistent objects:

   - *iManager*—In the Navigation frame, open the eDirectory Maintenance group and select Replica Ring Repair. Specify the server holding the Master replica for the partition and select the Send All Objects option.

   - *ConsoleOne*—Open the Partition and Replica view in ConsoleOne. Browse to and select the container on which you are going to work and select the Partition Continuity button from the toolbar. In the Partition Continuity table, highlight the replica you need to repair and select Receive Updates.

   - `ndsrepair`—Use the -P startup options to invoke Replica and Partition Operations. Enter the desired partition number to work with and select the View Replica Ring operation. Select the replica number to be repaired and choose Receive All Objects from the Master to This Replica.

4. Monitor the replica ring after making repairs to make sure that it is successfully sending updates between all replica-hosting servers. You can perform a send-updates operation from the Master replica by doing the following:

- *iManager*—In the Navigation frame, open the eDirectory Maintenance group and select Replica Ring Repair. Specify the server holding the Master replica for the partition and select the Send All Objects option.

- *ConsoleOne*—Open the Partition and Replica view in ConsoleOne. Browse to and select the container on which you are working and select the Partition Continuity button from the toolbar. In the Partition Continuity table, highlight the server with the Master replica and select Send Updates.

- `ndsrepair`—Use the -P startup option to invoke Replica and Partition Operations. Select the partition to work with, and then select View Replica Ring. Select the Master replica, and then Send All Objects to Every Replica in the Ring.

You should regularly use the preceding techniques to monitor synchronization activities and make sure that eDirectory is performing properly.

CHECK EXTERNAL REFERENCES

External references are pointers to eDirectory objects not stored in replicas on the current server. The check examines each external reference and makes sure that it links to a valid eDirectory object. Performing this check on a weekly basis makes sure that queries can traverse the tree properly.

You can do one of the following to check external references:

- *iMonitor*—In the Navigation frame, select Agent Process Status. Review the data under the External Reference Status heading.

- `ndsrepair`—Use the -C startup parameter to automatically perform the Check External References procedure.

One nice thing about the external reference check is that it will list any obituaries in your tree. *Obituaries* are references to deleted objects that are maintained until word of the deletion has been propagated to all servers hosting replicas of the affected partition. It is possible for obituaries and other types of external references to become corrupt or get stuck in the tree.

One thing that can cause this is problems with network addresses. To resolve network referral problems, do the following:

1. Identify the actual assigned IP address for each server involved.

   - *iMonitor*—In the Navigation frame, select Known Servers. Select the link for the server you want to look at, and then browse down and select Network Address in the left side of the navigation frame.

- `ifconfig`—Run this terminal utility on each Linux server you want to check.

- `CONFIG.NLM`—For mixed platform environments, run this console-based utility on each NetWare server you want to check.

2. Check network addresses to make sure that the addresses stored by eDirectory match those being reported by the servers in their SLP or SAP broadcasts. In iMonitor, click the Repair icon and select Advanced. Select Repair Network Addresses and click Start Repair. Use the Known Servers option in iMonitor to repeat this process for each server hosting eDirectory replicas in the network.

   This same procedure can be performed using `ndsrepair` through the `-N` startup option. Server addresses can be repaired individually, or the addresses for all known servers can be repaired.

3. More severe problems might require a rebuild of replicas that have received invalid network address information, as described in the previous section on verifying replica synchronization.

Checking external references in this way will help ensure the health and smooth operation of your eDirectory environment.

CHECK THE EDIRECTORY SCHEMA

Whenever you make changes to the eDirectory schema, confirm that all servers hosting eDirectory replicas are properly receiving schema updates. You can check the schema synchronization status in iMonitor by selecting Agent Process Status, and then reviewing the data under the Schema Sync Status heading.

It is possible that an eDirectory server, due to communication problems or corruption of synchronization timestamps, will fail to receive schema updates as they are applied to the eDirectory environment. The resulting schema inconsistencies can be resolved by doing the following:

- Identify the server that is reporting schema errors. This will be the server that has not received the schema updates properly. In iMonitor, force schema synchronization by clicking the Agent Configuration icon in the Header frame and then selecting Agent Triggers in the Navigation frame. Check the Schema Synchronization box and select Submit. Before doing this, make sure that DSTrace is configured to report Schema Sync messages and that it is currently logging in to iMonitor.

TIP

You can also view the schema sync in iMonitor as it occurs with Trace. Using Trace is described earlier in this chapter. For information on specific Trace options, see Appendix C.

- When the server has been identified, one potential solution is to declare a new epoch on the server. Start `ndsrepair` with the `-P -Ad` parameters. Select the partition with which you want to work, and then choose Repair Timestamps and Declare a New Epoch.

Unless you are making frequent changes to the schema, these types of activities shouldn't be necessary, but you should be aware of how such schema issues can be resolved.

REVIEW TREE FOR UNKNOWN OBJECTS

On a monthly basis, search eDirectory for unknown objects. You can do this from iManager by completing the following steps (you can also search for unknown objects from ConsoleOne):

1. In the Header frame, click the View Objects icon.
2. In the left pane, select the Search tab.
3. Select Unknown in the Type field. Make sure that you are searching from [Root] and that the Search Sub-containers option is checked.

Unknown objects can indicate resources that have not been properly installed or removed from the tree. However, they can also indicate that iManager or ConsoleOne does not have a snap-in capable of recognizing that object type, so don't immediately assume that unknown objects need to be deleted.

It is also possible to get eDirectory object and attribute inconsistencies when replicas of the same partition, for whatever reason, have different information stored about the same eDirectory object or object attribute. In order to isolate the server(s) that have the faulty information, it is necessary to unload eDirectory on other servers. This type of troubleshooting can only be done during off hours.

In order to troubleshoot this type of problem, do the following:

1. Identify all servers that host replicas of the partition, and note the type of replica on each server.

- *iMonitor*—In the Navigation frame, select Agent Synchronization. Select the Replica Synchronization link beside the partition with which you need to work.

- `ndsrepair`—Use the -P startup option to begin Replica and Partition Operations. Select the partition to work with and select View Replica Ring.

2. Select one of the servers and unload eDirectory by entering **/etc/init.d/ndsd stop** at the server console.

3. Use ConsoleOne to query the tree for the faulty objects and/or attributes. If they are still faulty, you know this server's replica is not the source of the error. Be sure to restart the ndsd (**/etc/init.d/ndsd start**) process after determining the validity of objects stored on that server.

4. Repeat steps 2 and 3 until the faulty server(s) is (are) found.

5. To attempt to repair the problem, first attempt to receive updates at the faulty server:

   - *iManager*—In the Navigation frame, open the eDirectory Maintenance group and select Replica Ring Repair. Specify the server that you want to receive correct replica information from the Master replica. Select the Receive All Objects option.

   - *ConsoleOne*—Open the Partition and Replica view in ConsoleOne. Browse to and select the container on which you are going to work and select the Partition Continuity button from the toolbar. In the Partition Continuity table, highlight the replica you need to repair and select Receive Updates.

   - `ndsrepair`—Use the -P startup parameter to begin Replica and Partition Operations. Select the partition to work with and select View Replica Ring. Select the replica to be repaired and enter Receive All Objects from the Master to This Replica.

6. If that fails, attempt to send all objects from one of the known good servers. If possible, use the Master replica for this operation.

   - *iManager*—In the Navigation frame, open the eDirectory Maintenance group and select Replica Ring Repair. Specify the server holding the Master replica for the partition and select the Send All Objects option.

   - *ConsoleOne*—Open the Partition and Replica view in ConsoleOne. Browse to and select the container on which you are working and select the Partition Continuity button from the toolbar. In the Partition Continuity table, highlight the server with the Master replica and select Send Updates.

- ndsrepair—Use the -P parameter to begin Replica and Partition Operations. Select the partition to work with and select View Replica Ring. Select the Master replica, and then Send All Objects to Every Replica in the Ring.

7. If that fails, the replica has to be destroyed. At this point you might want to involve Novell Technical Support, unless you are comfortable with the use of advanced ndsrepair options. Start ndsrepair with the -P -Ad parameters. Select the partition with which you want to work, and then select the Destroy the Selected Replica on This Server option.

These tasks will help you ensure the object health within your eDirectory tree and stay on top of the health of your eDirectory environment.

Using LDAP with eDirectory

Lightweight Directory Access Protocol (LDAP) services for eDirectory lets LDAP clients access information stored in eDirectory. LDAP is currently the preferred directory access protocol on the Internet. Because eDirectory lets you give different clients different levels of directory access, you can manage external, internal, and confidential information from the same directory. eDirectory also supports secure LDAP connections so that privileged users can access internal or private information securely without any special client software. All they need is a browser with LDAP support and connectivity to the LDAP server.

Installing LDAP Services

Novell LDAP Services for eDirectory are installed automatically during the OES Linux installation routine. For more information on OES Linux installation options, see Chapter 2.

Two types of objects are defined in the eDirectory schema to support LDAP Services:

- *LDAP Server object*—Use this object to configure the LDAP environment for a single LDAP server.

- *LDAP Group object*—Use this object to configure LDAP client access to eDirectory.

LDAP Services for eDirectory are an integrated component of **ndsd** and cannot be manually loaded and unloaded.

LDAP SERVER OBJECT

The LDAP Server object stores configuration information in eDirectory about an LDAP server. The LDAP Server object is created in the same container as your server object. Each LDAP Server object configures one LDAP server.

To configure an LDAP server, complete the following steps in iManager:

1. In the Navigation frame, open the LDAP group and select LDAP Overview.

2. Select the View LDAP Servers tab, and click the LDAP Server object with which you want to work.

3. Enter the configurable parameters in the property pages, and click the Refresh button to reset the LDAP server. Click OK when you're finished.

There are six pages of configuration parameters for the LDAP Server object:

- *Information*—Set the general configuration of your LDAP server on this page. The following entries are available:

  - *LDAP Group*—Specify the name of the LDAP group to which this server should belong.

  - *Dereference Aliases When Resolving Names*—Check this option to force the LDAP server to resolve to the actual object whenever it encounters an alias object.

- *Connections*—Sets the secure connection settings for this LDAP server with the following options:

  - *Server Certificate*—Specifies the digital certificate that is used for secure connections on this server. Certificate server creates this certificate during the server installation routine. You should not have to change this value.

  - *Client Certificate*—Specifies how the LDAP server will work with client certificates. Options include Not Requesting Certificates; Requesting, but Not Requiring Client Certificates; and Requiring Client Certificates.

  - *Trusted Root Containers*—Specifies the container(s) in which trusted root certificates are stored for those clients capable of using Transport Layer Security (TLS).

  - *Require TLS for All Operations*—Check this box to require TLS-protected connections for all LDAP server communications.

  - *Enable and Require Mutual Authentication*—Check this box to force the LDAP server to mutually authenticate when using SSL.

- *Enable Encrypted Port*—Sets the TCP port used for SSL connections on this server. Default is port **636**. This should not be changed unless another service is already using port **636** on this server. Uncheck this box to prevent LDAP clients from using secure connections on this server.

- *Enable Non-encrypted Port*—Sets the TCP port used for LDAP on this server. Default is port **389**. This should not be changed unless another service is already using port **389** on this server. Uncheck this box to force LDAP clients to use SSL connections on this server.

- *Concurrent Bind Limit*—Sets the maximum number of simultaneous LDAP connections. This should be set based on the amount of available memory in the LDAP server. Each LDAP request takes about 160KB of memory. Default is no limit.

- *Idle Timeout*—Defines the maximum time in seconds that an open LDAP connection can remain inactive before being closed. Default is no limit.

- *Bind Restrictions*—Specifies whether users must supply a username and password in order to connect. This is useful if you want to prevent anonymous or public access to eDirectory.

- *Searches*—Defines the search settings on this LDAP server with the following settings:

  - *Filtered Replicas*—If you have configured a Filtered replica with specific search data, such as a corporate directory, you can specify that LDAP uses this replica to perform its searches. If your Filtered replicas are configured for this purpose, they can improve search time significantly.

  - *Persistent Search*—Persistent search is an extension to the LDAP search operation that allows an LDAP client to receive active updates to a given query from the LDAP server. As data on the LDAP server changes, the client will be automatically notified of changes that affect its search. These settings let you enable/disable persistent searches, and limit the number of concurrent persistent searches.

  - *Restrictions*—Sets the maximum values for searches in both time and number of entries returned.

  - *Nonstandard Behaviors*—Two check boxes let you support ADSI and legacy Netscape schema requests, and provide operational as well as user attributes when a request for user attributes is made.

- *Events*—This page lets you enable event monitoring for external applications that may want to monitor certain eDirectory events. This monitoring can place a significant load on the LDAP server, so you can also specify a maximum server load for event monitoring.

- *Tracing*—This page lets you enable tracing of certain types of LDAP events. LDAP tracing can place a significant load on the LDAP server, so it should be used only when necessary to gather troubleshooting information.

- *Referrals*—This page lets you configure referral options that define how this LDAP server will react if it is unable to process an LDAP request directly:

  - *Default Referral URL*—Specify the LDAP URL that will point the LDAP client to another LDAP server when no specific referral information is available.

  - *Conditions Which Return Default Referral*—These three check boxes let you enable/disable situations under which this LDAP server will return a default referral to the client.

  - *Referral Options: Always Chain/Prefer Chaining*—Chaining causes the LDAP server to contact other LDAP servers to locate the requested data for the client, and then return the data to the client. Query work is server-intensive. *Always Refer/Prefer Referrals*—A *referral* is a message returned to the client that tells it where it can go to get the requested information. Both LDAP clients and servers must support referrals, but this eliminates the first LDAP server as a middleman for the LDAP request. The chaining and referral preferences can be set separately for eDirectory searches as opposed to other eDirectory operations.

Using the pages just described, you can configure the LDAP Server object as needed to fit your specific environment.

LDAP GROUP OBJECT

The LDAP Group object allows you to configure user access to the LDAP server. By default, an LDAP Group object will be created for each LDAP Server object, but if you want to use the same user configuration for multiple LDAP servers, you can combine them into a single LDAP group.

To configure the LDAP Group object, complete the following steps in iManager:

1. In the Navigation frame, open the LDAP group and select LDAP Overview.

2. Select the View LDAP Groups tab, and click the LDAP group object with which you want to work.

3. Enter the configurable parameters in the property pages, and click OK when finished.

There are four pages of configuration parameters for the LDAP Group object:

- *Information*—This page lets you set a couple of general settings for the LDAP Group:

  - *Server List*—Use this option to add or remove LDAP servers from this LDAP group.

  - *Proxy User*—Specifies the eDirectory user object to use as a proxy for anonymous LDAP bind requests. For more information, see "Connecting via LDAP," later in this chapter.

  - *Require TLS for Simple Binds with Password*—Check this option if you want to prevent unencrypted bind requests that contain a password. This is recommended to prevent passwords from being sent across the network in clear text.

- *Referrals*—This page lets you configure referral options that define how this LDAP server will react if it is unable to process an LDAP request directly:

  - *Default Referral URL*—Specify the LDAP URL that will point the LDAP client to another LDAP server when no specific referral information is available.

  - *Conditions Which Return Default Referral*—These three check boxes let you enable/disable situations under which this LDAP server will return a default referral to the client.

  - *Referral Options: Always Chain/Prefer Chaining*—Chaining causes the LDAP server to contact other LDAP servers to locate the requested data for the client, and then return the data to the client. Query work is server-intensive. *Always Refer/Prefer Referrals*—A *referral* is a message returned to the client that tells it where it can go to get the requested information. Both LDAP clients and servers must support referrals, but this eliminates the first LDAP server as a middleman for the LDAP request. The chaining and referral preferences can be set separately for eDirectory searches versus other eDirectory operations.

- *Attribute Map* and *Class Map*—These pages let an administrator associate LDAP schema classes and attributes to corresponding eDirectory schema classes and attributes. A default set of mappings is defined when the LDAP group is created, but it leaves many LDAP classes and attributes unmapped. If you have specific needs, you can map LDAP classes and attributes as needed.

NOTE

Because there are certain LDAP attributes (such as CN and Common Name) that map to the same NDS value, LDAP services support multivalue associations. However, the LDAP server will return the value of the first matching attribute it locates in the list. If you map multiple LDAP attributes to a single NDS attribute, make sure you order the list with the most important attributes at the top; they will take precedence.

Connecting via LDAP

All LDAP clients bind or connect to eDirectory as one of the following types of users:

- [Public] user (anonymous bind)
- Proxy user (proxy user anonymous bind)
- Directory user (eDirectory user bind)

The type of bind the user authenticates with affects the content the LDAP client can access. LDAP clients access a directory by building a request and sending it to the directory. When an LDAP client sends a request through LDAP Services for eDirectory, eDirectory completes the request for only those attributes to which the LDAP client has the appropriate access rights. For example, if the LDAP client requests an attribute value (which requires the Read right) and the user is granted only the Compare right to that attribute, the request is rejected.

Standard login restrictions and password restrictions still apply; however, any restrictions are relative to where LDAP is running. Time and address restrictions are honored, but address restrictions are relative to where the eDirectory login occurred—in this case, the LDAP server. Also, because LDAP does not support grace logins, users can log in to the server yet not be able to bind to LDAP.

CONNECTING AS A [PUBLIC] USER

An *anonymous bind* is an LDAP connection that does not contain a username or password. If an anonymous client requests an LDAP connection and the service is not configured to use a Proxy user, eDirectory authenticates the client as a [Public] user.

[Public] is an unauthenticated eDirectory user. By default, [Public] is assigned only the Browse right to the objects in the eDirectory tree. [Public] can see only objects; it cannot browse object attributes. This is typically too limited for most LDAP clients. Although you can change the [Public] rights, this will give those rights to all users. To avoid this, use Proxy user (anonymous bind).

CONNECTING AS A PROXY USER

Proxy user (anonymous bind) allows LDAP to connect as a predefined eDirectory user. This gives you the flexibility to offer an anonymous connection that may actually be useful for something—such as accessing public information—without potentially causing security problems by changing [Public].

The key concepts of Proxy user (anonymous bind) are as follows:

- All anonymous LDAP access is managed through the Proxy User object. Assign the Proxy user appropriate rights to all objects and attributes in eDirectory.

- The Proxy user cannot have a password or any password restrictions, such as password change intervals, because LDAP clients do not supply passwords during anonymous binds. Do not allow the Proxy user to change passwords.

- If desired, you can limit the locations from which a Proxy user can log in by setting address restrictions on the Proxy User object. For more information on creating and configuring eDirectory User objects, see Chapter 8.

The Proxy User object is enabled from the Information tab of the LDAP Group object, as described earlier in this chapter. There is only one Proxy User object for all servers in an LDAP group.

CONNECTING AS A DIRECTORY USER

LDAP clients can also connect using regular eDirectory User objects. When authenticated, the LDAP client is allowed access to any information to which the eDirectory user has rights.

The key concepts of eDirectory user binds are as follows:

- eDirectory user connections are authenticated to eDirectory with a username and password entered at the LDAP client.

- If secure connections are not required for password-based connections, the eDirectory password can be transmitted in clear text on the path between the LDAP client and LDAP server.

- If an eDirectory user password has expired, eDirectory bind requests for that user are rejected.

You have the flexibility to leverage any of these types of LDAP bind operations to give LDAP users access to eDirectory information they might need.

DNS and DHCP Services

DNS and DHCP services in OES Linux are provided by the traditional open source Bind and ISC DHCP Server programs. These programs are not installed by default in OES Linux, and if desired must be manually installed after the main server installation, or installed during a custom installation of OES Linux. Unlike OES NetWare, these components are not integrated into eDirectory or managed through iManager.

DNS and DHCP manage the assignment and discovery of IP addresses on a network. Both of these services are managed via YaST modules, under the Network Services category. Complete configuration of both of these services can be quite complex and is beyond the scope of the book. This section will provide a brief introduction to these services, as well as basic configuration information. For complete information on these services, refer to specific documentation for each service.

Installing DNS and DHCP Services

DNS and DHCP services can be installed as an optional service during the OES Linux installation routine. It can also be installed as a post-installation task through YaST.

To install DNS/DHCP services from YaST, each component (DNS and DHCP) must be installed separately. Complete the following steps to install the DHCP server:

1. Access YaST from a terminal using **yast**, or from a graphical environment using **yast2** or the YaST launcher from the application menu.

2. Select the Network Services category in YaST. From within this category, locate and select the DHCP Server module. This module will detect that the **rpm** for **dhcp-server** is missing and ask if you want to install it. Select Continue to install the necessary packages.

3. At the conclusion of the software installation, **SuSEconfig** is executed to update the system configuration. When this completes, the configuration of the DNS server will begin automatically.

4. The first step of configuring the DHCP Server is determining which interface the DHCP server will run on. Select the appropriate interface and click Next.

5. At the DHCP Global Settings page, enter the following information and click Next:

- *LDAP Support*—To store the DHCP configuration in LDAP, select this option. This is not normally used with eDirectory.

- *Domain Name*—Contains the domain name used when leasing addresses to clients.

- *Primary Name Server IP*—Enter the IP address of the primary DNS name server. If you're using DNS, this may be the address of the local server.

- *(Optional) Secondary Name Server IP*—Enter the IP address of a secondary DNS name server.

- *Default Gateway (Router)*—Enter the IP address of the default gateway on the current LAN segment.

- *(Optional) Time Server*—Enter the IP address of the NTP server used for synchronizing time.

- *(Optional) Print Server*—Enter the IP address of the print server to be offered to clients. If you are using iPrint, this is not necessary.

- *(Optional) WINS Server*—Enter the IP address of a Windows Internet Naming Service (WINS) server if desired.

- *Default Lease Time*—Enter the default amount of time an address is leased to clients. Use the drop-down box to select time in Days, Hours, Minutes, or Seconds.

6. At the Dynamic DHCP page, enter the following information and click Next:

- *First IP Address*—Enter the first valid IP address to be leased to clients.

- *Last IP Address*—Enter the last valid IP address to be leased to clients. This must reside on the same subnet as the First IP Address.

- *Default Lease Time*—Enter the default amount of time an address in the current address block is leased to clients. Use the drop-down box to select time in Days, Hours, Minutes, or Seconds.

- *(Optional) Max Lease Time*—Enter the maximum amount of time an address is blocked for use by a client. Use the drop-down box to select time in Days, Hours, Minutes, or Seconds.

7. After completing the configuration of DHCP, determine whether the DHCP server should start automatically at server power on, and press Finish to complete the installation.

After DHCP has been installed, complete the following steps to install the DNS server:

1. Access YaST from a terminal using yast, from a graphical environment using yast2, or from the YaST launcher from the application menu.

2. Select the Network Services category in YaST. From within this category, locate and select the DNS Server module. This module will detect that the rpm for bind is missing and ask if you want to install it. Select Continue to install the necessary packages.

3. At the conclusion of the software installation, SuSEconfig is executed to update the system configuration. When this completes, the configuration of the DNS server will begin automatically.

4. The first configuration item that must be configured is the Forwarder Settings. This option determines whether the PPP daemon is allowed to adjust the Forward configuration upon connection. For most installation, this should be left at Set Forwarders Manually. This option can also be adjusted after completing the installation. Make an appropriate selection and click Next.

5. At the DNS Zone configuration screen, the DNS zones that will be managed by this server can be configured. Any zones added during the installation can be edited after the fact. Also, additional zones can be modified after completing the DNS installation. If you are unsure of your DNS configuration, this screen can be left blank for the time being. When ready, click Next to continue.

6. The final installation screen for the DNS server Installation allows you to determine when the DNS server is started—during bootup or manually. If your DNS configuration is complete, select On; otherwise, select Off until the configuration is complete. To complete the installation of DNS, click Finish.

With DNS/DHCP services installed on the network, an IP client can establish a connection with the network by leasing an IP address from a pool of available addresses, rather than requiring that the workstation be assigned a fixed address individually. This makes IP address management much easier.

When the IP client is connected to the network, it can automatically detect available DNS name servers, through which it can translate domain names (for example, www.novell.com) into its corresponding IP address (for example, 137.65.168.1). This enables the client to communicate with the server properly. Domain names are a benefit to the human users of computers, not the computers themselves.

All DNS/DHCP configuration and management can be performed through direct configuration file editing from a terminal, or through the YaST management utility. For more information on the basics of YaST, see Chapter 6, "SUSE Linux Enterprise Server Management."

As DNS and DHCP can be extremely complex and customized for specific network needs, an in-depth discussion on these services does not fit within the scope of this book. However, the remaining content of this section will briefly discuss the basic configuration of both DNS and DHCP services. For more detailed information on these services, refer to the SLES online manual or the documentation installed with each service.

Configuring DHCP Services

Configuring the DHCP environment involves the following steps:

- Planning DHCP
- Configuring the DHCP server
- Starting DHCP services

PLANNING DHCP

Before using DHCP for the first time, you need to gather a lot of network information:

- Make a list of all IP hosts to be served by the DHCP server. Include all devices that use network addresses on every segment of your network.

- Compile a list of current IP address assignments. Organize your lists of hosts and IP addresses by geographic location. For example, if your network is spread over a WAN, make a list for each location to help you organize the distribution of DHCP resources.

- You must have a list of all permanently assigned network addresses. You might also want to make a list of devices that are to be denied IP addresses and those hosts that are to receive strict address limitations.

Another major issue is deciding how long to set your client leases. You must strike a balance between the amount of network traffic and the amount of flexibility in the system. The longest lease provided by a DHCP server determines the length of time you might have to wait before configuration changes can be propagated within a network. Consider the following issues when setting lease times:

- Keep leases short if you have more users than IP addresses. Shorter leases support more clients but increase the load on the network and DHCP server. A lease of two hours is long enough to serve most users, and the network load will probably not be significant. Leases shorter than this start to increase network and server load dramatically.

- Leases should be set twice as long as typical interruptions, such as server and communications outages. Decide how long your users should be able to go without contacting the DHCP server, and double it to get recommended lease duration.

- Hosts that are advertising services on the network, such as Web servers, should not have an IP address that is constantly changing. Consider permanent assignments for these hosts. The deciding factor should be how long you want the host to be able to keep an assigned address.

The default of three days is usually a pretty good balance between the need for a shorter and a longer lease.

CONFIGURING THE DHCP SERVER

Configuring the DHCP server is performed with the YaST DHCP Server module. If this is the first time you have used this module, you are presented with the same configuration wizard described in the DHCP Installation steps earlier in this chapter. When you launch the DHCP YaST module after having gone through the default configuration wizard, you are presented with the following general categories of options:

- *Start-Up*—Offers the option of starting the DHCP Server automatically upon server startup, or using a manual start setting.

- *Card Selection*—Allows you to specify the network interface card used for by the DHCP Server.

- *Global Settings*—Provides the same options outlined in the Global Settings section of the DHCP installation process earlier in this chapter.

- *Dynamic DHCP*—Provides the same options outlined in the Dynamic DHCP section of the DHCP installation process earlier in this chapter.

- *Host Management*—Used to manually register hosts and configure IP addresses for those hosts based on their hardware address.

- *Expert Settings*—Used to configure expert options for the DHCP server. After you've entered this category, you cannot return to the simplified view until the changes are saved and the module is restarted.

The configuration of the DHCP server is stored in the `/etc/dhcp.conf` file. If necessary, this file can be edited manually. After making any changes, be sure to restart the DHCP service for those changes to take effect.

STARTING DHCP SERVICES

When you have completed the configuration of the DHCP server, YaST should automatically start up the daemon. If necessary, you can also start the DHCP daemon by issuing the following command:

`rcdhcpd start`

This same command can stop the daemon with a **stop** command-line parameter. You typically won't need to do anything beyond this. If problems are encountered, check the system log file (`/var/log/messages`) for details.

To enable DHCP services on a client workstation, simply configure the TCP/IP properties to obtain an IP address automatically. The next time the client starts, it will send a request to the DHCP server for an IP address.

WARNING

Client configuration settings will override the configuration received from a DHCP server. The only exception is the hostname parameter set on the DNS Configuration tab of the TCP/IP Properties window.

For detailed information on DHCP configuration options, see the SLES online documentation.

Configuring DNS Services

Similar to DHCP, configuring the DNS environment involves the following steps:

- Planning DNS
- Configuring the DNS server
- Starting DNS services

PLANNING DNS

Consider the following issues and recommendations as you plan your DNS environment:

- You will configure a primary DNS name server, which is considered the authoritative source for DNS information. For load balancing and fault tolerance, plan to install one primary and at least one secondary name server.

- Secondary name servers receive their zone data from the primary name server. When it starts, and at periodic intervals, the secondary checks with the primary to see whether any information has changed. If the information on the secondary is older than that on the primary, a zone transfer occurs to update the secondary name server's information.

- If you are running a primary name server and providing DNS service for a zone, the size or geography of your network might require creating subzones within the zone.

- If a name server cannot answer a query, it must query a remote server. This is particularly relevant for Internet domain queries. The Bind DNS server allows you to configure primary and/or secondary name servers to act as forwarders. Forwarders that handle the off-site queries develop a robust cache of information. When using forwarders, configure the other name servers in your zone to direct their queries to the forwarder. The forwarder can typically respond to any given query with information from its cache, eliminating the need to pass an outside query to a remote server.

Considering the issues discussed here will help make sure your DNS environment is planned properly.

CONFIGURING THE DNS SERVER

Configuring the DNS server is performed with the YaST DNS Server module. If this is the first time you have used this module, you are presented with the same configuration process described in the DNS Installation steps earlier in this chapter. When you launch the DNS YaST module after having gone through the default configuration, you are presented with the following general categories of options:

- *Start-Up*—This selection offers the option of starting the DNS server automatically upon server startup or using a manual start setting. The DNS server can also be started and stopped directly from this screen. Finally, this screen also provides the option to enable LDAP support with the DNS server.

- *Forwarders*—This screen is used to allow the PPP daemon to automatically configure forwarders. Forwarders can also be set for manual mode and any manual forwarders can be directly entered into the forwarding list on this screen.

- *Basic Options*—This screen is used to configure basic options for the main DNS server configuration. Common options are available as a drop-down box and values for each option can be manually set and entered into the configuration file.

- *Logging*—This screen is used to configure logging options, including where the log files should be stored and what type of logging details are recorded.

- *ACLs*—This screen is used to configure Access Control Lists (ACLs) to provide security for zone access.

- *TSIG Keys*—This screen is used to configure TSIG keys, which are required for authentication when using Dynamic DNS.

- *DNS Zones*—This screen is used to add zones managed by the DNS server. After adding a zone, an additional option, Edit Zone, becomes available. Use this option to perform advanced zone customization—including adding resource records to the domain.

The general configuration of the DNS server is stored in the `/etc/named.conf` file. In addition to this configuration file, zone-specific information is written to configuration files found in the `/var/lib/named` directory structure. If necessary, you can edit these files manually. After making any changes, be sure to restart the DNS service for those changes to take affect.

STARTING DNS SERVICES

When you have completed the configuration of the DNS server, YaST should automatically start up the daemon. If necessary, you can also start the DNS daemon by issuing the following command:

`rcnamed start`

This same command can stop the daemon with a **stop** command-line parameter. When started, *named* should start responding to queries for the zone. If you encounter problems, check the system log file (`/var/log/messages`) for details.

To enable DNS services on a client workstation, simply configure the TCP/IP properties to obtain DNS server addresses automatically. The next time the client starts, it will dynamically query for DNS information on the network.

For detailed information on DNS configuration options, see the SLES online documentation.

## CHAPTER 8

Users and Network Security

Instant Access

Creating Users and Groups

- To create User and Group objects, use iManager.
- To set up a template so that all users you create receive a set of common characteristics, use iManager to create a Template object.

Ensuring Login Security

- To create account restrictions, access the user or group properties through iManager.
- To set or change passwords, access User object properties with iManager.

Working with eDirectory Security

- To view or change eDirectory object or property rights, use iManager.

Overview of Users in OES Linux

At its fundamental level, OES Linux provides file and print services and network-enabled application support to end users. These user-level services all require some method of locating a valid user account, and then authenticating the requested user to that account. When identity and permissions have been established, the service is started with the appropriate environment.

OES user accounts are all stored and managed within eDirectory. Not all applications and services, however, directly integrate or support eDirectory. To bring eDirectory functionality to as many applications as possible, OES Linux provides support for two primary methods of authentication:

- Native eDirectory
- LDAP

Native eDirectory

Native eDirectory-aware services are those services that understand the eDirectory Application Program Interface (API). Services that understand this API have the advantage of being able to directly communicate with eDirectory and leverage the many advanced features eDirectory has offered for years.

OES Linux offers several services that communicate directly to eDirectory through this API. Examples of this include iManager, Virtual Office, iFolder, the Novell Client, and many others. Through direct API communication with eDirectory, these services can leverage such things as advanced authentication mechanisms and complex permission structures offered on NSS volumes.

LDAP

Services that do not leverage the eDirectory API can still take advantage of eDirectory for user storage and account management. To accomplish this, services rely on an industry standard known as Lightweight Directory Access Protocol (LDAP).

LDAP is a protocol used to communicate with directories containing some form of information. In the case of eDirectory, the information being requested is quite often user account details. OES Linux installations with eDirectory automatically support LDAP connections for this purpose. LDAP-aware services can be configured to take advantage of this through the use of an LDAP connection to eDirectory. This connection is then used to locate and authenticate user accounts prior to the service being initiated.

OES Linux relies on this LDAP functionality for a number of important Linux services. One example of this is Samba. The Samba software suite provides Linux resources to Windows users as though the Linux server were actually running Windows. This functionality requires Windows users to authenticate to the Linux server just as they would with any other Windows machine. Traditionally, Samba stores users in a local file, unique to Samba. With OES Linux, Samba is configured to use LDAP to locate eDirectory users who are allowed access to Samba resources.

Another example of this situation is the integration of Pluggable Authentication Module (PAM) enabled services into eDirectory. As with Samba, eDirectory user objects are modified with OES to provide local Linux authentication to any PAM-aware service via LDAP and eDirectory. This is provided through the Linux User Management component of OES. Services that can use this functionality include such things as SSH, FTP, and local Linux logins.

It is important to understand that for these services that do not natively support eDirectory, the following three conditions must be met in order to support LDAP storage and authentication of accounts:

- *eDirectory with LDAP enabled*—By default, OES Linux configures eDirectory with LDAP support. This can be disabled, but additional configuration within eDirectory is not normally required.

- *LDAP-aware service*—Services that want to store accounts within eDirectory must be modified to support LDAP communication to a directory server. Most common services providing access to users already support this. (For specific configuration information, refer to the service or application documentation.)

- *Valid service account in eDirectory*—User accounts within eDirectory may not natively be valid accounts in an LDAP-aware service. In the case of Samba, eDirectory users must be modified to contain the required attributes of a Samba user. These modifications are performed via schema extensions as part of an OES Linux installation. Custom third-party applications may require additional schema modifications.

NOTE

More information on schema extensions required with supported LDAP-aware applications can be found in the "Provisioning Linux Users" section of this chapter.

When using LDAP-aware services, security enforcement is primarily handled by the respective service itself (Samba, FTP, SSH, and so on). eDirectory is still used to enforce user password requirements, account expirations, and other important abilities. However, advanced features such as eDirectory rights enforcement may not be available.

This does not mean that these services are insecure! On the contrary, integration with eDirectory actually provides another level of security to these applications. However, when given the choice between one access method versus another, you would be well advised to base your decision, at least in part, on the security of the access methods involved.

NOTE

The majority of this chapter will focus on eDirectory authentication and security. Following this, the "Provisioning Linux Users" section will fill in details regarding LUM and Samba.

eDirectory User-Related Objects

OES users are all stored as objects within eDirectory. In addition to replicating these objects across servers and providing basic account authentication services, eDirectory provides a solid security model that includes such things as trustee assignments, administrative roles, inherited rights, and rights filters. Understanding user-related objects, as well as the security model provided by eDirectory, is critical to implementing a secure user environment.

There are three main eDirectory objects that are used to organize your network users. You can use iManager to create and manage each of these types of objects (for more information on iManager, see Chapter 5, "OES Management Tools"):

- User object
- Group object
- Organizational role

These objects form the foundation from which eDirectory-based network services and privileges are ultimately delivered. After all, user-related objects define the human elements of your network. Immediately after a new OES Linux and eDirectory installation, the only eDirectory User object that exists is Admin (the root user does exist, but is stored as a local Linux user, rather than stored within eDirectory). Although it might be comforting to think of a network of one, you are going to have to create user accounts for every one of your users. After user accounts have been created, your users can begin working on the network. In most cases, users on a network will notice very little difference from working on a standalone computer. They still use the applications they were using before. They still open, save, and delete files the same way. They can still play the same games—but only if you let them!

And that's the goal of network security: to prevent users from taking some action, either unintentionally or intentionally, that might compromise the integrity of the network or expose network resources in such a way that can cause harm to the network or the organization. There are several levels of network security in today's networks, and OES Linux gives you a great deal of control over each.

The User Object

To create an eDirectory User object, complete the following steps:

1. Launch iManager. In the Navigation frame, open the Users group and select Create User (see Figure 8.1).

2. Specify the desired information and click OK. You should pay particular attention to the following fields:

FIGURE 8.1
Creating a new user in iManager.

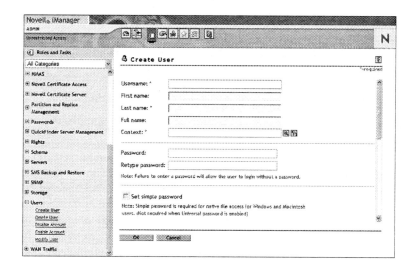

- *Username* (Required)—Enter the desired login name for this user. This is the name the user will enter when he or she authenticates to eDirectory.

- *Last Name* (Required)—Specify the last name of this user. This field is required so that you can perform name-based searches on eDirectory.

- *Context*—Specify the container in which the User object should be created.

- *Password*—Specify a password for the user.

WARNING

It is possible to create an eDirectory User object without a password, but it is highly discouraged due to the network security breach that results.

- *Create Home Directory*—If desired, specify a directory on an NSS volume to use as a home directory for the new user.

NOTE

The Create Home Directory option does not create a directory used as a home directory for LUM users. Home directories for LUM users will always be located beneath the /home directory.

3. After creating the eDirectory user account, you are prompted to enable the newly created user as a LUM user. If you are planning on using Linux User Management (LUM) or Samba, you should fill out this screen properly. The following fields are available on this screen, as shown in Figure 8.2:

- *Primary Group* (Required)—Enter the primary LUM group for the user. All Linux users must be associated with a Linux group. By default, a Linux group called lumgroup is created for this purpose.

- *Desired Shell Type* (Required)—Enter the default Linux shell for the LUM user. This field defaults to /bin/bash, which is a good choice for most general purposes.

- *Enable This User for LDAP (eDirectory) Authentication to Samba*—If this user will also be accessing server resources via Samba, select this check box to enable Samba Authentication.

FIGURE 8.2

Adding LUM and Samba attributes to new users.

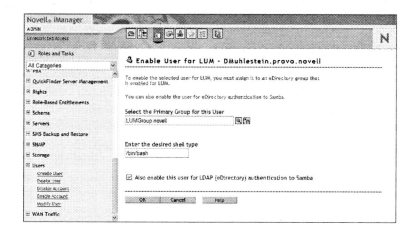

NOTE

More information on Samba and LUM is available in the "Provisioning Linux Users" section later in this chapter.

If you plan to assign certain identical properties to many of your users, you can use a User Template object. The Template object will automatically apply default properties to any new user you create using the template. However, it does not apply those properties to any users who existed before you created the user template. Network administrators often use a template to automatically grant default eDirectory and file-system rights to users.

To create a User Template object, complete these steps:

1. From iManager, select the View Objects icon in the Header frame.

2. In the Navigation frame, click any container object and choose Create Object from the task list.

3. Select Template from the list of available objects and click OK.

4. Specify the name of the Template object, and the context in which it should be created, and click OK.

After you have created the User Template object, you configure any of the common characteristics you want assigned to all users you create. To do this in iManager, browse to and select the object in the left frame. Modify the template by selecting the appropriate task and providing the desired information. You will specify most of the template information in the Modify Object and the Rights to Other Objects tasks.

NOTE

Template objects cannot be used to automatically create LUM and Samba accounts for new users.

The Group Object

Group objects are used to apply a common set of trustee rights to different User objects. User objects assigned to a group are made *security equivalent* to that group, meaning that any rights given to the Group object will also be applied to each of its member users.

When using LUM, groups are also used to provide a user's primary group for file ownership on the Linux filesystem. A primary group is required for all users within the LUM system.

Creating a group is very similar to creating a user. Complete the following steps to create a group and assign group membership to a user.

1. Launch iManager and select the View Objects icon in the Header frame.

2. In the Navigation frame, browse to and select a container object and choose Create Group from the task list.

3. Specify the name of the Group object, and the context in which it should be created, and click OK.

4. Click Modify to access the Group object properties pages. From there you can provide any object-specific information, and add members to the group by selecting the Members link. Click OK when finished to save the Group properties.

5. After creating the eDirectory group, you are prompted to enable the newly created group as a LUM group. If you are planning on using LUM, you should fill out this screen properly. To create a LUM group one of the following fields must be filled out:

    ■ *Linux Config Object*—To associate the group with all defined Linux Workstations, select this radio button and enter the Linux Config object in the corresponding field.

■ *Linux Workstation Object(s)*—To associate the group with one or more specific Linux Workstations, select this radio button and enter the group or groups in the corresponding field.

NOTE

More information on the Linux Config object, Linux Workstations, and other LUM objects and attributes is available later in this chapter.

The Organizational Role

Organizational roles function like groups of one. (They can have multiple occupants for process redundancy.) They use explicit security equivalence to provide specific rights to a user who needs to be able to perform a specific task. Organizational roles are generally used to grant some degree of administrative capability for a tree or branch of the tree. Although similar in some respects, an organizational role should not be confused with the role-based services of iManager. The iManager roles are much more flexible in their application than organizational roles. For more information on iManager roles, see Chapter 5.

Complete the following steps to create an organizational role and assign occupancy to a user:

1. Launch iManager and select the View Objects icon in the Header frame.
2. In the Navigation frame, browse to and select a container object and choose Create Object from the task list.
3. Select Organizational Role from the list of available objects and click OK.
4. Specify the name of the Organizational Role object and the context in which it should be created, and click OK.
5. Click Modify to access the Organizational Role object properties pages. From there you can provide any object-specific information, and specify the occupant of the Organizational Role. Click OK when finished to save the Organizational Role properties.

After you have created the organizational role, you can assign any User object to an organizational role to grant specific rights related to specific responsibilities within your organization.

eDirectory Authentication

Authentication provides the doorway for access to network resources. Without a strong authentication mechanism, sensitive network resources are essentially laid bare for anyone to access. The primary authentication method currently used with eDirectory is the username/password combination. Novell Modular Authentication Service (NMAS) makes it possible to integrate more advanced authentication and authorization techniques into your OES environment. Furthermore, NMAS offers *Universal Passwords*, which improve the traditional password-based authentication method.

Novell Modular Authentication Service

NMAS is designed to help you protect information on your network. NMAS offers a more robust framework for protecting your OES Linux environment. If you're not familiar with the different components of NMAS, you should get to know the following concepts. More information about each of these is provided in the OES Linux online documentation.

PHASES OF OPERATION

There are specific times when NMAS can be useful in helping to secure your network environment:

- *User identification* occurs prior to the actual authentication process. It provides a way to automatically gather a user's authentication information and use it to populate the Novell Login dialog in the Novell Client.

- *Authentication* is the opportunity for users to prove they are who they claim to be. NMAS supports multiple authentication methods.

- *Device removal detection* is the capability to lock down a workstation after authentication when it becomes clear that the user is no longer present.

Each of these phases of operation is completely independent. You can choose to use the same, or completely different, identification techniques for each phase. To provide this functionality, NMAS introduces a few additional concepts to eDirectory authentication:

- Login factors
- Login methods and sequences
- Graded authentication

LOGIN FACTORS

NMAS uses three approaches to logging in to the network, known as *login factors*. These login factors describe different items or qualities a user can use to authenticate to the network:

- *Password authentication*—Also referred to as "something you know," password authentication is the traditional network authentication method. It is still responsible for the lion's share of network authentication that goes on, including LDAP authentication, browser-based authentication, and most other directories.

- *Device authentication*—Also referred to as "something you have," device authentication uses third-party tokens or smart cards to deliver the secret with which you authenticate to the network.

- *Biometric authentication*—Also referred to as "something you are," biometric authentication uses some sort of scanning device that converts some physical characteristic into a digital pattern that can be stored in eDirectory. When users attempt to authenticate, their biometric patterns are compared against the stored version to see if they match. Common biometric authentication methods include fingerprint readers, facial recognition, and retinal scans.

LOGIN METHODS AND SEQUENCES

A *login method* is a specific implementation of a login factor. Novell has partnered with several third parties to create a variety of options for each of the login factors described earlier in this chapter. A *post-login method* is a security process that is executed after a user has authenticated to eDirectory. One such post-login method is the workstation access method, which requires the user to provide credentials in order to unlock the workstation after a period of inactivity.

NOTE

With OES Linux, NMAS provides only the Challenge Response and NDS login methods. Additional methods can be downloaded from http://support.novell.com. Search the Knowledge Base for "NMAS Methods" for a link to the downloadable methods.

When you have decided upon and installed a method, you need to assign it to a login sequence in order for it to be used. A *login sequence* is an ordered set of one or more methods. Users log in to the network using these defined login sequences. If the sequence contains more than one method, the methods are presented to the user in the order specified. Login methods are presented first, followed by post-login methods.

GRADED AUTHENTICATION

Another important feature in NMAS is *graded authentication*, which allows you to grade, or control, access to the network based on the login methods used to authenticate to the network. Graded authentication operates in conjunction with standard eDirectory and file-system rights to provide very robust control over data access in an OES Linux environment.

There are three main elements to graded authentication:

- *Categories*—NMAS categories represent different levels of sensitivity and trust. You use categories to define security labels. There are three secrecy categories and three integrity categories by default—biometric, token, and password.

- *Security labels*—Security labels are combinations of categories that assign access requirements to NCP and NSS volumes and eDirectory objects and properties. NMAS provides the following eight security labels:

  - Biometric and password and token

  - Biometric and password

  - Biometric and token

  - Password and token

  - Biometric

  - Password

  - Token

  - Logged in

NOTE

The security labels visible in iManager are directly dependent on the login methods installed on the server. To see all possible labels, ensure that all login methods have been downloaded from http://support.novell.com and installed on the local server.

- *Clearances*—Clearances are assigned to users to represent the amount of trust you have in them. In the clearance, a read label specifies what a user can read and a write label specifies locations to which a user can write. Clearances are compared to security labels to determine whether a user has access. If a user's read clearance is equal to or greater than the security label assigned to the requested data, the user will be able to view the data.

By configuring these elements of graded authentication, you can greatly increase the security of your network data, and apply different types of security to data of different levels of sensitivity.

UNIVERSAL PASSWORD

The final NMAS component that merits discussion is Universal Password. One of the many strong points of OES Linux is the ability to integrate user accounts for multiple services into one centralized eDirectory account. Although this sounds straightforward enough, there are several behind-the-scenes components used in making these services integrate well. Perhaps the best example of this is the situation surrounding user passwords.

Most network services have some native method of storing user accounts and authenticating users before providing access. Often these services are created with specific password requirements and encryption methods in mind. With OES Linux, user accounts in eDirectory must be configured in such a way as to provide account authentication using whatever method the specific service requires. In the past this has meant a specific password for each type of password encryption method used by these services. Although this does work, the obvious problem is how to keep all passwords in sync, should one of the stored passwords be modified. OES Linux resolves this concern through Universal Password.

Universal Password was created to address two general needs:

- *Unified password for eDirectory access*—Universal Password provides for a single, centralized password store for each user. If additional access methods requiring older-style passwords are in use, Universal Password synchronizes those password stores to ensure that a single password is used for each user.

- *Increased password security*—Universal Password brings advanced Password Policies to eDirectory. These policies provide password structure requirements to eDirectory. Possible requirements include such things as a minimum and maximum number of numeric and special characters, required password length, and blocking of specific words for passwords.

In addressing those needs, Universal Password has become the ideal method of providing authentication services to multiple network services. With OES Linux, Universal Password is required in order to ensure that users have a single password across all possible access methods. One example of where this requirement is particularly useful is with the Samba integration components.

Universal Password is managed via iManager. Although it's fully functional with default installations of OES Linux, you may want to alter its configuration to suit your specific password requirements. The following steps describe the process used to create new password policies or modify the default Universal Password configuration, as shown in Figure 8.3.

FIGURE 8.3
Advanced Password Rules page in iManager.

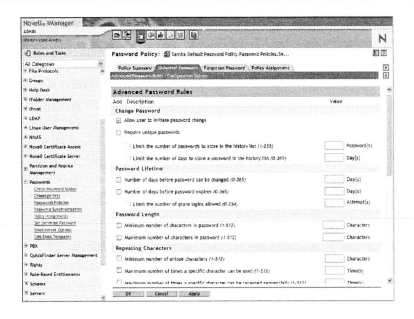

1. Launch iManager. In the Navigation frame, open the Passwords category and select Password Policies.

2. At this point, you can select the existing Samba Default Password Policy, or you can choose to create a new password policy. For the purpose of these instructions, ensure that the existing Samba Default Password Policy is selected and click Edit.

3. Select the Universal Password tab, then the Configuration Options sub-page. This page displays the following options for Universal Password:

- *Enable Universal Password*—This check box is used to enable or disable Universal Password. If Samba services are going to be offered on this OES Linux server, this setting should be enabled.

NOTE

When Universal Passwords are enabled, it is recommended that users change their password through the iManager self-service console, or the latest version of the Novell Client. Other utilities can be used to change user passwords, but only these utilities actually display the advanced password requirements set with Universal Password.

- *Enable the Advanced Password Rules*—This option is used to enable advanced rules that govern the creation of passwords. This is generally a welcome addition with Universal Password and is normally enabled.

- *Remove the NDS Password When Setting Universal Password*—This option is used to disable access from older Novell clients that do not recognize NMAS authentication methods. This is generally used to ensure that the advanced password rules of Universal Password are enforced.

- *Synchronize NDS Password When Setting Universal Password*—This option is used to synchronize the user's NDS password with the Universal Password during password changes. This option is normally enabled.

- *Synchronize Simple Password When setting Universal Password*—This option is used to synchronize the user's simple password during password changes. If Samba services are going to be offered on this OES Linux server, this setting should be enabled.

- *Synchronize Distribution Password When Setting Universal Password*—This option is used to synchronize the distribution password used by the DirXML engine with the Universal Password during password changes.

- *Allow User Agent to Retrieve Password*—This option is used when users access the Forgotten Password Self-Service feature of iManager. If this option is enabled, the user's password can be emailed to the user for retrieval.

- *Verify Whether Existing Passwords Comply with the Password Policy*—This option is used to enforce new password requirements for existing users. Users authenticating via NMAS-aware utilities will be notified if their passwords do not meet the password criteria. Users must change their password at that point.

4. After configuring the main Universal Password options, it is now time to configure the password requirements. Select the Advanced Password Rules subpage. This page displays the following categories and options for password requirements:

   - *Change Password*—This category has two check boxes used to determine whether users are allowed to change the password associated with their User object and whether unique passwords are required. If unique passwords are required, eDirectory tracks the specified number of recently used passwords with this account and prevents the user from reusing old passwords.

   - *Password Lifetime*—This category has two options used to determine the number of days before users are allowed to change their password, and when a password's lifetime has been exceeded and must be changed. If passwords are set to expire, the number of grace logins allowed is also set here.

   - *Password Length*—This category contains two options used to specify the minimum and maximum number of characters within passwords.

   - *Repeating Characters*—This category contains three options used to determine the minimum number of unique characters, as well as the maximum number of times a character can be used or repeated.

   - *Case Sensitive*—This category is used to determine the minimum and maximum number of upper- and lowercase letters used in password creation.

   - *Numeric Characters*—This category is used to determine whether or not numeric characters are allowed in passwords. If numeric characters are allowed, they can be disabled as the first or last character in a password. The minimum and maximum number of numeric characters is also set here.

   - *Special Characters*—This category is used to determine whether or not special characters are allowed in passwords. Special characters are defined as characters that are not numeric or alphabetic. If special characters are allowed, they can be disabled as the first or last character in a password. The minimum and maximum number of special characters is also set here.

- *Password Exclusions*—This category has one option used to list words that cannot be used for passwords. Commonly used passwords should be entered in this field. It is important to note that this is not intended to store a long list of words to prevent such things as dictionary attacks. A lengthy list of words would degrade server performance, and the same objective can be accomplished through requiring at least one numeric character.

5. After you configure the Advanced Password Rules, the Password Policy must be assigned to users or containers within eDirectory. Select the Password Policy subpage to make the assignment. On this page, select individual users, or the container that holds users you want to assign the password policy to. By default, newly created Samba users are automatically assigned to the Samba Default Password Policy. Click OK to complete the operation.

After you complete the configuration of Universal Password, new users in the container assigned to the password policy will automatically start using Universal Password. Existing users must have their Universal Password set in iManager, or they must change their password before being completely configured with a Universal Password.

NOTE

More information on Universal Password is available through the online documentation for NMAS.

Installing NMAS

NMAS requires both server- and client-side software in order to perform its authentication services. Installation of the NMAS client happens during the installation of the Novell Client, and is described in Chapter 4, "OES Linux Clients." On the server, NMAS is one of the default services and will be installed automatically with Novell eDirectory.

In order to use NMAS, several configuration options must be set, depending on your specific environment and needs. Server-side configuration is available through iManager. When the NMAS server options are configured, you can then configure the NMAS client to leverage NMAS capabilities. Generally, the process involves the following:

- *Create a login sequence*—This process identifies the specific login methods that will be used for login and post-login operations, and the order in which they will be applied if multiple login methods are specified.

- *Assign a login sequence to a user*—After a login sequence has been created, it is available for use by a user. A default login sequence can be defined, and users can be forced to use a specific login sequence, if desired.

- *Graded authentication*—With the login environment configured, you can now define those network resources that are available with each login method. Graded authentication lets you label network resources and require certain levels of authentication in order to access those resources.

- *Customize the user login*—The Novell Client supports several customization options based on the type of authentication that is being used. For more information on the Novell Client, see Chapter 4.

For more detailed information on each of these NMAS configuration steps, see the Novell online documentation.

eDirectory Login Controls

In addition to the actual login process, eDirectory provides a variety of login controls designed to help secure the network. Those controls are found in the properties of each User object. The various types of restrictions offered by eDirectory include

- Password restrictions
- Login restrictions
- Time restrictions
- Address restrictions
- Intruder lockout

NOTE

You will also see an Account Balance tab. This is a leftover from a NetWare server accounting feature that is not supported in OES Linux.

You can manage the various login controls from iManager or ConsoleOne. Login controls can be set on individual User objects, or they can be defined at the container level, where they will be automatically applied to all users in that container. To get to the login restrictions pages available through eDirectory, complete the following steps:

1. Launch iManager and select the View Objects icon. Locate the object for which you want to set login controls.

2. Click the object and select Modify Object.

3. Select the Restrictions tab and you will see a subpage for each of the controls listed previously. Select the appropriate page.

4. Make your desired changes and click OK to save your changes.

Each of the login control pages is described in more detail in the following sections.

PASSWORD RESTRICTIONS

The Password Restrictions page allows you to set password characteristics for eDirectory users. As mentioned previously, OES Linux uses Universal Password for password management. Universal Password configuration options include password settings available on this screen and additional features more advanced than the traditional eDirectory options available here. Because of this, the Password Restrictions screen should not be used to enforce password requirements with OES Linux.

NOTE

More information on configuring Universal Password is available in the "Novell Modular Authentication Service" section of this chapter.

LOGIN RESTRICTIONS

The Login Restrictions page allows you to control the capability of a user to log in to the network, as shown in Figure 8.4.

FIGURE 8.4
Login Restrictions page in iManager.

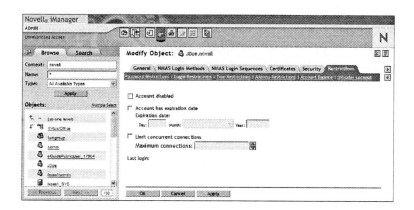

- *Account Disabled*—Checking this box disables the user account and prevents future login attempts. However, this will not affect a user who is currently logged in.

- *Account Has Expiration Date*—Checking this box allows you to set a date when the user account will be automatically disabled. This option might be used for contract employees or consultants who will be working for a predefined period of time.

- *Limit Concurrent Connections*—Check this box to define how many times the same account can be used to log in from different workstations simultaneously. If this option is enabled, the default is 1, but any value between 1 and 32,000 can be selected.

TIME RESTRICTIONS

The Time Restrictions page enables you to limit the time(s) of day when a user can access the network, as shown in Figure 8.5. By default, there are no restrictions.

To set a time restriction, click the box for which you want the restriction to occur, and then click Apply to reflect the change. To select a range of time, hold down the Shift key while moving the mouse over the time range. Each block is 30 minutes. When finished, make sure to select OK to save the new restrictions out to eDirectory. If a user is logged in when her lockout period is reached, she will be issued a five-minute warning, after which she will be automatically logged out.

FIGURE 8.5
The Time Restrictions page in iManager.

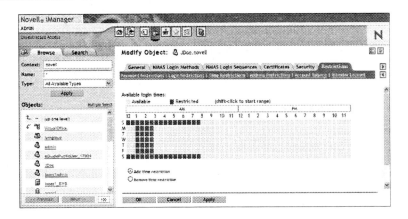

NOTE

One important caveat to time restrictions is that they are governed by the user's home time and not his current time. For example, if a user in New York takes a trip to Los Angeles, and is going to dial in to his home network, the time in New York rather than the time in Los Angeles will determine the time restriction. A time restriction of 6:00 p.m. EST would shut the user down at 3:00 p.m. PST. Although that might give your employee time to get in a round of golf, it might not be what you intended when configuring the time restriction in the first place.

ADDRESS RESTRICTIONS

The Address Restrictions page can be used to tie a user account to a specific workstation, thereby forcing users to log in from that hardware location, or network address only. Selecting to add a network address restriction invokes the dialog box shown in Figure 8.6. From this dialog box, specific address types (IP, TCP, UDP, and so on) can be selected, and then address information must be entered to configure the restriction.

FIGURE 8.6
Address Restrictions page in iManager.

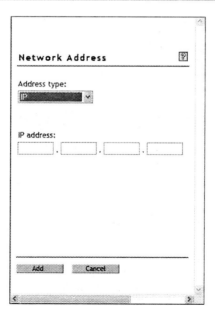

In today's world of dynamic addressing and roaming users, this option is not as useful as it once might have been, but in very security-conscious environments, it can still be necessary. However, TCP/IP functionality is severely limited by the fact that the utility assumes a Class B subnet mask (255.255.0.0) for all IP addressing—not very practical in today's overloaded IP world.

INTRUDER LOCKOUT

The Intruder Lockout page is useful only after a user account has been disabled. Intruder lockout refers to the disabling of a user account after a certain number of unsuccessful login attempts have been made. To re-enable a locked-out account, the administrator unchecks the Account Locked box on this page. The other three entries simply provide information about the status of the locked account.

The actual intruder detection system is configured at the container level rather than at the user level. In order to configure your intruder detection environment, complete the following steps:

1. Launch iManager and select the View Objects icon. Locate the container for which you want to set intruder detection.

2. Click the object and select Modify Object.

3. Select the Intruder Detection link, as shown in Figure 8.7.

4. Make your desired changes and click OK.

   ■ *Detect Intruders*—Check this box to enable the intruder detection system for this container. Associated with this check box are fields that allow you to set the number of incorrect login attempts before intruder lockout is activated—the default is 7—and the interval within which the unsuccessful attempts must occur—the default is 30 minutes.

   ■ *Lock Account After Detection*—Check this box to enable the account lockout feature. Associated with this check box are fields that allow you to specify the time period for which the account will remain locked—the default is 15 minutes. At the end of this period, the account will be reactivated automatically.

After the intrusion detection features have been configured, intruder lockout makes it much more difficult for would-be hackers to perform dictionary or other brute force attacks against one of your network accounts.

FIGURE 8.7
Enabling intruder detection features in iManager.

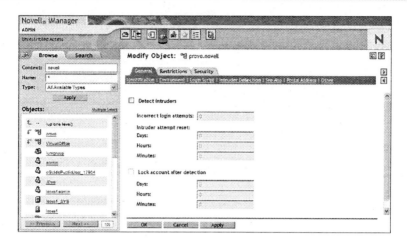

eDirectory Authorization

Now that users have authenticated to the network, you must provide them with access to all the resources they need. This also entails preventing them from accessing resources that they do not need. It wouldn't do to have sensitive documents describing future products open to and accessible to just anyone. The reality of the corporate world is that some resources must be maintained as "need to know."

Although determining exactly who needs access to what is a decision beyond most network administrators, Novell eDirectory provides powerful tools for implementing those decisions. This section discusses eDirectory access control concepts and how they work together to provide proper access to objects in the eDirectory tree.

Access Control Lists

Access control lists (ACLs) are stored in each eDirectory object to identify those other objects that have been granted some sort of control over it. Each object in an eDirectory tree maintains two types of access rights. The first set of rights is entry rights. Entry rights define how an object can be manipulated by other directory entities, as described in Table 8.1.

TABLE 8.1
Valid Entry Rights in eDirectory

ENTRY RIGHT	DESCRIPTION
Browse	Allows a trustee to discover and view the object in the eDirectory tree.
Create	This right applies only to container objects. It allows the trustee to create new objects within the container.
Delete	Allows a trustee to delete the object.
Rename	Allows a trustee to rename the object.
Supervisor	Allows a trustee full access to the object and its attributes.

The second set of rights is property rights. Property rights define how the attributes associated with an object can be manipulated. eDirectory property rights are described in Table 8.2.

TABLE 8.2
Valid Property Rights in eDirectory

PROPERTY RIGHT	DESCRIPTION
Compare	Allows a trustee to compare or to see if an attribute contains a given value.
Read	Allows a trustee to read an attribute value. This right confers the Compare right.
Write	Allows a trustee to add, delete, or modify an attribute value. This right confers the add or delete Self right to the attribute.
Self	Allows a trustee to add or delete its name as an attribute value (if applicable).
Supervisor	Assigns a trustee all attribute rights.

When entry and/or property rights are conferred on an eDirectory entity, it becomes a trustee of the conferring object. The list of trustees, and the specific object and property rights they have been granted, is maintained in an access control list associated with each eDirectory object. Figure 8.8 shows a representative ACL as seen from iManager.

As shown in Figure 8.8, the ACL maintains three pieces of information about a trustee assignment: object name, property name, and effective rights.

- *Object Name*—This field identifies the object that is being granted rights. It can also contain one of the special entry references outlined in Table 8.3.

FIGURE 8.8
eDirectory access control list in iManager.

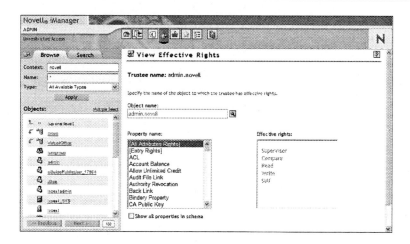

- *Property Name*—This field specifies the type of right that is being granted. It also specifies how that right is to be applied. Rights can be assigned to a specific property, to all properties, or to the object itself.

- *Effective Rights*—This field lists the rights that have been granted for a given property. In the eDirectory schema, most object classes specify a default access template that is used to create an ACL attribute for a new object. This default template provides basic access control for the new entry, allowing it to function in the directory. Different object classes have different default ACL templates to reflect their different needs. For example, the default ACL template for the User object grants the `Write` right to its own login script attribute. This allows users to change their personal login scripts as necessary.

TABLE 8.3
Special Trustee References in eDirectory

REFERENCE	DESCRIPTION
`Inherited rights filter`	eDirectory uses this reference to mask or filter privileges rather than granting rights.
`[Public]`	eDirectory uses this reference to grant rights to all objects in the eDirectory tree, including both authenticated and non-authenticated objects.

TABLE 8.3
Continued

REFERENCE	DESCRIPTION
[Root]	eDirectory uses this reference to grant rights to all authenticated entries.
Creator	eDirectory uses this reference to grant all rights to the client that created the object.
Self	eDirectory uses this reference to allow objects to add or delete themselves as values of attributes and to grant the object rights to its own attributes.

Inheritance

Inheritance is one of the most powerful—and sometimes frustrating—concepts in eDirectory security planning. It is similar to the security equivalence concepts (discussed previously) in that it deals with the determination of effective rights at any given point in the eDirectory tree. On the one hand, inheritance promises to save untold amounts of work by automating the assignment of rights in the eDirectory tree. On the other hand, because of the way that inheritance works, things sometimes don't happen exactly as you might have planned.

Novell has been using inheritance for a long time to apply rights to the NSS file system. If a user was granted rights at a specific directory, those rights implicitly applied to everything from that point down in the directory structure—until explicitly removed. The same principle applies to eDirectory: If a user is granted rights at a given container object, those rights are implicitly applied to each object in the tree from that point downward—until explicitly removed.

eDirectory implements inheritance through a dynamic model. This means that rights are calculated in real time whenever an eDirectory object attempts to perform any directory operation. To do this, eDirectory starts at [Root] and walks the tree down to the object, building a set of effective rights for that object along the way. If the effective rights for that object permit the requested operation, it is allowed to continue. If not, the operation is denied.

At first, it might seem very inefficient to traverse the eDirectory tree from [Root] each time effective rights need to be calculated—and it would be— except that eDirectory resolves this inefficiency through the use of external references.

External references exist to protect database integrity by storing information about partitions that do have local replicas. In other words, the Master replica of a child partition will maintain an external reference to [Root]. In order to determine the effective rights for a user, eDirectory need only consult the locally stored external references instead of potentially crossing the entire network to find the information it needs. This reduces network traffic and increases the speed of eDirectory tremendously. For more information on external references, see Chapter 7, "Novell eDirectory Management."

Inherited Rights Filters

Inherited Rights Filters (IRFs) are used to restrict inheritance in a directory tree. IRF use looks pretty straightforward on the surface, but it can cause all kinds of interesting situations to arise. Many calls have been logged to Novell's Technical Support groups because administrators got carried away with controlling every single aspect of eDirectory security instead of just trusting the environment to handle things properly.

WARNING

Don't implement IRFs unless you are absolutely sure you understand the consequences of doing so.

That said, it is sometimes desirable to limit the flow of rights through the eDirectory tree—either to segment administration or to isolate portions of the tree. If this becomes necessary, IRFs are the way to go. Just remember that less is usually more in this case. If you find yourself creating a large number of IRFs, it might be a sign of some fundamental eDirectory design issues. See Chapter 7 for more information on eDirectory tree design.

The first thing to recognize about IRFs is that they can filter supervisory rights in eDirectory, unlike supervisory rights in the NSS file system. This makes it possible to limit the control of Admin users higher up in the tree, but it also threatens to destroy your capability to administer the directory tree properly.

To configure an IRF, complete the following steps:

1. Launch iManager and select the View Objects icon. Locate the container or object for which you want to set an IRF.

2. Click the object and select Modify Inherited Rights Filter.

3. Click Add Property to create an IRF.

4. Select the property for which you want to define an IRF and click OK. You can create an IRF for entry rights, for all properties, or for specific properties.

5. Uncheck those rights that you want to be blocked by the IRF and select OK to save your changes. The page used to modify the IRF is shown in Figure 8.9.

FIGURE 8.9
Modifying IRF properties in iManager.

WARNING

It is very important to remember the dynamic nature of rights calculation in eDirectory. For example, if you are going to create a container administrator and filter administrative rights to that container from above, create the new Admin object first. If you set the IRF first, you will find yourself locked out—unable to define a user with administrative control for the container. An IRF is a two-edged sword.

After configuring IRFs, be sure to test your changes to ensure that the desired behavior was achieved. If problems are encountered, you may have to remove the IRF, and then re-add IRF components one at a time until you have isolated the misconfiguration.

Explicit Rights

Explicit rights are those specifically assigned to an object at some point in the eDirectory tree. When one object is given specific rights to another, it is called a *trustee*. To assign explicit rights, complete the following steps:

1. Launch iManager and select the View Objects icon. Locate the container or object for which you want to add a trustee.

2. Click the object and select Modify Trustees.

3. Click Add Trustee. Browse to the eDirectory object to which you want to assign trustee rights and click OK. You can select multiple objects if desired.

4. Click the Assigned Rights link next to each object, specify the appropriate rights for this trustee, and then click Done (see Figure 8.10).

   - *Property and Rights*—Specify the rights you want to grant for this trustee. If you want to assign specific property rights only, click Add Property to select specific properties from a list. You can assign entry rights, all property (attribute) rights, specific property rights, or any combination of the three.

   - *Inheritable*—If you are assigning a trustee to a Container object, you can check the Inheritable box if you want those rights to flow down to other objects within the container.

FIGURE 8.10
Assigning explicit trustee rights in iManager.

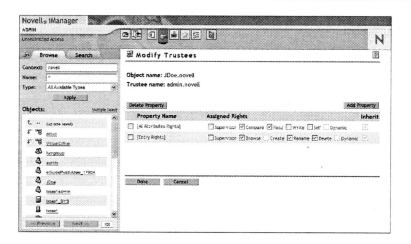

Assigning explicit rights is a very straightforward process, but as with IRFs, there are some caveats. For example, unlike security equivalence, explicit assignments are not cumulative. An explicit assignment pre-empts the implicit rights that a user might have had through inheritance. Making explicit rights assignments can easily eliminate rights that existed previously. Make sure you understand what is being provided through inheritance and security equivalence, and how your explicit assignment will affect those existing rights, before making manual changes to trustee rights.

Security Equivalence

Security equivalence in eDirectory is used to assign one object identical eDirectory rights to those already assigned to another object. eDirectory offers explicit and implicit security equivalence. Under the rules of inheritance described previously, security equivalence will continue to flow down from the point it is granted. In other words, if `JHarris` in `Provo.Quills` is granted equivalence to the Admin object, those rights will be granted at `[Root]` just as they are for Admin. Equivalence provides a method to grant users in one area of the eDirectory tree rights to objects in another.

TIP

Using security equivalence is not an efficient way to manage access. If you find yourself using lots of security equivalences, it is a strong indication of a poor eDirectory tree design. See Chapter 5 for more information on eDirectory design.

Implicit security equivalence occurs automatically when an object is inserted into the eDirectory tree. Every eDirectory object has security equivalence with the following objects:

- The `[Root]` object
- The `[Public]` trustee
- Each container between it and `[Root]`

Security equivalence to `[Root]` and `[Public]` provides basic access to eDirectory so that the new object can perform basic network tasks, such as navigating the directory, locating servers, and initiating an authentication request. All specific rights are derived from the inheritance from the container object(s) within which the object exists.

Explicit security equivalence is identical to implicit security equivalence, except the network administrator has to assign the equivalence manually. Use explicit security equivalence whenever one user needs explicit rights identical to another's rights, but cannot get those rights through normal inheritance or implicit security equivalence. To assign explicit security equivalence, complete the following steps:

1. Launch iManager and select the View Objects icon. Locate the container or object to which you want to grant security equivalence.

2. Click the object and select Modify Object.

3. Select the Security tab and click Security Equal To.

4. Specify the object to which this object will be security-equivalent and click OK.

5. Click OK to save the security equivalence.

Explicit security equivalence is most often used with Group objects, which were discussed earlier in this chapter. Each member of an eDirectory group is assigned as security equal to the Group object. In this way each user receives the rights associated with that group. Contrary to rights assignment, security equivalence is cumulative. This means that an object's implicit and explicit security equivalence will be added together in order to determine its effective rights.

THE DANGER OF EXPLICIT SECURITY EQUIVALENCE

Not all uses of explicit security equivalence are appropriate. For example, some administrators have used security equivalence to make their User object equivalent to the Admin object. This gives them all rights associated with the Admin object. The danger in this is that when you derive your rights from another object, those rights are never specifically recorded in your object. For example, if JHarris.Provo.Quills is security equal to Admin.Quills, whenever JHarris attempts to perform some directory operation, eDirectory will look at the effective rights of Admin. If Admin has sufficient rights to perform the operation, JHarris, as a security equal, is granted permission as well.

Can you see the danger? Some time down the road, JHarris is happily administering eDirectory. Why keep the Admin object around when it is never used? But the instant the object is deleted, JHarris loses all his administrative rights because they are derived from the Admin object and not explicitly assigned.

Even worse, unless some other object has been explicitly granted supervisory rights to the eDirectory tree, deleting the Admin object might delete the ability to administer eDirectory.

Explicit security equivalence can be a powerful tool, but you can end up laying a trap for yourself, or others who might come after you. In most cases, the explicit security equivalence should be restricted to use with Group objects. For applying specific rights to a single object, it is often best to assign those rights explicitly, rather than relying on another object to supply them.

Effective Rights

The whole point of all the preceding rights controls is to ensure that a given user, or other eDirectory object, has the appropriate rights on the network to do what's needed. Effective rights are the cumulative result of all the different rights tools working together. In the end, there are eight ways that one object can get rights to another:

- Object 1 is a trustee of Object 2. Therefore, Object 1 has explicit rights to Object 2.

- A parent container of Object 1 is a trustee of Object 2. Therefore, Object 1 has rights to Object 2 due to implicit security equivalence.

- Object 1 has explicit security equivalence to Object 3, which is a trustee of Object 2. Therefore, Object 1 has trustee rights to Object 2, which are equivalent to Object 3.

- [Public] is a trustee of Object 2. Therefore, Object 1 has rights to Object 2 through implicit security equivalence to [Public].

- [Public] is a trustee of a parent container of Object 2, and those rights flow down the tree due to inheritance. Therefore, Object 1 has rights to Object 2 through the combination of implicit security equivalence and inheritance.

- Object 1 is a trustee of one of Object 2's parent containers, and those rights flow down the tree to include Object 2 due to inheritance.

- A parent container of Object 1 is a trustee of a parent container of Object 2. Therefore, Object 1 has rights to Object 2 through a combination of explicit rights, implicit security equivalence, and inheritance.

- Object 1 is security equivalent to Object 3, which is a trustee of a parent container of Object 2. Therefore, Object 1 has rights to Object 2 through the combination of explicit security equivalence and inheritance.

NOTE

Inherited rights filters cannot affect the effective rights in the first four cases because no inheritance is being used. However, IRFs can modify or eliminate the effective rights provided in the last four cases because they depend on inheritance.

With eight ways to derive effective rights between two objects, it's easy to see how rights issues can get complicated very quickly. In most cases, the best solution is to let inheritance do the work of assigning rights wherever possible. The default combination of implicit security equivalence and dynamic inheritance is suitable for 90% of the directory installations out there.

Assign rights through containers and let them flow downward. As your directory tree evolves over time, situations can arise that cannot be satisfied by inheritance alone. If this happens, use groups, explicit assignments, and IRFs sparingly to address these exceptions.

When using IRFs, be careful that a single object doesn't become a point of failure. Consider what might happen if a User object is corrupted, or if that user becomes malicious. Always have a second or third option for accessing a branch of the tree that is restricted. Just as the military establishes a chain of command so that the mission can continue if one person is lost, eDirectory administrators have to make sure that proper access can continue—or at least be repaired—if the default method of access is lost.

TIP

One way of doing this is to create a secondary User object with full administrative rights, and then add a Browse IRF to that object. This effectively hides the secondary Admin from view but provides emergency administrative access should it be necessary.

Role-Based Administration

One exciting instance of authorization is the capability to assign specific administrative roles to users in the eDirectory tree. Although this was possible in a limited fashion with the use of organizational roles, iManager offers you a previously impossible level of control and ease of use. You can now define most any network activity as a *role*, and assign the eDirectory rights necessary to perform that activity to a user or group of users. For more information on configuring role-based administration with iManager, see Chapter 5.

File System Authorization

In addition to the authorization required for accessing eDirectory objects, OES Linux requires file-system-level authorization for accessing volumes, directories, and files. This level of security is only available on NSS volumes and does not apply to native POSIX file systems, such as resierfs and ext2/3. For more information on file system authorization with NSS, see Chapter 11, "OES Linux File Storage and Management."

Provisioning Linux Users

As mentioned at the beginning of this chapter, not all services support native eDirectory authentication. This is especially apparent within the services commonly associated with Linux environments.

Typical Linux servers provide user authentication for a number of services. Common examples of these are local logins, secure shell connections, Samba, NFS, and HTTP/FTP access. Managing user accounts across these access methods can be the most frustrating part of administration! Thankfully, OES Linux greatly simplifies this aspect of administration through enabling eDirectory as a central storage location for all user accounts across all services.

The central component of OES that provides this integration is Linux User Management.

Linux User Management

In a nutshell, Linux User Management (LUM) is a directory-enabled application that centralizes the storage and management of Linux user accounts. LUM uses eDirectory for the back-end repository of users and therefore benefits from the security, scalability, and reliability eDirectory users have come to expect.

LUM extends the capabilities of the Novell Account Management (NAM) software and includes the following components:

- *NAM Pluggable Authentication Module* (`pam_nam`)—This module provides eDirectory authentication through LDAP for all PAM-aware services. When authenticated, users have the same privileges as when authenticating through NIS, NIS+, or local files.

  Linux Administrators may equate this to the `pam_ldap` module. Although the primary purpose of `pam_nam` is to provide LDAP authentication, similar to `pam_ldap`, `pam_nam` offers a closer integration with eDirectory with the following additional benefits:

- Unique UIDs and GIDs across the LDAP tree, or LUM domain
- Advanced server access control based on LDAP access control lists (ACLs) in eDirectory
- Refined LDAP searches offering a more effective integration with eDirectory
- *NAM Name Service Switch* (`libnss_nam`) *redirector*—This redirector enables user lookup through an LDAP connection to eDirectory. This is used to enforce permissions when accessing system resources.
- *NAM Cache Daemon* (`namcd`)—This daemon caches all user lookups performed by NAM. This cache is checked first when performing user lookups. If the requested resource is located with the cache, the LDAP lookup against eDirectory will not be performed. This greatly increases name resolution performance.
- *Command-Line Utilities*—Many different command-line utilities exist to add Linux administrators. These utilities can be used in place of iManager for basic LUM administration. More information on these utilities will be available later in this section.

LUM-RELATED OBJECTS

In addition to the physical components of LUM, in order for LUM to integrate Linux authentication into eDirectory, the eDirectory schema must be extended. The extension takes place automatically during the LUM installation. LUM-specific extensions create both classes and attributes required for authentication by the Linux services. These extensions are used in creating LUM-specific objects used to configure LUM, and when modifying user and group objects to convert them to valid Linux users and groups.

The following list describes each of these required LUM objects:

- *Linux (UNIX) Config*—This object is used to store configuration information for a specific LUM domain. It contains such things as the next available GID and UID numbers and the context for Linux Workstations.

NOTE

A LUM Domain is simply a term used to describe one Linux Config object and all users and workstations associated with that object. By default, one Linux Config object and therefore one LUM Domain, is created during the installation of LUM. Into this one LUM Domain, additional Linux servers and workstations can be added using the namconfig utility.

If your network spans multiple sites, or LUM services will be offered to a large number of users, additional Linux Config objects (and therefore additional LUM Domains) can be created.

The namconfig utility is the only tool that can create Linux Config objects in eDirectory. When creating multiple Linux Config objects, ensure that all LUM domains exist in their own eDirectory partition. Also, due to the subtree LDAP search used with LUM, ensure that no LUM domain exists beneath another LUM domain in the eDirectory tree.

- *Linux (UNIX) Workstations*—Every Linux server or workstation relying on LUM authentication must have a Linux Workstation object in the eDirectory tree. This object maintains a link to all LUM groups that are allowed access to local services.

- *LUM User*—Normal eDirectory users are extended with a Linux-specific auxiliary class. This extension provides users with attributes required for Linux authentication. New attributes assigned to users include such things as the User ID (UID) number, primary Group ID (GID) number, default shell, and home directory location.

- *LUM Group*—eDirectory groups are also extended using a Linux-specific auxiliary class. This extension adds such attributes as the Group ID (GID) number, and Linux Workstations and users assigned to the group.

NOTE

During the installation of LUM, a default Linux Config, Linux Workstation, and LUM group are all configured automatically. However, LUM users must either be created manually during the creation of a new eDirectory user, or an existing eDirectory user must be converted to a LUM User prior to using LUM.

LUM INSTALLATION

The installation of LUM is normally performed during the main OES installation. If LUM was not selected during installation, follow these steps for adding LUM to your OES server.

1. On the OES server, launch YaST.

2. Select the Software category, and then click on the Install and Remove Software module.

3. Ensure that the Filter is set to Selections, and then select Novell Linux User Management in the Selection window. Click Accept to complete the installation. (You may be prompted to install additional software to satisfy software dependencies. If so, select Continue to finish the installation.)

4. After the LUM packages are installed, the LUM configuration must be completed. Ensure that the LDAP configuration for LUM is correct. Then enter the administrator's password in the appropriate field and click Next.

5. Ensure that the Linux User Management contexts for the Linux Config object and Linux Workstations are correct. If an LDAP proxy is desired, enter the required information and then click Next.

6. Select the PAM-enabled services you would like integrated with LUM. Selected services will now attempt to authenticate users via LUM prior to authenticating against the local account files. Click Next to complete the installation.

LUM ADMINISTRATION

LUM administration can effectively be divided into the following three categories:

- LUM configuration
- User and group administration
- Linux service administration

LUM CONFIGURATION

Although LUM is usable immediately after installation, it is a good idea to check the default LUM configuration prior to creating LUM users. The following steps describe checking the LUM configuration:

1. Launch iManager. In the Navigation frame, open the Linux User Management group and select Modify Linux/Unix Config Object (see Figure 8.11).

2. Locate the default UNIX Config object using the object selector. This object can be found in the same context as your server object. Click OK.

3. On the PosixConfigPage under the LinuxProfile tab, check the configured information and click OK. The default values are normally sufficient, but if necessary, the following fields may be changed:

- *Linux Workstation Contexts*—Enter the context or contexts where Linux Workstation objects should be located within the tree. When you use `namconfig` to add additional workstations to the tree, additional contexts will be automatically added.

- *uam Posix GID/UID Number Start*—Enter the first available number for Linux GID and UID numbers in these fields.

FIGURE 8.11
Modifying the Linux Config Object.

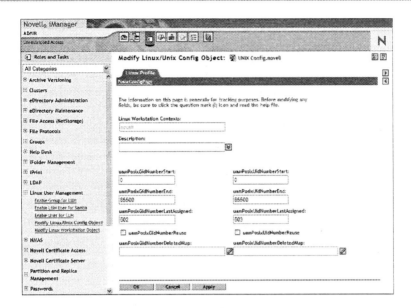

- *uam Posix GID/UID Number End*—Enter the last available Linux GID and UID numbers in these fields.

- *uam Posix GID/UID Number Last Assigned*—These fields contain the last GID and UID numbers assigned by LUM. Only change this field if you intend to skip a number range.

- *uam Posix GID/UID Number Reuse*—Check these options if you would like to reuse GID and UID numbers that belong to deleted users and groups.

WARNING

Reusing GID and UID numbers that were previously assigned to deleted users allows the new user or group to assume the Linux filesystem rights assigned to the previous user or group. Use this option only if you are familiar with Linux permissions and understand this risk.

- *uam Posix GID/UID Number Deleted Map*—These fields track the GID and UID of deleted users and groups. Normally, these fields should not be modified manually.

In addition to iManager-based configuration, there are some configuration options that you may want to set on the OES machine itself. One important option is regarding the configuration of the NAM Cache Daemon (namcd).

As explained earlier, the NAM Cache Daemon caches user and group lookups from eDirectory. By default this daemon uses a persistent cache that will be immediately available upon server restarts. For most implementations this is the desired behavior and will produce optimal performance. However, if you would like to use a nonpersistent cache, or modify the cache refresh or size settings, the configuration of namcd must be manually modified.

The configuration file for NAM is /etc/nam.conf. Within this configuration file, there are settings that determine the behavior of namcd. The primary settings regarding the namcd cache are as follows (see the nam.conf man page for more information):

- enable-persistent-cache=YES—Determines whether the namcd cache is maintained on the local server and kept persistent across server reboots. Valid values are "yes" or "no."

- persistent-cache-refresh-period=28800—Specifies the interval (in seconds) in which cached users and groups are refreshed from eDirectory. A longer interval reduces network traffic but can produce stale data. Valid settings range from 1 to 2147483647 seconds.

- persistent-cache-refresh-flag=all—Determines whether all user and group data is refreshed during a cache refresh, or just accounts that have been accessed during the current session. Valid values are "all" or "accessed."

NOTE

Do not confuse namcd (NAM Cache Daemon) with nscd (Name Service Cache Daemon). With LUM, namcd and nscd work together. The nscd daemon is used to cache hostnames and addresses. The namcd daemon specifically caches user and group names and IDs from eDirectory. Using namcd, performance of subsequent lookups of cached users and groups is significantly improved.

USER AND GROUP ADMINISTRATION

eDirectory users do not automatically have the attributes required for LUM authentication. In order for the user to be a valid LUM user, these attributes must either be added during the initial user creation from within iManager, or added after the fact by converting the existing user to a LUM user. Assigning the LUM attributes to users during user creation has already been described in the User Object section at the beginning of this chapter. The following steps describe how to convert an existing user to a valid LUM user.

1. Launch iManager. In the Navigation frame, open the Linux User Management group and select Enable User for LUM.

2. Locate the desired user object using the object selector or object history. Click OK.

3. To enable the user for LUM or Samba, the following fields must be filled out:

   ■ *Primary Group*—(Required) Enter the primary LUM group for the user. All Linux users must be associated with a Linux group. By default, a Linux group called lumgroup is created for this purpose.

   ■ *Enable Samba Authentication*—If this user will also be accessing server resources via Samba, select the check box to enable Samba Authentication. The user's Samba password must also be manually entered into the appropriate fields.

NOTE

Enabling a user for LUM during initial user creation will automatically enter the user's password into the Samba password fields. Converting a user after creation may result in non-synchronized passwords if the Samba password entered does not match the eDirectory password.

4. Click OK to save the modifications.

NOTE

Existing Linux implementations may want to migrate users directly from local, NIS, or NIS+ accounts. For information on this process, please see the man page for the unix2edir utility.

Linux requires every user to have a primary group associated with the user. LUM must also require a primary LUM group for users within eDirectory. As with user objects, eDirectory groups do not automatically have the attributes required for valid LUM groups. In order for the group to be a valid LUM group, these attributes must either be added during the initial group creation from within iManager, or added after the fact by converting the existing group to a LUM group. Assigning the LUM attributes to groups during user creation has already been described in the Group Object section at the beginning of this chapter. The following steps describe how to convert an existing group to a valid LUM group.

1. Launch iManager. In the Navigation frame, open the Linux User Management group and select Enable Group for LUM.

2. Locate the desired group object using the object selector or object history. Click OK.

3. To enable the group for LUM, one of the following options must be selected and filled out:

   - *Linux Config Object*—To associate the group with all defined Linux Workstations within the LUM domain, select this radio button and enter the Linux Config object in the corresponding field.

   - *Linux Workstation Object(s)*—To associate the group with one or more specific Linux Workstations, select this radio button and enter the group or groups in the corresponding field.

4. Click OK to save the modifications.

LINUX SERVICE ADMINISTRATION

During the installation of LUM, you can determine which PAM-aware services you would like LUM-enabled. Services available for selection are listed in Table 8.4.

TABLE 8.4
PAM-Aware Services Available for Integration with LUM

SERVICE	DESCRIPTION
login	Local authentications via programs such as mingetty.
ftp	File Transfer Protocol connections to programs such as vsftpd.
sshd	Secure Shell connections made to sshd.
su	Switched User authentications.
rsh	Remote command execution sessions with rsh.
rlogin	Remote shell sessions made with rlogin (not as secure as SSH).
passwd	Password changes made with the passwd command.
xdm	Graphical authentication used with local and remote graphical sessions.
openwbem	Authentication to openwbem providers on the local server. This is used for Health Monitoring within OES.

If these services were not configured during installation, you can use the YaST module for LUM to LUM-enable these services later. The following steps document this process:

1. On the OES server, launch YaST.

2. Select the Users and Security category, and then locate the Linux User Mgmt module. Click on this module to execute it.

NOTE

You may receive a warning about LUM already being configured on the OES server. Selecting "Yes" will cause the LUM components to be reinstalled and configuration can continue.

3. Ensure that the LDAP configuration for LUM is correct. Then enter the administrator's password in the appropriate field and click Next.

4. Ensure that the Linux User Management contexts for the Linux Config object and Linux Workstations are correct. If an LDAP proxy is desired, enter the required information and then click Next.

5. Select the PAM-enabled services you would like integrated with LUM. Selected services will now attempt to authenticate users via LUM prior to authenticating against the local account files. Click Next to complete the installation.

SECURING LUM

When you're using LUM, users can be authenticated to eDirectory using a secure or nonsecure LDAP connection. To increase security, it is a good idea to always use a secure LDAP connection. This is the default configuration of OES, but adding additional servers or workstations to the LUM domain will require a manual configuration. This process can also be followed on the current OES server to reconfigure LUM if configuration errors are encountered.

To enable secure LDAP connections with LUM, or to add an additional server or workstation to your LUM domain, execute the following command:

```
namconfig add -a <admin name and context> -r <Linux Config context> -w
➥<Server/workstation context> -S <Server DNS or IP Address>:389 -1 636
```

After determining the appropriate values for the admin name and context, Linux Config context, and server or workstation context, the command should look more like the following:

```
namconfig add -a cn=admin,o=novell -r ou=lum,o=novell -w
ou=ws,ou=nam,o=novell -S OESSERVER1:389 -l 636
```

The `namconfig` utility is used to configure NAM on Linux servers and workstations. This command configures the local server to communicate via SSL by modifying the `/etc/nam.conf` file and retrieving the server's SSL certificate from eDirectory. The server certificate is stored in the `/var/nam` directory as a hidden file named with the server name and a .der extension. If this certificate expires, it can be re-created using the following command:

```
namconfig -k
```

NOTE

For more information on `namconfig`, refer to the man page or to Novell's online documentation.

LUM COMMAND-LINE UTILITIES

The majority of LUM administration is performed through iManager. However, Linux administrators experienced with the command-line interface may find the command-line tools quicker than the browser-based interface of iManager.

Table 8.5 summarizes the command-line tools available for LUM administration on the OES machine.

TABLE 8.5
LUM Command-Line Utilities

UTILITY	DESCRIPTION
namconfig	This utility is used to add or remove LUM for a specified eDirectory context. This utility can also be used to adjust LUM configuration parameters and import the SSL certificate necessary for secure LDAP connections to eDirectory.
namuseradd	Creates a LUM user in eDirectory. Can also convert non-LUM eDirectory users to LUM users.
namuserdel	Used to delete a LUM user from eDirectory.
namuserlist	Used to connect and list valid LUM users from specified eDirectory contexts.
namusermod	Used to modify a LUM user's login information in eDirectory.

TABLE 8.5
Continued

UTILITY	DESCRIPTION
namgroupadd	Creates a LUM group in eDirectory. Can also convert non-LUM eDirectory groups to LUM groups.
namgroupdel	Used to delete a LUM group from eDirectory.
namgrouplist	Used to list valid LUM groups from eDirectory.
namgroupmod	Used to modify a LUM group's attributes in eDirectory.
unix2edir	Used to migrate local, NIS, or NIS+ accounts to eDirectory.
namutils.inp	Found in /var/nam, this configuration file is used to store default values for the various parameters of the nam utilities. This file is created upon running one of the nam utilities (except namuserlist and namgrouplist). After this file has been created, it can be modified to reduce the number of manually entered parameters required when using these utilities.
unix2edir.inp	Found in /var/nam, this configuration file is used to store default values for the various parameters of the unix2edir utility. This file is created upon running unix2edir. After this file has been created, it can be modified to reduce the number of manually entered parameters required when using this utility.

NOTE

More information on each of these utilities is available by accessing the man page for the respective utility.

AUTHENTICATION WITH LUM

With LUM configured, valid LUM users and groups created, and Linux services integrated into LUM, the authentication process a user goes through with LUM can finally be investigated.

LUM is specifically designed to take advantage of the Pluggable Authentication Module (PAM) infrastructure common with Linux servers. The primary benefit this offers is that all PAM-aware services have the potential to be integrated into eDirectory through LUM with relative ease. This section will describe the integration steps and processes of authentication with a PAM-aware service.

NOTE

It is possible to enable LDAP-aware services to integrate directly with eDirectory, but this configuration is specific to the application being integrated and beyond the scope of this book.

PAM INTEGRATION WITH LUM

As mentioned in the Login Process section of Chapter 3, "Working with SUSE Linux Enterprise Server 9," PAM utilizes a configuration file for every PAM-aware service. These files exist in the /etc/pam.d directory and are named after the respective service. The contents of these files are used to determine what modules are involved with the authentication process to ensure that the user is allowed access. As shown in Figure 8.12, the **pam_nam** module is used for all authentication services.

FIGURE 8.12

The pam_nam configuration used with the Login service.

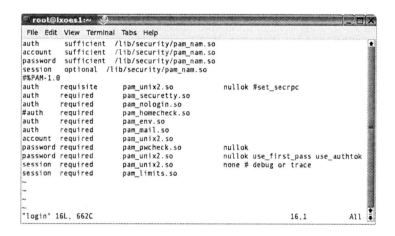

The control flag used with these services is normally set to **sufficient**. This causes the authentication process to halt upon successfully retrieving authentication, account, and password information from the **pam_nam** module.

If **pam_nam** is unable to fulfill the request, the remainder of the configuration file is used. This allows local accounts to authenticate after checking for the requested account in eDirectory. It is important to ensure that the service configuration file allows for local authentication for root-level access for administrators.

The `pam_nam` module relies on the `/etc/nam.conf` configuration file. This file contains information regarding the IP address of the eDirectory server, what credentials to use when authenticating to that server, and where in the eDirectory tree to search for LUM users and groups.

NOTE

For more information regarding the `nam.conf` configuration file, refer to the man page, or Novell's online documentation.

NAME SERVICES WITH LUM

After authentication, the ability to look up user and group names in eDirectory is still required. The process of resolving user, group, machine, and other identities in Linux is known as Name Services. When using LUM, the Name Services configuration must be altered to also look up names in eDirectory.

The configuration file for Name Services is `/etc/nsswitch.conf`. The main purpose of this file is to list possible databases of names being queried and where information regarding those names can be located. With LUM, the information we are concerned about is resolution of user and group names.

User and group lookup configuration can be found on the "passwd" and "group" database entries within the **nsswitch.conf** file. When you're using LUM on the local server, these two entries should contain the following configuration:

```
passwd: compat nam
group:  compat nam
```

This configuration causes the Name Service lookup to initially query the local files (using the default compatibility mode), and then query for names and groups using the `libnss_nam` library. This library uses LDAP to query eDirectory for user and group names. After being resolved, the names and IDs are cached by the NAM Cache Daemon (**namcd**) to reduce lookup time for subsequent requests.

One example of where this lookup is performed is when performing a file listing using the `ls` command. The `ls` command uses Name Services to translate the file and group owner IDs to usable names rather than the actual ID numbers. If the lookup is not successful, IDs rather than names will be displayed, and accurate permissions enforcement may be compromised.

Default installations of LUM should have this configuration performed automatically. However, if additional servers or workstations are added to the LUM domain outside of an OES installation, after adding the machine using namconfig, the nsswitch.conf file must be manually configured as in the preceding example in order for name lookups to be successful.

Samba User Management

The Samba program suite provides access to local resources through the Microsoft SMB/CIFS protocol. This effectively allows Windows, Linux, and other operating systems to connect to those resources as though they were residing on a Windows-based computer. To do this, Samba must use an authentication method that is compatible with Windows authentication. Samba provides this authentication through a local store of Samba users—in addition to those same users being stored as local Linux accounts. Although this default configuration does work, it can result in unsynchronized passwords, and an environment that is difficult to maintain. OES Linux resolves this situation by leveraging the LUM infrastructure to provide Samba authentication as well.

Samba User Management requires the LUM component to be fully operational. All Samba users must first be valid LUM users. It is a good idea to fully test LUM using local logins prior to beginning Samba configuration.

NOTE

With OES, a user's Samba password is stored as two specific attributes of each Samba user. This password can only be synchronized when users change their password from within Virtual Office. If you expect users to change their password from other utilities, you must enable the Universal Password component of NMAS.

When Universal Password is enabled, the Universal Password is used in place of the Samba password during user authentication. This ensures a single user password across all authentication methods, including Samba, and synchronization is not an issue.

For more information on Universal Password, see the "Universal Password" section earlier in this chapter.

SAMBA COMPONENTS

The Samba suite that comes with OES is the same version of Samba that is available through other Linux distributions, such as SLES 9, with one notable exception. In order to integrate with LUM, the OES version of Samba has been compiled using the --with-ldapsam and --with-ssl switches. These switches are necessary to leverage the LDAP storage of user accounts, and to provide secure access to those accounts.

In order to access LDAP directories, Samba also relies on the OpenLDAP client libraries. These libraries are `libldap.so` and `libldap_r.so`. The default configuration of the OpenLDAP client is to provide a connection to eDirectory through a secure (SSL) LDAP session.

SAMBA INSTALLATION

The installation of Samba is normally performed during the main OES installation. If Samba was not selected during installation, follow these steps to add Samba to your OES server.

1. On the OES server, launch YaST.

2. Select the Software category, and then click on the Install and Remove Software module.

3. Ensure that the Filter is set to Selections, and then select Novell Samba Configuration in the Selections window. Click Accept to complete the installation. (You may be prompted to install additional software to satisfy software dependencies. If so, select Continue to finish the installation.)

4. After the Samba packages are installed, the Samba configuration must be completed. Ensure that the LDAP configuration for Samba is correct. Then enter the administrator's password in the appropriate field and click Next.

5. Ensure that the Novell Samba Configuration is accurate, including the LDAP server host, base context for Samba users, eDirectory tree name, and the proxy user and password for the LDAP queries. When the configuration is complete, click Next.

SAMBA ADMINISTRATION

Administration of Samba services within OES can be divided into the following three basic categories:

- General Samba configuration
- Samba user administration
- Samba resource administration

GENERAL SAMBA CONFIGURATION

The main configuration file for Samba is `/etc/samba/smb.conf`. This file contains the necessary information for Samba to connect to eDirectory. The following list contains a few of the parameters required for Samba integration with LUM:

- `passdb backend`—This field contains the connection information to the eDirectory server.

- `ldap admin dn`—The eDirectory administrator's name and context, in LDAP format, must be specified with this parameter.

- `ldap suffix`—This field contains the LDAP search base context to be used when locating Samba users. This is normally the same context where the Linux Config object can be found.

- `ldap passwd sync`—This option determines whether the Samba password should be synchronized via LDAP. This should be set to **on** with OES.

- `security`—This field should be set to **user** with OES. This ensures that a valid username and password combination is required, prior to the user gaining access to Samba shares.

- `encrypt passwords`—This option configures the server to recognize the encrypted passwords used with OES.

- `netbios name`—This option configures the NetBIOS name the Samba server will be known as. OES appends `-W` to the host name for this entry. This is required to prevent a conflict with NCP server name.

SAMBA USER ADMINISTRATION

As mentioned, Samba users are simply LUM users with an additional set of attributes associated with each user. During user creation within iManager, you are automatically prompted to convert the new user to both a LUM and Samba user. If user conversion is done at this time, the user's Samba password field will be automatically filled in with the new user's password. If the user is not converted at this time, the user will have to be manually converted later and the password must be re-entered manually.

Normal users cannot be converted directly to a Samba user without being also converted to a LUM user. For information on this process, refer to the LUM user section earlier in this chapter.

If you have a LUM user who was not designated as a Samba user, the LUM user must be manually converted to a Samba user through the following steps:

1. Launch iManager. In the Navigation frame, open the Linux User Management group and select Enable LUM User for Samba.

2. Locate the desired user object using the object selector or object history. Click OK.

3. To enable the user for Samba, the user's Samba password must be entered and confirmed. After entering the password, click OK to convert the user.

When this process has been completed, the user is now a valid Samba user and can access any Samba resources configured on the server.

SAMBA RESOURCE ADMINISTRATION

Samba resources include such things as local files and printers. With OES, iPrint is the recommended method of printer sharing as the iPrint solution is much more complete than printer sharing under Samba.

File sharing with Windows users can be accomplished through either Samba or using the Novell Client to access NCP server resources. The NCP server provides a more complete filesystem permission structure than Samba, and NCP-based permissions are fully integrated with eDirectory. However, Samba shares are a commonly used method of sharing files and may be the best option based on your requirements.

Configuring Samba file shares with OES is identical to configuring shares without OES. The YaST administration tool provides access to a Samba server configuration module. This module should be used to configure all Samba shares. The following steps document this process:

1. On the OES server, launch YaST.

2. Select the Network Service category and then click on the Samba Server module. At this point, you may be prompted to install the **samba-winbind** package. If so, select OK to install the required package and continue.

3. Select the Shares tab and click Add to configure a new share. In the subsequent dialog, provide the following information and click OK:

   - *Share Name*—Enter a name clients will use to access the shared directory.

   - *Share Description*—Enter a description for the new share. This description will be available to clients when they attempt to access the share.

   - *Share Type*—Select Directory as the share type, and then enter the local directory you want to share.

4. Select Finish to save the Samba configuration and restart the Samba service to enable the new share.

NOTE

Samba can be quite complex. For more information regarding the many options for configuring Samba resources, refer to the main Samba documentation found at http://www.samba.org.

## CHAPTER 9

OES Clustering Services

Instant Access

Installing Novell Cluster Services

- You can install Novell Cluster Services (NCS) from YaST. OES Linux ships with a license for a two-node cluster. Clusters of a larger size require additional licenses, which are purchased separately.

- If you are upgrading an existing NetWare cluster environment to OES Linux, perform a *rolling conversion* by upgrading one node at a time.

Configuring Clusters

- Configure your cluster environment from the Cluster Options page in iMonitor.

- Cluster-enable a storage pool by selecting New Cluster Pool from the Cluster Options page in iManager.

- Cluster-enable an application or service by creating a new cluster resource from the Cluster Options page in iManager.

- Configure parameters for individual cluster resources in iManager by accessing the resource properties from the Cluster Options page.

Monitoring Clusters

- Monitor your cluster environment from the Cluster Management page in iManager.

- View the status of the cluster and the various cluster resources from the Cluster Management page in iManager.

In order to remain competitive, your organization needs to provide customers and employees uninterrupted access to data, applications, websites, and other services 24 hours a day, 7 days a week, 365 days a year.

This makes high availability of your organization's services more than a technical issue. It's a business issue that requires a reliable solution.

Novell Clustering Services (NCS) is a multinode clustering system for OES Linux that is integrated with Novell eDirectory. NCS ensures high availability and manageability of critical network resources including data (server volumes), applications, and OES Linux services. NCS supports failover, failback, and migration (load balancing) of individually managed cluster resources.

NOTE

A license for a two-node NCS cluster is included with OES Linux. Licenses for additional cluster nodes must be purchased separately from Novell.

Clustering Benefits

NCS allows you to configure up to 32 OES Linux servers into a high-availability cluster, where resources can be dynamically switched or moved to any server in the cluster. Resources can be configured to automatically switch or move to another node in the event of a server failure. They can also be moved manually, if necessary, to troubleshoot hardware or balance server workload.

One of the best things about NCS is that it enables you to create a high-availability environment from off-the-shelf components. You don't have to spend millions when you create a cluster, and you can add servers to the cluster as your needs change and grow over time.

Equally important is the capability to greatly reduce unplanned service outages that result from server failures of some sort. You can even reduce the frequency of planned outages for software and hardware maintenance and upgrades because individual nodes can be removed from the cluster without affecting service availability to network users.

NCS provides the following advantages over a nonclustered environment:

- Increased availability
- Improved performance
- Low cost of operation
- Scalability
- Disaster recovery
- Data protection
- Shared resources

Because of these advantages, clustering systems are becoming mandatory for environments in which system availability is a must.

Clustering Fundamentals

Suppose you have configured a two-node cluster, with a web server installed on each of the nodes. Each of the servers in the cluster hosts two websites. All the content for all four websites is stored on a shared disk subsystem connected to each of the servers in the cluster. Figure 9.1 shows how such an environment might look.

During normal operation, each clustered node is in constant communication with the other nodes in the cluster through periodic polling. In this way, a node can quickly detect whether something happens to another node in the cluster.

If node 2 fails due to some hardware or software problems, users currently attached to the web server will lose their connections. The IP address associated with node 2 and all its services are migrated to node 1. Users would likely have to reload their web pages, which would be available from the new node within a few seconds.

After the problem in node 2 is located and repaired, it is restarted and automatically re-inserts itself into the cluster. Node 1 detects the return of node 2 and seamlessly passes back all the addresses and services originally assigned to node 2. The cluster returns to its normal configuration without any administrator intervention.

FIGURE 9.1
The basic cluster architecture.

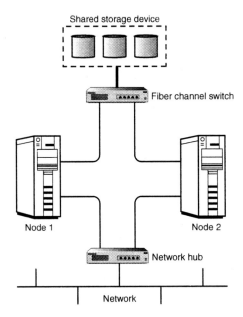

Shared storage device

Fiber channel switch

Node 1

Node 2

Network hub

Network

Clustering Terminology

We all know that clustering provides a high-availability platform for your network infrastructure. High availability is becoming increasingly important for two purposes: file access and network services. The following sections discuss NCS configuration for both of these situations. However, before you start working with an NCS cluster, you should be familiar with the terms described in the following sections.

Master Node

The first server that comes up in an NCS cluster is assigned the cluster IP address and becomes the *master node*. (Other nodes in the cluster are often referred to as *slave* nodes.) The master node updates information transmitted between the cluster and eDirectory, and monitors the health of the cluster nodes. If the master node fails, NCS migrates the cluster IP address to another server in the cluster, and that server becomes the master node.

Cluster-Enabled Volume

A *cluster-enabled* volume is an NSS volume configured to provide location-transparent access to OES Linux file services. The volume is associated with an eDirectory virtual server object that provides a unique secondary IP address for locating the volume on the cluster's shared storage device. The volume provides read-write file access to users.

NOTE

OES Linux clusters failover storage pools. This means you can migrate more than one volume at a time to another node if they are part of the same storage pool. For more information on Novell Storage Services (NSS), see Chapter 11, "OES Linux File Storage and Management."

Cluster Resource

A *cluster resource* is an object in eDirectory that represents an application or other type of service (such as DHCP or the master IP address) that you can migrate or fail over from one node to another in an NCS cluster. The cluster resource object includes scripts for unloading the service from one node and loading it on another node. In most cases, make sure the service is installed on all nodes in the cluster that will host the service.

Heartbeats and the Split-Brain Detector

NCS uses heartbeats on the LAN and a Split-Brain Detector (SBD) on the shared storage device to keep all services highly available on the cluster when a node fails. NCS determines when a node fails over the LAN and casts off the failed node through the following process:

- Every second (by default), each node in an NCS cluster sends out a heartbeat message over the network.

- The master node monitors the heartbeats of all other nodes in the cluster to determine whether they are still functioning.

- If a heartbeat is not received from a node during a predefined timeout (eight seconds by default), that node is removed (cast off) from the cluster, and migration of services begins.

NOTE

If the master node fails to send a heartbeat within the predefined timeout, it is cast off, and another node takes over as the master node.

NCS also uses the SBD to determine when a node fails through the following process:

- Each node writes an epoch number to a special SBD partition on the shared storage device. An epoch occurs each time a node leaves or joins the cluster. The epoch number is written at half the predefined timeout value (four seconds by default).

- Each node reads all epoch numbers for all other nodes in the SBD partition.

- When the master node sees an epoch number for a specific node that is lower than the others, it knows that the node has failed, and the node is cast off.

Fan-Out Failover

When a node fails in an NCS cluster, the cluster-enabled volumes and resources assigned to that node are migrated to other nodes in the cluster. Although this migration happens automatically, you must design and configure where each volume and resource migrates during failover.

TIP

You will probably want to distribute, or *fan out*, the volumes and resources to several nodes based on factors such as server load and the availability of installed applications. NCS relies on you to define where clustered resources will be assigned should a failure occur.

Installing Novell Cluster Services

The following list specifies the minimum hardware requirements for installing NCS:

- A minimum of two OES servers.

- At least 512MB of memory on all servers in the cluster. This provides sufficient memory to support failover of multiple applications to the same server node.

- At least one local disk device on which the root filesystem will be installed for each node.

- A shared disk system, either Storage Area Network (SAN) or iSCSI, is required for each cluster in order for all cluster data to be available to each node. This is how high availability of data is achieved.

NOTE

NCS will create a special cluster partition using one cylinder of one drive of the shared disk system. This will require roughly 20MB of free disk space on the shared disk system for creating the cluster partition.

WARNING

Be aware that it is possible to access shared disk systems by servers both in and out of the cluster. With NCS, this can cause corruption and possibly loss of the entire volume. To avoid this problem, ensure that only servers within the cluster access the shared disk system. If a noncluster server must access the same disk system, ensure that access is only granted to noncluster volumes.

- Make sure the disk system is installed and configured in accordance with the manufacturer's instructions.

- Make sure that the disks in the shared disk system are configured in some type of fault-tolerant configuration, such as mirroring or RAID 5. If this is not done, a single disk error can potentially cause a volume failure across the entire cluster.

Configuring the Shared Disk System

Prior to installing NCS, access to the shared disk system should be configured. One of the easiest methods of accessing a shared disk is through iSCSI. iSCSI is a new standard that makes it possible to transmit SCSI communications over a network by encapsulating them in standard TCP/IP data packets. This enables you to create a low-cost Storage Area Network (SAN) using regular high-speed network hardware, and avoid the considerable costs previously associated with fiber-based SAN architectures.

ISCSI BASICS

Two main components are required for iSCSI access to a shared disk:

- *iSCSI Initiator* software is installed on each server that will use the shared iSCSI storage. The initiator software allows an OES Linux server or cluster to communicate with an iSCSI storage server or other iSCSI target over a normal TCP/IP network.

- *iSCSI Target* can either be a dedicated iSCSI router or a software-based iSCSI controller. NetWare servers offer a software-based iSCSI controller that allows external iSCSI initiators to access to local disks.

Configuring your Linux server as an iSCSI target is beyond the scope of this book. However, access to a shared disk is required for fully utilizing NCS. The remainder of this section will explain how to configure access to a NetWare-based iSCSI target using an iSCSI initiator on the OES Linux server. For information on configuring the NetWare iSCSI target, see the online OES NetWare documentation.

INSTALLING AND CONFIGURING ISCSI INITIATORS

To configure an OES Linux server as an iSCSI initiator, you must first load the initiator software on the server using YaST. The following steps describe this process:

1. Access YaST from a terminal using **yast**, or from a graphical environment using **yast2** or the YaST launcher from the application menu.

2. Select the Software category in YaST. (This is typically the category selected by default.) From within the Software category, click on the Install and Remove Software module.

3. Use the Filter drop-down box to select the Search category.

4. In the Search window (left pane of the main window), enter **linux-iscsi**.

5. Click Accept to begin the software installation. At this point you may be prompted to install a few additional packages to satisfy dependencies. If so, select to continue the installation to install all required packages.

6. At the conclusion of the software installation and **SuSEconfig** process, select Finish to exit the Add and Remove Software module.

With the **linux-iscsi** package installed on your OES Linux server, you are now ready to configure access to the iSCSI target. Accessing an iSCSI target on NetWare can be accomplished either with or without LDAP Access Control. The following steps document the required configuration process:

1. In order to use LDAP Access Control with an iSCSI target, create an iSCSI initiator object in eDirectory for each Linux server you want to access the iSCSI target. If LDAP Access control is not in use, skip to step 4.

2. Assign the newly created iSCSI initiator objects as trustees of the iSCSI target objects in eDirectory.

3. Using your favorite text editor, edit the /etc/initiatorname.iscsi file on the OES machine. Locate the InitiatorName entry, which should resemble the following:

   InitiatorName=iqn.1987-05.com.cisco:01.23bcc5247683

   Modify this entry to contain the LDAP distinguished name of your iSCSI initiator object as follows:

   InitiatorName=iqn.1987-05.com.cisco:cn=InitiatorObject,o=Novell

   Replace cn=InitiatorObject,o=Novell with the distinguished name of your initiator object in LDAP format.

4. Using a text editor, edit the /etc/iscsi.conf file. Add the following information to this file:

   DiscoveryAddress=iSCSI_Target_Server_IPAddress

   After you enter the correct information, the iscsi.conf entry should appear as follows:

   DiscoveryAddress=192.168.1.150

5. In order to connect to the iSCSI target, start the initiator using the following command:

   /etc/init.d/iscsi start

6. After starting the initiator, use the iscsi-ls command on the OES machine to verify connectivity. If everything has been configured properly, the iSCSI target information will be displayed following the iSCSI driver version. If no targets are displayed, you may have a configuration error on the NetWare side.

With the initiator configured and started, you can access the iSCSI disk subsystem as if it were a directly attached resource on each OES Linux server configured as an initiator for that iSCSI device. Mapping drives, trustee rights, and directory and file attributes will all work identically to a directly connected storage device.

Installing Novell Cluster Services

Novell Cluster Services can be installed during the original OES Linux installation, or can be added to an existing server after the fact using YaST. To add NCS to an existing OES installation, complete the following steps:

1. Access YaST from a terminal using `yast`, or from a graphical environment using `yast2` or the YaST launcher from the application menu.

2. Select the System category in YaST. From within this category, locate and select the Novell Cluster Services (NCS) module. This module will detect that the RPMs for NCS are missing and ask if you want to install them. Select Continue to install the necessary packages.

3. At the conclusion of the software installation, `SuSEconfig` is executed to update the system configuration. When this completes, the configuration of the OES component will begin automatically.

4. At the Novell Cluster Services (NCS) LDAP Server Configuration screen, enter the following information and click Next:

   - *Local or Remote Directory Server*—Select the radio button, which indicates whether eDirectory is running on the local server, or a remote server.

   - *Directory Server Address*—If a remote eDirectory server is in use, enter the IP address for this server.

   - *Admin Name with Context*—Enter the eDirectory administrator's credentials using fully qualified dot notation, for example, `cn=admin.o=novell`.

   - *Admin Password*—Enter the password for the administrator user.

   - *Port Details*—If necessary, select this button to change the configured ports for the eDirectory server that you specified earlier. The default LDAP port for unencrypted communications is **389**, and port **636** is used for SSL-encrypted communications.

5. At the Novell Cluster Services (NCS) Configuration screen, enter the required information (see Figure 9.2), and click Next.

   - *New or Existing Cluster*—Select whether this server will be added to a new or existing cluster. The Configure Later option is normally only used during the main OES installation, when the final configuration of NCS is being postponed until after the server is fully installed.

   - *Cluster FDN*—If the server is being added to a new cluster, enter the fully distinguished name of the new cluster. If the server is being added to an existing cluster, enter the fully distinguished name of the existing cluster.

- *Cluster IP Address*—If you are creating a new cluster, enter a unique IP address for the new cluster. This address must be separate from the server's IP address, and is required to be a static address on the same subnet as all cluster servers.

- *Optional Device for SBD Partition*—If you are creating a new cluster, enter the device where the SBD partition will be created. If you are not using a shared disk system, leave this field blank.

FIGURE 9.2

Novell Cluster Services (NCS) configuration options.

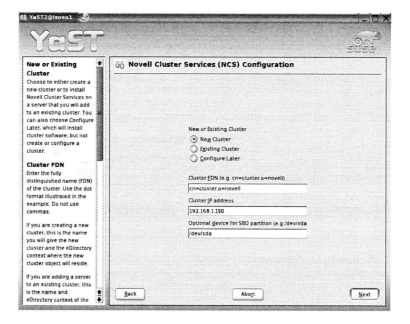

WARNING

As previously mentioned, you must have roughly 20MB of free (unpartitioned) space on one of the shared disk drives to create the cluster partition. If no free space is available, Novell Cluster Services can't use the shared disk drives.

6. If the server has multiple IP addresses configured, ensure that the IP address to be used for clustering with the current node is selected. In order for NCS to be active, select Start Clustering Services now. Click Next to finish the installation of NCS.

When NCS is installed and running, you will use the Clusters category within iManager for the remaining configuration tasks. To start and stop NCS manually, use the following init script with a **start** or **stop** command-line parameter:

```
/etc/init.d/novell-ncs <parameter>
```

Converting NetWare Clusters to Linux

If you have an existing NCS cluster, using NetWare 6.5 Cluster Services, you can convert NetWare nodes to OES Linux through a *rolling conversion* process. This process allows you to convert one server at a time, without bringing the cluster down.

NOTE

NetWare 5.1 and NetWare 6 clusters must first be upgraded to NetWare 6.5 clusters before they can be converted to OES Linux clusters.

In the *rolling conversion* process, nodes in the NetWare cluster are converted one at a time to OES Linux. During this process, normal failover of the cluster will ensure that user access is not lost in this process. To perform the *rolling conversion*, execute the following tasks:

1. Shut down the NetWare server you are converting to OES Linux. Cluster resources running on this server should fail over to other nodes in the cluster.

NOTE

If a cluster node holds the Master replica of any eDirectory partitions, convert other servers in the cluster first. The Master replica holder should be among the last servers converted to OES Linux.

2. In eDirectory, remove any references to the downed NetWare server. This includes the Cluster Node object, the Server object, and all other objects referencing the server.

3. Run DSRepair on the server holding the Master replica of the partition in which the downed server existed. The eDirectory tree should be fully synchronized and free from error prior to installing the new OES Linux server. If problems are reported, run DSRepair multiple times to ensure that the tree is clean. If problems persist and cannot be resolved, contact Novell Technical Support before proceeding.

4. Install OES Linux on the downed server, or replacement hardware. During the OES Linux installation, do not install Novell Clustering Services as this will be installed later. Optionally, the new server can be installed using the same IP address and server name as the NetWare server it is replacing. See Chapter 2, "Installing OES Linux," for information on installing OES Linux.

5. Set up and verify SAN connectivity on the new Linux server. These steps are specific to the SAN being used. For more information, refer to documentation supplied by your SAN vendor.

6. Install Novell Cluster Services to your OES Linux server, and select to add the server to your existing NetWare cluster. See "Installing Novell Cluster Services" earlier in this chapter for more information.

7. Execute `sbdutil -f` via a terminal on the OES Linux server to verify connectivity to the cluster (SBD) partition on the SAN.

8. Start NCS by executing `/etc/init.d/novell-ncs start`.

After the conversion process completes, cluster resources will automatically fail back to the Linux server if the following conditions are met:

- The failback mode of the cluster resources is set to Auto.
- The new Linux server is using the same node number as the replaced NetWare server.

If necessary, manually migrate cluster resources to the new Linux server to complete the conversion process.

The same eight conversion steps can now be restarted on additional NetWare 6.5 nodes in the cluster, or the cluster can be left using both NetWare and Linux. If all nodes in the NetWare 6.5 cluster are converted to Linux, the cluster conversion process must be finalized by writing the cluster resource load and unload scripts into eDirectory. This must be performed on one OES Linux server after all servers in the cluster have been converted from NetWare. The following two steps are required for this process:

1. From a terminal on one OES Linux server in the converted cluster, execute **cluster convert preview <*resource_name*>**. This will display the resource load and unload script changes that will be made when the conversion is committed.

2. Execute **cluster convert commit** from a terminal on one OES Linux server to perform the script conversion and finalize the NetWare to Linux conversion.

After the `cluster convert commit` command has been executed, all load and unload scripts will be permanently converted to Linux scripts, and your conversion will be complete.

Configuring Novell Cluster Services

There are some general configuration options for your NCS environment of which you should be aware. All of these configuration options are available from the Cluster Options page in iManager, shown in Figure 9.3.

FIGURE 9.3
Cluster Options page in iManager.

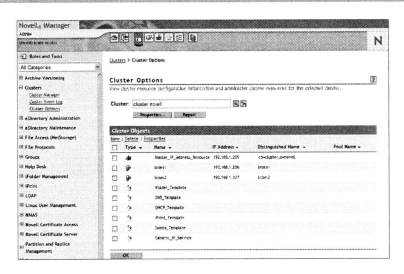

To access the Cluster Options page in iManager, perform the following steps:

1. From within iManager, select the Cluster Options link, found under the Clusters category.

2. In the right pane, use the Object Selector or Object Browser tools to locate your cluster object. After you select the cluster object, the current page will automatically reload.

From this page, configuration parameters used to configure the entire cluster environment can be accessed. To view these options, select the Properties button from the Cluster Options page. This will open the Cluster Properties page, shown in Figure 9.4. The various configuration settings available from this page are described next.

FIGURE 9.4
Cluster Properties page in iManager.

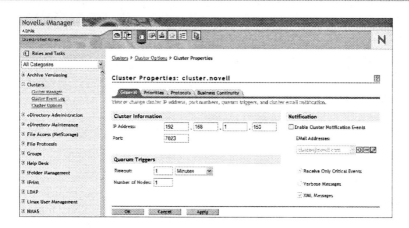

IP Address/Port

You can view and change the IP address and port assigned to the Cluster object when you installed NCS. The Cluster IP address normally does not need to be changed, but can be if needed.

The default cluster port number is **7023**, and is automatically assigned when the cluster is created. The cluster port number should not be changed unless there is a TCP port conflict with another resource using the same port. If there is a conflict, you can change the port number to any other value that doesn't cause a conflict.

Quorum Triggers

The Quorum Triggers configuration is used to define two trigger values that are used during the startup of the cluster.

- *Timeout*—Timeout specifies the amount of time to wait for the number of servers defined in the Membership field to be up and running. If the timeout period elapses before the quorum membership reaches its specified number, resources will automatically start loading on the servers that are currently up and running in the cluster.

- *Number of Nodes*—This represents the number of nodes in the quorum that must be running in the cluster before resources will start to load. When you first bring up servers in your cluster, NCS reads the number specified in the Number of Nodes field and waits until that number of servers is up and running in the cluster before it starts loading resources. Set the number to a value greater than 1 so that all resources don't automatically load on the first server that is brought up in the cluster.

Notification

NCS can automatically send out email messages for certain cluster events such as cluster and resource state changes or nodes joining or leaving the cluster.

- *Enable Cluster Notification Events*—Check this box to enable cluster email notifications. If this is not checked, all remaining fields are grayed out.

- *Email Addresses*—Specify the email address that should receive notifications in the field provided. Repeat this process for each address you want on the notification list. You can provide up to eight email addresses.

- *Receive Only Critical Events*—Select this radio button if you want administrators to receive notification of only critical events like a node failure or a resource going comatose.

- *Verbose Messages*—Select this radio button if you want administrators to receive notification of all cluster state changes, including critical events, resource state changes, and nodes joining and leaving the cluster.

- *XML Messages*—Check this box if you want administrators to receive notifications in XML format. XML messages can be interpreted and formatted in a way that lets you customize the message information for your specific needs.

NOTE

NCS uses Postfix for sending email alerts. If you are also running cluster resources that use SMTP, the port configured for Postfix must be changed to avoid port conflicts between the two services. You can modify the port used by Postfix by editing the /etc/postfix/main.cf file. For more information on performing this change, refer to http://www.postfix.org.

Priorities

The Priorities page allows you to control the order in which multiple resources start on a given node when the cluster is brought up, or during a failover or failback. For example, if a node fails and two resources fail over to another node, the resource priority will determine which resource loads first. This is useful for ensuring that the most critical resources load first and are available to users before less critical resources.

To adjust the priority of a resource, select the resource in the priority list. After selecting the resource, use the up and down arrow buttons to move the resource to a higher or lower priority. Click Apply when finished.

Protocols

You can use the Protocol link to view or edit the transmit frequency and tolerance settings for all nodes in the cluster, including the master node.

- *Heartbeat*—Specifies the amount of time between transmits for all nodes in the cluster except the master. For example, if you set this value to 1, nonmaster nodes in the cluster will send a signal that they are alive to the master node every second.

- *Tolerance*—Specifies the amount of time the master node gives all other nodes in the cluster to signal that they are alive. For example, setting this value to 4 means that if the master node does not receive an "I'm alive" signal from a node in the cluster within four seconds, that node will be removed from the cluster.

- *Master Watchdog*—Specifies the amount of time between transmits for the master node in the cluster. For example, if you set this value to 1, the master node in the cluster will transmit an "I'm alive" signal to all the other nodes in the cluster every second.

- *Slave Watchdog*—Specifies the amount of time the master node has to signal that it is alive. For example, setting this value to 5 means that if the nonmaster nodes in the cluster do not receive an "I'm alive" signal from the master within five seconds, the master node will be removed from the cluster and one of the other nodes will become the master node.

- *Maximum Retransmits*—This option is not currently used with Novell Cluster Services but will be used for future versions.

The master node is generally the first node brought online in the cluster, but if that node fails, any of the other nodes in the cluster can become the master.

Cluster Node Properties

In addition to editing the configuration of the entire cluster, it is also possible to adjust the IP address of an individual cluster node. This can also be accomplished using the Cluster Options page in iManager. To adjust this setting for an individual node, complete the following steps:

1. From within iManager, select the Cluster Options link, found under the Clusters category.

2. In the right pane, use the Object Selector or Object Browser tools to locate your cluster object. After you select the cluster object, the current page will automatically reload.

3. In the Cluster Objects list, locate and select the check box for the desired cluster node. When the node has been marked, select Properties in the header of the Cluster Objects window.

4. The IP address for the selected node is the only item that can be adjusted here. Make any necessary changes, and select OK to save your changes and exit back to Cluster Options page.

From the main Cluster Options page, it is also possible to delete a node from the cluster. To delete a cluster node, select the check box beside the cluster node and click Delete in the header of the Cluster Object window.

After a node is deleted, you must unload and reload NCS on each server in the cluster in order for the node deletion to take effect. To do this, run `rcnovell-ncs restart` from the console of each server in the cluster.

Always-Available File Access

To make network data constantly available through your newly created cluster, you need to create and configure shared cluster pools and volumes. Shared volumes can be any of the traditional Linux filesystems (Reisfer, EXT2/3, and so on) or NSS. Shared NSS volumes must be created on shared NSS pools. NSS pools can be designated as sharable either during or after creation. This is possible through both iManager and the command-line `nssmu` utility. To create a cluster-enabled NSS pool during pool creation via iManager, complete the following steps:

1. From within iManager, select the Pools link, found under the Storage category in the left navigation frame.

2. In the right pane, use the Object Selector or Object Browser tools to locate your cluster object. After you select the cluster object, the current page will automatically reload.

3. Select New to create a new pool.

4. Enter the name of the NSS pool, and click Next.

NOTE

Because periods are used as delimiters in fully qualified names in eDirectory, periods cannot be used in the naming of your NSS pool. If spaces are used in the name, eDirectory will convert those spaces to underscores.

5. Check the box next to the device on which the NSS pool should be created. Also enter the size of the new NSS pool. If desired, select the Mount on Creation check box to make the pool available after creation.

6. Select Finish to create the new NSS pool. For more information on NSS pools, see Chapter 11.

7. You can either select to cluster-enable the pool now or later. You *must* cluster-enable a pool in order for it to fail over during a failure. If you choose to cluster-enable the storage pool now, you have to provide the following information:

- *Virtual Server Name*—Change the name of the default Virtual Server object. When you cluster-enable a pool, the Virtual Server object is named by combining the Cluster object name and the Pool object name. For example: `QuillsCluster_SharePool_Server`.

- *CIFS Server Name*—If you select CIFS as an advertisement protocol, specify a server name that CIFS clients will see for this storage when browsing the network.

- *IP Address*—Each cluster-enabled pool requires its own IP address. This IP address is used to provide access and failover capability to the pool. It is assigned to the storage pool and associated with volume within the pool. All volumes in the storage pool share the same IP address.

- *Advertising Protocols*—Specify how you want the shared storage pool to advertise its existence to clients. AFP is used by Macintosh clients, CIFS is used by Microsoft Windows, and NCP is used by the Novell client.

Cluster-Enabling a Volume After Pool Creation

When you have created the NSS pool, you can add sharable NSS volumes. Shared volumes can be created with either iManager or `nssmu`. The following steps can be used to create a shared volume using iManager:

1. From within iManager, select the Volumes link, found under the Storage category in the left navigation frame.

2. In the right pane, use the Object Selector or Object Browser tools to locate your cluster object. After you select the cluster object, the current page will automatically reload.

3. Select New to create a new volume.

4. Enter a name for the new volume and click Next.

5. Check the box next to the pool on which the NSS volume should be created. Also enter the size of the new NSS volume.

6. Select the desired NSS attributes for the volume. Also, designate a mount point and select whether to mount and activate the volume on creation. Click Finish to complete the volume creation.

The whole point in creating a cluster is to provide constant access to network resources. Because one of the principal resources on a network is data, cluster-enabling a storage pool will likely be one of the things you do first.

NOTE

To cluster-enable a non-NSS volume, create the Linux partition on the shared storage system as you normally would. After creation, create a cluster resource with the proper load and unload script to provide access to the partition.

Cluster-Enabling a Storage Pool After Creation

If you chose not to cluster-enable a storage pool when it was initially created, you can do so after the fact from iManager. Make sure you deactivate the pool and dismount the volume(s) before cluster-enabling them. To cluster-enable an existing pool, complete the following steps:

1. From within iManager, select the Cluster Options link, found under the Clusters category in the left navigation frame.

2. In the right pane, use the Object Selector or Object Browser tools to locate your cluster object. After you select the cluster object, the current page will automatically reload.

3. Select New from the Cluster Objects window.

4. Specify Pool as the new object type, and then click Next.

5. Enter the name of the pool you would like to cluster-enable, or browse and select one. After a pool has been selected, complete the following information and click Next:

- *Virtual Server Name*—Enter the name of the Virtual Server object. When you cluster-enable a pool during pool creation, the Virtual Server object is named by combining the Cluster object name and the Pool object name, for example: `QuillsCluster_SharePool_Server`.

- *CIFS Server Name*—If you select CIFS as an advertisement protocol, specify a server name that CIFS clients will see for this storage when browsing the network.

- *IP Address*—Each cluster-enabled pool requires its own IP address. This IP address is used to provide access and failover capability to the pool. It is assigned to the storage pool and associated with volume within the pool. All volumes in the storage pool share the same IP address.

- *Advertising Protocols*—Specify how you want the shared storage pool to advertise its existence to clients. AFP is used by Macintosh clients, CIFS is used by Microsoft Windows, and NCP is used by the Novell client.

- *Online Resource After Create*—Select this check box to automatically start the volume resource immediately after object creation.

- *Define Additional Properties*—Select this check box to continue cluster configuration of the pool following object creation.

You can delete cluster-enabled volumes and pools in the same way that you delete standard NSS volumes and pools. When a cluster-enabled resource is deleted, NCS will automatically modify its load scripts to remove that resource.

Modifying Node Assignment for a Storage Pool

When you cluster-enable a storage pool, all nodes in the cluster are automatically assigned to the pool. The order of assignment is the order in which the nodes appear in the list. To assign or unassign nodes, or to change the failover order, complete the following steps:

1. From within iManager, select the Cluster Options link, found under the Clusters category in the left navigation frame.

2. In the right pane, use the Object Selector or Object Browser tools to locate your cluster object. After you select the cluster object, the current page will automatically reload.

3. Select the check box next to the storage pool whose start and failover modes you are changing. When the check box is selected, click the Properties link in the Cluster Objects window to access the properties of the storage pool.

4. Select the General tab.

5. From the list of unassigned nodes, select the server you would like to assign the storage pool to. Click the right arrow to move the server to the Assigned Nodes list. This process should be repeated for all servers that should be assigned to the resource.

6. Click the up and down arrows to adjust the failover order of the servers assigned to the storage pool. Click Apply or Finish to save your changes.

The first server in the Nodes list will be the preferred node for the cluster-enabled storage pool. Failover will occur sequentially down the list.

Configuring Storage Pool Policies

After a storage pool has been cluster-enabled, you can configure the start, failover, and failback parameters. To do this, complete the following steps:

1. From within iManager, select the Cluster Options link, found under the Clusters category in the left navigation frame.

2. In the right pane, use the Object Selector or Object Browser tools to locate your cluster object. After you select the cluster object, the current page will automatically reload.

3. Select the check box next to the storage pool whose start, failover, or failback modes you would like to edit. Then click the Properties link in the Cluster Objects window.

4. Select the General tab, and configure the following options:

   ▪ *Resource Follows Master*—Check this box if you want the resource to run only on the master node in the cluster. If the master node fails, the resource will fail over to whichever node becomes the master.

   ▪ *Ignore Quorum*—Check this box if you don't want the cluster-wide timeout period and node number limit enforced. This makes sure the resource is launched immediately as soon as any server in the Assigned Nodes list is brought online. You can modify the quorum values from the Cluster Configuration page in iManager.

5. Continue with the storage pool configuration by adjusting the following options:

   ▪ *Start*—When this option is set to Auto, the resource will start automatically whenever the cluster is brought online. When this option is set to Manual, you must start the device after the cluster comes online. The default is Auto.

- *Failover*—When this option is set to Auto, the resource will automatically move to the next server in the Assigned Nodes list if the node it is currently running on fails. When this option is set to Manual, you will intervene after a failure and reassign the resource to a functioning node. The default is Auto.

- *Failback*—When this is set to Auto, the cluster resource will migrate back to its preferred node when it comes back online. The preferred node is the first node listed in its Assigned Nodes table. When this option is set to Manual, the cluster resource will not fail back until you allow it to happen. When this option is set to Disable, the cluster resource will not fail back to its most preferred node when the most preferred node rejoins the cluster. The default is Disable.

6. Click Apply to save the configuration changes.

Adjusting these settings gives you granular control over the behavior of your clustered storage pool.

Always-Available Network Services

When you are ready to start loading applications and services in a clustered environment, there are some extra steps you have to take beyond the standard installation and configuration provided by the application or service. As with a cluster volume, you will most likely need to cluster-enable the application or service. You might also have to make some changes to the Cluster object and the cluster nodes so that they can properly support the new application or service.

Cluster Resource Applications

When creating a resource for an NCS cluster, you need to be familiar with the following types of applications:

- *Cluster-aware*—Cluster-aware applications are specifically designed to take advantage of a clustered environment. These applications and services recognize when they are running on a cluster. They will automatically tweak their internal settings to be more tolerant of communication lapses that occur in a clustered system.

- *Cluster-naive*—Although you can cluster-enable any application, if it is not designed to recognize that it is running on a cluster, the application is referred to as *cluster-naive*. For a cluster-naive application or service, NCS does all the work to ensure that the resource is reloaded on another node if the assigned cluster node fails.

Many OES Linux services, and some third-party applications as well, are designed to take advantage of Novell Clustering Services when it is detected. For example:

- Apache Web Server and Tomcat Servlet Engine
- GroupWise (MTA, POA, GWIA, WebAccess)
- iFolder
- iManager
- iPrint
- Novell clients (Windows 98 and Windows XP/2000)
- NetStorage

As you can see from this list, you can leverage the advantages of clustering with many types of applications, thereby making your entire network more resilient to failures.

Cluster-Enabling an Application

You cluster-enable a service or application by creating a Cluster Resource object for it in eDirectory.

To create a cluster resource for an application, complete the following steps:

1. From within iManager, select the Cluster Options link, found under the Clusters category in the left navigation frame.

2. In the right pane, use the Object Selector or Object Browser tools to locate your cluster object. After you select the cluster object, the current page will automatically reload.

3. Select New from the Cluster Objects window.

4. Specify Resource as the new object type, and then click Next.

5. At the New Resource screen, supply the necessary information and click Finish.

   - *Resource Name*—Specify a name for the new cluster resource.

   - *(Optional) Template*—If a resource template already exists for the resource you are creating, use the Object Selector to locate and select the template.

   - *Online Resource After Create*—Select this check box to automatically make the service available after resource creation.

- *Define Additional Properties*—Check this box so that you can set the Cluster Resource object properties, such as Load and Unload scripts, after it is created. This causes the Finish button to change to Next, and opens several additional screens to configure resource properties, just as if you were configuring an existing cluster resource through the properties of the resource.

NOTE

NCS includes resource templates for DHCP, DNS, Generic IP services, iFolder, iPrint, and Samba. The generic IP service template can be used when configuring certain server applications to run on your cluster. You can edit and customize any of the templates for your specific needs. New templates can also be created in the same manner as creating cluster resources.

The cluster resource includes a unique IP address, which lets it be migrated from node to node within the cluster, as necessary. Cluster resources are created for both cluster-aware and cluster-naive applications.

Assign Nodes to the Cluster-Enabled Resource

When you create a cluster-enabled resource, all nodes in the cluster are automatically assigned to the resource. The order of assignment is determined by the order in which the nodes appear in the Assigned Nodes list. To assign or unassign nodes, or to change the failover order for the resource, complete the following steps:

1. From within iManager, select the Cluster Options link, found under the Clusters category in the left navigation frame.

2. In the right pane, use the Object Selector or Object Browser tools to locate your cluster object. After you select the cluster object, the current page will automatically reload.

3. Select the check box next to the resource whose start and failover modes you are changing. Then click the Properties link in the Cluster Objects window to access the properties of the cluster resource.

4. Select the General tab.

5. From the list of unassigned nodes, select the server you would like to assign the resource to. Click the right arrow to move the server to the Assigned Nodes list. This process should be repeated for all servers that should be assigned to the resource.

6. Click the up and down arrows to adjust the failover order of the servers assigned to the resource. Click Apply or Finish to save your changes.

The first server in the Nodes list will be the preferred node for the cluster-enabled resource. Failover will occur sequentially down the list.

Configure Clustered Resource Policies

After a resource has been cluster-enabled, you can configure the start, failover, and failback parameters. To do this, complete the following steps:

1. From within iManager, select the Cluster Options link, found under the Clusters category in the left navigation frame.

2. In the right pane, use the Object Selector or Object Browser tools to locate your cluster object. After you select the cluster object, the current page will automatically reload.

3. Select the check box next to the resource whose start, failover, or failback modes you would like to edit. Then click the Properties link in the Cluster Objects window.

4. Select the General tab, and configure the following options:

   ■ *Resource Follows Master*—Check this box if you want the resource to only run on the master node in the cluster. If the master node fails, the resource will fail over to whichever node becomes the master.

   ■ *Ignore Quorum*—Check this box if you don't want the cluster-wide timeout period and node number limit enforced. This makes sure the resource is launched immediately as soon as any server in the Assigned Nodes list is brought online. You can modify the quorum values from the Cluster Configuration page in iManager.

5. Continue with the resource configuration by adjusting the following options:

   ■ *Start*—When this option is set to Auto, the resource will start automatically whenever the cluster is brought online. When this option is set to Manual, you must start the device after the cluster comes online. The default is Auto.

   ■ *Failover*—When this option is set to Auto, the resource will automatically move to the next server in the Assigned Nodes list if the node it is currently running on fails. When this option is set to Manual, you will intervene after a failure and reassign the resource to a functioning node. The default is Auto.

- *Failback*—When this option is set to Auto, the cluster resource will migrate back to its preferred node when it comes back online. The preferred node is the first node listed in its Assigned Nodes table. When this option is set to Manual, the cluster resource will not fail back until you allow it to happen. When this option is set to Disable, the cluster resource will not fail back to its most preferred node when the most preferred node rejoins the cluster. The default is Disable.

6. Click Apply to save the configuration changes.

Adjusting these settings give you granular control over the behavior of your clustered resource.

Migrating a Cluster Resource

A node doesn't have to fail in order to migrate a resource from one node to another. To migrate a cluster resource, complete the following steps:

1. From within iManager, select the Cluster Manager link, found under the Clusters category in the left navigation frame.

2. In the right pane, use the Object Selector or Object Browser tools to locate your cluster object. After you select the cluster object, the current page will automatically reload.

3. Select the check box next to the resource you would like to migrate to another node. Then click the Migrate link in the Cluster State View window.

4. Select the server you would like to migrate the resource to and click OK to migrate the resource.

NOTE

If you click Offline instead of Migrate, the resource will be unloaded, and will not load again until it is manually reloaded into the cluster. If you need to modify the resource configuration, Offline lets you take the resource out of the cluster in order to do so. Cluster resources can't be modified while loaded or running in the cluster.

You might want to do this in order to perform some type of maintenance on one of the nodes or just to balance out the node workload if one is getting too busy.

Configuring Load and Unload Scripts

Load scripts are required for each resource or volume in your cluster. The load script specifies the commands to start the resource or mount the volume on a node. Unload scripts are used to ensure that when a resource is removed from a node, all modules and resources are properly cleaned up in the process.

TIP

Load and unload scripts are created automatically for disk pools when they are cluster-enabled. Because of this, you shouldn't have to mess with scripts for cluster-enabled volumes and pools.

To create a resource load or unload script, complete the following steps:

1. From within iManager, select the Cluster Options link, found under the Clusters category in the left navigation frame.

2. In the right pane, use the Object Selector or Object Browser tools to locate your cluster object. After you select the cluster object, the current page will automatically reload.

3. Select the check box next to the resource you are creating or editing a load script for. Then click the Properties link in the Cluster Objects window to access the properties of the cluster resource.

4. Select the Scripts tab. Select either the Load Script or the Unload Script link.

5. Edit or add the necessary commands to the script to load or unload the resource on a node. Sample commands are as follows:

```
SAMBA_ROOT=/mnt/samba
exit_on_error mount -t reiserfs /var/smb $SAMBA_ROOT
ignore_error del_secondary_ipaddress ipaddress/subnet
```

6. Specify a timeout value. The timeout value determines how much time the script is given to complete. If the script does not complete within the specified time, the resource becomes comatose. The default is 600 seconds (10 minutes).

Resource load scripts are simply Linux shell scripts. Therefore, you use the same commands in a load script that you would use to create any other Linux shell script file that runs from a server terminal. Applications and services will often include prebuilt startup scripts for loading and unloading application modules. You can use these as a template for creating load and unload scripts. Consult the application or service documentation for information on necessary load and unload commands.

Understanding Resource States

When running or testing an NCS cluster, you can view valuable information about the current state of your cluster, and its various resources, from the Cluster Management view in iManager (see Figure 9.5).

FIGURE 9.5
View of cluster status in iManager.

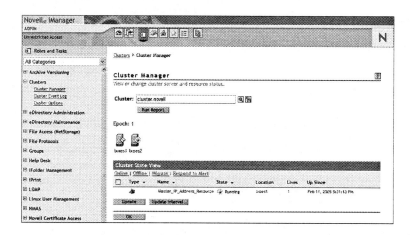

In order for the Cluster Manager to report your cluster configuration, you must locate and select your cluster object from eDirectory using the Cluster link. After you select the object, the Custer Manager page will refresh and display information on the current cluster.

Some of the specific cluster information you can gather from the Cluster Manager view includes the following:

- An icon represents each node in your cluster. The yellow disk indicates the node that is functioning as the master server in the cluster. The master server can change over time due to failover or migration events that take place.

- Epoch indicates the number of times the cluster state has changed. The epoch number will increment each time a node joins or leaves the cluster.

- The Run Report link provides a detailed report of your cluster. This report includes the cluster settings, quorum member information, and load and unload scripts.

- In the Cluster State View window, each node of the cluster is listed along with its node type and associated resource state.

Table 9.1 describes different resource states you might see in the Cluster State View window of the Cluster Manager page in iManager and provides some possible actions for each state.

TABLE 9.1
Cluster Resource States

RESOURCE STATE	DESCRIPTION	ACTION
Alert	One of the resource policies has been set to Manual. The resource is waiting for admin instructions.	Click the Alert Status indicator and you will be prompted to start, fail over, or fail back the resource.
Comatose	The resource is not running and requires administrator intervention.	Select the Comatose Status indicator and take the resource offline. After resource problems are resolved, the resource can be put back online.
Unloading	The resource is unloading from the server on which it was running.	None.
Running	The resource is in a normal running state.	Select the Running Status indicator, and you can choose to migrate the resource to a different node or take the resource offline.
Loading	The resource is loading on a server.	None.
Unassigned	None of the nodes in the Assigned Node list are currently online.	Select the Unassigned Status indicator and you can take the resource offline. This will prevent the resource from running on any of its preferred nodes should one or more of them rejoin the cluster.
NDS_Sync	The properties of the resource have changed and the changes are still being synchronized in eDirectory.	None.

RESOURCE STATE	DESCRIPTION	ACTION
Offline	The resource is shut down or is in a dormant or inactive state.	Select the Offline Status indicator and, if desired, click the Online button to load the resource. NCS will choose the best node possible, given the current state of the cluster and the resource's Assigned Nodes list.
Quorum wait	The resource is waiting for a quorum to be established so that it can begin loading.	None.

For more information on NCS, refer to the online OES Linux documentation.

## CHAPTER 10

Identity Manager Bundle Edition

Instant Access

Installing Identity Manager Bundle Edition

- Install the Identity Manager engine from the Identity Manager Bundle Edition CD-ROM using the command-line installation program.

- Install Identity Manager drivers and management plug-ins (for iManager) from the Identity Manager Bundle Edition CD-ROM at the application server or workstation destination.

Configuring Identity Manager Bundle Edition

- Use the Identity Manager management plug-ins to configure and manage your Identity Manager environment from iManager.

Originally released in the fall of 2001 as DirXML, Identity Manager has become an award-winning and groundbreaking tool for integrating the diverse systems in today's modern networks. OES Linux includes a fully functional version of Identity Manager suitable for linking some of today's most common directory systems into a cohesive whole.

NOTE

The rename of DirXML to Identity Manager was a fairly recent change. As such, a number of utilities still reference Identity Manager as DirXML. For all practical purposes, these two terms are synonymous.

Derived from Nsure Identity Manager 2, Identity Manager Bundle Edition enables you to bidirectionally synchronize data and passwords between Novell eDirectory, Microsoft Active Directory, and Microsoft Windows NT domains.

How Identity Manager Works

Identity Manager Bundle Edition allows you to link your disparate network data sources together using Novell eDirectory as the central repository for sharing data, as shown in Figure 10.1.

FIGURE 10.1
Logical architecture of Identity Manager—Hub and Spoke.

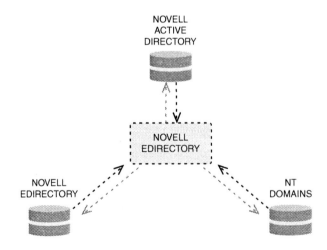

The Identity Manager architecture consists of several components that work together to achieve effective data and password synchronization:

- *Identity Manager Engine*—Running on OES Linux, the Identity Manager engine functions as the communications hub that provides data and password synchronization between your central eDirectory tree and any participating external systems. The Identity Manager engine uses Extensible

Markup Language (XML) to create object models of any data event. It then applies a set of rules to determine if, and how, the data modifications are sent to participating systems. The centralized Identity Manager engine makes sure that data events are processed consistently throughout your network environment.

- *Identity Manager Drivers*—Customized to each system that will participate in Identity Manager synchronization, the Identity Manager drivers act as communications "spokes" or channels between your central eDirectory tree and any participating external systems. Identity Manager drivers are configured to subscribe to data changes made in the central eDirectory tree, and publish data changes that occur locally to the central eDirectory tree. This publish/subscribe model gives you complete control over the nature and direction of data synchronization.

NOTE

To simplify configuration, Identity Manager Bundle Edition provides configuration files that you can import into a driver during installation to automatically set up driver rules, filters, and transformation documents that dictate what data from this system should be exchanged with other systems and how this data should be exchanged.

- *Filters*—Filters specify which objects and attributes can be shared between the central eDirectory tree and a given target system. Each Identity Manager driver supports two sets of filters. The Subscriber filter determines the objects and attributes that are shared from eDirectory to the target system. The Publisher filter determines the objects and attributes that are shared from the target system to eDirectory. A list of default attribute mappings for Active Directory and NT Domain drivers is provided in Table 10.1.

- *Rules*—Rules are used to specify requirements for the management of object creation, matching, and placement that take place as part of a data synchronization event. For example, a Creation rule might specify that any User object created through a synchronization event must first have certain attributes defined, such as Surname and Email address.

- *Style Sheets*—Style Sheets use Extensible Stylesheet Language Transformations (XSLT) documents to transform XML events and data as needed to suit the needs of the various Identity Manager[nd]integrated systems. For example, XSLT can be used to transform data received from one system into a format consumable by another system to which the data must be synchronized. You will likely not have to work with XSLT directly because it is built in the background by the Identity Manager graphical configuration tool.

- *Password Synchronization Filters and Agents*—PasswordSync filters capture changes to passwords and pass these changes to PasswordSync agents over secure channels. PasswordSync integrates with Identity Manager drivers to determine how password changes should be applied across systems. For example, changing the password for JHARRIS in an NT domain could mean that the new password should be sent to JLHARRIS.PROVO.QUILLS.COM in the eDirectory environment.

- *Remote Loader Service*—The Remote Loader Service is a communications mechanism whereby the Identity Manager engine and central eDirectory tree can effectively communicate with an Identity Manager driver that is actually loaded and running on a separate server. For example, the Identity Manager engine leverages the Remote Loader Service to communicate with the Identity Manager driver for Active Directory, which is loaded on a Windows 2000 Active Directory server.

TABLE 10.1
Object Attributes Identity Manager Sets for Bidirectional Synchronization

EDIRECTORY OBJECT ATTRIBUTES	ACTIVE DIRECTORY	NT DOMAINS
User	User	User
CN	userprincipalName	Name
Description	description	Comment
Identity Manager-ADAliasName	SAMAccountName	NT4AccountName
Facsimile Telephone Number	facsimileTelephone Number	FullName
Full Name	displayName	
Given Name	givenName	
Group Membership	memberOf	
Login Disabled	userAccountControl	Logon Disabled
nadLoginName	nadLoginName	nadLoginName
Owner	managedBy	
Password Allow Change		PasswordChange
Password Required		PasswordRequired
Physical Delivery		
Office Name	I	
Postal Code	postalCode	
Post Office Box	postOfficeBox	
S	st	
SA	streetAddress	
See Also	seeAlso	
Surname	sn	
Telephone Number	telephoneNumber	
Title	title	
Unique ID	mailNickname	

EDIRECTORY OBJECT ATTRIBUTES	ACTIVE DIRECTORY	NT DOMAINS
Group	Group	
CN	cn	
Member	member	
Organizational Unit	Organizational Unit	
OU	ou	

Installing the Identity Manager Engine

Identity Manager Starter Pack components are installed on those servers that will participate in the data synchronization process. iManager components must also be installed on your iManager server if it is different from the server running the Identity Manager engine. To install the Identity Manager engine on your OES Linux server, complete the following steps:

1. At the OES Linux server where you want to install Identity Manager, insert the Identity Manager Bundle Edition CD-ROM.

2. Mount the CD-ROM, and then locate and execute the installation program `/linux/setup/dirxml_linux.bin`. You must execute this command as the root user.

3. Review the Welcome information and press Enter to continue.

4. At the License Agreement screen, review the agreement and enter **Y** to accept the usage terms.

5. Specify the appropriate number (1–4) for the components you want to install. The DirXML Server (option 1) must be installed on the local OES server. Remember that Identity Manager drivers and management components can be installed on separate servers from the Identity Manager engine, if you like. To install multiple components on the local server, either perform the installation multiple times, or select option 4 and customize the component installation list.

6. (Optional) Depending on the options you entered, you may be prompted for LDAP credentials or the server's SSL port.

7. Verify the summary information and press Enter to begin the package installation. If you have selected to install the DirXML server, your eDirectory server will be shut down during the installation.

8. After the installation has completed, press Enter to close the installation program.

9. (Optional) If you only installed the DirXML engine, repeat the installation and install the web-based Administrator Server components (option 3) on your iManager server. This is required to install the DirXML plug-ins for iManager. After installing the plug-ins, restart Apache using `rcapache2 restart` before the plug-ins will take effect.

After completing the installation, the eDirectory daemon should be automatically restarted. However, if you installed iManager plug-ins, you will be required to manually restart the Apache server, as documented in step 9. After everything has been restarted, iManager is the administrative tool used to configure Identity Manager. Accessing iManager should now show two new categories in iManager's Navigation frame—`DirXML` and `DirXML Utilities`. The options available beneath these categories are used to configure the actual data synchronization process and are described later in this chapter.

Installing Remote Loaders and Drivers

With the Identity Manager engine installed, you are ready to start configuring your Identity Manager environment. The first step in doing this is to make sure that the Remote Loader is installed on any systems that will use it. For both Active Directory and NT domain synchronization, the Identity Manager driver and Remote Loader must be installed on an appropriate Domain Controller. The Domain Controller should have the following characteristics:

- *Active Directory*—Domain Controller running Windows 2000 Server with Support Pack 1 and Internet Explorer 5.5 or later

- *NT Domain*—Primary Domain Controller (PDC) running Windows NT 4 with Service Pack 6a or later

To install Remote Loader and Identity Manager driver on a Windows 2000 server running Active Directory, complete the following steps. For more information on performing the same type of installation on an NT 4 server, see the OES Linux online documentation.

1. At the Windows 2000 server that will host the driver, insert the Identity Manager Bundle Edition CD-ROM. After a few moments, the Identity Manager Bundle Edition Installation screen will appear. Click Next.

2. At the License Agreement screen, select the appropriate language to view the license agreement. When you have reviewed the agreement, click I Accept.

3. If necessary, review the Identity Manager overview pages. Click Next to continue to the next overview page, and then Next again to continue the installation.

4. At the Components screen, deselect DirXML Server, DirXML Web Components and Utilities. Then select DirXML Connected System, to install the Identity Manager Remote Loader and Drivers, and click Next.

5. At the Location screen, specify the path to which the Remote Loader will be installed, and click Next. It is usually best to just accept the default path.

6. At the Select Drivers for Remote Loader Install screen, select the Remote Loader Service and the DirXML Driver for Active Directory, and then click Next.

7. Review the information on the Installation Summary screen, and click Finish. You may see a warning about LDAP conflicts. If so, click OK to close the message box.

8. At the Create Shortcut screen, click Yes. This will create a shortcut on your Windows desktop to the DirXML Remote Loader Console.

9. At the Installation Complete screen, click Close.

10. Launch the Identity Manager Remote Loader Configuration Wizard using `dirxml_remote.exe` found in the directory specified in step 5, typically `c:\Novell\RemoteLoader`. At the Welcome page, click Next.

11. At the Command Port screen, click Next. This is the port that will be used by this instance of the remote loader to listen for Identity Manager activity. Novell recommends keeping the default port.

12. At the Configuration File screen, click Next. This is the name and location of the log file that will be used to record Remote Loader configuration options.

13. At the DirXML Driver screen, select Native and make sure that `ADDRIVER.DLL` is listed in the drop-down list. Click Next.

14. At the Connection to Identity Manager screen, provide the required information and click Next.

- *Port*—Specify the port that Remote Loader will use to listen for the Identity Manager engine. Novell recommends keeping the default port.

- *Address*—Specify the IP address that Remote Loader will use to communicate with the Identity Manager engine.

- *Use SSL*—Check the Use SSL box if you want secure communications between the Identity Manager engine and Remote Loader. You will have to provide the self-signed certificate from the Identity Manager server in order to use SSL. For more information on using SSL, see the OES Linux online documentation.

15. At the Tracing screen, specify the level of tracking data that you want recorded, the location of the trace file, and click Next. You will likely want to set up tracing while installing and configuring your driver. However, when the driver configuration is complete, you will probably want to set the trace level to 0 to prevent the log file from growing to fill your entire hard drive over time.

- *Level 0*—No information display or tracking

- *Level 1*—General informational messages about processing

- *Level 2*—Displays messages from level 1 plus the XML documents that are passed between the engine and driver

- *Level 3*—Displays messages from level 2 plus documents sent and received between the Remote Loader and the Identity Manager engine

- *Level 4*—Displays messages from level 3 plus information about the connection between the Remote Loader and the Identity Manager engine

16. At the Install as a Service screen, check Install the Remote Loader Instance as a Service, and click Next. Doing this lets Remote Loader continue to run even after you have logged out of the Windows system.

17. At the Passwords screen, specify the password you want to set for access to Remote Loader and the Driver object, and click Next.

18. At the Summary screen, review your configuration settings, and click Finish. When prompted, click Yes to start the Remote Loader service.

With Remote Loader configured, Identity Manager will now be able to synchronize data between your central eDirectory tree and your secondary Active Directory environment. Data is mapped from one directory structure to the other as discussed previously (see Table 10.1).

To view the Remote Loader trace screen, which shows you the communication activities between the two directory environments, or to edit the configuration of your Remote Loader Driver, use the Remote Loader Console (as shown in Figure 10.2). An icon for this utility should have already been created on your desktop during the installation process.

FIGURE 10.2
Remote Loader Console.

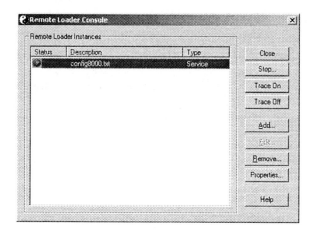

The Remote Loader Console provides access to the complete Remote Loader environment. From this console, you can start and stop driver instances, access trace screens, edit the properties of Remote Loader drivers, and add or delete drivers. When using this utility, keep in mind that some actions are only available if the selected driver is in a particular state, such as running or stopped. For example, to edit a driver's configuration, stop the driver and select the Edit button. This will invoke the Remote Driver Configuration page, as shown in Figure 10.3, where all the parameters entered during the Remote Loader Configuration Wizard process can be modified.

To create additional Remote Loader Drivers, the Add button on the Remote Loader Console can be used. Or, if you prefer, the Remote Loader Configuration Wizard can be manually started and used for the creation of additional drivers.

Installing Identity Manager on a Secondary eDirectory Tree

Each eDirectory tree that you want to synchronize with Identity Manager must have an Identity Manager driver installed and configured on a replica server of the secondary eDirectory tree. The first Identity Manager driver for eDirectory was installed as part of the Identity Manager engine installation, described previously. The Identity Manager driver installation for eDirectory will vary based on the platform that the host server is running. Identity Manager supports the following operating systems:

- NetWare 6.0 SP3 or later
- NetWare 6.5
- Windows NT/2000
- Red Hat AS/ES 2.1, AS 3.0
- SUSE Linux Enterprise Server 8 or 9
- Solaris 8 or 9
- AIX 5.2L

For more information on installing the Identity Manager driver in a secondary eDirectory tree, see the OES online documentation.

FIGURE 10.3
Remote Driver Configuration page.

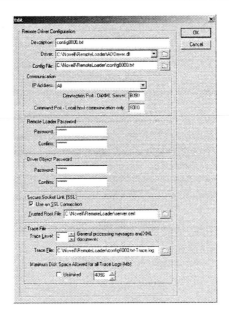

Configuring an Identity Manager Driver

Now that all the Identity Manager components are in place, you can do the actual Identity Manager driver configuration. This is done through the iManager plug-ins for Identity Manager that were installed previously. You can also use ConsoleOne to do the Identity Manager configuration if desired.

To simplify the configuration process, you can import the preconfigured driver settings that you have copied to your systems as part of the Identity Manager installation process, described previously. To import a preconfigured Identity Manager driver, complete the following steps:

1. Launch iManager from the server where the Identity Manager plug-ins have been installed.

2. Open the DirXML Utilities link in the Navigation frame and click Import Drivers.

3. Select the radio button next to In a New Driver Set, and click Next.

4. Provide the required information and click Next.

   - *Name*—Provide a name for the driver set.

   - *Context*—Specify the context in which you want the driver set object to be created.

   - *Server*—Specify the server object on which Identity Manager is installed.

   - *Create a New Partition on This Driver Set*—Selecting this option will create a new directory partition in which Identity Manager data will be stored, where it can be isolated from the rest of the day-to-day eDirectory activity. Novell recommends that you configure Identity Manager in this way.

5. Select the specific driver configuration file you want to import and click Next. You can select multiple drivers, if desired.

6. Provide the required information to configure the driver and click Next. If you have selected multiple drivers, you will have to fill out the appropriate configuration information for each driver. For more information on the specific information requested by each driver type, see the OES online documentation.

7. Provide the required information to configure administrative rights for the Identity Manager driver and click Next.

- Click Define Security Equivalence, add Admin, and click OK. This grants the Identity Manager driver security equivalence to Admin in eDirectory so that sufficient rights are granted the driver to perform its synchronization operations.

- Click Exclude Administrative Roles, add Admin, and click Next. You should add any objects with administrative roles to this list in order to avoid problems with similar objects that may exist in other directories. Typically, administrative roles are specific to a given directory tree and don't need to be synchronized.

8. At the Summary screen, click Finish. You can also click Finish with Overview if you want to view a synopsis of the driver's settings, as shown in Figure 10.4.

FIGURE 10.4
Identity Manager (DirXML) Overview screen.

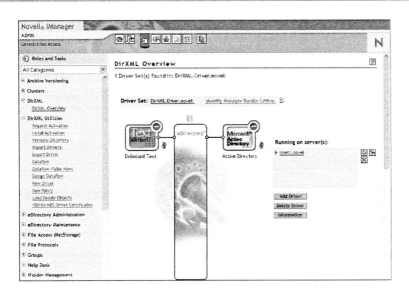

With the Identity Manager driver configured, you will see a new driver set in the Identity Manager (DirXML) Overview screen (Figure 10.4). This screen is accessible from the DirXML Overview link within the DirXML category of iManager. From this overview you can enable the driver and perform synchronization tests to make sure the driver is functioning properly. You can use the driver's trace screen to monitor activities as well as the Trace options in iMonitor. For advanced settings and detailed information on Identity Manager driver configuration, see the OES online documentation.

Identity Manager Password Synchronization

In addition to the synchronization of data between disparate systems such as eDirectory, Active Directory, and NT domains, Identity Manager Bundle Edition also enables you to synchronize passwords between these systems. Identity Manager Password Synchronization for Windows, known as PasswordSync, allows passwords to be transparently and securely synchronized between eDirectory and the Active Directory/NT domains for which you have Identity Manager drivers configured.

PasswordSync uses filters and agents to capture changes to passwords and securely pass those changes to included systems. Identity Manager is capable of understanding object mappings across systems so that each user object is associated with the proper object in every other system. Because of this, synchronizing passwords across the systems becomes much easier.

The specifics of how PasswordSync is installed depends on the systems involved. For example, because Microsoft clients forward password change requests to their respective Domain Controllers for processing, PasswordSync Filters are installed on all Domain Controllers in Active Directory and NT environments. On the other hand, because Novell clients never send passwords across the network, PasswordSync filters for eDirectory are installed on the client workstation and are part of the Novell clients that ship with OES NetWare.

Unfortunately, because password synchronization with Identity Manager relies on PasswordSync filters and agents communicating the changes throughout the environment, if a password is synchronized through an unsupported mechanism, the synchronization will not occur. One example of this is an LDAP client such as Novell eGuide. If you use an LDAP client to change your eDirectory password, the change will not be synchronized to your Active Directory and/or NT Domain environments because the PasswordSync filters are never involved in the process. Similarly, if a password is changed from a non-Windows environment, the change will not be synchronized.

Bottom line here: Use PasswordSync if you can be confident that password changes will only occur in one of the Windows methods supported by PasswordSync. For example:

- Workstation running the Novell client
- Workstation not running the Novell client
- Windows server or workstation running Microsoft Management Console
- Windows workstation or server running ConsoleOne
- Workstation or server running Novell iManager

For more information on configuring and using PasswordSync, see the OES online documentation.

PART III

Open Enterprise Server User Access

## CHAPTER 11

OES Linux File Storage and Management

Instant Access

Managing Logical Volumes

- To create, delete, or enlarge a logical volume, use the volume management options in iManager, or the console-based nssmu.

- To mount/dismount or activate/deactivate a logical volume, use the volume management options in iManager, or the console-based nssmu.

- To verify or rebuild a logical volume or pool, use the console-based ravsui.

Managing Disk Space

- To manage file compression, use nsscon to set file compression parameters.

- To limit users' disk space, use volume management options in iManager.

Managing Files

- To salvage or purge deleted files, use the NetWare Utilities option in the Novell Client or ConsoleOne.

- To display information about files and directories, view the NetWare Info tab of the file or directory properties using the Novell Client.

NSS Directory and File Security

- To view or change filesystem trustee assignments, use the `rights` command-line utility. The Novell Client and NetStorage can also be used.

- To view or change directory and file attributes, use `chmod` or NetStorage.

Backing Up and Restoring Files

- To back up and restore network files, use `nbackup` from the server console. For a more comprehensive backup/restore solution, use a third-party backup product that is SMS-compliant.

File storage and management are the core of any network server, and Novell NetWare has long offered the capability to manage files in many ways. The primary tool for file management has been Novell Storage Services (NSS). With OES Linux, Novell has brought this powerful filesystem to the Linux world.

This chapter looks at the various file storage capabilities and options available in OES Linux and discusses the advantages and potential pitfalls of each. This chapter also covers the SMS backup services offered with OES.

Novell Storage Services

Novell Storage Services (NSS) is a powerful storage and filesystem that provides an efficient way to use all the space on your storage devices. NSS cannot be used for the OES Linux root filesystem, which contains the SLES operating system files, but it can be used for any other storage space you would like to allocate.

NSS is now one of many different filesystems offered on Linux platforms. Although every filesystem's primary goal is to provide access to disk storage, each filesystem has its own particular features. NSS is no different and offers a wide range of features not available with any other filesystem.

Some of the main features of NSS are complete integration with eDirectory, extended Access Control Lists (ACLs), rights inheritance and filtering, support for multiple name spaces, and much, much more. Many of those capabilities are only possible through an NSS feature known as a backlink.

With NSS, each file or directory is backlinked to the parent directory. This means that not only does the parent know what objects are beneath it, but the child also knows what parent directories are above it. This feature is unique to NSS and offers several powerful capabilities. One benefit of this is visible when browsing directories with varying permissions. In non-NSS filesystems, all directories are visible even if you do not have permission to enter the directory. With NSS, backlinks are used to ensure directory visibility is confined to just the directories you have access to.

Another benefit is seen when assigning permissions. To provide access to a file several levels deep in a directory tree, NSS only requires that rights be assigned at that specific file or location. There is no need to traverse the tree, either manually or automatically, and assign rights. Through backlinks, NSS automatically determines the visibility of parent directories and ensures that users are able to traverse to the location where rights have been assigned.

NSS also offers many additional capabilities over traditional Linux filesystems. This does not mean that NSS is always the best choice, but understanding the capabilities of NSS should help you to make the right filesystem choice for whatever filesystem needs you may have. NSS is particularly useful in conjunction with other OES components, such as Novell Clustering Services (NCS) and the Novell Client. NSS is a powerful addition to your OES Linux infrastructure, and an important component to understand.

The first concept with which you should become familiar in the NSS filesystem is the *volume*. An NSS volume is the highest level in the filesystem hierarchy, and is the structure within which directories and files are maintained. From a Linux perspective, a volume is just another term for a filesystem or formatted partition.

NOTE

OES Linux has support for both NSS and NCP volumes. All OES Linux servers (with eDirectory) will have at least one NCP volume, known as SYS. This is actually the /usr/novell/sys directory, which is served to NCP-based clients as a volume. This directory contains files used in conjunction with NCP access to the server. More information regarding NCP volumes is available later in this chapter.

OES Linux does not automatically create any NSS volumes. These volumes can be created as needed using iManager or the command-line utility nssmu.

The volume is the last link in the NSS chain. Figure 11.1 gives a high-level view of the NSS architecture.

FIGURE 11.1
A high-level view of the NSS architecture.

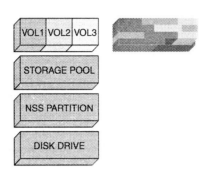

- *NSS partitions*—A *partition* is a logical organization of space on a hard disk, and represents the lowest level of organization for disk storage. Partitions prepare space on storage devices to be used in an organized and structured way by defining the ways in which the filesystem will interact with the storage devices.

- *NSS storage pools*—NSS storage pools are created in partitioned space. A *storage pool* is a specified amount of space you obtain from all your storage devices. Within the storage pool, you will create the NSS volumes you need on the server. Only one storage pool can exist on a partition, but you can create an unlimited number of NSS volumes in each storage pool, thereby removing partition constraints on the number of volumes that can be created.

- *NSS volumes*—The volumes you create from NSS storage pools are called *logical volumes*. As shown in Figure 11.1, they are logical volumes because the space used to create a given volume can come from a variety of storage devices. It is not contiguous space. A logical volume can be set to a specific size, or allowed to grow dynamically according to the amount of physical space assigned to the pool. This lets you add and store any size or any number of files you need without having to create other partitions. You can add any number of volumes to a storage pool as long as you have available physical space in the pool.

Beyond these three NSS building blocks, you should be aware of several concepts related to the configuration and management of NSS volumes:

- *NSS management*—You will use iManager for configuring and managing your NSS environment. It gives you the ability to control and change your server's storage characteristics from any place with an Internet connection. In addition to iManager, there are terminal-based management tools, such as nssmu, as well. These utilities must be used from terminals on the OES machine.

- *Overbook your storage pool*—Individual logical volumes cannot exceed the size of a storage pool. However, because you can create multiple logical volumes in a single storage pool, OES Linux permits the total space allocated to logical volumes to exceed the actual pool size. This feature, called *overbooking*, can be an efficient way to manage your filesystem because it lets your volumes grow organically over time instead of being locked into a rigid structure that can leave space unused.

- *Deactivate/activate logical volumes and storage pools*—You might need to temporarily prevent user access to storage pools or volumes to perform maintenance. Instead of bringing down the server, you can deactivate individual storage pools. When you deactivate a storage pool, users will not have access to any of the volumes in that pool.

- *Fast error correction and data recovery*—Because NSS is a journaled filesystem, it can quickly recover data after a filesystem crash. Instead of scanning the filesystem for corruption, NSS replays the latest set of changes to make sure they were written correctly. The filesystem either recovers the changed information or returns it to its original condition prior to the transaction.

- *Immediately save data to disk*—The Flush Files Immediately feature saves your file data to disk immediately after you close the file instead of caching it in memory and waiting for the next disk write cycle. This prevents your data from being at risk between disk write cycles, at the cost of slower filesystem performance overall.

- *Retain previously saved files (Snapshot)*—The File Snapshot feature keeps an original copy of all open files so they can be archived by your backup utility. By capturing the most recent closed copy of the file, Snapshot guarantees that you still have a solid copy of the file with which to work.

- *Salvage Files*—This option causes deleted files to be marked as purgeable space on the pool. Deleted files can be salvaged until the purgeable space is reclaimed as free space. This can be done manually by an administrator or automatically through the Purge Delay time.

- *Transaction Tracking System (TTS)*—Transaction Tracking System protects database applications by backing out transactions that are incomplete due to a system failure. To enable TTS for an NSS volume, select the User-level Transaction Model option in the Volume properties page of iManager.

- *Review the modified file list*—NSS maintains a list of files that have been modified since the previous backup. To save time, your backup utility only has to review this list rather than scanning the entire filesystem for modified files.

- *Enable file compression*—NSS supports file compression. This lets you decide whether to compress the files in your volumes for more efficient use of storage device space. When it's enabled, however, you cannot disable file compression without re-creating the volumes.

- *Data shredding*—The data shredding feature overwrites purged disk blocks with random patterns of hexadecimal characters. This is a security option that helps prevent the use of a disk editor to attempt to recover purged files. You can require up to seven random shred patterns to be written over deleted data.

- *User space restrictions*—From iManager, you can now limit the amount of space available to an individual user on a logical volume.

- *Directory space restrictions*—From iManager, you can now limit the space that can be assigned to a given directory or subdirectory.

- *Repair storage pools instead of individual volumes*—Use the repair utility `ravsui` to perform a verify or rebuild operation to repair the NSS systems. The verify and rebuild operations function on the pool level rather than the individual volume level. These utilities should be used only as a last resort to recover the filesystem after data corruption.

  - *Verify*—Checks the filesystem integrity of an NSS pool by searching for inconsistent data blocks or other errors. This operation indicates whether there are problems with the filesystem.

  - *Rebuild*—Verifies and uses the existing leaves of an object tree to rebuild all the other trees in the system.

NOTE

In order to perform either a verify or rebuild operation, the NSS pool must be deactivated and marked as being in a maintenance mode. This will deactivate all volumes in the pool automatically.

- *RAID support*—NSS provides software support for RAID 0 (data striping), RAID 1 (data mirroring), and RAID 5 (data striping with parity) to give you a robust set of options for protecting your server data. You can create and manage software RAID through iManager or through the console-based NSS Management utility (nssmu).

Understanding these NSS concepts will make it easier for you to plan and manage your NSS filesystem.

Planning the Filesystem

Now that you know a little about NSS, you can start planning your OES Linux filesystem. Throughout the planning phase, keep in mind that this is not referring to the root filesystem, where your operating system and Linux applications are traditionally installed. Plan your NSS file structure around shared applications and network storage that are yet to be created. After implementing your NSS plan, you can create and configure these applications and data repositories for use by the appropriate OES component. With that in mind, consider the following tips for creating a robust, accessible, and easy-to-manage filesystem:

- NSS filesystems under Linux can be used in two distinct modes—NetWare mode and Linux mode. In *Linux mode*, NSS volumes are accessed using local Linux user accounts. In this mode, the extended trustee capabilities of NSS are not available, and NSS behaves like any other Linux filesystem, with regard to permissions. In *NetWare mode*, user accounts are redirected back to eDirectory. This allows eDirectory to control permissions and enables the advanced trustee framework available with NSS. When implementing NSS volumes, you should plan your layout according to the mode the volumes will be used with. Each NSS volume should only be accessed using one of these modes—not both.

WARNING

Accessing an NSS volume through both eDirectory-based user accounts (such as admin) and local accounts (such as root) will result in unpredictable behavior of permissions. Data will be consistent across access methods, but eDirectory trustee assignments are much more complex than POSIX permissions and are not entirely compatible. Plan your NSS volumes to ensure that only one access method is used.

- To simplify data backup, separate your applications and data into distinct volumes. Application volumes will be relatively stable over time, so they can be backed up less frequently than a data volume in which files are changing constantly. For more information about backing up files, see the "Backing Up and Restoring Files" section later in this chapter.

- If different applications will be available to different groups of users, try to organize the applications' directory structures so that you can assign comprehensive rights in a parent directory. This can help prevent you from having to create multiple individual rights assignments at lower-level subdirectories. More information on filesystem rights is available later in this chapter.

- If you want to use file compression to compress less frequently used files, try to group those types of files into directories separate from other files that are used more often. That way you can turn on compression for the less frequently used directories and leave it turned off for the frequently used directories. For more information about file compression, see the "File Compression" section later in this chapter.

- Decide whether you want users' daily work files to reside in personal directories, in project-specific directories, or in some other type of directory structure. Encourage your users to store their files on the network so that the network backup process can back up those files regularly, and so the files can be protected by NSS security.

These tips can help you effectively plan your filesystem. In addition, you must also understand how OES Linux provides access to NSS volumes. When you understand client access methods, you may need to adjust your NSS volume layout accordingly. These issues are described in the following sections.

ACCESSING NSS VOLUMES

At their fundamental level, NSS volumes are simply formatted filesystems. However, clients can potentially access these filesystems through several different methods. These access methods are typically specific to the OES component involved, like NetDrive or iFolder, but there is one access method that was specifically designed with NSS volumes in mind—NCP.

The Novell NetWare Core Protocol (NCP) has been an important client/server networking protocol in Novell networks for years. Once based on IPX, this protocol runs over IP and provides login and file access capabilities, among other services, to NetWare servers and client workstations. The most prevalent example of the power of NCP is the Novell Client.

As explained in Chapter 4, "OES Linux Clients," the Novell Client is one of the primary methods of accessing NetWare resources from a workstation. The Client performs this function through the NCP protocol. The Client uses NCP to communicate directly with eDirectory for login and authentication. It is also through NCP that such things as file-level permissions and printer access control are obtained by the Client. With OES Linux, it was important to maintain those capabilities, and also bring the additional features, like login scripts, to the Linux platform. This goal was accomplished through the NCP Server component of OES Linux.

The NCP Server is actually an integrated component of Novell eDirectory. However, its role is separate from the traditional view of eDirectory. The main purpose of the NCP Server is to provide NCP services, such as file and print, to workstations running the Novell Client. The NCP Server is therefore an important component with regard to file access.

Using the NCP Server, directories on your OES Linux server can be shared over NCP as an NCP volume. These NCP volumes on Linux then appear exactly like volumes that are available on a NetWare server. This means that a workstation running the Novell Client can access any NCP volume using just the server name and NCP volume name.

One user-accessible NCP volume is created by default with OES Linux—SYS. The directory on the local filesystem for the SYS volume is /usr/novell/sys. This directory is referred to as the *mount point* of the NCP volume, although no separate partition is required to be mounted there. Workstations running the Novell Client can directly access that directory by mapping a local drive through the Client to the SYS volume.

The SYS volume is important for Novell Client workstations due to the directories stored there. By default, the following two directories can be found on the SYS NCP volume:

- PUBLIC holds the Novell tools necessary to log in and map drives to NCP resources.
- LOGIN holds those files required for user access even though they are not yet logged in to the Novell environment. This includes the basic utilities necessary to help accomplish an eDirectory login.

The method used by the NCP Server for sharing a local directory as an NCP volume is the same method used to make NSS volumes available to client workstations. This is important as it means that NSS volumes must first be mounted locally, and then exported (automatically) as NCP volumes.

Because the volumes are mounted into the root filesystem, access to the volume can be granted through any possible method of accessing the local disk. This includes such things as through NFS and Samba shares. To allow for access through multiple methods, you may want to adjust the mount point of the NSS shares to match requirements imposed by other services.

NOTE

Accessing NSS volumes through traditional Linux methods, such as NFS or Samba, does not automatically put the volume into Linux mode. Whether an NSS volume is in Linux mode or NetWare mode is completely dependent on where the user account is being stored. If Samba authentication is being redirected to eDirectory, the NSS volume is still being used in NetWare mode and the advanced trustee capabilities of NSS are available.

NSS VOLUME CONSIDERATIONS

With an understanding of how clients will access the NSS volumes, it is possible to plan your volume layout. This layout should include what NSS volumes you would like to create, and possibly what directory structure should exist on that volume.

One consideration should be whether to have one volume or many. For the most part, applications should not require a dedicated volume. However, multiple volumes allow you to tune volume-wide settings for optimal performance of a specific application. Care should be taken to not overdo this, though, as too many volumes may result in unwanted administrative overhead.

It is also possible to create separate directory structures for each application or storage location. This is true for both single volume and multivolume configurations. Through a properly planned file structure, it is much easier to assign trustee rights that grant users access to what they need, but without granting them access to things they don't. For example, general-use applications can be organized in an **APPS** volume, each in its own subdirectory. With this configuration, rights to these applications can be easily assigned high in the directory structure where they will flow down, through inheritance, to all subdirectories. More information on filesystem rights is available later in this chapter.

If an application requires that it be installed at the root of a filesystem, NSS gives you the flexibility of installing the application where it makes sense and then creating a root drive mapping to fool the application into thinking it is operating from a root location in the filesystem. Creating a root drive mapping requires the redirector capabilities of either the Novell Client or the NetDrive Client. See Chapter 4 for more information on the Novell Client. See Chapter 12, "OES Linux File Access," for more information on NetDrive.

You can create a map root from the client, but if it is needed for a large number of users, a much better way is to include the **map** command in the appropriate login script. The eDirectory login script is a batch file that outlines basic operations that should be performed every time the user logs in to the network. Login script operations can include environment variables, drive mappings, program execution, and message display.

Through a login script, a **map** operation can be performed automatically when each user logs in, and changes to every workstation will not be necessary. For example, you can add the following command to a container login script to root map a drive for all users within the container:

```
MAP ROOT X:=VOL1:APPS\ABC
```

For more information about login scripts, see the online OES documentation.

If you decide to host an application from the Linux server, you should flag the application's executable files as Shareable, Read-Only (S, Ro). This allows the application to be used by multiple users simultaneously, but prevents users from inadvertently deleting or modifying it. This is an additional layer of protection beyond that provided by restricting access to the files at the directory level. More information on filesystem rights is available later in this chapter.

Working with NSS Volumes

You can create NSS storage structures as needed, both during the installation process and after the server installation is complete. Given that, it is probably a good idea to understand the technology and storage concepts a little before you start doing a lot of storage management. You can configure and manage NSS after installation with iManager or the console-based NSS Management utility (**nssmu**).

With NSS, you use partitions, storage pools, and logical volumes. You create logical volumes in storage pools that are composed of free space from the various storage devices in your server.

NSS uses free space from multiple storage devices. NSS allows you to mount up to 255 volumes simultaneously and store up to 8 trillion files in a single volume—up to 8TB (terabytes) in size.

The main components of the NSS filesystem were introduced at the beginning of this chapter. The following sections explain how to install, create, and work with NSS resources.

INSTALLING NSS

NSS is normally installed during the main OES Linux installation. However, NSS can be added after the main installation using YaST. The following steps document this process:

1. Access YaST from a terminal using **yast**, or from a graphical environment using **yast2** or the YaST launcher from the application menu.

2. Select the System category in YaST. From within this category, locate and select the NSS module. This module will detect that the RPMs for NSS are missing and ask if you want to install them. Select Continue to install the necessary packages.

3. At the conclusion of the software installation, **SuSEconfig** is executed to update the system configuration. When this completes, the configuration of the OES component will begin automatically.

4. At the Novell Storage Services LDAP Server Configuration screen, enter the following information and click Next:

   ■ *Local or Remote Directory Server*—Select the radio button that indicates whether eDirectory is running on the local server or a remote server.

   ■ *Directory Server Address*—If a remote eDirectory server is in use, enter the IP address for this server.

   ■ *Admin Name with Context*—Enter the eDirectory administrator's credentials using fully qualified dot notation, for example, **cn=admin.o=novell**.

   ■ *Admin Password*—Enter the password for the administrator user.

   ■ *Port Details*—If necessary, select this button to change the configured ports for the eDirectory server you specified earlier. The default LDAP port for unencrypted communications is **389** and port **636** is used for SSL-encrypted communications.

5. At the NSS Unique Admin Object screen, enter a fully qualified name for the NSS administrator object. Each server in the eDirectory tree must have its own NSS administrator object. After entering the name, click Next to complete the installation.

6. In order for NSS to be active, you should restart the Linux server. If you would like to start NSS services manually, you can execute **/etc/init.d/novell-nss start**.

NOTE

Unlike other startup scripts, the NSS startup script (/etc/init.d/novell-nss) only accepts the **start** command-line parameter. This is due to the kernel module requirements of this component. If you want to completely disable NSS, you must use **insserv** or **chkconfig** to remove this service from your Linux startup process.

PARTITIONS

With NSS, you probably won't have to manage partitions directly because they are automatically created to support the storage pools you define. However, if you want to create non-NSS partitions, you can do so from YaST by following these steps:

1. Access YaST from a terminal using **yast**, or from a graphical environment using **yast2** or the YaST launcher from the application menu.

2. Select the System category in YaST, and select the Partitioner module.

3. At the Expert Partitioner page, you can create a new partition by clicking the Create button.

4. Select the device on which the partition should be created, and designate the partition as a primary or extended partition. At the Create Partition page, specify at least the following information (see Figure 11.2):

   - *Size*—Adjust the partition size by designating the appropriate start and end cylinders. The start cylinder is not normally adjusted, and the end cylinder can be determined automatically be entering sizes in the format of +2.7GB (for a 2.7-Gigabyte volume).

   - *Mount Point*—Select or enter the directory that will be used as the mount point for this partition.

   - *Format*—Select Format to automatically format the new partition with the designated filesystem type. Possible options are EXT2/3, FAT, JFS, Reiser, XFS. If this partition should be an encrypted filesystem, select the Encrypt FileSystem check box.

FIGURE 11.2
Creating non-NSS partitions using YaST.

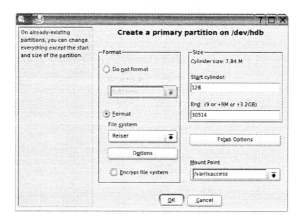

NSS leverages the Enterprise Volume Management System (EVMS) to bring NSS support to Linux. As such, common EVMS utilities such as `evmsgui` can be used to create and manage NSS partitions. This also allows traditional Linux filesystem utilities, such as `mkfs` and `mount`, to format and mount NSS volumes. Linux gurus may find the traditional utilities more favorable, but iManager is generally a more user-friendly way of working with NSS.

iManager automatically creates NSS partitions when NSS pools and volumes are created. This significantly reduces the complexity of managing disk partitions. For more information on low-level management of NSS partitions, see the online OES Linux documentation.

STORAGE POOLS

A *storage pool* is a specific amount of space you obtain from one or more storage devices in your server. OES Linux has integrated the partition-creation process into the process for creating storage pools. NSS storage pools provide the flexibility of NSS. They can be created to span one or multiple partitions on the hardware side, and can be divided into one or multiple logical volumes on the user side.

After a pool is created, you can add storage devices to your server and then expand the pool to include the space available on the new storage device. To create a new storage pool, complete the following steps:

1. Launch iManager, open the Storage link, and select Pools in the Navigation frame.

2. At the Pool Management page, specify the server with which you want to work. This will bring up the storage pool information for that server, as shown in Figure 11.3.

3. Click New to create a new storage pool.

4. Specify the name of the storage pool and click Next. Make sure to follow the naming conventions as outlined.

5. At the Select Device and Space page, choose the storage device(s) from which the new storage pool will get its space, specify the amount of space for each device, and then click Finish. Check Activate on Creation if you want the pool to be available as soon as it is created.

After creating the pool, you will be returned to the Pool Management page, from which you can perform various configuration tasks on storage pools and view the characteristics of pools that have been created. Configuration options include the following:

- *New*—Allows you to create new storage pools, as described previously.
- *Delete*—Allows you to delete an existing storage pool.
- *Rename*—Allows you to rename an existing storage pool.
- *Activate*—Makes a pool, and all volumes associated with that pool, available for use.
- *Deactivate*—Removes a pool, and all volumes associated with that pool, from service. Users cannot access data on an inactive pool. This might be done so that you can perform maintenance on the pool or its associated volumes.
- *Increase Size*—Allows you to add space to a storage pool.
- *Snapshot*—This pool-level feature is not available on Linux-based NSS pools.
- *Update eDirectory*—If you have modified or renamed a storage pool, use this option to update the eDirectory pool object with the new information and characteristics.
- *(Conditional) Deleted Volumes*—If you have deleted volumes from a storage pool, you can use this option to salvage or purge those deleted volumes.
- *(Conditional) Offline*—This pool-level feature is not available on Linux-based NSS pools.

FIGURE 11.3
Managing storage pools from iManager.

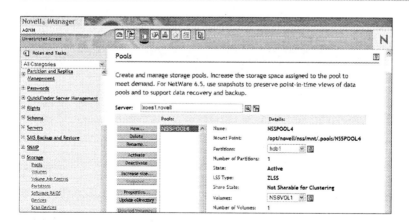

These options give you granular control over the management and performance of the storage pools on your OES Linux server.

LOGICAL VOLUMES

After a storage pool has been created, you are ready for NSS logical volumes. NSS volumes can be set to a specific size or set to grow dynamically within the storage pool according to the amount of storage space that is needed over time. When set to grow dynamically, NSS volumes can automatically take advantage of new storage devices when their space is added to their associated storage pool.

After you've created the volume, you must mount it before network users can access it. To create and mount a new NSS volume, complete the following steps:

1. Launch iManager, open the Storage link, and select Volumes in the Navigation frame.

2. At the Volume Management page, specify the server with which you want to work. This will bring up the volume information for that server, as shown in Figure 11.4.

3. Click New to create a new volume.

FIGURE 11.4
Managing server volumes from iManager.

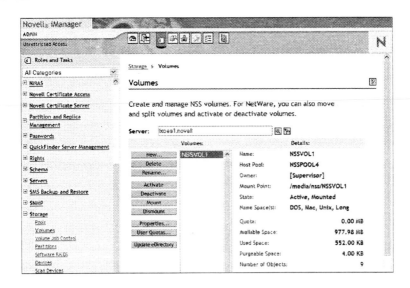

4. Specify the name of the volume and click Next. Be sure to follow the naming conventions as outlined.

5. At the Select a Pool and Volume Quota page, provide the required information and click Next. The required information includes:

- *Storage Pool*—Check the box next to the storage pool from which the volume will be created. You can also click the New Pool button to create a new storage pool for this volume. Doing this will drop you into step 4 of the storage pool creation process, discussed previously.

- *Allow Volume Quota to Grow to Pool Size*—If you don't want to specify a volume quota, check this box to let the volume grow dynamically to fit the available pool space.

6. At the Attribute Information page, make your desired selections and click Finish. The selections you can make include:

- *Backup*—This option marks the volume data for backup, similar to setting the Archive bit on a file or directory.

- *Compression*—Turns data compression on for this volume. Compression will use volume space much more efficiently at the cost of read performance. If volume data is not used constantly, compression can be a good idea.

- *Data Shredding*—Instructs NSS to overwrite deleted data with random characters to prevent recovery with disk reader software. Specify how many overwrite passes to make (1–7).

- *Directory Quotas*—Sets a limit on the amount of space that any directory can occupy. This might be useful for restricting the size of application, log, or user directories you don't want to grow beyond a certain point.

- *Flush Files Immediately*—Instructs NSS to write data to disk immediately upon file close, rather than waiting for the next write cycle.

- *Migration*—Enables support for near-line storage, such as optical subsystems. Migration creates a lookup key in the volume's File Allocation Table (FAT) that describes how to retrieve the data from the near-line storage system.

- *Modified File List*—Displays a list of files modified since the last backup cycle. This is useful for archive utilities, so they don't have to scan the entire volume for changed files.

- *Salvage*—Instructs NSS to keep deleted files until the space is needed for new data, so they can be recovered if necessary.

- *Snapshot - file level*—Instructs NSS to keep a copy of the last closed version of each open file in this volume. That way, archive utilities can save the copy to provide some protection in the event of data loss.

- *User Space Quotas*—Allows you to set usage limits for individual eDirectory users. When a quota is reached, users will be unable to save any more files until they have made space for them by removing other files.

- *User-Level Transaction Model*—Enables Novell's Transaction Tracking System (TTS) for the volume. This helps protect databases from corruption that might occur if a failure happens during a database transaction. With TTS turned on, an incomplete transaction is completely backed out and restored to its original state prior to the transaction. TTS protects data by making a copy of the original data before it is overwritten by new data. Then, if a failure of some component occurs in the middle of the transaction, TTS restores the data to its original condition and discards the incomplete transaction.

- *On Creation*—This section allows you to specify whether to activate and/or mount the new volume upon creation. Activating a volume is what makes it available for use. Mounting a volume associates that volume with a directory on the OES root filesystem. If you select to mount the volume, you must also identify a directory used as a mount point.

After the volume has been created, you will be returned to the Volume Management page, from which you can perform various configuration tasks on existing volumes and view the characteristics of volumes that have been created. Configuration options include the following:

- *New*—Allows you to create new volumes, as described previously.

- *Delete*—Allows you to delete an existing volume. All data on a deleted volume is removed, but salvage and purge options for deleted volumes are available at the storage pool level.

- *Rename*—Allows you to rename an existing volume.

- *Activate*—Makes a volume available for mounting and use by the server.

- *Deactivate*—Makes a volume temporarily unavailable for use by the server. A volume cannot be mounted while it is deactivated.

- *Mount*—Makes a volume available for use by network users, who can then access the volumes through any of the access methods supported by OES Linux.

- *Dismount*—Makes a volume temporarily unavailable for use by network users.

- *Properties*—This option lets you make changes to volume attributes, as defined when the volume was created. Volume attributes were discussed previously, during the volume creation process.

- *User Quotas*—If you have enabled the User Space Restrictions attribute on a volume, use this option to set those space restrictions. This is often useful for limiting the amount of space available to users' home directories.

- *Update eDirectory*—If you have modified or renamed a volume, use this option to update the eDirectory volume object with the new information and characteristics.

These volume configuration options give you granular control over the management and performance of the NSS volumes on your OES Linux servers.

Console-Based NSS Management Utilities

Traditional NSS management utilities are console-level tools written for the NetWare platform. With NSS now available on Linux, these same tools have been brought over to the OES Linux platform. The two main console tools for NSS are the NSS Management Utility and the NSS Console.

NSS MANAGEMENT UTILITY (nssmu)

The NSS Management Utility, or **nssmu**, is the primary tool for creating NSS pools and volumes from the command line. This utility also has the ability to enable RAID configurations and manage storage devices and partitions. iManager offers the same general features of **nssmu** and is the preferred tool for managing NSS.

The NSS Management Utility is installed to the **/sbin** directory and can be executed by entering **nssmu** via a terminal by an administrative user. For more information on **nssmu**, see the man page for **nssmu** (man 8 nssmu) or view the online OES Linux documentation.

NSS CONSOLE (nsscon)

The NSS Console, **nsscon**, was created to make the NetWare NSS console commands available on Linux. These commands are used to both manage the available NSS resources and tune the many NSS configuration parameters. The NSS Console will also act as a running log of NSS activity and can be used in troubleshooting NSS problems.

The NSS Console is installed to the /sbin directory and can be executed by entering **nsscon** via a terminal by an administrative user. After **nsscon** is started, you are presented with the **nsscon** prompt, which is the name of the server followed by a greater-than (>) sign. All commands entered at this prompt must be in the following format:

```
nss <PARAMETER>
```

NSS pools and volumes can be displayed using the following syntax:

```
nss pools
```

```
nss volumes
```

NSS parameters can also be adjusted by locating the specific parameter and configuring a new value using the following syntax:

```
nss /AllocAheadBlks=30
```

To view a list of the most commonly used NSS configurable parameters, execute the following command:

```
nss help
```

All **nsscon** parameters are case insensitive and can be abbreviated as long as there is no ambiguity in the parameter name. Also, parameters can be set on system startup by adding the parameter setting to the NSS configuration file: /opt/novell/nss/conf/nssstart.cfg.

To exit the NSS Console, enter **exit** at the **nsscon** prompt. For more information on the NSS Console, see the online OES Linux documentation.

OTHER NSS CONSOLE UTILITIES

The NSS Management Utility and Console are not the only command-line tools for NSS with OES Linux. Table 11.1 lists the remaining console-based utilities used with NSS. More information regarding these utilities is available through the online OES Linux documentation.

TABLE 11.1
Console-Based NSS Utilities

COMMAND	DESCRIPTION
nss	Used to list, activate, and deactivate NSS pools.
nssmu	NSS Management Utility used to create and delete NSS partitions, pools, and volumes. Can also be used to enable RAID configurations.
nsscon	NSS Console used to adjust tuning parameters of NSS.

COMMAND	DESCRIPTION
nssscan	Maintenance utility used to scan or restore an NSS pool.
nssmount	Used to mount NSS volumes.
nssupdate	Used to update eDirectory information for NSS pools.
ravsui	The Rebuild And Verify Simple User Interface utility is used to perform maintenance on NSS pools.
ravview	The Rebuild And Verify Viewer utility is used to view report files generated through maintenance procedures with ravsui.

Repairing NSS Pools

When a problem occurs in the NSS environment, repairs are made at the storage pool level rather than at the volume level. There are two basic types of repair operations for NSS pools:

- *Verify*—This operation checks the filesystem integrity for an NSS pool by searching for inconsistent data blocks or other errors. This process will indicate if there are problems with the filesystem.

- *Rebuild*—This operation actually makes repairs to the NSS storage pool should they prove necessary.

NOTE

The rebuild process should be a last resort and is seldom necessary. The NSS filesystem is *journaled*, meaning that it keeps a log of disk activities while they are executing. When a disk crash or other problem occurs, NSS automatically rolls the filesystem state back to a known good state and then re-executes the operations in the journal to bring the system back up to date.

Verify and rebuild operations can only be performed on deactivated pools that are designated as being in a maintenance mode. Pools can easily be deactivated through iManager (using the Storage, Pools page), but the nsscon utility must be used to designate a pool in maintenance mode. The nsscon utility can also be used to deactivate a pool. As such, it may be easier to perform both operations directly through nsscon. To deactivate and mark a pool in maintenance mode using nsscon, perform the following steps:

1. From a terminal on the OES machine, launch nsscon.

2. From the nsscon command prompt, enter **nss pools** to retrieve a listing of all NSS pools.

3. Using a pool name located in step 2, deactivate the pool by entering **nss /PoolDeactivate=<*POOL_NAME*>** at the nsscon prompt.

4. To mark the pool as being in a maintenance mode, enter **nss /PoolMaintenance=<*POOL_NAME*>** at the nsscon prompt.

5. While the pool is in maintenance mode, perform the verify or rebuild operation using ravsui. (This is explained in more detail following these steps.)

6. To reactivate the pool, enter **nss /PoolActivate=<*POOL_NAME*>** at the nsscon prompt.

7. When the pool is reactivated, you can activate and mount volumes through iManager, or by entering **nss /VolumeActivate=<*VOLUME_NAME*>** at the nsscon prompt. To view a list of volumes through nsscon, enter **nss volumes**.

As previously mentioned, NSS maintenance can only be performed while the pool is in maintenance mode. After setting maintenance mode on a pool, you can execute a verify operation, which is a read-only assessment of the storage pool, by typing the following command at a server console:

```
ravsui verify <NSS_POOL_NAME>
```

Should it become necessary, you can perform a rebuild by entering the following command at the server console:

```
ravsui rebuild <NSS_POOL_NAME>
```

The rebuild operation verifies and accounts for all data blocks in the storage pool. If there are any errors, the errors appear on the screen and are also recorded in rebuild log files. The verify operation also records log files of the operation. All ravsui log files are written to the /var/opt/novell/log/nss/rav directory. However, these logs are written in XML format and are not intended to be directly viewed. To view these log files properly, use the ravview utility.

The ravview utility is used to view both verify and rebuild log files. However, the utility must be told what type of log file is being viewed. This is accomplished with the following startup switches:

```
ravview rtf <REBUILD_LOG_FILE>
```

```
ravview vbf <VERIFY_REPORT_FILE>
```

The most recent log files corresponding to a specific pool can also be viewed by using the following syntax:

```
ravview rtfn <POOL_NAME>
```

```
ravview vbfn <POOL_NAME>
```

After reviewing log files and completing any rebuild or verify operations, remember to reactivate and mount the pool and volume(s). Users will be unable to access data until this final step is completed.

NOTE

For more information on `ravsui`, `ravview`, and other NSS command-line functions, see the utility help screen (`-help`) and OES Linux online documentation.

Saving Disk Space

OES Linux offers a few simple features to help you to conserve disk space if it becomes an issue:

- NSS file compression, which compresses less frequently used files, has been shown to conserve up to 63% of your hard disk space. However, your specific experience will vary depending on the types of files being stored on the server.

- Restricting users' disk space enables you to decide how much room user data can consume on a given volume.

- Purging files from NSS volumes lets you free up disk space by removing files that have been deleted but are still retained in a salvageable state. (You can also salvage deleted files, instead of purging them, but of course that doesn't free up any disk space.)

Although none of these is a replacement for adding disk space to your server, they can help you keep things running smoothly while you prepare to upgrade your hardware.

FILE COMPRESSION

File compression typically can save up to 63% of the server's hard disk space by compressing unused files. Compressed files are automatically decompressed when a user accesses them, so the user doesn't necessarily know that the files were compressed.

Volumes are automatically enabled to support compression if you enable that attribute when the volume is created. You can also enable support for compression after the fact by modifying a volume's properties with iManager.

After compression is enabled on a volume, it cannot be disabled, except by deleting and re-creating the volume. However, through proper management of volume compression, it is possible to nearly prevent files from being compressed.

By default, when a volume is created with compression turned on, files and directories are compressed automatically after they've been untouched for 14 days.

You can change several aspects of file compression, however, such as how long the files wait before being compressed, the time of day the compression activity occurs, and which files never get compressed. To control file compression, you can use two directory attributes and several **nsscon** commands.

To specify compression for specific volumes or directories, you can assign them the following attributes with the Novell Client. To do this, access the NSS volume through the Novell client, and view the properties of the volume or directory using the right-click menu. Select the NetWare Info tab and modify the following attributes:

- *Don't Compress*—Instructs NSS to never compress the directory, even if compression is turned on for a parent directory.
- *Immediate Compress*—Instructs NSS to compress the directory immediately, without waiting the standard inactivity period.

The **nsscon** commands that affect file compression let you control compression characteristics for all enabled volumes on the server. You can set options such as when compression happens, how many files can be compressed at the same time, how many times a file must be accessed before it is decompressed, and so on. You must use **nsscon** to view and change these parameters.

NOTE

Remember that if you change a compression parameter using nsscon, the change affects all files and directories in all volumes on the server that have been enabled for compression.

To change the compression parameters, complete the following steps:

1. From a terminal on the OES machine, launch **nsscon**.
2. Modify any of the NSS parameters by entering the following at the **nsscon** prompt:

   nss *<Parameter>*=*<Value>*

NSS parameters are not case sensitive. To view a complete list of parameters, use nss ? at the nsscon prompt. All parameters, as well as their current settings, are displayed on the screen. Compression-related parameters are as follows:

- /CompressionDailyCheckStopHour=HOUR—Specifies the hour when the file compressor stops searching volumes for files that need to be compressed. If this value is the same as the Compression Daily Check Starting Hour value, the search starts at the specified starting hour and goes until all compressible files have been found. The default is 6 (6:00 a.m.). Values range from 0 (midnight) to 23 (11:00 p.m.).

- /CompressionDailyCheckStartingHour=HOUR—Specifies the hour when the file compressor begins searching volumes for files that need to be compressed. The default is 0 (midnight). Values range from 0 to 23 (11:00 p.m.).

- /MinimumCompressionPercentageGain=NUMBER—Specifies the minimum percentage that a file must be able to be compressed in order to remain compressed. The default is 20. Values range from 0 to 50.

- /(No)EnableFileCompression—When this option is set to On (/EnableFileCompression), file compression is allowed to occur on volumes that are enabled for compression. If this option is set to Off (/NoEnableFileCompression), file compression won't occur, even though the volume is still enabled for compression. The default is On.

- /MaximumConcurrentCompressions=NUMBER—Specifies how many volumes can compress files at the same time. Increasing this value can slow down server performance during compression times. The default is 2. Values range from 1 to 8.

- /ConvertCompressedToUncompressedOption=NUMBER—Specifies how a compressed file is stored after it has been accessed. The default is 1. Values range from 0 = always leave the file compressed; 1 = leave the file compressed after the first access within the time frame defined by the Days Untouched Before Compression parameter, and then leave the file uncompressed after the second access; 2 = change the file to uncompressed after the first access.

- /DecompressPercentDiskSpaceFreeToAllowCommit=NUMBER— Specifies the percentage of free disk space that is required on a volume before committing an uncompressed file to disk. This helps you avoid running out of disk space by uncompressing files. The default is 10. Values range from 0 to 75.

- `/DecompressFreeSpaceWarningInterval=TIME`—Specifies the interval between warnings when the volume doesn't have enough disk space for uncompressed files. The default is 31 min 18.5 sec. Values range from 0 sec (which turns off warnings) to 29 days 15 hours, 50 min 3.8 sec.

- `/DeletedFilesCompressionOption=NUMBER`—Specifies how the server handles deleted files. The default is 1. Values range from 0 = don't compress deleted files; 1 = compress deleted files during the next day's search; 2 = compress deleted files immediately.

- `/DaysUntouchedBeforeCompression=DAYS`—Specifies how many days a file or directory must remain untouched before being compressed. The default is 14. Values range from 0 to 100000. Setting this value to 100000 effectively disables file compression.

3. When finished, enter **Exit** to quit the `nsscon` utility.

These configuration parameters give you robust control over the compression process. However, you should always remember that enabling compression can lead to slower filesystem performance due to the processor-intensive nature of file compression/decompression.

RESTRICTING USERS' DISK SPACE

You can restrict how much disk space a user can fill up on a particular volume. This can help prevent individual users from using an excessive amount of disk space. NSS volumes let you enable/disable this support through the User Space Restrictions attribute.

To set space restrictions, open the Volumes page in iManager (in the Storage group). Click User Quotas to open a page from which you can select users and assign them a maximum amount of disk space they can use on a given volume (see Figure 11.5). You can also see how existing restrictions have been set and how much space each user has available in their quota.

PURGING AND SALVAGING FILES

When files are deleted from an NSS volume, they are not actually removed from the server's hard disk. Instead, they are retained in a salvageable state. Deleted files are usually stored in the same directory from which they were originally deleted. If the directory itself was also deleted, the deleted directory must be salvaged prior to gaining access to any deleted files within that directory.

FIGURE 11.5
Using iManager to set and view user volume quotas.

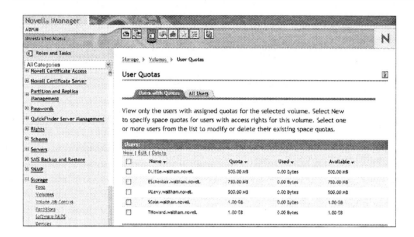

EXCEPTIONS TO THE SALVAGEABLE STATE
Deleted files are maintained in this salvageable state unless one of the following occurs:

- The file is salvaged, restoring it to its original form.

- The server runs out of free space on the disk and begins to overwrite files that have been deleted for a specified period of time. The oldest deleted files are overwritten first. A configurable NSS parameter defines the amount of time a file must remain deleted before it can be overwritten.

- The administrator or user purges the file. (When purged, a file is completely removed from the disk and cannot be recovered.) You can purge files with the Novell Client and ConsoleOne.

- The Immediate Purge attribute can be set at the file, directory, or volume level to prevent files from being salvaged. You can set this attribute with the Novell Client and ConsoleOne.

- The administrator sets the NSS parameter /ImmediatePurgeOfDeletedFiles. All volumes on that server will immediately purge deleted files. (The default for this parameter is Off. To disable immediate purge, set the NSS parameter /NoImmediatePurgeOfDeleteFiles.)

If any one of these events occurs, the file is no longer salvageable.

PURGING AND SALVAGING FILES

You, or any user, can use the Novell client utilities to either purge or salvage a deleted file or directory. To do so, right-click the red N in the system tray, select NetWare Utilities, and choose either Salvage or Purge.

You can also use ConsoleOne to salvage and purge files by completing the following steps:

1. Launch ConsoleOne and browse to the directory containing the files or directories you want to salvage or purge.

2. From the View menu, select Deleted File View.

3. In the View window (right side), select a file or directory.

4. Click either the Salvage or Purge button on the ConsoleOne toolbar, as shown in Figure 11.6.

FIGURE 11.6
Using ConsoleOne to salvage or purge deleted files.

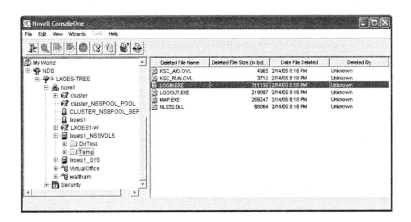

5. If you salvage files from an existing directory, the files are restored to that directory. In order to salvage files from a deleted directory, the deleted directory itself must first be salvaged. After the directory has been salvaged, additional deleted files within that directory can be salvaged.

This provides both users and administrators with a tool for recovering deleted files.

NOTE

If you have data shredding enabled, it will occur when a file is purged, not when it is deleted. If you have very sensitive materials on which you want to use data shredding, it might be a good idea to enable the Immediate Purge attribute for the file or directory where such data is stored.

NSS Data Security

One of the most important features of NSS is its flexible, yet powerful, security model. This security is integrated with eDirectory and offers comprehensive security management through command-line utilities, NetStorage, or the Novell Client. As mentioned earlier in this chapter, NSS operates in two modes, NetWare mode and Linux mode. NetWare mode requires that eDirectory user accounts be used to access NSS volumes. This allows for integration with eDirectory, and is the only way to provide for the advanced security capabilities described in this section. Linux mode refers to accessing NSS volumes using local user accounts. In this mode, you are limited to the traditional POSIX permissions seen with other Linux filesystems. Information about POSIX permissions can be found in Chapter 3, "Working with SUSE Linux Enterprise Server 9."

With an NSS filesystem in NetWare mode, you can implement two types of security tools in the filesystem, either together or separately, to protect your files:

- *Trustee rights*—These are equivalent to entry rights for eDirectory objects. Trustee rights enforce access control that defines the possible actions that can be taken with Volume, Folder, and File objects and who or what can perform those actions.

- *Attributes*—Attributes define the characteristics of individual Folder or File objects. Because attributes trump trustee rights, they control the activities of all users, regardless of which trustee rights are assigned.

Filesystem Trustee Rights

Filesystem trustee rights allow eDirectory users and groups to work with files and directories on NSS volumes in specific ways. Each right determines whether a user can do things such as see, read, change, rename, or delete the file or directory. NSS filesystem rights obey inheritance rules just like eDirectory rights. When rights are assigned to a file, they define a user's allowable actions for that file only. When rights are assigned to a directory, they affect a user's allowable actions on not only the directory itself but also everything stored within that directory.

Although filesystem rights are similar in nature to the eDirectory rights for objects and properties (described in Chapter 8, "Users and Network Security"), they are not the same thing. Filesystem rights are separate from eDirectory rights. They affect only how users work with files and directories. eDirectory rights affect how users work with other eDirectory objects.

There are eight filesystem trustee rights. You can assign any combination of those filesystem rights to a user or group, depending on how you want that user or group to work.

Table 11.2 describes the available filesystem rights and how they affect directory and file access.

TABLE 11.2
Filesystem Rights

FILESYSTEM RIGHT	ABBREVIATION	DESCRIPTION
Read	r	Directory: Allows the trustee to open and read files in the directory. File: Allows the trustee to open and read the file.
Write	w	Directory: Allows the trustee to open and write to (change) files in the directory. File: Allows the trustee to open and write to the file.
Create	c	Directory: Allows the trustee to create subdirectories and files in the directory. File: Allows the trustee to salvage the file if it was deleted.
Erase	e	Directory: Allows the trustee to delete the directory and its files and subdirectories. File: Allows the trustee to delete the file.
Modify	m	Directory: Allows the trustee to change the name, directory attributes, and file attributes of the directory and its files and subdirectories. File: Allows the trustee to change the file's name or file attributes.

FILESYSTEM RIGHT	ABBREVIATION	DESCRIPTION
File Scan	f	Directory: Allows the trustee to see the names of the files and subdirectories within the directory. File: Allows the trustee to see the name of the file.
Access Control	a	Directory: Allows the trustee to change the directory's IRF and trustee assignments. File: Allows the trustee to change the file's IRF and trustee assignments.
Supervisor	s	Directory: Grants the trustee all rights to the directory, its files, and its sub-directories. It cannot be blocked by an IRF. File: Grants the trustee all rights to the file. It cannot be blocked by an IRF.

NOTE

Trustee assignments are the only way to enforce access control on NSS volumes under Linux. Using the traditional Linux permission tools, such as chown or chgrp, will not affect access from eDirectory users. These tools should only be used when accessing Linux volumes in Linux mode.

INHERITING FILESYSTEM RIGHTS

Just like eDirectory rights, NSS filesystem rights can be inherited. This means that if you have filesystem rights to a parent directory, you can also inherit those rights and exercise them in any file and subdirectory within that directory. Inheritance keeps you from having to grant users filesystem rights at every level of the filesystem.

You can block inheritance by removing the right from the IRF of a file or subdirectory. As with directory objects, every directory and file has an inherited rights filter, specifying which filesystem rights can be inherited from a parent directory. By default, file and directory IRFs allow all rights to be inherited.

Inheritance can also be blocked by granting a new set of trustee rights to a subdirectory or file within the parent directory. As with the eDirectory rights, inherited and explicit filesystem rights are not cumulative. Explicit assignments replace the inherited rights from a parent directory.

FILESYSTEM SECURITY EQUIVALENCE

Security equivalence for NSS filesystem rights works the same way as security equivalence for eDirectory rights (explained in Chapter 8). You can assign one user to have the same eDirectory rights and filesystem rights as another user by using the Security Equal To Me tab in an object's properties page.

NOTE

Remember: You are still subject to the shortcomings of security equivalence as described in Chapter 8.

FILESYSTEM EFFECTIVE RIGHTS

Just as with eDirectory rights, determining which NSS filesystem rights a user can actually exercise in a file or directory can be confusing at first. A user's *effective filesystem rights* are the filesystem rights that the user can ultimately execute in a given directory or file. The user's effective rights to a directory or file are determined in one of two ways:

- A users' inherited rights from a parent directory, minus any rights blocked by the subdirectory's (or file's) IRF

- The sum of all rights granted to the user for that directory or file through direct trustee assignment and security equivalences to other users

WORKING WITH FILESYSTEM TRUSTEE RIGHTS

iManager can't yet take you into the NSS or NCP filesystem. You can assign rights at the volume level, but not at the directory or file level. Use NetStorage, the Novell Client, or the command-line **rights** utility to work with filesystem rights.

MANAGING RIGHTS WITH THE NOVELL CLIENT

To see or change a user's trustee assignments with the Novell Client, complete the following steps:

1. From a workstation, log in to the server using the Novell Client. If necessary, map a drive to the NSS volume you would like to modify trustees on.

2. Using a file manager, browse to the point in the filesystem, volume, folder, or file with which you want to work.

3. Right-click the folder or file and select Properties, and then select the NetWare Rights tab.

4. The Effective Rights box displays your effective rights to the selected object, as shown in Figure 11.7. The Trustees box contains all current trustee assignments on the current object.

FIGURE 11.7
Working with filesystem trustee rights through the Novell Client.

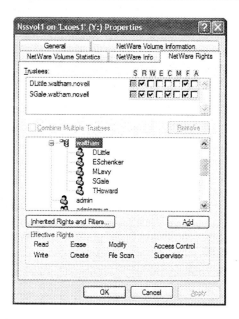

You can make a user a trustee of a FileSystem object using the NetWare Rights tab of the Novell Client by doing the following:

1. From the eDirectory tree view in the center of the page, locate and select the desired User object. Click Add to add the user as a trustee.

2. In the Trustee box at the top of the page, check those explicit filesystem rights that you want to grant the user and click OK or apply.

If the user is already a trustee, simply highlight the appropriate User object in the Trustees box and perform step 2.

MANAGING TRUSTEES AT THE COMMAND LINE
To see or change a user's trustee assignments at the command line, you cannot use the normal Linux **chown** utility. Although this utility can manipulate the

POSIX ownership for an NSS volume in Linux mode, it is unable to view or modify the extended trustee assignments available with NSS in NetWare mode. To adjust the NSS trustee assignments, you must use the `rights` command-line utility.

The `rights` utility can be used to view effective rights; view, modify and delete trustee assignments; and modify the inherited rights filter.

To view trustee assignments using the `rights` utility, execute the following command:

```
rights -f <File_Or_Directory> show*
```

To view the effective rights of a particular eDirectory user, the following command may be used:

```
rights -f <File_Or_Directory> effective <Username>
```

Finally, to add or delete trustee assignments, the following commands can be used:

```
rights -f <File_Or_Directory> trustee <Username>

rights -f <File_Or_Directory> delete <Username>
```

For more information on the `rights` command, use `rights --help`.

NetStorage can also be used to adjust file and directory trustee assignments. This option is available through the properties of files and directories while logged in to NetStorage. For more information on NetStorage, see Chapter 12.

File and Directory Attributes

Another important NSS security tool for securing files and directories is attributes. *Attributes* are properties of NSS files and directories that control what can happen to those files or directories. Attributes, which are also called *flags*, are different from trustee rights in several ways:

- Attributes are assigned directly to files and directories, whereas rights are assigned to users.

- Attributes override rights. In other words, if a directory has the Read-Only attribute, you can't delete the directory even if you've been granted the Erase right.

- Likewise, attributes don't grant rights. Just because a file has the Read-Write attribute doesn't mean you can write to it if you don't have the Write right.

- Attributes affect all users, including the Admin user.

- Attributes affect some aspects of the file that rights do not, such as determining whether the files in a directory can be purged immediately upon deletion.

Knowing these distinctions between NSS file attributes and trustee rights will help you better understand the behavior of the NSS filesystem.

There are twelve NSS attributes that apply to either files or directories. However, there are only four core attributes that are configurable using traditional POSIX utilities from a Linux terminal. These attributes are listed in Table 11.3.

TABLE 11.3
File and Directory Attributes

ATTRIBUTE	DESCRIPTION
Read-Only	Allows files to be opened and read, but not modified. Using some Linux-based utilities, like vi, it is possible to write changes to a read-only file if you have the proper trustee assignments. Directories use this attribute to allow listing of directory contents.
Read-Write	Allows files to be opened, read, and modified. Allows directory contents to be modified.
Execute	Marks a file as executable and allows execution of the file. Directories always have this attribute set to allow access to the directory itself.
Hidden	Hides the file or directory so that it is not listed by NCP-based clients, like the Windows File Manager, and can't be copied or deleted.

These four attributes can be used in combination with each other to produce several possible configurations of file attributes. Each combination of attributes can be assigned using the Linux utility chmod. This utility is used to assign *file permissions* on traditional Linux filesystems and *file attributes* on NSS.

On traditional Linux filesystems, you must specify the permissions for the user owner, group owner, and all other Linux users when assigning permissions with chmod. On an NSS volume, the permissions are managed through trustee assignments and are not settable through chmod. Therefore, the file or directory ownership, visible when listing files from a terminal, has no real relevance to the permissions users have to the object. Because the ownership does not matter, it is also not necessary to specify the user, group, and other permissions when assigning file attributes on an NSS volume through chmod. Specifying the file attributes using the user owner field only is sufficient.

In other words, on a traditional Linux filesystem, chmod 700 would give the user owner full permissions to the file and no permissions would be granted to the group owner or other category of users. That same command on an NSS volume would assign specific attributes on the file, for all trustees of the file. Displaying the file using the ls command would also display these attributes as though all categories of users were assigned the attributes—not just the user owner category. The end result of this is that the chmod 700 command produces the same attribute assignment as chmod 755, or chmod 722.

Setting NSS file attributes using chmod relies on the same octal system when used on traditional filesystems. Possible combinations of attributes are listed in Table 11.4.

TABLE 11.4
POSIX Representations of NSS File and Directory Attributes

OCTAL CODE OF ATTRIBUTES	FILE MODE DISPLAY	ENABLED NSS ATTRIBUTES	DESCRIPTION
000	-----	Hidden Read-Only	Prevents files from being displayed (from NCP clients) or modified.
100	--x--x--x This must say hyphen-hyphen-x three times - as in: --x--x--x	Hidden Read-Only	Prevents directory contents from being displayed (from NCP clients) or modified.
400	r--r--r-- This must say r-hypen-hypen three times - as in: r--r--r--	Read-Only	Allows files to be read, but does not allow modification.
500	r-xr-xr-x	Read-Only Execute	Allows files to be read and executed. No modification is allowed. Allows directories to be entered and renamed. Directory contents can be displayed, but cannot be modified.

OCTAL CODE OF ATTRIBUTES	FILE MODE DISPLAY	ENABLED NSS ATTRIBUTES	DESCRIPTION
600	rw-rw-rw-	Read-Write	Allows files to be read and modified.
700	rwxrwxrwx	Read-Write Execute	Allows files to be read, modified, and executed. Allowed directories to be entered, renamed, or deleted. Directory contents can be listed and modified.

NOTE

The chmod permissions of 200 and 300 are not designed to be used. They create a hidden file that can be written to with the proper trustee assignments, but they offer no benefit over the 000 setting.

There are additional NSS attributes, which can be used for specific requirements. These attributes can be set or adjusted using NetStorage, or the NSS command line utility /sbin/attrib. Although you can set these additional attributes on files and directories, some attributes are only applicable to one or the other. A list of commonly used NSS attributes can be found in Table 11.5.

TABLE 11.5
Common NSS File and Directory Attributes

ATTRIBUTE	FILE	DIRECTORY	DESCRIPTION
Read-Only	X	X	Allows the file to be opened and read, but not modified. Assigning the Read-only attribute automatically assigns Delete inhibit and Rename inhibit.
Archive	X		Indicates that the file has been changed since the last time it was backed up.
Hidden	X	X	Hides the file or directory so that it isn't listed by NCP-based connections, such as the Windows File Manager, and can't be copied or deleted.

TABLE 11.5
Continued

ATTRIBUTE	FILE	DIRECTORY	DESCRIPTION
Sharable	X		Allows the file to be used by more than one user simultaneously. Useful for utilities, commands, applications, and some database files. Most data and work files should not be sharable, so that users' changes do not conflict.
Transactional	X		When used on database files, allows Novell's Transaction Tracking System (TTS) to protect the files from being corrupted if the transaction is interrupted.
Purge Immediate	X	X	Purges the file or directory immediately upon deletion. Purged files can't be salvaged.
Compress Immediate	X	X	Compresses the file or directory immediately.
Do Not Compress	X	X	Prevents the file or directory from being compressed.
Rename Inhibit	X	X	Prevents users from renaming the file or directory.
Delete Inhibit	X	X	Prevents users from deleting the file or directory.
Copy Inhibit	X	X	Prevents the file or directory from being copied.
Compressed	X		This attribute is not settable by users. It is set by NSS itself to indicate that a file has been compressed. This option is only valid for volumes supporting compression.

To assign advanced NSS attributes to a file or directory using NetStorage, complete the following steps:

1. Launch NetStorage by accessing the following URL:

   http://<OES_Server_IP_Address_Or_DNS_Name>/NetStorage/

2. Enter your user credentials and click OK. Using an eDirectory administrator will allow you to adjust attributes on any NSS file.

3. Use the left-hand navigation frame to locate the NSS_Volumes folder. All NSS volumes should be listed beneath this folder. Expand the folder structure under the desired NSS volume to locate the directory where file attributes are to be adjusted.

4. Select the check box by file or directory in the right-hand pane, and then select File, Properties. NSS Attributes will be displayed on the NetWare Info tab as shown in Figure 11.8. Check the desired attributes and select Apply.

FIGURE 11.8
Working with file and directory attributes in NetStorage.

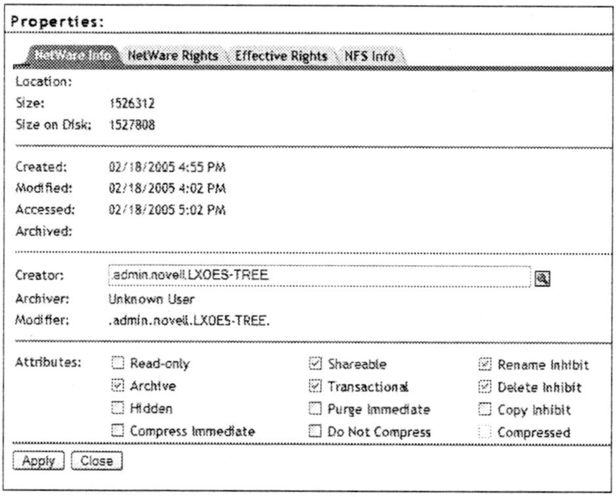

5. Click Close to return to the main NetStorage window.

It is also possible to use the terminal-based utility /sbin/attrib to set file and directory attributes. This utility can be used to set advanced attributes not listed off in Table 11.5. For information on using this utility, execute /sbin/attrib -help, or see the online OES documentation. For additional information on NetStorage, see Chapter 12.

Backing Up and Restoring Files

Although current storage technologies, such as RAID, hot-swappable hard drives, and network-attached storage are making servers ever more secure in their capability to maintain data, there are still many ways in which data can be lost or corrupted. For those situations, it is necessary to have a backup of your network data so that lost files can be recovered.

OES Linux provides a data backup-and-restore infrastructure known as Storage Management Services (SMS). SMS makes it possible to copy your network data, including files, directories, the eDirectory database, and even data from other servers and clients, to an offline storage system such as tape or optical disk. With a well-developed backup strategy, you can be confident that you will always have a current copy of your network data, so you can restore files should the unthinkable occur.

There are several network backup solutions for Linux on the market today. Unfortunately, at the time of this writing, none of them builds upon this SMS foundation to deliver a comprehensive backup solution. This means that with third-party backup tools on Linux, you will be able to back up your filesystem, but extended data, like NSS ACLs, cannot be part of that backup. However, SMS is designed with networking environments in mind. Because of this, SMS-compliant backup programs running on other operating systems can effectively back up OES Linux servers. This means that another operating system, NetWare or Windows, is required for an enterprise-level backup solution, but obtaining complete backups is worth the trouble.

OES Linux does include a fairly basic Linux server-based, SMS-aware backup interface called nbackup. This utility will back up the data correctly—including extended data—but it lacks many of the conveniences, such as flexible scheduling options, that third-party products have. This situation shouldn't last long, as third-party vendors are expected to release native Linux backup programs supporting SMS in the near future.

A solid backup strategy is critical to the well-being of your network. The following section describes backup strategies that can be employed to protect your valuable data. Although the majority of these strategies are explained from the perspective of using an enterprise-level backup software program, the essential features of nbackup are also discussed.

Planning a Backup Strategy

Planning is critical to developing an effective backup strategy. A well-planned backup strategy will avoid those headaches associated with finding and restoring files if that becomes necessary. It will reduce the time it takes to perform data backups and help keep your network humming along. When planning your backup strategy, consider the following:

- How frequently should you make backups?
- What type of medium are you going to use to back up your data?
- How should you rotate your backup media?
- Where will your backup copies be stored?
- How and when will you test the restore procedure?

TIP

Although it is possible to back up eDirectory database files, restoring them is a prescription for major grief. Rather than trying to restore eDirectory objects from tape, use partition replication to restore objects to a server. For more information on eDirectory design and replication, see Chapter 7, "Novell eDirectory Management."

PLANNING A BACKUP SCHEDULE

An important part of determining how often you need to back up your data revolves around how rapidly significant changes to your data occur, and how important those changes are. A lot of this depends on your line of business. If your data changes rapidly, and those changes must be protected, you should plan on daily backups of that information. If your data changes more slowly, or if re-creating the lost data isn't a big deal, perhaps a weekly backup schedule will do the trick.

Enterprise backup products let you determine not only when to back up your network, but also what types of information you back up each time. There isn't much point in backing up all your network data every night if only a few of the files are changing each day.

If you don't need a full backup every time, you can perform what is known as an *incremental* backup. In an incremental backup, changed files are detected, and only those files are backed up. One particularly efficient way of backing up your network involves both incremental and full backup routines.

One day a week, you perform a full backup of the network. Then, on each subsequent day during that week, perform an incremental backup of only those files that have changed. Using this strategy, you can restore your entire system, if necessary, by first restoring the weekly backup, and then applying each daily backup to get your files back to their state the day prior to the system failure. This achieves full data protection while minimizing the time it takes to perform the daily backup routines.

Finally, a *differential* backup is a twist on the incremental backup. Differential backups are the same as incremental backups except that the archive bit is not reset as part of the backup process. This means that each differential backup will include all changed data since the last full backup, eliminating the need to restore multiple backup sessions in order to recover all file changes since the last full backup.

TIP

Backup products that are NSS-aware can speed up incremental backups significantly by leveraging the NSS Modified File List (MFL). The MFL maintains a list of changed files so that the backup software doesn't have to review every file manually to see which files have changed since the last backup.

Another tip for minimizing backup time is to organize your directory (folder) structure so that often-changed files are separate from seldom-changed files. For example, there's no point in wasting your time by frequently backing up files such as applications and utilities, which seldom change. If you put applications in one directory and work files in another, you can skip the application directory completely during incremental backups, making the process go faster.

Finally, be sure to document your backup schedule and keep a backup log. A written record of all backups and your backup strategy can help someone else restore the files if you aren't there.

CHOOSING YOUR BACKUP MEDIUM

Before purchasing a backup device, you must decide what kind of backup medium you want to use. Many manufacturers' backup products can back up data onto a variety of storage media, but it's a good idea to know what you want before you buy something that limits your choices. The medium you choose will probably depend on the following factors:

- How much you're willing to spend.
- How large your network is.
- How long you need to retain your backed-up data. (Some media deteriorate after a few years; other media have a 100-year guarantee.)

Tape is still the most common backup medium in use today, especially in small- to medium-sized businesses. Tapes are relatively easy to use, can be used in any size network, and are fairly inexpensive.

NOTE

One of the downsides of tape is that backup manufacturers may use different, proprietary tape formats that aren't compatible with each other. Two tape standards have been established (one from Novell and another from Microsoft), so some efforts have been made to standardize on one or the other, but there are still differences between manufacturers. Be sure any backup product you buy is compatible with any other system with which you need to share tapes.

You should study the pros and cons of the various tape formats to find the best balance between cost and performance before making a decision.

If you are interested in very long-term storage, tapes suffer because they will break down over time. Optical storage such as writeable CDs and DVDs provide a storage medium that is much more resistant to the ravages of time. However, these solutions typically are significantly more expensive than tape solutions.

If you are unsure about the best storage medium for you, talk to your resellers about your specific needs, and let them help you choose the best fit for your storage needs. You should also verify that your backup server and software support the hardware you are planning to use.

PLANNING THE MEDIA ROTATION

When you are using rewriteable media, such as tapes, plan to have multiple sets of backup media that can be rotated. This way you keep multiple datasets available at all times. If your current backup is corrupted for any reason, you can still fall back to an older copy. Many network administrators use three or more sets of backup media and cycle through them, one each week. That way, three or more backup datasets are available at any given time. The number of tapes or disks you need depends on the rotation schedule you select.

Some backup products offer preset rotation schedules for you. They will automatically prompt you for the right set of media and keep track of the schedule.

DECIDING WHERE TO STORE THE BACKUPS

Another important aspect of your backup strategy is to plan where to store your backups. If you have backups of noncritical data, you might be comfortable keeping them onsite. However, when storing backups onsite, you should at least store them in a room separate from the server's room. If a fire breaks out in the server room, your backup tapes won't do you much good if they're lying melted beside the server.

For mission-critical data, you might need to keep backups in an off-site location. That way, if a physical disaster occurs (such as a fire, flood, or earthquake), they'll be safe. If the data is critical enough to store off-site, but you also want to have immediate access to it, consider making two copies and storing one off-site and the other on-site.

TESTING THE RESTORE PROCESS

A backup is useful only if the data in it can be restored successfully. Too many people discover, too late, a problem with their backups when they're in the middle of an important data restore process. One way to avoid this is to practice restoring files in a lab environment. This will not only familiarize your staff with the process, but will also test the quality and integrity of your backup data. By practicing, you can identify problems you didn't realize you had. Don't wait until it's too late.

The correct frequency for testing your restore process is dependent upon the frequency of your backups and the criticality of your data. For very sensitive systems, monthly tests might be necessary, but for most environments, a quarterly test of your restore process will probably be sufficient.

Storage Management Services (SMS)

As previously mentioned, Storage Management Services (SMS) provides a data backup-and-restore infrastructure to OES Linux. This infrastructure is built upon two main components:

- *Storage Management Data Requester (SMDR)*—The Storage Management Data Requester is responsible for providing connectivity between a backup application and a Target Service Agent (TSA). The daemon responsible for this process is smdrd. As incoming requests are received by smdrd, new processes are spawned to handle each request. Each process then loads the TSA required for the backup operation.

- *Target Service Agent (TSA)*—A Target Service Agent is responsible for providing backup capabilities for a specific resource. This resource could be a filesystem (such as NSS) or application (such as GroupWise). The TSA does this by abstracting the data of the resource and providing that data to the backup service using the ECMA standard System Independent Data Format (SDIF). The TSA provided with OES is tsafs, which provides TSA services for the NSS filesystem.

The most important aspect of the SMS infrastructure is that the TSA understands details of the backup target that normal, file-only backup services cannot understand. More specifically, `tsafs` understands extended characteristics of NSS because it was written to communicate with NSS through NSS APIs. The end result is that a backup taken through an SMS-aware backup program will be able to preserve NSS characteristics that normal, file-only backups will miss.

TUNING SMS COMPONENTS

Both the SMDR and TSA components can be tuned for operational and performance reasons. This tuning is normally performed through iManager, as shown in Figures 11.9 and 11.10.

FIGURE 11.9
SMDR Configuration page in iManager.

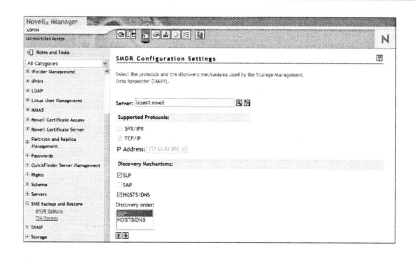

The main configuration file for the SMDR daemon is `/etc/opt/novell/sms/smdrd.conf`. If necessary, this file can be edited manually. If any changes are made to this file, refresh `smdrd` using the `rcnovell-smdrd refresh` command.

The main configuration file for the filesystem TSA is `/etc/opt/novell/sms/tsafs.conf`. If necessary, this file can be edited manually. If any changes are made to this file, refresh the TSA using the `smsconfig` utility. The syntax for refreshing the TSA using `smsconfig` is `smsconfig -r tsafs`.

FIGURE 11.10

TSA Configuration page in iManager.

THE nbackup UTILITY

The **nbackup** is a console-based utility that is included in the SMS component of OES Linux. This utility is an SMS-compliant backup that is intended to provide basic backup services for OES Linux.

By default, this utility is located in the **/opt/novell/sms/bin** directory (along with all the other SMS binaries). This directory is not normally on your path, so it must be executed using the full path (that is, **/opt/novell/sms/bin/nbackup**). To avoid this situation, you can add this directory to your path using the following command:

```
export PATH=$PATH:/opt/novell/sms/bin
```

As mentioned before, at the time of this writing, **nbackup** is the only Linux-based SMS-aware backup utility. As **nbackup** is intended for basic backup functions, it may be difficult to build an entire enterprise-level backup process around this utility. If you want a more complete solution, any SMS-aware backup product, running on any OS, should be able to connect to the local TSA and back up your OES Linux NSS volumes.

Proper usage of **nbackup** is demonstrated later in this chapter. For more information on **nbackup**, and the other SMS components, see the online OES Linux documentation.

Preparing to Back Up

There are four major steps involved in configuring an SMS backup system for use:

1. Install the Storage Management Services (SMS) on your OES Linux server. SMS is the collection of files and utilities that comprise the OES backup solution. It also provides a foundation and common interface for third-party vendors that allow their backup applications to communicate with OES.

2. Set up a *host server* (backup server) by installing a backup device and loading any required device's drivers. This can be a server or any workstation with the appropriate software.

NOTE

Although this server can be your OES Linux server, be aware that the only SMS-aware backup utility for Linux is nbackup. For additional flexibility and features of a comprehensive backup product, you may want to use a NetWare or Windows machine as your backup server.

3. Configure your OES Linux server by loading the SMS components. If additional servers or workstations are to be backed up, ensure that they have the proper TSAs loaded. These servers and workstations are called *targets*.

4. Begin the backup using a Storage Management Engine (SME) on either the host server or a workstation. The SME is the interface from which you will run backup and restore operations. nbackup is an SME that is available with OES Linux.

You will perform these basic steps whether you choose to use nbackup or some other utility as your preferred SME. Several third-party vendors offer backup/restore utilities that function as SMEs. Should you choose a third-party backup solution, ensure it is SMS-compliant.

The following sections provide details on each of these four documented backup steps.

INSTALLING STORAGE MANAGEMENT SERVICES

You can install SMS during the installation of OES Linux, by choosing it as an optional OES service. You also can install SMS after the fact through YaST. To install SMS through YaST, complete the following steps:

1. Access YaST from a terminal using **yast**, or from a graphical environment using **yast2** or the YaST launcher from the application menu.

2. Select the System category in YaST. From within this category, locate and select the SMS module. This module will detect that the RPMs for SMS are missing and ask if you want to install them. Select Continue to install the necessary packages.

3. At the conclusion of the software installation, **SuSEconfig** is executed to update the system configuration. When this completes, the configuration of the OES component will begin automatically.

4. At the SMS LDAP Server Configuration screen, enter the following information and click Next:

   - *Local or Remote Directory Server*—Select the radio button that indicates whether eDirectory is running on the local server or a remote server.

   - *Directory Server Address*—If a remote eDirectory server is in use, enter the IP address for this server.

   - *Admin Name with Context*—Enter the eDirectory administrator's credentials using fully qualified dot notation, for example, **cn=admin.o=novell**.

   - *Admin Password*—Enter the password for the administrator user.

   - *Port Details*—If necessary, select this button to change the configured ports for the eDirectory server you specified earlier. The default LDAP port for unencrypted communications is **389** and port **636** is used for SSL-encrypted communications.

With SMS installed, you are now ready to configure the backup/restore environment on your OES Linux server.

SETTING UP THE HOST SERVER

Before you can perform any type of backup, you must first prepare the host server that will be responsible for performing the backup and writing data to the backup media. The following steps summarize this process:

1. Attach the backup device (tape or disk drive) to the host server, following the manufacturer's instructions.

2. Load the necessary backup device drivers on the host server, again following manufacturer's instructions. For example, to manually load the driver for a generic SCSI tape device, execute the following command:

   ```
   modprobe st
   ```

3. Confirm that the device is loaded, and recognized using the `mt` command as follows:

```
mt -f /dev/st0 status
```

TIP

To load the SCSI tape device modules upon system startup, edit the `/etc/sysconfig/kernel` file and add the module names to the `MODULES_LOADED_ON_BOOT` directive. For example, for the generic <u>st</u> device, this entry should appear as:

```
MODULES_LOADED_ON_BOOT="st"
```

When these steps are completed, the host server is prepared, and the target server must be configured. For more information on configuring your host device, refer to the documentation supplied with your backup hardware.

SETTING UP TARGETS

Backup targets can be your OES Linux server, or any other server or workstation with the necessary TSA. The following steps describe the process for configuring your OES Linux server as a backup target:

1. Load the SMDR daemon on your OES Linux server using the following command:

```
rcnovell-smdrd start
```

This will load the SMDR daemon (**smdrd**) and register the NSS TSA (**tsafs**) with SMDR. These components were explained earlier in this chapter.

If you would like these services to be loaded upon server startup, use `insserv` to add this service to the startup process of your OES machine. The syntax for this command is

```
insserv novell-smdrd
```

2. *(Optional)* If you are going to back up any other target servers, you need to load the appropriate TSA(s) on each target. The SMS modules for other OES Linux servers must all be loaded as explained in step 1. For other NetWare servers that might be functioning as a target server, load the following modules:

- TSAFS—Load on OES NetWare target servers.
- TSA600—Load on NetWare 6 target servers.
- TSA500—Load on NetWare 5 target servers.
- TSA410—Load on NetWare 4 target servers.

When these steps are completed, the target preparation is complete, and the target server is ready to be backed up.

BACKING UP FILES WITH nbackup

After you've loaded the necessary drivers and software on the host server and loaded a TSA on the OES Linux target server (or other servers or workstations), you are ready to back up the target's files. OES Linux provides **nbackup** as a console-based utility for backing up network data.

To use **nbackup** to back up files, complete the following steps:

1. Identify the backup target you would like to back up. This should be the full path to a location under the mount point of the NSS volume. To back up a specific directory, use the full path to the directory itself. To back up all data on an NSS volume, use the full path to the mounted volume, followed by an asterisk (*). For example, to back up all files on **NSSVOL1**, which is mounted at **/media/nss/NSSVOL1**, the backup target would be **/media/nss/NSSVOL1/***.

2. Determine the filename or backup device you would like to write the data to. If you are writing the backup to a backup device, the device name should be in the format of **/dev/st0**.

3. Determine a username to use for authentication to the TSA. This is normally your eDirectory admin user. This name should be entered in the format of **admin.novell**.

4. Begin the **nbackup** process using the information retrieved in steps 1–3. The command line should appear as follows:

   nbackup -cvf *<Backup_File_Or_Device>* -U *<Username>* *<Backup_Target>*

nbackup can also be used to restore backup archives using the **-x** command-line parameter in place of **-c**. The **-t** command-line parameter can be used to view the contents of backup files and tapes.

Although **nbackup** is not a full-featured backup product, it does have one advantage. It is completely command-line-driven and therefore fully useable through scripts. These scripts can then be scheduled for execution through CRON. This combination makes for a simple, yet effective, backup solution. For more information on **nbackup**, see the **man** page or online OES Linux documentation.

## CHAPTER 12

OES Linux File Access

Instant Access

Using NetStorage

- NetStorage provides a WebDAV server interface for all OES Linux files and directories.

- Use any WebDAV-compliant application, such as web browsers, Windows Explorer (My Network Places), or Office 2000 to access OES NetWare files and folders.

- NetStorage can provide clientless access to iFolder files.

- NetStorage provides the WebDAV support for the NetDrive client.

Working with NetDrive

- NetDrive client is available online by searching for `netdrive` at http://support.novell.com/filefinder.

- NetDrive supports access to OES Linux files and folders using standard protocols: FTP, WebDAV, or iFolder.

Synchronizing Files with Novell iFolder

- Synchronize files between remote clients and a centralized iFolder server, so that user data is available anytime, from anywhere.

- Configure and manage iFolder server through the iFolder management console, available at https://<*iFolder server DNS or IP address*>iFolderServer/Admin after iFolder is installed.

- Use iFolder client to provide synchronization between the iFolder server and regularly used machines.

- If you are using a machine for one-time access, use NetStorage to access the iFolder server without having to synchronize all files.

- Use NetDrive to access the iFolder server without synchronizing the entire directory. Useful when the desktop application is not WebDAV-aware.

- iFolder access requires that the iFolder server be installed and configured prior to use.

Introduction to Novell File Access

One of the major tenets of Novell's oneNet philosophy is that users should have access to their files and data at any time, from anywhere. To help you reach this goal, OES Linux includes a host of methods for accessing network data.

In keeping with Novell's open-standards approach to network services, these access methods are designed to use Internet standards, web browsers, and thin clients, thereby minimizing the need to add large amounts of workstation software in order to access network resources. Those access methods that do require a client of some sort make installation and configuration as easy as possible, so users can get on with their business.

This chapter takes a look at the new and nontraditional forms of file access available in OES Linux. These include

- NetStorage
- Novell NetDrive
- Novell iFolder
- FTP server

NetStorage

NetStorage provides a transparent WebDAV interface to OES files. Effectively, NetStorage allows you to access files on an OES Linux server without a Novell client. NetStorage is integrated with iFolder, NetDrive, and Virtual Office to make accessing your network files as easy and seamless as possible—all without using the traditional Novell Client.

NetStorage leverages a middle-tier architecture, also called *XTier*, to provide its services. This same architecture is used to support some of the functionality for Novell's ZENWorks line of management solutions.

Installing NetStorage

NetStorage can be installed during the installation of the OES Linux server, or after the fact through YaST. Typically, you will need to install NetStorage only on one OES Linux server in your eDirectory tree, or on one server at each geographical site, although very heavy usage might require more than one per site.

To install NetStorage through YaST, complete the following steps:

1. Access YaST from a terminal using `yast`, or from a graphical environment using `yast2` or the YaST launcher from the application menu.

2. Select the Network Services category in YaST. From within this category, locate and select the NetStorage module. This module will detect that the RPMs for NetStorage are missing and ask if you want to install them. Select Continue to install the necessary packages.

3. At the conclusion of the software installation, `SuSEconfig` is executed to update the system configuration. When this completes, the configuration of the OES component will begin automatically.

4. At the NetStorage LDAP Server Configuration screen, enter the following information and click Next:

   ■ *Local or Remote Directory Server*—Select the radio button that indicates whether eDirectory is running on the local server or a remote server.

   ■ *Directory Server Address*—If a remote eDirectory server is in use, enter the IP address for this server.

   ■ *Admin Name with Context*—Enter the eDirectory administrator's credentials using fully qualified dot notation, for example, `cn=admin.o=novell`.

   ■ *Admin Password*—Enter the password for the administrator user.

   ■ *Port Details*—If necessary, select this button to change the configured ports for the eDirectory server you specified earlier. The default LDAP port for unencrypted communications is **389** and port **636** is used for SSL-encrypted communications.

5. At the NetStorage Configuration screen, enter the required information (see Figure 12.1), and click Next. You can change these settings after the installation through iManager by opening the NetStorage link and selecting Authentication Domains.

FIGURE 12.1

NetStorage Configuration options.

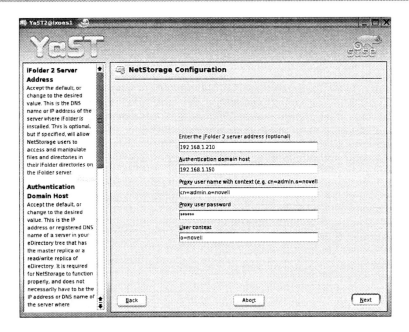

- *(Optional) Enter the iFolder 2 server address*—Specify the DNS name or IP address of your iFolder 2.x server if you want users to be able to access iFolder data through NetStorage. More information on iFolder is available later in this chapter.

- *Authentication Domain Host*—Specify the DNS name or IP address of a server in your eDirectory tree that hosts a master or a read/write replica of eDirectory. This does not have to be the server where NetStorage is being installed. NetStorage will use this server to authenticate users when they attempt to log in to NetStorage.

- *Proxy user name with context*—Enter a fully distinguished user proxy name for use with NetStorage. This is required and must be a user who has sufficient rights to read and save users' iFolder passphrases. The default user is the eDirectory admin user.

- *Proxy user password*—Enter the password for the proxy user.

- *User context*—Specify the base context in which valid NetStorage users may be located. Users found in the subtree beneath this context will be able to use NetStorage. If you want to use the entire tree, specify the root context, for example, o=novell.

6. In order for NetStorage to be active, select to restart XTier, Apache, and Tomcat when prompted.

The NetStorage installation is now complete and additional configuration can now be performed.

Configuring NetStorage

Use iManager to configure and manage your NetStorage environment by opening the File Access (NetStorage) link in the Navigation frame. There really isn't much in the way of required configuration, but it's nice to understand the control you do have over NetStorage.

- *Authentication Domains*—This page enables you to add, remove, and modify authentication domains to NetStorage. These are eDirectory servers that NetStorage will search for user authentication information.

- *Current Sessions*—This page shows a list of current NetStorage sessions.

- *Files*—This page enables you to actually view the available NetStorage files. You will be required to authenticate as a valid user, and the user must exist in one of the authentication domains defined for this NetStorage server.

- *iFolder Storage Provider*—This page enables you to review and change basic iFolder parameters that relate to its operation with NetStorage. In most cases you won't have to change any of these, but they are accessible if necessary.

- *NetWare Storage Provider*—This page enables you to review and change basic parameters related to the use of NetWare-mapped drives with NetStorage. In most cases you won't have to change any of these, but they are accessible if necessary.

- *NetStorage Options*—This page enables you to do some configuration of the XTier server configuration. In most cases you won't have to change any of these, but they are accessible if necessary.

- *NetStorage Statistics*—This page displays a report with information about server up time, login failures, number of NetStorage sessions, and so on.

- *Resource Usage*—This page shows server resources being used in support of the NetStorage middle-tier server environment. It is useful for keeping track of how server resources are being used for troubleshooting server issues.

- *WebDAV Provider*—This page lists the location of the NetStorage WebDAV provider (`XDAV.NLM`) and the location of NetStorage template files used for building the NetStorage web interfaces.

■ *Storage Location*—Use the Storage Location links to access pages where you can create, delete, and modify storage location objects in your eDirectory tree. Storage location objects are pointers to NetWare directories that can be given more useful names than those typically seen when looking at NetStorage resources. This is particularly useful for common directories shared by multiple users.

For more detailed information on any of these parameters, see the OES online documentation.

Using NetStorage

In order to avoid timestamp issues and confusion over the most current version of a file, Novell recommends that the date and time on the NetStorage server and the WebDAV client be reasonably close, within a few hours of each other.

You can access NetStorage from any WebDAV client, two of the most obvious of which are web browsers and Microsoft Windows web folders. However, there are WebDAV clients for Linux and Macintosh systems as well. The following process is equally applicable to those environments.

1. From your WebDAV client, enter the NetStorage URL, which is the DNS name or IP address of your NetStorage server with /oneNet/NetStorage appended to the end. Remember to include the http:// prefix and remember that URLs are case sensitive. For example:

   http://prv-serv1.quills.com/oneNet/NetStorage

NOTE

To use web folders in Windows XP/2000, open My Network Places (the Windows WebDAV client) and select Add Network Place. This opens a wizard for creating a new folder in My Network Places.

2. At the authentication screen, specify your eDirectory username and password. This User object must be accessible from the eDirectory server(s) you specified during the NetStorage installation.

After being authenticated, your WebDAV client displays the network files and folders that are currently accessible. To do this, NetStorage reads the user's Novell login script to determine drive mappings, reads eDirectory User object properties to determine the path to the user's home directory, and then displays a list of files and folders based on mapped drives and home directories. Figure 12.2 shows NetStorage views from both a web browser and Windows web folders.

FIGURE 12.2

Accessing NetWare folders through NetStorage.

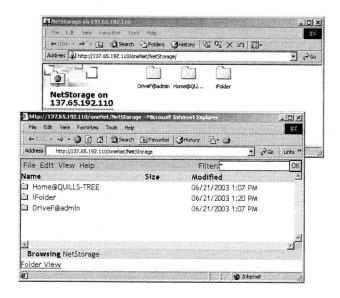

TIP

If you specified multiple Authentication Domains, NetStorage will read the user login script from only the primary eDirectory server when calculating mapped drives to display. However, NetStorage will read User object properties from all trees and display multiple home directories—as long as the User object has the same name in each tree. This is useful if a user normally logs in to more than one eDirectory tree.

If you have an iFolder account, you will see an iFolder folder in addition to your mapped drives and home directory, as shown in Figure 12.2. The first time you open the iFolder folder, all you will see is a file called PASSPHRASE.HTM. To access the contents of your iFolder directory, open PASSPHRASE.HTM, as shown in Figure 12.3, and specify the passphrase of your iFolder account.

This allows NetStorage to decrypt your iFolder files so that it can interpret them properly. The passphrase for NetStorage is stored as an encrypted attribute on your User object, so it is not at risk of discovery.

FIGURE 12.3

Specifying your passphrase to access iFolder from NetStorage.

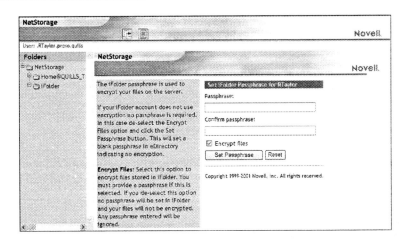

When you're connected to your OES files through WebDAV, you have full access to them. You can browse, open, and close folders; copy files to your local drive; and open files with WebDAV-compliant applications such as web browsers, Microsoft Office 2000, and so on.

In addition, if you use Microsoft Windows web folders, you can use all the normal Windows mechanisms for copying, cutting, pasting, and renaming files. To perform similar actions from a browser interface, click the down arrow next to the file or folder with which you want to work.

If you need to use a file with a non-WebDAV application, you will need to copy the file to your local drive so that the application can use normal operating-system mechanisms for working with the file. This is the only real drawback to NetStorage: It does not provide low-level integration with the operating system, such as creating a drive letter that allows applications to access the files as if they were local.

Novell helps you resolve this issue for Windows workstations with NetDrive, which is described in the next section. The trade-off is having full access to network files as if they were local versus having a clientless solution for accessing your network files.

Novell NetDrive

Novell NetDrive enables you to map a network drive to any OES Linux server without using Novell client software. This means that with NetDrive, you can access and modify your files from any workstation using just an Internet connection. After a network drive is mapped, the drive letter that you assigned during the mapping appears in Windows Explorer and functions just like those that are mapped through Novell client. Basically, the capability to map drives has been extracted from the Novell client where it can be used independent of all the other Novell client features. For more information on the Novell client, see Chapter 4, "OES Linux Clients."

NetDrive Prerequisites

NetDrive runs on any Windows workstation, including Windows 95/98/Me and Windows XP/2000/NT. You need only 2MB of available space on your hard drive to install and run the NetDrive client.

WARNING

If you are installing the NetDrive client on a Windows 95 workstation, make sure you have installed the Winsock 2 update from Microsoft. It is available on the Microsoft website.

NetDrive supports three protocols for accessing network files:

- *WebDAV*—NetDrive integrates with NetStorage to provide a comprehensive file access solution with very little client overhead. NetStorage must be installed and configured prior to using NetDrive with WebDAV.

- *FTP*—NetDrive can access network files using the standard File Transfer Protocol (FTP). An FTP server must be installed and configured on your network before using NetDrive with FTP. With OES, you can use one of the optional FTP servers, described later in this chapter, to provide this type of access.

- *iFolder*—NetDrive can access files from your directory on the iFolder server. iFolder must be installed, and your iFolder account configured, prior to using NetDrive with iFolder.

The choice of protocol depends largely on your network environment. One is not preferable to another. Use the protocol that best fits your network strategy.

Using NetDrive

The latest version of the NetDrive client is available by searching on `netdrive` at http://support.novell.com/filefinder. If you need help installing the NetDrive client, see Chapter 4.

With the NetDrive client installed, you can access files on your OES Linux servers using standard Internet protocols. However, not every protocol is supported on every version of Windows.

- *iFolder*—Windows NT and XP/2000
- *FTP*—Windows 95, 98, NT, and XP/2000
- *WebDAV (HTTP)*—Windows 95, 98, NT, and XP/2000
- *Secure WebDAV (SSL)*—Windows NT and XP/2000

The NetDrive installation inserts an icon in the Windows system tray (lower-right corner of the Explorer window). To configure NetDrive and begin using it to access your network files, complete the following steps:

1. Click the NetDrive icon in the system tray.

2. From the main NetDrive window, as shown in Figure 12.4, you can create new sites, map network drives, and configure and manage the websites to which you have mapped drives.

Each of these functions is discussed in the following sections.

FIGURE 12.4
The NetDrive 4.1 configuration window.

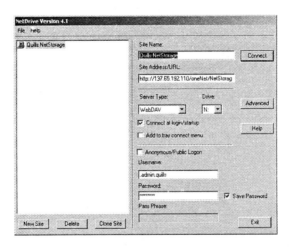

Adding a Site to NetDrive

Adding a site to NetDrive makes an OES Linux site available to NetDrive so that drive mapping can take place. To add a site to NetDrive, complete the following steps:

1. In the main NetDrive window, click New Site.

2. At the Add New Site screen, enter the requested information, and click Finish.

   - *Name for Your New Site*—Enter a descriptive name for the new NetDrive site.

   - *Address/URL*—For an FTP connection, specify the DNS name or IP address of your FTP server (ftp://ftp.quills.com/files). For a WebDAV connection, specify the DNS name or IP address of the server where NetStorage is installed, along with the NetStorage access path (http://prv-serv1.quills.com/oneNet/NetStorage). For iFolder, specify the DNS name or IP address of your iFolder service (http://ifolder.quills.com). If you omit the FTP or HTTP prefix, NetDrive defaults to FTP. If you want to use a nonstandard HTTP port, make sure you append it to the end of the URL.

NOTE

If you want to connect with WebDAV and SSL encryption, remember to specify the HTTPS prefix as part of the URL.

After you have created a site, the name of the new site and the URL of the OES Linux server are listed in the main NetDrive window. The rest of the page defaults to common connection options for the file protocol you have chosen (refer to Figure 12.4). However, you can change any of this information after the fact:

- *Server Type*—Specify the protocol that you will use to access this site.

- *Drive*—Specify the drive letter that you want to use for the mapped drive.

- *Connect at Login/Startup*—Check this box to have NetDrive map its drive automatically when your workstation starts.

- *Add to Tray Connect Menu*—If you right-click the NetDrive icon in the system tray, you will see a Connect To option. Check this box to add the site to those listed in the Connect To menu.

- *Anonymous/Public Logon*—Check this box to bypass user authentication for an FTP connection. Both WebDAV and iFolder access require specific user authentication. Leave this box unchecked if you want to require authentication in order to access the site. If you do this, you will have to enter a valid username and password.

- *(Conditional) Pass Phrase*—If you are connecting to an iFolder server, enter a passphrase. This is used to encrypt your files as they are transferred over the Internet. iFolder is discussed later in this chapter.

- *Save Password*—Check this box if you want NetDrive to remember your authentication password.

Click the Advanced button to set optional download, caching, and file-locking parameters for the NetDrive site. You won't normally have to do anything in the Advanced area.

When you are finished configuring site properties, click Connect to actually map the drive. When NetDrive maps the drive, Windows opens a new window corresponding to the drive letter that you have just mapped.

After NetDrive has successfully mapped a drive to the site, the Monitor window appears. It provides you with connection status, file transfer statistics, and a connection log. With the newly mapped drive, you can copy, cut, and paste files as you would in any other Windows drive.

TIP

If you have problems viewing the mapped directory or connecting to a server using FTP, specify the server IP address instead of the URL. You might also need to enable passive mode if the problem does not go away. Click Advanced and select PASV–Passive Mode. Then try connecting to the web server again.

For more information on the advanced options available with NetDrive, see the OES online documentation.

Novell iFolder

Novell iFolder gives you automatic, secure, and transparent synchronization of files between your hard drive and the iFolder server, which results in easy access to personal files anywhere, anytime.

Being able to access your files from any computer, in any location, eliminates mistakes and the updating that is frequently necessary when your local files are not accessible over the network.

Novell iFolder has three components:

- *iFolder server software*—After you have installed the iFolder server software on your server, users can install the iFolder client in order to access their iFolder files. Administrators use the iFolder Management console and the iFolder website to manage iFolder user accounts.

NOTE

The iFolder Management console enables you to perform administrative tasks for all iFolder user accounts. From the iFolder website, iFolder users download the iFolder client. It is also where you can access the Java applet and view your iFolder files from a browser. The iFolder website can, and should, be customized to fit the look and feel of your organization.

- *iFolder client software*—Novell iFolder client is compatible with Windows 95/98, Windows XP/2000/NT, and Linux workstations. The iFolder client must be installed on every workstation that you will use to access your iFolder files. When the iFolder client is installed, it does three things:

    - It creates a shortcut to your iFolder directory on your desktop. The iFolder directory, which by default on a Windows client is located in `My Documents\iFolder\userid\Home`, is where you will keep the files you want to synchronize with the iFolder server. When a file is placed in the iFolder directory, it is synchronized out to the iFolder server, from which it can be accessed by all workstations that are logged in to your iFolder account.

    - On Windows workstations, an iFolder icon is placed in the workstation system tray. Right-clicking the system tray icon gives users access to their user-configurable preferences and the iFolder status screen, which displays a history of the transactions that have occurred between the iFolder server and the client.

    - A user account is created on the iFolder server. iFolder user accounts are created automatically when a user downloads and installs the iFolder client. When you log in, iFolder asks you for a username and a password. Next, iFolder prompts you for a passphrase. This passphrase is used to encrypt files that are uploaded to the server.

NOTE

Uninstalling the iFolder client does not delete the associated user account on the iFolder server. This can be done only from the iFolder Management console.

- *iFolder Java applet*—Use the iFolder Java applet to access iFolder files from a workstation on which the iFolder client is not installed.

iFolder Prerequisites

Remember the following prerequisites when you are installing iFolder:

- iFolder requires Internet Explorer 5.5 or higher to be installed on every Windows workstation where you are installing the iFolder client.
- You need 10MB of free space on the root volume where you plan to install iFolder.
- Novell provides an iFolder client for both Windows and Linux desktops. For more information on configuring iFolder on a Linux desktop, see the OES online documentation.

NOTE

If you are installing the iFolder client on a Windows 95 workstation, make sure you have installed the Winsock 2 update from Microsoft. It is available on Microsoft's website.

Installing iFolder

Novell iFolder can be installed on a dedicated server using the Novell iFolder Server installation pattern or as an optional component during the OES Linux server installation. iFolder can also be installed after the fact through YaST. To install iFolder with YaST, complete the following steps:

1. Access YaST from a terminal using **yast**, or from a graphical environment using **yast2** or the YaST launcher from the application menu.

2. Select the Network Services category in YaST. From within this category, locate and select the iFolder 2.x module. This module will detect that the RPMs for iFolder are missing and ask if you want to install them. Select Continue to install the necessary packages.

3. At the conclusion of the software installation, **SuSEconfig** is executed to update the system configuration. When this completes, the configuration of the OES component will begin automatically.

4. At the iFolder 2.x LDAP Configuration screen, enter the following information and click Next:

- *Local or Remote Directory Server*—Select the radio button that indicates whether eDirectory is running on the local server, or a remote server.

- *Directory Server Address*—If a remote eDirectory server is in use, enter the IP address for this server.

- *Admin Name with Context*—Enter the eDirectory administrator's credentials using fully qualified dot notation, for example, `cn=admin.o=novell`.

- *Admin Password*—Enter the password for the administrator user.

- *Port Details*—If necessary, select this button to change the configured ports for the eDirectory server you specified earlier. The default LDAP port for unencrypted communications is **389** and port **636** is used for SSL-encrypted communications.

5. At the iFolder 2.x Web Configuration screen, as shown in Figure 12.5, provide the required information and click Next.

FIGURE 12.5
iFolder 2.x Web Configuration options.

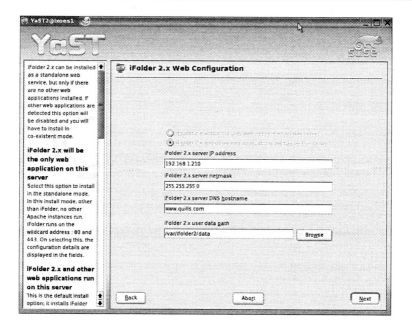

- *iFolder 2.x will be the only web application on this server —or— iFolder 2.x and other web applications will run on this server*—If no other OES services are currently installed on this server, you have the option to decide whether iFolder will be the only web application running locally. If it is the only web application, iFolder will bind to all available addresses and service all incoming requests on ports 80 and 443. On the other hand, if iFolder will be running alongside other web applications, the Apache configuration must be modified to bind iFolder to a unique IP address. This IP address must be manually configured, and should be reserved only for use with iFolder.

- *iFolder 2.x server IP address*—Specify the IP address of the server on which iFolder services will be running.

- *iFolder 2.x server netmask*—Specify the netmask used on the iFolder server.

- *iFolder 2.x server DNS hostname*—Specify the DNS hostname of the server on which iFolder services will be running.

- *iFolder 2.x user database path*—Enter the path to the directory where you want the iFolder user data to be stored on the iFolder server. This defaults to `/var/ifolder2/data`.

6. At the iFolder 2.x configuration, admin user's screen, enter any users you would like to designate as iFolder admin users and click Next.

7. At the end of the installation, click Yes to restart Apache.

iFolder is now installed and ready for further configuration through the administration interface.

Configuring iFolder

The first time the iFolder client is installed, a user account is automatically created on your iFolder server. In addition to the default iFolder website, another website is available for performing server management.

After iFolder is installed, you can access the iFolder Management console through the following URL: https://<*iFolder server DNS or IP address*> iFolderServer/Admin. For example:

https://prv-serv1.quills.com/iFolderServer/Admin

The initial view of iFolder Management console shows you the types of tasks you can perform, but you won't be able to actually do anything until you log in via LDAP. Use an administrative user account you specified during the iFolder installation. After you have authenticated using an administrative account, you will get a new authenticated view of iFolder Management console that allows you to actually perform the various iFolder administrative tasks (see Figure 12.6). There are four types of iFolder management activities:

- Global settings
- User management
- System monitoring
- Reporting

FIGURE 12.6
iFolder Management console.

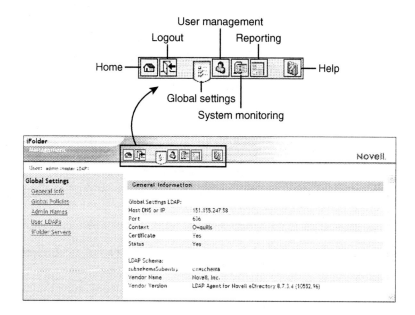

GLOBAL SETTINGS

Global Settings is the default page when you first log in to the iFolder Management console. You will see five links in the Navigation frame (see Figure 12.6):

- *General Info*—The General Info link provides basic information about the iFolder server, including DNS name or IP address, port being used, and so on.

- *Global Policies*—With the Global Policies page, you can set both server and client policies by clicking the appropriate button. These settings define the default configuration for the iFolder environment.

- *Admin Names*—This page allows you to modify the list of Admin objects defined for iFolder. These objects must be located in the Admin context defined during the installation of iFolder.

- *User LDAPs*—The User LDAPs page allows you to define the LDAP server that iFolder will use to authenticate users. By default, iFolder will not search subcontexts for potential iFolder users. You can configure the contexts that iFolder should search for users on this page.

- *iFolder Servers*—This page allows you to add new iFolder servers to the iFolder environment as they are installed.

Use the global settings links to configure the primary characteristics of your iFolder environment.

USER MANAGEMENT

Before your users can start using iFolder, you have to enable their User objects from the User Management button in the iFolder Server Management console. You can select users individually or in groups. To enable user objects to work with iFolder, complete the following steps:

1. Launch iFolder Server Management and click the User Management button in the Header frame.

2. Click Advanced Search in the Navigation frame.

3. Specify how you want iFolder to search for users and then click Search. You can search by a name, a portion of a name, the context, or even the entire server. After you perform the search, all user objects located within your defined criteria will be listed (see Figure 12.7).

4. Click Enable All Found Users as iFolder Users to allow the User objects that have been found to use iFolder. Alternatively, you can check the boxes next to only those user objects for which you want to provide iFolder access and click Enable Checked Users as iFolder Users.

NOTE

As new User objects are configured on your network, you will have to add those users in order for them to have access to iFolder. iFolder access is not granted by default.

FIGURE 12.7
Configuring iFolder users with the iFolder Management console.

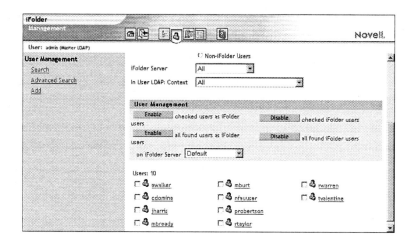

SYSTEM MONITORING

The System Monitoring button provides a real-time view of the status of your iFolder environment. From this page, you can see a list of all iFolder and LDAP servers in your environment, along with important characteristics of each.

REPORTING

The Reporting button allows you to take the information you can see from System Monitoring and capture it in report format. You can create reports in four categories:

- *General Information*—This report gives you information about the status of your entire iFolder environment.

- *iFolder Servers*—This report provides configuration information for each iFolder server in your environment.

- *User LDAPs*—This report provides configuration information for each LDAP server being used by your iFolder environment for user authentication.

- *User Accounts*—This report provides information about each user object that is using your iFolder environment and how it is making use of iFolder resources.

You can configure the iFolder reporting environment to fit the needs of your network environment.

Using iFolder

After iFolder is installed and configured on the server and user access has been defined, your users can begin to take advantage of iFolder's file synchronization capabilities. The first thing iFolder users need to do is install the iFolder client. The iFolder client is available on the iFolder web page, which is http://<*iFolder server DNS or IP address*>iFolder. For example:

http://prv-serv1.quills.com/iFolder

To install the iFolder client, complete the following steps:

1. From the iFolder web page, select Download Windows Client in the Navigation frame. You can download the Linux client for use with Linux desktops as well. For more information on using iFolder with Linux, see the OES online documentation.

2. At the File Download screen, choose to either save the client file to disk or run it directly from the server, and then click OK. If you are accessing the server from a remote location, it will probably be faster to download the file prior to installing the iFolder client. If you do this, specify a location for the file. After the download is complete, execute the file you downloaded.

3. At the Welcome screen, click Next.

4. At the License Agreement Language screen, select the language in which to view the license agreement and click Next. This will open a browser window with the iFolder license agreement. To continue the installation, close the browser window.

5. At the License Agreement screen, click Yes to accept the agreement.

6. At the Destination Location screen, specify the location where you want the iFolder client files to be installed and click Next.

7. At the Installation Complete screen, select Yes, I Want to Restart My Computer Now, and click Finish.

8. After your workstation reboots, you will see a Setup Complete message, with instructions on using iFolder. Click Continue to finish the installation.

9. The Login screen will be displayed, as shown in Figure 12.8. Specify the required information and click Login. You will provide a username (typically your NetWare username) and password. Typically, the iFolder server information will be provided for you.

FIGURE 12.8
The iFolder Login screen.

10. At the iFolder Location screen, specify the location on your local drive to which your iFolder files will be synchronized and click OK.

11. At the iFolder configuration screen, make your desired selections and click OK.

   - *Enable Automatic Login at Startup*—Select this option if you want iFolder to start automatically when you boot up your computer.

   - *Encrypt Files*—Select this option if you want to encrypt files that are stored on the iFolder server.

12. (Conditional) If you elected to encrypt files, specify a passphrase. The passphrase is used as a cryptographic key to encrypt your files on the iFolder server. You can also specify a hint to help remember the passphrase if you forget it.

13. Select Enable Pass Phrase Recovery if you want your admin to be able to recover your passphrase for you. Click OK.

When you log in, you will see new iFolder icons on your desktop and in the Windows system tray (lower-right corner of the desktop). The desktop icon is a shortcut to your iFolder files. The system tray icon gives you access to iFolder user account information and configuration parameters. To access them, right-click the iFolder icon that appears on the system tray of your workstation. The following major menu options are available:

   - *Logout/login*—If you are currently logged in, the Logout option is displayed, which will log you off the iFolder server and stop all iFolder synchronization. If you are currently logged out, the Login option is displayed, which allows you to log in to the iFolder and initiate synchronization activities.

- *Sync Now*—Forces synchronization between the workstation and the iFolder server to begin immediately.

- *Account Information*—This option allows you to view account settings and synchronization activity, as well as allowing you to set account synchronization preferences. The Account Information screen is shown in Figure 12.9. From the Account Information screen, you can work with the following options:

  - *Account Information tab*—Displays basic account information, including username, iFolder directory location, iFolder servername, account space statistics, and to-be-synchronized statistics.

  - *View Activity tab*—Lets you view, save, and clear your iFolder account activity log. The log is automatically cleared each time you log in to iFolder.

  - *Preferences tab*—Lets you enable/disable automatic synchronization and define how often files will be synchronized to/from the iFolder server. You can also choose to have the iFolder client remember your iFolder password and passphrase so that you don't have to type them each time you log in.

FIGURE 12.9
The iFolder Account Information screen.

- *Open iFolder*—Opens the iFolder directory associated with your iFolder client account. This is equivalent to double-clicking the iFolder icon that is created, by default, on the Windows desktop.

- *View Conflict Bin*—The conflict bin exists to save files that were deleted or changed during an iFolder synchronization. You can manually review the files in the conflict bin to make sure that the correct version of the file has been synchronized.

- *About iFolder*—Provides version information for the iFolder client.

- *iFolder website*—Selecting this option opens the iFolder website associated with your iFolder server. From this page, you can download the iFolder client, view iFolder product information and instructions, and access your iFolder account via a web browser.

- *Help*—Opens the iFolder client help file.

- *Exit*—This option closes the iFolder client interface and effectively logs you out of the iFolder server. The icon will disappear from the system tray, so in order to restart the iFolder client, you have to click Start, Programs, Novell iFolder, iFolder Client.

As you can see, nearly every feature needed by a user is available through the iFolder icon in the Windows system tray.

ACCESSING IFOLDER THROUGH A BROWSER

iFolder has a browser-based option that eliminates the need for the iFolder client in order to access files in your account on the iFolder server. With iFolder web access, you can download only the files that you need, as opposed to synchronizing the entire directory. With the iFolder web access, all you need is Internet access to get to your iFolder account.

To access your iFolder account through a web browser, complete the following steps:

1. Open the iFolder applet, which is found at the following URL:
   http://<*iFolder server DNS or IP address*>/iFolder/applet/java.htm

2. At the Login screen, provide your iFolder username, password, and passphrase, and click Connect.

When you're logged in, you will see your iFolder files listed in a directory structure in the browser window (see Figure 12.10). Expand folders by double-clicking them.

FIGURE 12.10
iFolder Java WebAccess interface.

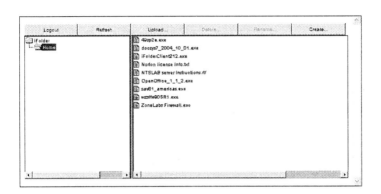

From the browser interface, you can download, upload, delete, create, and rename files. However, after you download a file, changes will not be synchronized automatically. Make sure you upload files after making changes, so they can be synchronized to all other workstations where you have installed the iFolder client.

ACCESSING IFOLDER FROM NETSTORAGE OR NETDRIVE

Accessing an iFolder server from either NetStorage or NetDrive was described earlier in this chapter in the sections for each of those products. However, the important thing to remember is that you are accessing files on the server only. You don't get the effects of synchronization between client and server as you do with the iFolder client.

The advantage of this scenario is that you can access files from any workstation without fear of accidentally leaving data on a foreign machine. This might lead some to consider using iFolder without installing the iFolder client. This is a possible solution, but remember that files are not replicated to multiple locations. If the server experienced a problem, files on the iFolder server could become lost or unrecoverable.

TIP

The best solution is one that uses each technology where it makes sense, without relying too heavily on only one type of file-access solution.

FTP Server

Several FTP servers are available for the Linux platform. With SLES, two commonly used FTP servers are Pure-FTP (**pure-ftpd**) and VSFTP (**vsftpd**). Both of these FTP servers are included with SLES distributions and may be optionally installed during the OES installation.

The Pure-FTP server is intended to provide fast, lightweight FTP access to a Linux server. It offers a focus on tight integration with the Linux kernel and a standards-compliant and security-aware design.

The VSFTP server, or Very Secure FTP server, is an FTP server that was coded with a focus on security. Given the focus of this server, it is the FTP server most commonly used with SLES and will be the center of this discussion.

Regardless of the server you select, the purpose of an FTP server is to provide a means of easily transferring files over network connections. All File Transfer Protocol (FTP) servers communicate over TCP/IP and should conform to RFC 959. The VSFTP server meets these requirements. When the primary VSFTP server daemon (**vsftpd**) is started, you can perform file transfers from any FTP client to the OES Linux Server. This is normally done by authenticating as a local user to the FTP server. However, if you are also using the LUM component of OES, FTP users can be configured for redirection back to your Novell eDirectory tree. Without LUM, the FTP server will be limited to authenticating locally stored users only. For more information on LUM, please see Chapter 8, "Users and Network Security."

The VSFTP server is a fully functional FTP server with many features, such as those in the following list. This section provides basic installation and configuration information so that you can use FTP file access with NetDrive.

- *xinetd-based service management*—The Internet Super Daemon Extended, or **xinted**, manages the **vsftpd** process. This allows **xinetd** to provide an additional security layer for **vsftpd**. As incoming requests are encountered, **xinetd** verifies the request, and if allowed, spawns the **vsftpd** process. With this integration, FTP service management is performed via the YaST Network Services (**inetd**) module.

- *Authenticated user access*—Local user access can be used to provide local and LUM users with complete access to private files. These accounts can be locked into their home directory through the use of a **CHROOT** jail.

- *Anonymous user access*—Anonymous user accounts can be set up to provide users with basic access to public files. Using a **CHROOT** jail, anonymous access can be locked into a specific directory structure to reduce potential security risks.

- *Firewall support*—If the FTP client is behind a firewall, FTP server supports passive mode data transfer and the configuration of a range of passive data ports.

- *FTP logs*—The FTP service maintains a log of several activities, including FTP sessions, unsuccessful login attempts, active session details, and system error—and FTP server—related messages.

For detailed information on all VSFTP server features, see the VSFTP homepage at http://vsftpd.beasts.org/.

Installing FTP Server

The VSFTP server can be installed as an optional component during the OES Linux installation or it can be installed later through YaST. To install VSFTP using YaST:

1. Access YaST from a terminal using `yast`, or from a graphical environment using `yast2` or the YaST launcher from the application menu.

2. Select the Search category in YaST. From within the Search category, enter **vsftpd** and click Search.

3. In the right pane, the **vsftpd** package should be displayed. Click the check box to mark **vsftpd** for installation.

4. Click Accept to start the software installation. At this point you may be prompted to install a few additional packages to satisfy dependencies. If so, select to continue the installation to install all required packages.

5. At the conclusion of the software installation, `SuSEconfig` is executed to update the system configuration. After this completes, select Finish to exit the Install and Remove Software module.

6. After being installed, the FTP service must be enabled through `xinetd`. From within YaST, select the Network Services category and locate and select the Network Services (`inetd`) module.

7. From within the Network Services Configuration (`xinetd`) screen, locate and select `ftp` in the Currently Available Services list, and then click on the Toggle Status (On or Off) button to enable the FTP service (see Figure 12.11). Select Finish to update the FTP configuration file and restart the `xinetd` service.

When the VSFTP server has been installed, and enabled within `xinetd`, you are ready to configure the FTP server.

FIGURE 12.11
YaST Network Services (xinetd) configuration for FTP.

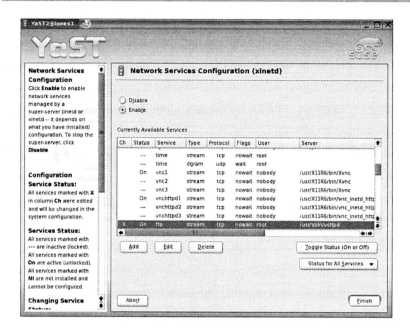

Configuring the FTP Server

Before you start the vsftpd server daemon, you should configure it by adjusting the configuration parameters found in the configuration file. The default configuration file is /etc/vsftpd.conf. The parameters in this configuration file do include comments; however, full descriptions, including default values for parameters, are only available through the man page (man 5 vsftpd.conf).

The vsftpd server daemon can be run in two modes: standalone or behind xinetd. From a security perspective, running vsftpd behind xinetd is a commonly used configuration. However, if the FTP service is expected to be heavily used, or if additional security is not necessary (LAN-only accessible location), running the FTP server in standalone mode is an option.

When you configure vsftpd, some options are only applicable to the standalone mode of vsftpd. For example, the IP address the FTP server will listen on can be configured via the listen_address parameter within vsftpd.conf. However, this parameter will only be recognized in standalone mode. When protected by xinetd, the IP address configuration is performed within xinetd.

The vsftpd server daemon reads the default configuration file /etc/vsftpd.conf upon daemon startup and configures itself accordingly. If any change is made to this file, the next FTP connection will cause xinetd to spawn a new session of the FTP daemon and the new configuration will automatically take affect.

GENERAL SETTINGS

The General section of the configuration file is used to configure system-wide behavior of the VSFTP server. Table 12.1 lists the available General server settings, with a brief description and the default setting in the configuration file.

TABLE 12.1
General Settings Parameters in vsftpd.conf

PARAMETER	DEFAULT VALUE	DESCRIPTION
write_enable	NO	Determines whether or not any type of write command will be allowed.
dirmessage_enable	YES	Activates directory messages that are displayed to users upon entering certain directories.
nopriv_user	nobody	Non-privileged user that the FTP server can use as a secure user.
ftpd_banner	None – Default vsftpd banner	Welcome message displayed to users upon connecting to FTP server. It is recommended that you change this to reduce the likelihood of users knowing the type of FTP server being used.
hide_ids	NO	Causes all user and group ownership information to be displayed as "ftp".

TRANSFER SETTINGS

The Transfer section of the configuration file is used to configure file transfer behavior of the VSFTP server. Table 12.2 lists the available Transfer server settings, with a brief description and the default setting in the configuration file.

TABLE 12.2
Transfer Settings Parameters in `vsftpd.conf`

PARAMETER	DEFAULT VALUE	DESCRIPTION
connect_from_port_20	YES	Ensures that data transfer connections originate on Port 20.
idle_session_timeout	300	Default amount of time (in seconds) a client can remain idle before being disconnected.
data_session_timeout	300	Default amount of time (in seconds) a data transfer can stall before being disconnected.
pasv_enable	YES	Enables PASV method for data transfers.
pam_service_name	vsftpd	Identifies the string PAM uses to integrate vsftpd. (This should not be changed.)

LOCAL USER SETTINGS

The Local User section of the configuration file is used to configure the FTP capabilities and environment for local users. These settings also apply to LUM users if the LUM component of OES is enabled. Table 12.3 lists the available Local User settings, with a brief description and the default setting in the configuration file.

TABLE 12.3
Local User Settings Parameters in `vsftpd.conf`

PARAMETER	DEFAULT VALUE	DESCRIPTION
local_enable	NO	Determines whether or not local users are allowed to authenticate.
local_umask	077	The umask variable used during local user FTP sessions.
chroot_local_user	NO	Determines whether or not local users are locked in a CHROOT jail during the FTP session.
chroot_list_enable	NO	Determines if a list of users to CHROOT is configured on the server.

TABLE 12.3
Continued

PARAMETER	DEFAULT VALUE	DESCRIPTION
chroot_list_file	/etc/vsftpd. chroot_list	If the chroot_list_enable parameter is set to YES, this parameter must contain a list of users who should be locked in a CHROOT jail.

ANONYMOUS USER SETTINGS

The Anonymous User section of the configuration file is used to configure the FTP capabilities and environment for anonymous, or guest, users. Table 12.4 lists the available Anonymous User settings, with a brief description and the default setting in the configuration file.

TABLE 12.4
Anonymous User Settings Parameters in vsftpd.conf

PARAMETER	DEFAULT VALUE	DESCRIPTION
anonymous_enable	YES	Determines whether anonymous connections are allowed.
anon_world_readable_only	YES	Causes anonymous users to only be allowed access to files that are readable to everyone.
anon_upload_enable	NO	Determines whether or not anonymous connections are allowed to upload files to the server.
anon_umask	077	The umask variable used during anonymous FTP sessions.

LOG SETTINGS

The Log Settings section of the configuration file is used to configure the logging behavior of the FTP server. Table 12.5 lists the available Log settings, with a brief description and the default setting in the configuration file.

TABLE 12.5
Log Settings Parameters in `vsftpd.conf`

PARAMETER	DEFAULT VALUE	DESCRIPTION
syslog_enable	YES	Causes vsftpd messages to be sent to syslog rather than tracked in the default vsftpd.log file.
log_ftp_protocol	NO	Causes all FTP requests and responses to be logged.
xferlog_enable	NO	Causes all FTP uploads and downloads to be logged.
vsftpd_log_file	/var/log/ vsftpd.log	If syslog is not used for logging, this parameter is used to adjust the default location for the vsftpd logfile.

With a basic FTP server running, NetDrive can be used by OES clients to access FTP resources, as described earlier in this chapter. For more information on using an FTP server in more general situations, see the SLES online documentation, or the **vsftpd** documentation at http://vsftpd.beasts.org/.

## CHAPTER 13

OES Printing Services

Instant Access

Installing and Configuring iPrint

- Install iPrint as part of the server installation, or install it after the fact through YaST.

- Configure the Driver Store, iPrint Manager, and Printer objects through iManager.

- The Driver Store and iPrint Manager daemons are automatically started after configuration. If necessary, the /etc/init.d/novell-idsd and /etc/init.d/novell-ipsmd scripts can be used to start and stop the daemons.

- Use the Manage Printers page in iManager to configure printer objects.

Working with iPrint

- The iPrint client is required to access and manage iPrint printers. Install the client by going to the iPrint home page on your OES Linux server at http://<server_IP_address or DNS_name>/ipp.

Defining Print Options

- To tell the printer how to print a job (the paper form to use, format, and so on), open iManager and choose Manage Printer. Specify the printer and select the Configurations page to change printer configuration.

Printing Jobs

- To print files from within an application, simply follow the application's normal printing procedures (making sure the application is configured to print to a network printer).

- To cancel or move a print job, open iManager and choose Manage Printer. Specify the printer and select Printer Control, Jobs.

Introduction to OES Printing

Along with file sharing, printer sharing was one of the original value propositions of Novell NetWare back in the early 1980s. OES Linux continues this on a Linux platform by delivering a powerful printing solution that allows users to print to any network printer to which they have been given rights—even if that printer is on the other side of the world! OES Linux uses iPrint as its default print environment. iPrint leverages the powerful foundation of Novell Distributed Print Services (NDPS), but puts a web face to printing and removes the dependence on the Novell client for print services. With iPrint, mobile employees, business partners, and even customers can access your printers through existing Internet connections. iPrint uses the Internet Printing Protocol (IPP), an industry standard, to make it possible to print seamlessly over the Internet, thus making location-based printing a reality.

The benefits of IPP include the following:

- IPP enjoys broad vendor support.
- IPP works over local networks as well as the Internet.
- IPP provides encrypted print services via SSL or TLS.
- IPP provides accessibility to print services from any platform (Windows, Macintosh, Linux, Unix, and so on).

Because iPrint is implemented on the foundation of NDPS, you also get all the advantages of robust network printing services coupled with the interoperability and ease-of-use of an Internet standard. So, through the combination of IPP and NDPS, you gain the following capabilities:

- Global access to printers managed through eDirectory
- Web-based printer location tool and driver installation
- Capability to print from anywhere to anywhere
- Web-based user controls and printer status
- Printers don't have to be IPP-aware to function with iPrint

When your iPrint environment is configured, you can enjoy powerful printing options suitable for the web-based business world, such as:

- *Printing across the Internet*—Remote employees can actually print directly to a printer located at the office because iPrint resources are available as standard web URLs. Simply enter the appropriate URL for a company's print services, locate the printer to which you want to print, and iPrint takes care of the rest—including the installation of the iPrint client software, if necessary.

- *Printing away from "home"*—Setting up printing when visiting a different company location used to be an ordeal. No more. Now, simply access the company's print services URL, browse to the office at which you are currently located, and use the office map to locate the printer closest to you. Selecting the printer will install the necessary driver software automatically.

- *Printing instead of faxing*—Because you can now print across the Internet, you can effectively print instead of faxing. All you need is an iPrint printer to which you can connect. With the web-based iPrint tools, it is possible to monitor the print job remotely and then email the intended recipient when the print job has finished.

iPrint provides the robust printing environment you expect from Novell while at the same time integrating with modern printing standards that extend printing capabilities to the Internet.

iPrint Components

Because iPrint leverages NDPS, traditional Novell administrators might recognize several of the components that have been around since NetWare 5. In order to properly manage and route network print jobs from multiple users to multiple printers, NDPS uses the following software components:

- *Printer Agent*—A printer agent is simply software that manages a printer. Every printer must have a printer agent in the iPrint world. A printer's printer agent does the following:

  - Manages the printer's print jobs

  - Responds to client queries about print jobs or printer capabilities

  - Communicates with the printer and is notified when something goes wrong, or when some other monitored event occurs so that it can be communicated to those interested in the printer status

- *iPrint Gateway*—The Gateway handles communication between the Print Manager and the printer. With OES Linux, the Gateway provides this functionality through LPR over TCP/IP. The Gateway also uses SNMP to monitor printer status.

- *iPrint Manager*—The iPrint Manager controls all printer agents configured on a given server. One iPrint Manager can provide print services to multiple printers. If necessary, additional iPrint Managers can also be added to the eDirectory tree. Although multiple iPrint Managers can be configured on a single server, only one iPrint Manager at a time can be running on a server.

In addition to the NDPS components already mentioned, iPrint adds the following components:

- *IPP Server*—The IPP Server is responsible for processing all IPP requests and sending those requests to the iPrint Manager or iPrint Driver Store.

- *iPrint Driver Store*—The iPrint Driver Store is a centralized repository of printer drivers. As clients configure printers for the first time, the iPrint Manager automatically downloads the appropriate driver from the iPrint Driver Store and caches it locally for future installations.

- *iPrint web pages*—These pages are used to install the iPrint client software and printers, and to view and manage print jobs. The look and feel of these pages is customizable with any HTML editor you might want to use.

- *Print provider and Web browser plug-ins*—These are the only client-side pieces necessary to leverage the iPrint environment. As previously mentioned, the Novell client is not required.

TIP

If you are managing printers at multiple sites, you should plan to have an iPrint Manager at each geographical location to reduce printing-related traffic over your WAN links. You may also choose to configure additional iPrint Driver Stores, but keep in mind that each store must be individually updated as new printer drivers become necessary.

With this introduction to iPrint components, you are now ready to start working with the printing capabilities of OES Linux.

Installing iPrint

If you didn't select iPrint during the server installation, you can install it after the fact from YaST. To install iPrint from YaST, complete the following steps:

1. Access YaST from a terminal using `yast`, from a graphical environment using `yast2`, or from the YaST launcher from the application menu.

2. Select the Network Services category in YaST. From within this category, locate and select the iPrint module. This module will detect that the `rpms` for iPrint are missing and ask if you want to install them. Select Continue to install the necessary packages.

3. At the conclusion of the software installation, `SuSEconfig` is executed to update the system configuration. When this completes, the configuration of the OES component will begin automatically.

4. At the iPrint LDAP Server Configuration screen, enter the following information and click Next:

   - *Local or Remote Directory Server*—Select the radio button, which indicates whether eDirectory is running on the local server or a remote server.

   - *Directory Server Address*—If a remote eDirectory server is in use, enter the IP address for this server.

   - *Admin Name with Context*—Enter the eDirectory administrator's credentials using fully qualified dot notation, for example, `cn=admin.o=novell`.

   - *Admin Password*—Enter the password for the administrator user.

   - *Port Details*—If necessary, select this button to change the configured ports for the eDirectory server specified previously. The default LDAP port for unencrypted communications is **389** and port **636** is used for SSL-encrypted communications.

5. At the iPrint Configuration screen, enter the eDirectory tree name and click Next.

6. In order for iPrint to be active, select restart Apache when prompted.

With iPrint installed on your OES Linux server, you are now ready to start configuring your iPrint environment.

Configuring iPrint

A few general tasks are involved in setting up an iPrint environment—all of which can be performed through iManager:

- Create an iPrint Driver Store.
- Create an iPrint Manager.
- *(Optional)* Set up—Although DNS is not technically required, it will be a lot easier for your users to access web-based iPrint tools if DNS is configured on your network. Otherwise, they will have to specify IP addresses to get to iPrint services. If the IP address changes for any reason, users will have to reinstall their printers. For more information about configuring DNS, see Chapter 7, "Novell eDirectory Management."
- Create printer objects.
- Install iPrint support on workstations.

The following sections take a look at each of these tasks and describe how you can accomplish each of them.

CREATE AN IPRINT DRIVER STORE

To create a new iPrint Driver Store for your iPrint environment, complete the following steps from iManager:

1. In the Navigation frame, open the iPrint group and select Create Driver Store.
2. On the Create Driver Store page in the Content frame, provide the necessary information and click OK (see Figure 13.1).
   - *Driver Store Name*—Specify a name for the Driver Store object.
   - *Container Name*—Specify a location for the Driver Store object in the eDirectory tree.
   - *Target Server*—Specify a DNS name or IP address for the server that will host the driver store.
   - *eDir Server*—Specify the eDirectory server you want the driver store to be associated with.
3. Click OK to complete the process.

When the iPrint Driver Store configuration is complete, it is written to the /etc/opt/novell/iprint/conf/idsd.conf configuration file. This configuration file can be manually edited to perform such tasks as configuring multiple Driver Stores, modifying the eDirectory server assignment, and adding secondary eDirectory servers to the Driver Store. For information regarding the syntax of this file, refer to the **/etc/opt/novell/iprint/conf/ idsd-template.conf** file.

FIGURE 13.1
Creating an iPrint Driver Store in iManager.

The initialization script for the iPrint Driver Store is **/etc/init.d/ novell-idsd**. This script should be used to automatically start the Driver Store daemon after configuration within iManager. This script should also be configured to start automatically upon server startup. If necessary, this script can be used with a **start** or **stop** command-line parameter to manually load and unload the driver store.

NOTE

The iPrint Driver Store can also be shut down using the Manage Driver Store link within iManager. After locating and opening the Driver Store object, select the Driver Store Control page and select Shutdown to unload the store.

OES Linux ships with many printer drivers for common printers. As printer manufacturers release new printers and updated drivers, however, you might need to add a driver that is not included with the default set that shipped with OES Linux.

To see the list of existing printer drivers, and to add a new driver to the store, complete the following steps in iManager:

1. In the Navigation frame, open the iPrint group and select Manage Driver Store.

2. In the Content frame, specify or browse to your iPrint Driver Store object and click OK.

3. Select the Drivers tab to add a driver to the store, as shown in Figure 13.2.

FIGURE 13.2

Adding a new printer driver to the iPrint Driver Store with iManager.

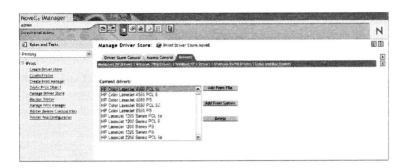

4. Select the subpage for the operating platform (Windows XP, Linux and Mac, and so on) for the printer driver. A list appears, showing all printer drivers currently available.

5. Click Add from File or Add from System and specify the driver you want to add. Click OK and follow the prompts to add the driver to your store. Add from File means that you have a separate driver available. Add from System means that you want to extract the appropriate resource driver from system files.

NOTE

You are only allowed to use the Add from System option for the operating system that matches the workstation you are currently using. For all other operating systems, you must use the Add from File option.

Also, in iManager printer drivers can only be added from workstations running the iPrint client. If necessary, install the iPrint client prior to performing this operation.

The new driver will appear in the list of available resources in the Driver Store database.

CREATING AN IPRINT MANAGER

After you have created and populated your Driver Store, you are ready to create an iPrint Manager on your server. To do this, create an iPrint Manager object in the eDirectory tree and then load the iPrint Manager on the server by completing the following steps in iManager:

1. In the Navigation frame, open the iPrint group and select Create Print Manager.

2. In the Content frame, provide the necessary information and click OK (see Figure 13.3).

   - *Print Manager Name*—Specify a name for the iPrint Manager object.

   - *Container Name*—Specify a location for the iPrint Manager object in the eDirectory tree.

   - *Target Server*—Specify a DNS name or IP address for the server where the iPrint Manager will be located.

WARNING

It is strongly recommended that the server's DNS name be specified in the Target Server field of the iPrint Manager. If an IP address is used, and the server's IP address is modified, all clients using printers managed by the iPrint Manager will need to be reconfigured with the new IP address. Using a DNS name ensures that clients are not affected if these types of changes become necessary!

   - *eDir Server*—Specify the eDirectory server you want the iPrint Manager to be associated with.

   - *Driver Store Name*—Specify the name of the Driver Store object that has already been created.

3. Click OK to return to the iManager home page.

FIGURE 13.3
Creating a Print Manager in iManager.

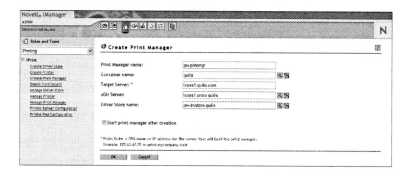

When the iPrint Manager configuration is complete, it is written into the /etc/opt/novell/iprint/conf/ipsmd.conf configuration file. If the eDirectory server assignment needs to be changed, or additional eDirectory servers need to be added to the server list, this file can be manually edited. For information regarding the syntax of this file, refer to the /etc/opt/novell/iprint/conf/ipsmd-template.conf file.

The initialization script for the iPrint Manager is /etc/init.d/novell-ipsmd. This script is used to start the iPrint Manager upon object creation in iManager. This script should also be configured to automatically start upon server startup. If necessary, this script can be used with a **start** or **stop** command-line parameter to manually load and unload the iPrint Manager.

NOTE

The iPrint Manager can also be shut down and moved to another server using the Manage Print Manager link within iManager. After locating and opening the iPrint Manager object, select the Manager Control page and select Shutdown to unload the store. To move the manager to another server, select the Move option.

After successful configuration, the Print Manager will control all printer agents that you install on your OES Linux server. This task is accomplished with the help of an iPrint database. The database is used to track information regarding all configured iPrint servers managed by this specific iPrint Manager.

The iPrint database is stored in the /var/opt/novell/iprint directory as psmdb.*. To help protect against configuration loss, this database is backed up every time a printer is added or deleted from the current iPrint Manager. The database is also backed up every night at midnight. The backup database is named psmdbsav.*. In the event of damage to the current database, the backup version can be manually restored using the following steps:

1. Ensure that the iPrint Manager is stopped by executing
   /etc/init.d/novell-ipsmd stop

2. Rename the current iPrint database:
   cd /var/opt/novell/iprint
   mv psmdb.* psmdbold.*

3. Restore the backup database:
   mv psmdbsav.* psmdb.*

4. Start the iPrint Manager by executing
   /etc/init.d/novell-ipsmd start

CREATING NETWORK PRINTERS

To create an iPrint printer, you must first create a Printer object in the eDirectory tree, and you must have already created an iPrint Manager object. To create a Printer object using iManager, complete the following steps in iManager:

1. In the Navigation frame, open the iPrint group and select Create Printer.

2. In the Content frame, provide the necessary information and click Next.

   - *Printer Name*—Specify a name for the Printer object.

   - *Container Name*—Specify a context where the Printer object will be located.

   - *Print Manager Name*—Specify the name of the Print Manager that will manage this printer.

   - *DNS Name or IP Address*—Specify the DNS name or IP address of the physical printer.

   - *Location*—(Optional) Specify descriptive information that will help iPrint clients determine where this printer resides.

   - *Description*—(Optional) Specify a description for the printer.

   - *LPR Printer Name or Port 9100*—These two fields are used to specify the connection type to the printer. Enter the LPR Printer Name for all printers except those that only support port 9100. Select Port 9100 for printers that only support access through port 9100. (HP JetDirect printers are one example of printers that normally use port 9100.)

3. Select the appropriate printer driver(s) from the driver list and click Next. You can select a driver for each type of Windows workstation platform: Windows XP, Windows 2000, Windows NT 4, or Windows 95/98, as well as Linux/Mac. These are the drivers that will be automatically downloaded to the client workstations when they install the printer.

4. Click OK to return to the iManager home page.

IPP support is enabled automatically when a new printer object is created. However, you can enable/disable secure IPP support (requires SSL/TLS) from the iPrint Support subpage of the Client Support tab for each printer object. You can also enable/disable LPR/LPD client support on the LPR Support subpage beneath that same Client Support tab.

When your printers have been installed, managing them is relatively easy. Everything you need is located in iManager. The Printer Management links, shown in the left side of the navigation frame in Figure 13.3, are a one-stop shop for managing user access, printer configuration, and print service support.

PRINTER POOLING

iPrint lets you create a pool of printers to share print duties. Users install one of the printers associated with a pool. When a print job is sent, if the installed printer is busy, the Print Manager can automatically redirect that print job to an idle printer in the pool. Pool printers need to use the same print driver and be of a similar make and model to be sure that print jobs will print correctly. All printers in a pool must be assigned to the same Print Manager.

To create a printer pool, complete the following steps in iManager:

1. In the Navigation frame, open the iPrint group and select Printer Pool Configuration.

2. Specify the Print Manager for which you are creating a printer pool. Select Create Printer Pool from the drop-down list, and click OK.

3. Specify a name for the printer pool, and select the printers that should be included in the pool. Click Next.

4. Click OK to return to the iManager home page.

After the printer pool has been created, it will transparently share jobs among all printers in the pool when necessary.

PRINTER BANNERS

iPrint also lets you configure print banners, or cover sheets, which can be assigned to specific iPrint printers. Thanks to the integration of eDirectory into the iPrint system, these banners can even include information such as the print owner's email address, location, or full name.

NOTE

In order for eDirectory attributes to be used in print banners, the iPrint Manager must have the necessary eDirectory rights to read the desired attributes. This can easily be solved using iManager and assigning the iPrint Manager the appropriate trustee rights to the containers where user objects can be found.

Banners are associated with a specific iPrint Manager. When assigned to a manager, printers managed by the iPrint Manager can then be assigned to one of the configured banners.

To create a custom banner, complete the following steps in iManager:

1. In the Navigation frame, open the iPrint group and select Printer Banner Configuration.

2. Specify the Print Manager for which you are creating a banner. Select Create Custom Banner from the drop-down list, and click OK.

3. Specify a name for the banner, and select the page location for the banner text.

4. Select the items you would like displayed on the banner. Each item can also be configured with a relative font size. eDirectory attributes are all displayed using an eDir designation at the beginning of the attribute name.

5. Click Next and then OK to return to the iManager home page.

After creating the banner, you must associate it with a printer in order to perform a function. The following steps outline the process of assigning a print banner to a printer:

1. In the Navigation frame, open the iPrint group and select Printer Banner Configuration.

2. Specify the Print Manager for which you are assigning a banner. Select Assign Custom Banner from the drop-down list, and click OK.

3. Select a banner from the Custom Banner drop-down list, and then select printers for which the banner should be active. When finished assigning banners to printers, click Next.

4. Click OK to return to the iManager home page.

Accessing iPrint Printers

In order for users to use iPrint, they need two components:

- The Novell iPrint client
- A printer to which they can print

When a user selects a printer to be installed by iPrint, iPrint determines whether the Novell iPrint client is installed. If it is not installed, iPrint will walk the user through the client installation. Following this, the printer driver is downloaded and the printer is installed on the user's workstation.

iPrint client files and printers can be quickly and easily installed from a web page.

TIP

The iPrint client and appropriate printer drivers can also be distributed using ZENworks for Desktops (Windows workstations), and ZENworks for Linux Management (Linux workstations). If you have either of these additional Novell products, consult the Novell online documentation for more information on automating client delivery and installation with ZENworks.

Users simply browse to the iPrint URL, which, by default, is the following: http://<*server_IP_address or DNS_name*>/ipp. Figure 13.4 shows a sample iPrint printers home page.

FIGURE 13.4
A sample iPrint printers home page.

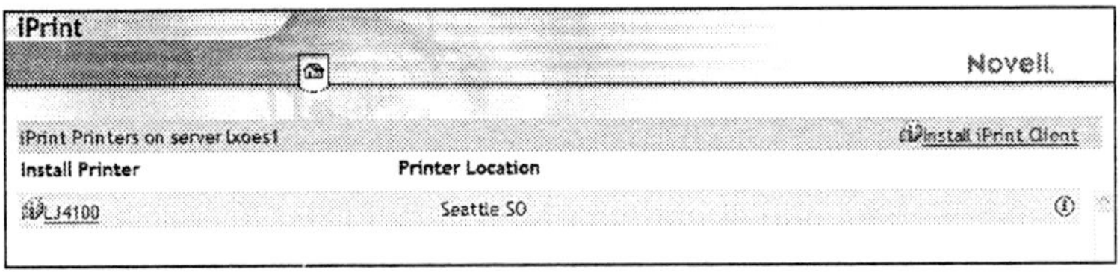

The iPrint printers home page displays a listing of available printers and a link to install the iPrint client. Users simply select Install iPrint Client and follow the prompts to complete the client installation. If they try to install a printer before installing the iPrint client, they will be prompted to install the client first.

NOTE FOR WINDOWS WORKSTATIONS

When using the iPrint client in a Windows environment, the workstation must normally reboot to complete the installation. To remove the iPrint client from a Windows workstation, either the standard Remove Programs option in the Windows Control Panel or the Uninstall shortcut under the Novell iPrint program group can be used.

NOTE FOR LINUX WORKSTATIONS

In a Linux workstation environment, the iPrint client is downloaded in rpm format. After the client is downloaded, the root account must be used to install the rpm. To avoid this requirement, ZENworks for Linux Management (ZLM) can be used to push the client out to Linux workstations. Otherwise, download the rpm to the user's home directory and install the client manually.

Linux workstations do not require a reboot after installing the iPrint client. However, iPrint browser plug-ins will not be recognized until the user's browser is restarted after installing the client. If you are using the Konqueror browser, the iPrint plug-in can be registered by choosing Settings, Configure Konqueror, Plugins, Scan for New Plugins.

After the client is installed, users return to the same iPrint URL to install the necessary printer support. If you have associated a printer driver with each of your iPrint printers, it is automatically installed on the users' workstations. If a printer driver already exists on the workstations, it will be overwritten.

When the printer driver installs on a Windows workstation, a Printer icon is added to the users' Printers folder. From that point on, users access the printer through all the normal avenues.

DEFAULT PRINTER DRIVER OPTIONS

You can control how printer driver options are set when the printer driver is installed on a workstation. To use this functionality, you must configure Location-Based Printing with the iPrint Map Designer.

As part of the iPrint Map Design process, you must configure the properties of all printers being made available through iPrint maps. Table 13.1 shows the supported parameters for iPrint printers.

TABLE 13.1
Supported Printer Parameters for iPrint Printers

PARAMETER	SUPPORTED VALUES
orientation	Landscape, portrait
papersize	Letter, lettersmall, tabloid, ledger, legal, statement, executive, A3, A4, A4small, A5, B4, B5, folio, quatro, 10x14, 11x17, note, env_10, env_12, env_14, csheet, dsheet, esheet, env_dl, env_c5, env_c4, env_c3, env_c65, env_b5, env_b6, env_italy, env_monarch, env_personal, fanfold_us, fanfold_std_german, fanfold_lgl_german, iso_b4, japanese_postcard, 9x11, 10x11, 15x11, env_invite, letter_extra, legal_extra, tabloid_extra, A4_extra, letter_extra_transverse, a_plus, b_plus, letter_plus, A4_plus, A5_transverse, B5_transverse, A3_extra, A5_extra, B5_extra, A2, A3_transverse, A3_extra_transverse
copies	Enter the number of copies you want printed
color	Yes=color; no or false=monochrome
duplex	Simplex, horizontal, vertical
collate	Yes or true=collate; no=do not collate

More information on the iPrint Map Design process is available later in this chapter.

IPRINT CLIENT UPDATES

Periodically, users will need to update their iPrint client. Each time a user starts his or her workstation, the iPrint client checks with the default printer to determine whether a newer version of the iPrint client exists. If necessary, a newer version of the client can be installed. You can control how this update takes place with the `iprint.ini` file.

The `iprint.ini` file is stored in `/var/opt/novell/iprint/htdocs` on each server where iPrint is installed. It lets you specify whether the user should be prompted before a new client is installed, or if the update should be a "hands-free" process.

Descriptive text for each entry in `iprint.ini` is included in the file. You can view and edit the file using a text editor.

WARNING

The `iprint.ini` file should be synchronized across all servers on which iPrint is running.

Location-Based Printing

Location-based printing is one of the key values of iPrint. It lets users easily locate and install printers using one of two methods:

- *Printer list views*—With list views, you configure printer lists so that they make the most sense for your users, such as by building, by office location, or by eDirectory context.

- *Printer maps*—Using the iPrint Map Designer, you can create maps of printer locations by using drag-and-drop methods. Then you can post the maps on a web server for users to access. By looking at the maps, they locate a printer close to their location and simply click the Printer icon. The printer driver and iPrint client, if necessary, are then installed on the users' workstations.

Each of these methods is discussed in the following sections.

CREATING PRINTER LISTS

iPrint provides a default list of printers organized by the iPrint Manager. To create a custom list, you can modify the HTML of the iPrint page and create links to individual printers' IPP URLs. When you create an iPrint printer, a URL is listed in the accepted IPP URL list. This is the URL you will specify when creating a customized printer list.

Using the iPrint Map Designer tool, you can quickly create a map showing printer locations. The tool lets you import floor plans so that you can drag and drop printers to actual locations. These maps are then published on a web server so that users can install printers that are closest to their location.

CREATING PRINTER MAPS

Creating printer maps requires that you have the iPrint client installed on the workstation from which you will be creating the maps. You must also access the Map Designer using Internet Explorer 5.5 or later.

The iPrint Map Designer lets you create maps showing the physical locations of printers in a building by using background images of the building's floor plan. After creating the maps, use the iPrint Map Designer to modify or update your maps as necessary.

To create a printer map for your iPrint users, complete the following steps:

1. Get graphic images of your building floor plan(s). iPrint supports images in JPEG, GIF, and BMP formats. Copy all of the floor plan images to your iPrint servers and store them in `/var/opt/novell/iprint/htdocs/images/maps`.

   You can also use custom printer icons within your maps. To do this, copy the desired images into the `/var/opt/novell/iprint/htdocs/images/printers` directory.

2. To access the iPrint Map tool, use Internet Explorer to access http://<*server address*>/ippdocs/maptool.htm.

3. From the bottom of the Navigation frame, select the background image from the Background drop-down list. Select a floor plan image from those you have copied to `/var/opt/novell/iprint/htdocs/images/maps`. Alternatively, you can retrieve and modify an existing map file by selecting Open and specifying (browsing to) the directory where the map is located.

4. To add a printer to the map, provide the following information:

   ▪ *Printer icon*—Select the type of printer icon you want to use.

   ▪ *Printer list*—Click the Browse icon and enter the IP address or DNS name of the OES Linux server where the iPrint Manager is running. Click OK. From the printer list, select the printer agent you want associated with this printer icon. If the printer is not listed, make sure you have IPP enabled for that printer.

NOTE

To add printers from different Print Managers to the same map, first add the printers from the first Print Manager, and then click the Browse icon, select the next Print Manager, and repeat the process.

5. Drag and drop your printer icon to the desired location on the map. When you have completed this, the following three fields become enabled and must be filled out:

   - *Printer URL*—The URL created for the IPP printer will populate this field automatically. You should not need to change the URL.

   - *Mouse over Text*—This field is populated automatically by the printer agent's name. You can override this information and enter any descriptive text you want to display when a user moves the mouse over the Printer icon.

   - *(Optional) Printer Caption*—Enter the information to display, using Enter to parse the information onto multiple lines.

6. When the printer has been correctly placed on the map, click on the Driver Settings option in the menu bar to configure default printer options, such as orientation, paper size, and so on. Possible options were explained in the "Default Printer Driver Options" section earlier in this chapter. These options can also be manually added to the map file after the map has been generated. For information on this, see the DRIVER-OPTIONS section of the `example.htm` file in `/var/opt/novell/iprint/htdocs`.

7. Click Save, and save the map. If you have Samba access to your server, you can save the file directly to `/var/opt/novell/iprint/htdocs`. Otherwise, you will have to save the file to a local directory, and transfer the map to the server manually.

WARNING

If you click Refresh or close your web browser without saving the map, all changes made since the last time the map was saved will be lost.

Repeat step 4 for each printer you want to place on your map. You can edit a printer's information at any time by clicking the appropriate printer icon and changing the printer information fields as required. If you need to add or modify printers from a previously used Print Manager, click a printer icon from that manager and the printer list will be populated with printers from that manager.

HOSTING THE MAPS ON A WEB SERVER

After creating your maps, you need to post them on a web server in order for your maps and iPrint to work properly. This web server can be a new or existing web server, or it can be the OES server itself. To use a new or existing web server, copy the contents of the /var/opt/novell/iprint/htdocs directory and its subdirectories to the web server directory structure. You can then link to your maps from your company's internal web page or send the URL out to your users.

To use the OES server itself, simply copy the map file to the /var/opt/novell/iprint/htdocs directory. The map file then must be linked to an existing website, or published to end users. The URL for the map will be http://<server address>/ippdocs/<map>.

Printer Availability on Workstations

Sometimes you might want printers to remove themselves automatically from a workstation. For example, suppose you have a printer in your lobby for a customer to use. When the customer leaves, you want the printer to be removed from the customer's laptop. Setting the persistence of the printer allows you to automatically remove the printer when the customer reboots his or her laptop.

To configure a printer's persistence, you must be using Location-Based Printing. When configuring the location maps, you have the opportunity to configure the driver settings for each printer. If you would like to modify a printer's persistence, configure the persistence attribute to one of the values listed in Table 13.2.

TABLE 13.2
Possible Options for Printer Persistence

PARAMETER	SUPPORTED VALUES
persistent	The printer will not be automatically removed.
volatile-reboot	The printer will be removed when the workstation is rebooted.
volatile-date-time	The printer will be removed at the specified time. The time should be entered in the following numeric format: year,month,day,hour,minute

As with other driver parameters, this can also be manually entered into existing maps by following the syntax in the example.htm file found in /var/opt/novell/iprint/htdocs.

Setting Up a Secure Printing Environment

iPrint is designed to take full advantage of eDirectory security and ease of management. Setting up a secure printing environment can be done on two levels:

- *Print access control*—Create a secure printing management infrastructure by assigning users to User, Operator, or Manager roles. This restricts the list of those who can control printers, iPrint Managers, and Driver Stores.

- *Securing iPrint with SSL*—This option not only encrypts print communications over the wire, but also requires users to authenticate before installing and printing to a printer.

These levels are discussed in the following sections.

Print Access Control

Printer security is ensured through the assignment of the Manager, Operator, and User Access Control roles, and by the strategic placement of printers and printer configurations. For more information on eDirectory access control in general, see Chapter 7.

The access controls for iPrint allow you to specify the access each User, Group, or Container object will have to your printing resources. It is important to remember that all iPrint print roles function independently. For example, assigning someone as a printer manager does not automatically grant said person the rights of a printer user.

In most cases, the default assignments will prevent any problems that this role independence might cause. For example, a printer manager is automatically assigned as a printer operator and user for that printer. Similarly, a printer operator is automatically assigned as a user of that printer as well. You cannot remove the user role from an operator, and you cannot remove the operator and user roles from a manager.

The creator of an iPrint object is automatically assigned to all supported roles for the type of object being created.

You can assign multiple Printer objects to a given printer agent, but simultaneously make different access control assignments to each Printer object. This means that users in different containers can be assigned different trustee rights to the same printer.

PRINTER ROLES

As previously alluded to, three roles are associated with iPrint printing services: Manager, Operator, and User. Table 13.3 describes the rights granted to each role.

TABLE 13.3
NDPS Print Roles and Their Associated Rights

ROLE	ASSOCIATED RIGHTS
Manager	Tasks performed exclusively by the printer manager are those that require the creation, modification, or deletion of Printer objects, as well as other eDirectory administrative functions. Printer managers are automatically designated as printer operators and users as well, so they can perform all tasks assigned to the operator role. Typical manager functions include the following: Modifying and deleting Printer objects Adding or deleting operators and users for a printer Adding other managers Configuring interested-party notification Creating, modifying, or deleting printer configurations
Operator	Print operators cannot create, modify, or delete eDirectory objects or perform other eDirectory administrative functions. Their management tasks include the following: Performing all of the functions available through the Printer Control page Pausing, restarting, or reinitializing printers Reordering, moving, copying, and deleting jobs Setting printer defaults, including locked properties Configuring print job spooling
User	Print users only have rights to submit and manage print jobs that they own. Users cannot copy, move, reorder, or remove jobs they do not own. To simplify administration, the container within which a printer resides is automatically assigned as a user for that printer. That way, all users in that container inherit printer user rights. You can delete the Container object as a printer user in order to block access to the printer for users in that container.

To define the role assignment for a printer, complete the following steps in iManager:

1. In the Navigation frame, open the iPrint group and select Manage Printer.

2. In the Content frame, specify the printer for which you want to configure access controls and click OK.

3. At the Manage Printer page, select the Access Control tab, as shown in Figure 13.5.

4. Make your desired changes by adding or deleting members from the User, Operator, and Manager roles for this printer. eDirectory objects that can be assigned in these roles include User, Group, or Container objects. Click OK to save your changes.

FIGURE 13.5
Access Control tab for defining printer management roles in ConsoleOne.

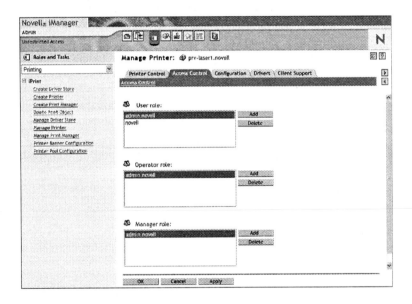

Following these changes, printer access will be granted according to the access controls you have defined.

IPRINT MANAGER ACCESS CONTROLS

iPrint Manager security is provided exclusively through the printer manager role in iManager. The printer manager role was discussed previously in the "Printer Roles" section. Refer to Table 13.3 for more information on iPrint

administrative roles in iManager. For more information on role-based administration with iManager, see Chapter 5, "OES Management Tools." Common
administrative tasks related to the print manager include the following:

- Creating printer agents and iPrint Manager objects
- Adding or deleting operators and users for a printer
- Adding other managers
- Configuring interested-party notification
- Creating, modifying, or deleting printer configurations

You should plan on assigning users who need to perform these types of tasks as
occupants of the printer manager role.

IPRINT DRIVER STORE ACCESS CONTROLS

Two roles are associated with the Driver Store object. The printer manager role
was discussed previously in the "Printer Roles" section. Refer to Table 13.3 for
more information on iPrint administrative roles in iManager:

- *Manager*—Tasks performed exclusively by the Driver Store manager
  require the creation, modification, or deletion of Driver Store objects, as
  well as those that involve other eDirectory administrative functions.
  Typical manager functions include the following:

  - Creating, modifying, and deleting Driver Store objects
  - Adding other managers
  - Enabling or disabling Driver Stores

- *Public access user*—A public access user is a role assigned to all individu-
  als on the network who are users of printers receiving services and
  resources provided by the Driver Store. This role is assigned by default
  and does not require specific administrative action by the Driver Store
  manager.

Securing iPrint with SSL

Secure printing takes advantage of SSL, which requires users to authenticate
using their eDirectory usernames and passwords. Users must authenticate once
per eDirectory tree per session. The print data is encrypted, and all print communications use port 443. Without secure printing, the printer is available to
anyone on the local network and print communications are not encrypted.
Secure printing works in conjunction with the security level set for the printer.

Prior to implementing SSL for iPrint, the following considerations must be noted:

- *Enabling SSL changes the printer URL.* Implementing SSL will modify the printer URL. Clients currently configured to access the printer will need to delete and reinstall the printer in order to be operational.

- *SSL uses LDAP authentication.* When users authenticate to the printer, this authentication is performed using LDAP access to eDirectory. LDAP then performs a search for the requested user starting from the root of the tree. If your eDirectory tree is large, the search base can be manually configured to decrease the time necessary for this search. To make this change, edit the `AuthLDAPURL` parameter within the `iprint_ssl.conf` file found at `/etc/opt/novell/iprint/httpd/conf`.

To enable SSL support for a given printer, complete the following steps in iManager:

1. In the Navigation frame, open the iPrint group and select Manage Printer.

2. In the Content frame, specify the printer for which you want to enable IPP printing.

3. On the Client Support tab, select the iPrint Support subpage. To enable SSL, click the check box for Enable Secure Printing.

4. Click OK to return to the iManager home page.

When this configuration is complete, SSL printers will require user authentication and encrypt communication between the client and server. Depending on the security of your network and the material being printed, this may not be a required step.

Open Enterprise Server Web Services

## CHAPTER 14

OES Foundations

Instant Access

Installing Apache Web Server and Tomcat Servlet Engine

- Apache Web Server and Tomcat Servlet engine are installed with most configurations of OES Linux. If necessary, they can also be installed later using YaST.

Managing Apache Web Server

- To manage Apache Web Server, use the httpd.conf and various configuration directories beneath /etc/apache2.

- Apache Web Server can also be managed using the HTTP Server module in YaST.

- Virtual Hosting should be used to add custom content to the existing instance of Apache used for OES administration.

- Use the Apache Server logs to view errors and access attempts. Important log files include

  - /var/log/apache2/access_log
  - /var/log/apache2/error_log

Managing Tomcat Servlet Engine

- Use the Tomcat logs to view configuration information and errors. Important log files for Tomcat are

  - `/var/log/apache2/mod_jk.log`

  - `/var/opt/novell/tomcat4/logs/catalina.out`

  - `/var/opt/novell/tomcat4/logs/localhost_log.*`

This chapter looks at Apache Web Server and Tomcat Servlet Engine. Together, they form the foundation necessary for delivering web services on the OES Linux platform:

- *Apache Web Server*—Apache Web Server is an open-source (read: *free*) web server that is responsible for serving more than 60% of all web content on the Internet. In OES Linux, Apache provides support for all OES Linux web-based management tools, and support for regular web server functionality for providing web services and applications.

- *Tomcat Servlet Engine*—Tomcat was developed by the same folks who gave us Apache and is used to serve web applications. As with Apache, Tomcat is used internally for OES Linux web-based management tools, and can be used externally to provide web-based services.

Several powerful OES Linux services rely on Apache and Tomcat, including

- iManager
- iFolder
- iPrint
- QuickFinder
- Virtual Office

The following sections will discuss Apache Web Server and Tomcat Servlet Engine and their possibilities with OES Linux.

Apache Web Server

Apache Web Server is the primary HTTP stack provided for OES Linux. Apache is an open-source web server used by more than two-thirds of the Internet's web servers. As such, it runs on all major server platforms and can scale to support thousands of simultaneous connections.

Apache Web Server is a complex and full-featured product, so there is a lot more to it than can be covered here. However, because Apache is an open-source application, almost anything you want to know about it is available on the web. You should take some time to look through the Apache documentation in order to become familiar with architecture and capabilities, particularly if you are going to implement a more complex web environment. The Apache Web Server documentation is available online at http://httpd.apache.org/docs-2.0.

Apache Web Server can be used in a few different ways on OES Linux. First, Apache is installed automatically as a dedicated web server to support the administrative tools for OES Linux and its related products and services. You can find all files related to this instance of Apache in the `/etc/opt/novell/httpd/conf.d` directory. This administrative web server supports iManager, Virtual Office, iPrint, and other OES Linux services that need a web interface.

If you are using iFolder, a customized configuration of Apache is required. Normally, this is accomplished by installing iFolder on its own dedicated server (with no other OES components). However, it is possible to install other OES components on the same server. To ensure that iFolder is usable in both configurations, a separate, dedicated instance of Apache is used. The configuration file used by the iFolder instance of Apache can be found in the `/etc/opt/novell/ifolder/conf` directory. A separate binary (`/usr/sbin/httpd2-worker`) is also used for the iFolder version of Apache.

NOTE

The iFolder version of Apache is highly customized and specific to the iFolder process. Configuration files for this instance of Apache should not be modified manually. For more information on iFolder, see Chapter 15, "OES Web Services."

Another way Apache is commonly used with OES is to host your own custom web content. In this situation, you should not load another instance of Apache, but rather customize the administrative instance of Apache to recognize a virtual server, or separate document root directory. This is covered later in this chapter.

When you use iManager, accessible from any web browser, it is the Admin configuration of the Apache Web Server that serves the data between the web browser and OES Linux.

Installing Apache Web Server

If you are interested in using Apache only as the foundation for your OES Linux tools and services, you don't have to do anything to get Apache up and running. The **admin** server configuration of Apache is installed automatically during most OES Linux installations.

However, if you chose to perform a custom installation of OES, or are adding OES components to an existing SLES9 server, you may want to install Apache manually. To install Apache Web Server manually through YaST, complete the following steps:

1. Access YaST from a terminal using **yast**, or from a graphical environment using **yast2** or the YaST launcher from the application menu.

2. Select the Software category in YaST. (This is typically the category selected by default.) From within the Software category, click on the Install and Remove Software module.

3. Use the Filter drop-down box to select the Selections category.

4. In the Selection window (left pane of the main window), select Simple Webserver. (You can select the entire category, or just the Apache2 package in the right pane.)

5. If you'd like to install Tomcat Servlet Engine, change the Filter drop-down box to Search, and search on "Tomcat." In the right pane window, locate and select **novell-tomcat4**.

NOTE

OES Linux also includes Tomcat 5 Servlet Container (through the **jakarta-tomcat** package). Tomcat 5 is an update to Tomcat 4 that includes new features and fixes over Tomcat 4.x. OES Linux components require version 4, but you can use Tomcat version 5 in your custom web services environment. To do this, select it in the query results screen, along with Apache Web Server and Tomcat 4 Servlet Container (**novell-tomcat4**). Post-installation tools and processes are identical for the two versions.

6. Click Accept to begin the software installation. At this point you may be prompted to install a few additional packages to satisfy dependencies. If so, select to continue the installation to install all required packages.

7. At the conclusion of the software installation and **SuSEconfig** process, select Finish to exit the Add and Remove Software module.

After Apache Web Server and Tomcat Servlet Engine are installed, you can use the following initialization scripts to start Apache and Tomcat:

```
/etc/init.d/apache2
/etc/init.d/novell-tomcat4
```

NOTE

If you also installed Tomcat 5, the initialization script for use with that version is /etc/init.d/tomcat.

These initialization scripts accept command-line parameters of **start** and **stop**, which determine what action the scripts will perform on each service. Also, the installation process will configure both of these daemons to automatically start in runlevels 2 through 5.

Apache Web Server Configuration

Apache Web Servers are managed through a primary configuration file called httpd.conf and a secondary file called default-server.conf. In addition to these two main configuration files, Apache is also designed to load external service-specific configuration files stored in the /etc/apache2/conf.d directory, and virtual server configuration files found in the /etc/apache2/vhosts.d directory.

When implementing a custom web server, your configuration changes could be written directly to the global configuration files for Apache. However, rather than directly editing these files, it is usually better to create new configuration files containing only your new configuration. These files can then be stored in the Apache configuration directories and easily removed or edited should the need arise.

OES Linux also follows this recommendation by placing a configuration file called nnls_httpd.conf in the /etc/apache2/conf.d directory, which in turn causes Apache to load all configuration files found in the /etc/opt/novell/httpd/conf.d directory. This setup separates the OES-specific configuration into manageable files for each service. This is useful from a troubleshooting perspective because it reduces the complexity of each individual file, but it also reduces the chance that a configuration error in one file will cause widespread problems throughout the Apache server.

Configuring OES components through iManager may modify some of the configuration files found in the OES-specific directories. These configuration files, however, should not normally be adjusted manually.

It is possible, and perhaps likely, that you will want to adjust the global, non-OES configuration files for Apache. Any configuration change you may want to implement can be performed through manually editing the configuration files, or through the YaST HTTP Server module (shown in Figure 14.1).

FIGURE 14.1
HTTP Server YaST Module.

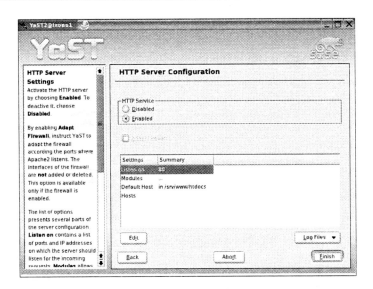

The HTTP Server module within YaST can be used to adjust most of the commonly modified parameters of Apache. To use this module, execute the following steps:

1. Access YaST from a terminal using **yast**, or from a graphical environment using **yast2** or the YaST launcher from the application menu.

2. Select the Network Services category in YaST. From within this category, locate and select the HTTP Server module. This invokes the HTTP Server Configuration page shown in Figure 14.1.

Using the HTTP Server module is fairly straightforward, but important configuration options should be explained before attempting to adjust these options. Some of the more common options are explained further in the remaining sections of this chapter.

Storing Web Content

The most important aspect of running a web server is making sure that the various web pages are available to your web users. Although the art of creating web pages is beyond the scope of this book, you need to know the basics about storing files on Apache Web Servers so that pages will be available as needed. To do this, you should become familiar with three main web server directory features: Document Root, Additional Document Directories, and User Home Directories.

DOCUMENT ROOT

The home page associated with your web server's IP address and/or DNS name is stored in the document root directory and named `index.htm` (or `index.html`). From the home page, you can create links to other pages, graphics, and applications as needed. Secondary resources can have any filename.

The document root, also called the *primary document directory*, is where a web server will start looking for requested web pages and resources. By default, Apache Web Server document root is set to the following location:

`/srv/www/htdocs`

Because it's not necessarily a good idea to use the root filesystem for storing your web pages, you can choose to partition out this directory during the OES installation, or simply change the document root to another partition and directory by completing the following steps:

NOTE

For the best web server performance, you should keep the document root as high in the directory structure as possible to reduce document search times.

1. From within the HTTP Server module (as described in the preceding section), select the Default Host parameter in the lower portion of the HTTP Server Configuration page, and then select Edit.

2. Select the Directory option containing the default path (`/srv/www/htdocs`) and select Edit. Enter the new Document Root path and adjust any directory options if necessary. When finished, click OK.

3. Select the DocumentRoot option and select Edit. Enter the new Document Root path and click OK.

4. Select OK to return to the main page, and then click Finish to save your changes.

YaST makes performing these type of changes a rather trivial task, but it is also important to understand how to perform these changes from a terminal. To adjust the DocumentRoot manually from a terminal, complete the following steps:

1. Open a terminal and connect to your Open Enterprise Server.

2. Edit the `/etc/apache2/default-server.conf` file using your favorite text editor. Locate the `DocumentRoot` directive and replace the existing directory with the absolute path to the new web directory in the following format: `/<directory>/<subdirectory>`. For example:

   `/apache2/docs`

NOTE

The path specified for the document root must exist prior to starting Apache. Apache will not automatically create this directory.

3. After saving your modifications, restart the Apache daemon using the following command:

   `/etc/init.d/apache2 restart`

After restarting Apache, you will be able to access your web content at the new directory.

ADDITIONAL DOCUMENT DIRECTORIES

You can also create additional document directories for those who want to publish their own content, but to whom you don't want to grant access to the document root. This also lets you easily distribute the responsibility of web content to those responsible for it.

This functionality requires the use of the `Alias` directive. This directive is used to map a local file system directory to a `url-path`. When the `url-path` is accessed, Apache automatically replaces the normal `DocumentRoot` directory with the directory specified in the `Alias` configuration.

To create an additional document directory manually using the `Alias` directive, you must add an `Alias` definition and `Directory` configuration entry into one of the Apache configuration files, such as `default-server.conf` or a custom configuration file in `/etc/apache2/vhosts.d`. This entry should be configured as in the following example:

```
Alias /marketing /var/web/marketing
<Directory /var/web/marketing>
```

```
    Order allow,deny
    Allow from all
</Directory>
```

The `Alias` directive in this example links the `/marketing url-path` to the `/var/web/marketing` directory. When clients access a URL, such as http://OES_SERVER/marketing/reports.html, rather than accessing the `reports.html` file from the normal `DocumentRoot` directory, the file access is redirected to the `/var/web/marketing` directory.

USER HOME DIRECTORIES

This feature enables you to set up document directories for each local user, and any LUM user in your eDirectory tree. These document directories are then used as personal websites for your users.

In order to use this feature, the `mod_userdir` Apache module must be installed and configured. This is performed automatically, with the OES installation, and if necessary can be double-checked through the Add and Remove Software module of YaST. If you'd like to adjust the default configuration of this module, you must edit the `/etc/apache2/mod_userdir.conf` configuration file. The following are some important directives found within this file:

- `UserDir disabled <usernames>`—List of users who are not allowed a public web directory. By default, this just contains the root user. If no usernames are specified, access to all users' web directories is denied.

- `UserDir enabled <usernames>`—List of users who are explicitly allowed a public web directory. This directive is normally only used in conjunction when the `UserDir disabled` directive is denying access to all users.

- `<Directory /home/*/public_html>`—This is the main definition for the behavior of the public directory. This directive defines which directory is associated with each user's website, and also what rights and operations are permitted in the directory. For more information on how to configure this option, see the `online mod_userdir` documentation at http://www.apache.org.

After adjusting any parameters in this file, restart Apache for your changes to take effect. Using the default configuration, users' web directories can be found in the `public_html` directory beneath each user's home directory. To view the contents of that directory, use a web browser to access the server domain name, followed by a slash (/), followed by `~username`. For example:

`http://www.quills.com/~jharris`

NOTE

Before attempting to access the web directory for LUM users, ensure that they have logged in at least one time. Logging in will create their home directory and the public_html directory beneath their home directory that is required for web access.

If you want to avoid encountering a listing of the contents of the public_html directory, each user should create an index.html file as a placeholder in this directory. To configure this automatically for all new users, create a default index.html file and place it in /etc/skel/public_html. All new users will automatically receive a copy of this file during their home directory creation.

Hosting Multiple Websites

Apache supports *virtual servers* to host multiple websites on a single physical server. This lets a single OES Linux server potentially host all your web server needs. This is useful if you need to let different divisions or departments host their own web resources, or if you are an ISP and need to host multiple websites for your clients without having a separate physical server for each one of them.

You can host two types of virtual servers on your Linux server:

- *IP-based Virtual Hosts*—This option lets you define multiple IP addresses and assign each to a different document root. IP-based Virtual Hosts can be configured using one single instance of Apache, or with one instance per virtual server. With OES, a single shared instance is the recommended configuration. This requires fewer system resources than multiple instances of the web server, but this configuration also causes all virtual servers to share the same configuration.

NOTE

You can use YaST to create a virtual IP address for use by an IP-based virtual server. Edit the configuration of an existing network controller (under Network Devices, Network Card) and choose to add a Virtual Alias in the Advanced options.

- *Name-based Virtual Hosts*—This option lets you map a single IP address to multiple server names by assigning each server a DNS name. Each Name-based Virtual Host then associates each DNS name with a specific home page. For this configuration to be successful, each client browser must report the desired hostname as part of the HTTP headers. Some older browsers may not support this, but for the most part this should not cause any issues.

NOTE

Due to requirements of SSL, Name-based Virtual Hosting is not compatible with SSL communication. If SSL is a requirement, you must use IP-based Virtual Hosting.

In order to configure either of these types of virtual servers, you should create a configuration file for each virtual host (named after each host with a `.conf` extension), and place the configuration file in the `/etc/apache2/vhosts.d` directory. You can also create a new host from within the HTTP Server module in YaST by following these steps:

1. Access YaST from a terminal using `yast`, or from a graphical environment using `yast2` or the YaST launcher from the application menu.

2. Select the Network Services category in YaST. From within this category, locate and select the HTTP Server module.

3. From HTTP Server Configuration page, select the Hosts parameter in the lower portion of the HTTP Server Configuration page, and then select Edit.

4. Click Add to create a new host. This will invoke the New Host Information page, as shown in Figure 14.2.

   Enter the following information and click OK:

   - *Server Name*—The DNS name used to access this web server content.
   - *Server Contents Root*—The DocumentRoot directory for this host.
   - *Administrator Email*—Enter the email address of the site administrator.
   - *Server Resolution*—This host can be accessed using a specific IP address or DNS hostname. Enter the server's IP address, and select the access method that will be used to access this host.

5. Select OK to return to the main page, and then click Finish to save your changes.

FIGURE 14.2

HTTP Server Module—New Host Information page.

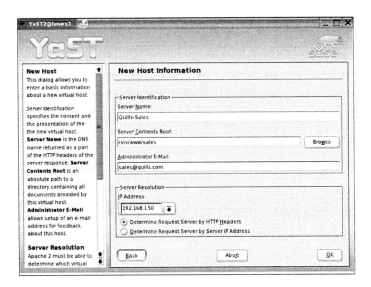

The next time Apache is started, this directory will be read in the initialization process and your virtual servers will be activated. For help with the syntax of these virtual host files, and information on important directives within them, see the sample `vhosts.template` file in `/etc/apache2/vhosts.d`.

NOTE

For more information on both of these virtual server options, see the Apache documentation at http://httpd.apache.org/docs-2.0/vhosts/.

Apache Modules

Apache Web Server has been developed with a component architecture that permits functionality to be added through the addition of a functionality-specific module. A *module* is a specially developed extension for Apache Web Server that provides new or expanded functionality.

Requests directed to an Apache Web Server pass through a series of stages as they are handled. Some of the Apache stages include authentication, authorization, and access control. Modules can be inserted at these, or any other, stage to provide increased functionality.

Several modules are available for use with Apache Web Server on OES Linux:

- mod_userdir enables web access to users' home directories.

- mod_cache enables an HTTP content cache that can be used to cache either local content or content available through a proxy.

- mod_perl enables support for the Perl scripting language on Apache Web Server.

- mod_php enables support for the PHP scripting language on Apache Web Server.

- mod_dav provides WebDAV (Web-based Distributed Authoring and Versioning) functionality for the Apache Web Server.

Each of these modules can be installed via the Install and Remove Software module of YaST. For more information on using Apache modules, see the Apache Web Server documentation site at http://httpd.apache.org/docs-2.0/mod/.

Adding Content to Your Website

After Apache Web Server has been installed and enabled, you can immediately access a sample web page and some subpages that are included for demonstration. The default website used with OES is a collection of OES component Welcome pages. These pages offer links to many of the management utilities that are available with OES. This content is accessed using the HTML data stored at the default document root at /srv/www/htdocs.

To view the default OES Welcome pages, open a client web browser on a workstation in your network and enter your OES server's IP address or DNS name. For example:

http://prv-serv1.quills.com

When your web server is running, you can start posting content for your web server audience to access—whether that's your department, your company, or the whole world. Do this by placing files in the web server's primary or additional document directories.

For example, suppose you created a new HTML file called mktg_docs.html that includes links to the marketing collateral for your organization. You would probably copy that file to the additional document directory assigned to the marketing organization; for example, /srv/www/htdocs/marketing.

After the file is stored in the additional document directory, users can access the file by entering the web server's DNS name together with the additional document directory identifier and the filename. For example:

http://www.quills.com/marketing/mktg_docs.html

The same general process governs the creation of any web content, whether that content is an Internet site, a corporate intranet, a departmental page, or even a personal web page. What differentiates one web site from another is how it is available (internally versus externally) and what type of server it is running on. External sites and larger corporate sites are usually run on dedicated web servers or hardware virtual servers, whereas smaller departmental sites work well on software virtual servers where users can easily create personalized pages, if necessary.

Publishing Content to a Website

When you are configuring an internal website, you will often have areas of a website that are available for contributors to publish their content. This makes it possible for users to communicate within a department, share information with other departments, and communicate items of general interest.

NOTE

Virtual Office is a powerful new feature for OES Linux that makes it much easier to create temporary or ad-hoc portals for information-sharing purposes. For more information on Virtual Office, see Chapter 15.

Web content contributors have several options for publishing content to your web server. For example:

- Mapping a network drive and creating or copying the content to the desired directory
- Using Internet Explorer 5.0 or higher
- Using Novell NetDrive to map a drive

Additionally, users who are familiar with web publishing tools can choose any of those with which they are familiar.

PUBLISHING CONTENT USING A MAPPED DRIVE

If your contributors are using the Novell Client, this is one way of providing access to web content areas. Use iManager to assign the appropriate rights to web content contributors and provide users with the correct network path so that they can map a drive to the content directory. For use with mapped drives in this manner, the web content area should be stored on an NSS volume. With this configured, you can set up automatic drive mapping through a login script. For more information on login scripts, see the OES online documentation.

PUBLISHING CONTENT USING WEBDAV

Web-based Distributed Authoring and Versioning (WebDAV) is an industry-standard protocol that enhances HTTP, turning the web into a document database that enables collaborative creation, editing, and searching from remote locations.

WebDAV support is provided on OES Linux through NetStorage. With NetStorage enabled, you can publish content directly to a specified document directory from any WebDAV-enabled browser, for example, Internet Explorer. For more information on NetStorage, see Chapter 12, "OES Linux File Access."

PUBLISHING CONTENT WITH NETDRIVE

Novell NetDrive lets you map a drive to any server without using the traditional Novell Client. This means that with NetDrive, you can access your files on any server and modify them through standard Windows utilities such as Windows Explorer. The NetDrive client can be installed from the Novell client's CD-ROM. For more information on NetDrive, see Chapter 12.

Apache Web Server Management

Managing Apache Web Server on a day-to-day basis should not consume a lot of an administrator's time. However, there are a few concepts and additional configuration options that might make management tasks even less of a difficulty. The following sections describe the remaining important files and configuration options useful from this perspective.

SERVER CONFIGURATION

The main area of concern for most administrators is the basic configuration of their Apache server. Although this has been covered briefly in previous sections of this chapter, there are a few additional areas you may want to investigate and customize for your environment.

PERFORMANCE TUNING

Performance within Apache is not normally an issue. However, if you have customized your web configuration to include a large amount of data, or are expecting your server to be under a heavy load, it may be worth your time to investigate this subject.

Apache-specific performance tuning options are mainly specified in the /etc/apache2/server-tuning.conf file. Some of the options specified here include the number of server processes to spawn at daemon startup, and the maximum number of simultaneous client requests. Adjusting these parameters can increase the performance of Apache, but incorrect modification of this file can also quickly lead to performance and operational problems. Before adjusting this file, you should review all relevant material on the Apache documentation website at http://httpd.apache.org/docs-2.0.

MIME TYPES

Also known as context labels, MIME (Multipurpose Internet Mail Extension) types specify the file types that Apache Web Server recognizes and supports. The MIME types configuration file is /etc/apache2/mime.types. This file is actually just a symbolic link to the same mime.types file used by SLES (/etc/mime.types). It is important that this file contain the definitions of all file types used on your Apache server. For example, if you want to put MP3 files on your server, you must add the MP3 extension to your MIME types. If this extension is not added, the server transfers the file to the user as text, instead of as a sound file.

To add a new MIME type to your web server, add a new entry into the /etc/mime.types file containing the following two fields:

- MIME Type—Specify the type of content for which you are creating a new MIME type. When a web server sends a document to a client, it includes metadata that identifies the document's type so that the client can handle the document correctly. Possible MIME types include

  - text/plain
  - text/html
  - image/jpeg
  - image/gif
  - application/x-tar
  - application/postscript
  - application/x-gzip
  - audio/basic
  - lang (used to specify a specific language)
  - enc (used to specify that the file is compressed)

NOTE

The official list of context types is maintained by the Internet Assigned Numbers Authority (IANA) and can be found at www.iana.org.

- **Extension**—In the Extension field, enter the file extension associated with the context label you have specified.

NOTE

To add a new extension to an already defined MIME type, just add the new extension to the existing MIME definition. Separate multiple extensions with spaces.

After making the changes, save the updated file and the new MIME type will be recognized at the next Apache restart.

LISTEN PORTS

The `/etc/apache2/listen.conf` file is used to configure the various IP addresses and ports that Apache Web Server uses to listen for incoming requests.

If you have to adjust these settings, you should be aware of which ports may already be in use by other OES components. Some port assignments in the OES Linux environment can be reassigned, whereas others are permanent. Table 14.1 shows the default port assignments for OES Linux web services as a starting point for any adjustments you may have to make.

TABLE 14.1
OES Linux Default Port Assignments

SERVICE	PORT NUMBER(S)	CONFIGURABLE
Apache	80 and 443	Yes
Domain Name Service (DNS)	53	No
File Transfer Protocol (FTP)	20 and 21	No
iFolder	Uses LDAP and Apache ports	Indirectly by changing LDAP and/or Apache ports
iMonitor	80	Yes
iPrint	631 and Apache SSL port (443)	Indirectly by changing the Apache SSL port
Lightweight Directory Access Protocol (LDAP)	389 and 636	Yes

TABLE 14.1
Continued

SERVICE	PORT NUMBER(S)	CONFIGURABLE
NetWare Core Protocol (NCP)	524	No
Novell File System	20, 111, and 2049	Only 2049 is configurable
NetWare Remote Manager (NRM)	8008 and 8009	Yes
Network Time Protocol (NTP)	123	No
Service Location Protocol (SLP)	427	No
Simple Network Management Protocol (SNMP)	161	No
Telnet	23	No
Tomcat	8080	Yes

ERROR RESPONSES

Typical HTTP error messages are pretty generic and do not give much information. Use the /etc/apache2/errors.conf file to customize error messages and potentially redirect the client to a location where more help is available. When a server cannot complete a request, it typically sends one of the following four error messages to the client:

- *Unauthorized (HTTP 401)*—Occurs when a user tries unsuccessfully to access a file in a secure area of the web server.

- *Forbidden (HTTP 403)*—Occurs when the server does not have file system rights sufficient to read the requested data.

- *Not found (HTTP 404)*—Occurs when a user tries to access data that does not exist.

- *Server (HTTP 500)*—Occurs when the server is improperly configured or when a fatal error occurs (such as the system running out of memory).

In place of these generic errors, there are many situations in which you might want to use custom messages. For example, if users are denied access, instead of receiving a message that simply says "Unauthorized," they could receive a custom error message that explains the reason they were denied access and points them to the help desk to have an account created.

The default installation of Apache already employs custom error pages. These pages are defined in `errors.conf` and found in the `/usr/share/apache2/error` directory. To further change the error response for your server, the error pages found in this directory can be customized, or the error code and new action can be manually defined in the `errors.conf` file. Manual changes to `errors.conf` must be in the following format:

```
ErrorDocument <Error_Code> <Action>
```

Possible actions include a custom message enclosed in quotes, the absolute path to an HTML page or script, and the URL of another page to redirect the user to. After you make any changes, the Apache server must be restarted.

SERVER LOGS

In addition to configuration changes and website updates, monitoring your web activity through log files is necessary to track down errors, and an excellent way to locate security breaches. Apache Web Server provides two types of logs for tracking what is happening in your web server environment: access logs and error logs.

ACCESS LOG

The access log records information about web clients that access your web server, and records client information such as IP addresses and date and time of access. By default, the access log is `/var/log/apache2/access_log`.

The access log is configured in a number of places because the access log is normally specific to each virtual server. However, there is still a default, site-wide configuration for the access log. This configuration is found in the `/etc/sysconfig/apache2` file. In this file, the `APACHE_ACCESS_LOG` directive defines where the default log is located.

ERROR LOG

The error log records diagnostic information related to errors that occurred while processing requests. The error log is very important because it often contains details of what went wrong and how to fix it. By default, the error log is `/var/log/apache2/error_log`. If necessary, this location can be adjusted in the `httpd.conf` configuration file.

If necessary, the logging level of the error log can be adjusted using the `APACHE_LOGLEVEL` directive in the `/etc/sysconfig/apache2` file. Care should be taken when adjusting this to track more information as performance may suffer because of the logging of unnecessary details.

Tomcat Servlet Engine

As with Apache, Tomcat is an open-source application. (It is also known by its open-source project name, Jakarta. For more information on the Jakarta project, see http://jakarta.apache.org.) Its specific function is as a servlet container. A *servlet* is a server-side program that generates dynamic web pages based upon user input. Tomcat provides a runtime environment within which servlets can execute and be managed. Apache Web Server depends on Tomcat to process servlets and Java Server Pages (JSP).

As with Apache, two instances of Tomcat can be loaded on an OES Linux server. The first is an `admin` instance that is used in conjunction with the Apache `admin` server to support the various management tools and other services available with OES Linux. The `admin` instance of Tomcat is loaded automatically when OES Linux is installed.

The second instance is a public copy that is used in support of web applications that are served from the OES Linux server. You will use this version to build your own web environment.

NOTE

Tomcat provides basic servlet and JSP support for OES Linux. For a more robust web application development environment, Novell offers Novell exteNd Application Server. For more information on Novell exteNd offerings, see the OES Linux online documentation, and visit http://www.novell.com/solutions/extend/.

Installing and Configuring Tomcat

Because Tomcat is useless without a web server with which to interoperate, Tomcat is normally installed in conjunction with Apache Web Server. For information on installing Apache and Tomcat, see the Apache installation section earlier in this chapter.

By default, OES Linux installs Tomcat 4 configuration files into the `/etc/opt/novell/tomcat4` directory structure. If a second instance or public version of Tomcat is installed, these configuration files will normally be installed in the `/etc/tomcat` directory.

The admin (OES-specific) version of Tomcat requires no additional configuration in order to be operational. However, it is still a good idea to understand the important configuration files for Tomcat. The following list contains the most important configuration files for the `admin` instance of Tomcat:

- `server.xml`—Main configuration file for Tomcat. This file is located in the `/etc/opt/novell/tomcat4` directory.

- `jk_module.conf`—The main configuration file for the Jakarta-Apache plug-in. This file is located in the `/etc/opt/novell/httpd/gconf.d` directory.

- `workers.properties`—Contains configuration information that connects servlets to Tomcat worker processes. This file is located in the `/etc/opt/novell/httpd/gconf.d` directory.

The public version of Tomcat uses the same configuration files; however, they are typically located within the `/etc/tomcat` directory. For more information on configuring Tomcat for use outside of OES, refer to the Tomcat documentation.

Managing Tomcat

Tomcat does not require much management with OES as the configuration should be completed by the OES installation, and the Tomcat service should be started automatically at server startup. However, you may encounter a situation where you want to start or stop the Tomcat service manually. To do so with the `admin` version of Tomcat, the following `init` script must be executed with a `start` or `stop` command-line parameter:

`/etc/init.d/novell-tomcat4`

If you are also running a public version of Tomcat, the `init` script for that instance of Tomcat is normally as follows:

`/etc/init.d/tomcat`

Tomcat Log Files

Another important aspect of managing Tomcat is analyzing and troubleshooting any errors that might be encountered. In the event errors are seen, understanding the important log files used by Tomcat will lead to much quicker identification and resolution of any problems.

Table 14.2 lists the important log files used by Tomcat 4 and each log file's purpose.

TABLE 14.2
Important Tomcat Log Files

LOG FILE	LOCATION	DESCRIPTION
mod_jk.log	/var/log/apache2	Contains all errors associated with the Tomcat plug-in for Apache. Use the JkLogLevel directive in jk_module.conf to increase the log level if more information is required.
catalina.out	/var/opt/novell/ tomcat4/logs	Contains Tomcat startup information. Use this file to verify port configuration or troubleshoot any startup or shutdown problem.
localhost_log	/var/opt/novell/ tomcat4/logs	These files contain servlet-specific messages and errors.

TIP

For more information on Tomcat, see the OES Linux online documentation, and visit the comprehensive Tomcat documentation site at http://jakarta.apache.org.

## CHAPTER 15

OES Web Services

Instant Access

Using Virtual Office

- Use preconfigured services to make OES Linux files, as well as common services such as NetStorage, iPrint, and email, available through a single portal website.

- Access Virtual Office at https://*<server name or IP address>*/vo.

- Configure Virtual Office through Administration links visible within Virtual Office to users with eDirectory administrative rights.

- *Virtual teams* are a specialized instance of Virtual Office that you can use to create ad-hoc portals to support a community, group, or team focused on a specific project or topic of discussion.

Working with Novell QuickFinder

- QuickFinder creates a web search engine for use by internal users (indexes relevant Internet websites) or by external users (indexes your web server information so that it can be effectively searched).

- QuickFinder can be configured and managed through the QuickFinder Server Manager pages, which are accessible at https://*<server name or IP address>*/qfsearch/admin. Links to this management page are also available via iManager.

Working with eGuide

- eGuide provides robust and secure LDAP white pages to access company information.

- Access the eGuide search page at https://*<server name or IP address>*/eGuide.

- Access the eGuide Administration Utility at https://*<server name or IP address>*/eGuide/admin/index.html.

Novell Virtual Office

Novell Virtual Office allows network administrators to quickly and easily provide browser-based access to network resources. Effectively, Virtual Office enables you to create personalized user portals through which users can access their data and applications from a single website. Not only that, but Virtual Office also provides the capability to create *virtual teams*, or ad-hoc shared portals that can support a project or any other group that needs access to shared resources.

Virtual Office provides services that allow you to access network resources through the Virtual Office interface. *Services* are little Java-based servlets or applications that provide access to specific types of network resources. OES Linux includes several default Virtual Office services for accessing network resources and performing common network tasks:

- *NetStorage*—Provides access to the Novell NetStorage service. NetStorage provides Internet-based access to file storage on an OES server, including access to iFolder. Both NetStorage and iFolder were discussed in Chapter 12, "OES Linux File Access."

- *iPrint*—Provides access to Internet printing via iPrint. For more information on iPrint, see Chapter 13, "OES Printing Services."

- *Email*—Provides support for popular email applications and protocols, including Novell GroupWise, Microsoft Exchange, Lotus Notes, Novell NetMail, POP3, and IMAP.

- *eGuide*—Provides a simplified screen to access phone numbers and other user information stored in eDirectory. eGuide is discussed in more detail later in this chapter.

- *Change Password*—Links to a page where users can change their password in eDirectory.

- *Web Search*—Provides integration with a Novell Web Search, or QuickFinder, server. QuickFinder is discussed in more detail later in this chapter.

- *ZENworks*—Provides integration with Novell ZENworks for Desktops functionality, such as application delivery, through the Virtual Office interface.

Perhaps most important to you as a network administrator, Virtual Office doesn't require any complicated web development or programming. It's pretty much ready to go right out of the box.

Installing Virtual Office

Virtual Office can be installed on a dedicated server using the Novell Virtual Office Server installation pattern or as an optional component during the OES Linux installation. Virtual Office can also be installed later through YaST.

NOTE

For most networks, you will need to install Virtual Office on only one server in each eDirectory tree.

The only requirement for Virtual Office, beyond the minimum requirements for an OES Linux server, is a web browser. To install Virtual Office using YaST, complete the following steps:

1. Access YaST from a terminal using `yast`, or from a graphical environment using `yast2` or the YaST launcher from the application menu.

2. Select the Network Services category in YaST. From within this category, locate and select the Virtual Office module. This module will detect that the RPMs for Virtual Office are missing and ask if you want to install them. Select Continue to install the necessary packages.

3. At the conclusion of the software installation, `SuSEconfig` is executed to update the system configuration. When this completes, the configuration of the OES component will begin automatically.

4. At the Virtual Office LDAP Server Configuration screen, enter the following information and click Next:

    - *Local or Remote Directory Server*—Select the radio button that indicates whether eDirectory is running on the local server or a remote server.

    - *Directory Server Address*—If a remote eDirectory server is in use, enter the IP address for this server.

- *Admin Name with Context*—Enter the eDirectory administrator's credentials using fully qualified dot notation, for example, `cn=admin.o=novell`.

- *Admin Password*—Enter the password for the administrator user.

- *Port Details*—If necessary, select this button to change the configured ports for the eDirectory server you specified earlier. The default LDAP port for unencrypted communications is **389** and port **636** is used for SSL-encrypted communications.

5. At the Virtual Office Configuration screen, enter the required information (see Figure 15.1), and click Next.

FIGURE 15.1
Virtual Office Configuration options.

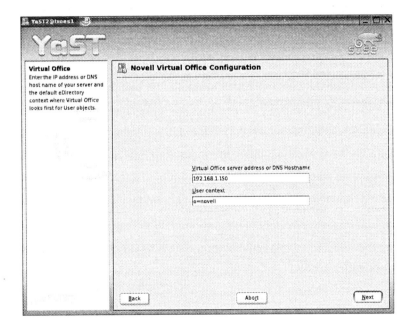

- *Virtual Office Server Address or DNS Hostname*—Specify the DNS name or IP address of your Virtual Office server.

- *User Context*—Specify the base context in which valid Virtual Office users may be located. Users found in the subtree beneath this context will be able to use Virtual Office. If you want to use the entire tree, specify the root context, for example, `o=novell`.

6. In order for Virtual Office to be active, select to restart Apache and Tomcat when prompted.

After installing Virtual Office, you can access a default Virtual Office web page by pointing your browser to the following page: https://<server DNS name or IP address>/vo. For example:

```
https://wa1-serv1.quills.com/vo
```

This page will include links to all the gadgets you can use from the Virtual Office portal.

Preparing Virtual Office for Use

Configuring your Virtual Office environment has two aspects: configuring Virtual Office itself and configuring Virtual Office services. Both of these are discussed in the following sections.

CONFIGURING VIRTUAL OFFICE

To perform the initial configuration of Virtual Office, complete the following steps:

1. Launch the Virtual Office web interface (https://<*virtual office server*>/vo) and authenticate as a user with administrative rights in eDirectory (for example, Admin).

2. When the Virtual Office page loads for administrative users, you will see a set of Administrative links in the Navigation frame that are not present for normal users, as shown in Figure 15.2.

FIGURE 15.2
Virtual Office administration view.

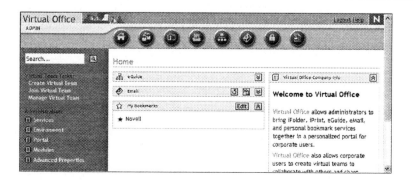

3. Select Environment in the Navigation frame.

4. Configure Virtual Office as required for your environment and click OK to save your changes. Three tabs are available in the Environment page:

- *Team Configuration*—Virtual teams let you create virtual ad-hoc groups that can share resources and information through a centralized portal dedicated for that purpose. More information on virtual teams is provided later in this chapter. To configure your virtual team environment, provide the requested information and click Save.

  - *Virtual Teams*—Enables/disables virtual team functionality.

  - *Allow Access to Existing Teams*—Enables/disables access to existing virtual teams. When this option is enabled, existing teams are accessible, even if virtual teams and/or new team creation is disabled.

  - *Enable Team Creation*—Enables virtual team creation. This option is enabled by default. When this option is disabled, no virtual team functionality is available.

  - *Manage Team Access*—Click Edit to specify those users who have rights to create virtual teams.

  - *Team File Share*—Click Edit to specify the location where virtual team members will be allowed to store shared files. File sharing requires the use of Samba integration with OES Linux because the location where virtual team files will be stored must be configured as a CIFS/SMB share point. For more information on Samba with OES Linux, see Chapter 11, "OES Linux File Storage and Management."

  - *SMTP Address*—Click Edit to specify the IP address or DNS name of your SMTP mail server. This is required if you want Virtual Office to be able to send email notifications to virtual team members.

  - *Chat Server IP Port*—Specifies the TCP port that will be used for chat communications for virtual teams.

- *Portal Information*—On this page, you define how your Virtual Office portal can be used. This page has three options:

  - *Portal Containers*—Sets those contexts from which users can log in and access Virtual Office. Effectively, this restricts the list of potential Virtual Office users to those within the contexts you specify.

- *Portal Locations*—If you are running Virtual Office on multiple servers, make sure that all portal addresses are listed here. Remember, you can specify the same storage location for multiple Virtual Office portals.

- *Teams*—Lists all virtual teams that have been created on the selected Virtual Office portal.

- *Logging*—On this page you configure the information that will appear in Virtual Office log reports. Virtual Office logs can help you track service usage and diagnose problems. Typically, you won't use logging because of the overhead that it requires, but it is useful for gathering environment and troubleshooting information.

  - *Logging*—Check this box to enable logging.

  - *Logging Level*—Sets the level of logging that will be performed. There are three levels of information you can obtain from the logging report. It's counter-intuitive, but selecting Low will log all available information, Medium limits logging output, and High restricts log output even more.

  - *Logging Modules*—Lets you specify the specific Virtual Office modules that you want to include in the logging. Leave the field blank to log all modules.

  - *Logging to Standard Error*—Check this box to log to the defined Standard Error device. By default, this is the Tomcat logger screen.

  - *Logging to Standard Out*—Check this box to log to the defined Standard Out device. By default, this is the Tomcat logger screen.

  - *Logging to File*—Check this box to send the log to a file. By default, the log file is `/var/opt/novell/tomcat4/webapps/vo/WEB-INF/debug.xml`.

When you have completed the initial configuration of Virtual Office, you can move on to the configuration of the services available through the Virtual Office portal.

CONFIGURING VIRTUAL OFFICE SERVICES

Several Virtual Office services ship with OES Linux, but in order to use each you must perform some basic configuration, primarily centered on enabling the service and specifying the location of the service on the network.

NOTE

If you are interested in doing more advanced customization, or in developing your own Virtual Office services, you can use the Novell exteNd development tools for doing this. For more information on exteNd, see the OES online documentation.

To configure the various Virtual Office services, complete the following steps:

1. Launch the Virtual Office web interface (https://<*virtual office server*>/vo) and authenticate as a user with administrative rights in eDirectory (for example, Admin).

2. Select Services in the Navigation frame to open the Services configuration page.

3. Use the tabs provided on the Services page, as shown in Figure 15.3, to configure Virtual Office services. If you don't select Enable on one or more of these tabs, that service will be removed from your Virtual Office web page.

FIGURE 15.3
Virtual Office services configuration.

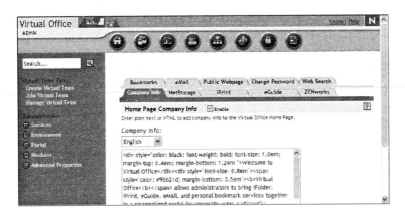

- *Company Info*—Use this option to specify the information that will appear in the News field in the Virtual Office web page. Enter regular text or HTML in the text box to specify the information that should appear in the News field.

- *NetStorage*—You must have NetStorage installed and configured before enabling this service. For more information on NetStorage, see Chapter 12. Specify the location of the NetStorage service to be used by Virtual Office. You can run NetStorage from the same server that is running Virtual Office, or from a different server, or you can specify a custom location for the NetStorage service. Unless you are using the default local location for NetStorage, you will have to provide the complete IP or DNS path to the NetStorage service.

- *iPrint*—You must have Novell iPrint installed and configured before enabling this service. For more information on iPrint, see Chapter 13. Specify the location of the iPrint service to be used by Virtual Office. You can run iPrint from the same server that is running Virtual Office, from a different server, or specify a custom location for the iPrint service. Unless you are using the default local location for iPrint, you will have to provide the complete IP or DNS path to the iPrint service.

- *eGuide*—You must have eGuide installed and configured before enabling this service. More information on eGuide is available later in this chapter and in the OES Linux online documentation. Specify the location of the eGuide service to be used by Virtual Office. You can run eGuide from the same server that is running Virtual Office, from a different server, or specify a custom location for the eGuide service. Unless you are using the default local location for eGuide, you will have to provide the complete IP or DNS path to the eGuide service.

- *ZENworks*—You must have ZENworks for Desktops installed and configured before enabling this service. When enabled, certain ZENworks services can be accessed through Virtual Office, such as application distribution. For more information, see the OES online documentation.

- *Bookmarks*—Virtual Office allows you to specify default web links that you want to appear on the Virtual Office Navigation bar and/or a user's Virtual Office Web page.

- *Email*—You must have an email service installed and configured before enabling this service. There are two steps to making a user's email available through Virtual Office: First, you specify the type of email system with which Virtual Office will integrate, and then you click the Edit button next to the server link to specify the type and location (IP or DNS name) of the mail server to which Virtual Office should attach.

- *Public Web Page*—Enables/disables users' ability to configure personal web pages that will be accessible through Virtual Office. Users will do the Public Web Page configuration if you enable the service.

- *Change Password*—Enables/disables users' ability to change their passwords, both regular and universal, through Virtual Office. This can be an important self-service tool to reduce burden on your help desk.

- *Web Search*—Configures access to QuickFinder web search through Virtual Office. You must have QuickFinder installed and configured prior to accessing it through Virtual Office. You can run QuickFinder from the same server that is running Virtual Office or from a different server. Unless you are using the default local location for QuickFinder, you will have to provide the complete IP or DNS path to the QuickFinder service.

When you have configured the various Virtual Office services to your satisfaction, Virtual Office is ready to use.

Virtual Teams

A *virtual team* is an ad-hoc shared portal that can support a project or any other group that needs access to shared resources. To create a virtual team, complete the following steps:

1. Launch the Virtual Office web page, which is available at https://*<server DNS name or IP address>*/vo by default.

2. Select Create Virtual Teams in the Navigation bar.

3. Specify a name for the new virtual team and click Create. You can also enter a description for the team you are creating.

Within a virtual team, team members can exchange information, share files, and maintain a calendar of events. Virtual Office enables you to create and manage your own virtual teams and/or become a member of teams created by others.

CONFIGURING VIRTUAL TEAM SERVICES

Certain services are available only within the context of a virtual team. These special services are designed to enhance communication and productivity between the members of a virtual team. Clicking the icon for your newly created team in the My Virtual Teams section of the Navigation frame will open a web page (see Figure 15.4) from which the following team-specific services are available:

FIGURE 15.4
Default virtual team portal in Virtual Office.

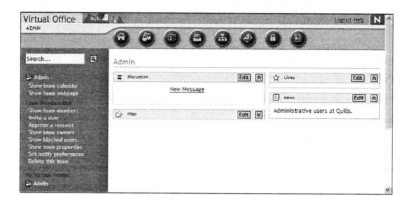

- *Discussion*—Team members can use the Discussion service as a web log of sorts to capture online discussions, and exchange ideas and messages. The discussion threads are accessible by all members of the team.

- *Files*—Team members can use the Files service as a web-based file-sharing tool. Files can be created, uploaded, deleted, and browsed through this service. The Files service uses the Team File Share location specified during the configuration of Virtual Office, discussed previously.

- *News*—The News area contains information provided by the owner of the Virtual Team. This is intended to be used as a tool for sharing important information quickly to all team members.

- *Links*—The Links service enables you to create a list of team-related links that can be shared among team members to facilitate research or collaboration.

In addition to the team-specific services available through the Virtual Team link, two other resources are available to virtual team members:

- *Calendar*—From the Navigation frame, select Show Team Calendar. From this page, you can schedule team-related events and appointments and share this information with team members.

- *Team Webpage*—From the Navigation frame, select Show Team Webpage. The team web page provides basic information about the virtual team, including its purpose, team members, and lists of published web links and files that the team wants to make readily available.

MANAGING VIRTUAL TEAMS

As the owner of a virtual team, you have several management tasks available to you for configuring and managing your virtual team. When you have created a virtual team, open the team web page to perform one or more of the following tasks:

- *Show Team Members*—From the Team Membership column, select Show Team Members, and then click Membership.

- *Invite a User*—From the Team Membership column, select Invite a User, and then click Add. When invited, a user can choose to accept or reject the invitation.

- *Approve a Request*—From the Team Membership column, select Approve a Request, and then click Approve or Deny.

- *Show Team Owners*—From the Team Membership column, select Show Team Owners, and then click Add. After being added, new team owners have the same rights you do, including the capability to remove you as an owner! For this reason, make sure team ownership is handed out carefully.

- *Show Blocked Users*—From the Team Membership column, select Show Blocked Users, and then click Add. This option enables you to manage team membership by exception, rather than having to specify each user who should be a member.

- *Show Team Properties*—From the Team Membership column, select Show Team Properties. From this page, you can update the name, description, or services associated with a virtual team.

- *Set Notify Preferences*—From the Team Membership column, select Set Notify Preferences and select each event for which you want team members automatically notified via email.

- *Delete This Team*—From the Team Membership column, select Delete This Team, and then click Delete twice more. When a virtual team has served its purpose, you can delete it very easily.

As you can see from this list, virtual team owners have several tools at their disposal to manage the operation of the team portal, control access to the team portal, and make sure that usage of the team portal is only for designated purposes.

JOINING A VIRTUAL TEAM

You must be a member of a virtual team to have access to information and services associated within that virtual team. To request membership in a virtual team, complete the following steps:

1. Launch the Virtual Office web page, which is available at https://*<server DNS name or IP address>*/vo by default.

2. Select Join Virtual Team in the Navigation frame.

3. Select the team you want to join from the list of available teams, and click Join.

4. Click Request to request permission to join the team of the team's owner. Click OK to finish the team joining process.

After the owner approves your request, you become a member of the team and will have access to the virtual team resources. Any user can request membership to virtual teams, but membership is granted only when approved by the virtual team owner.

Novell QuickFinder

Although QuickFinder isn't a required web service for OES Linux, it is all about making your web resources available to employees and customers as quickly and accurately as possible. Supporting everything from simple internal search solutions to complex search services that you can offer to organizations for a fee, QuickFinder is one of the fastest and most accurate search engines currently available.

Novell QuickFinder, previously called Novell Web Search, offers a powerful, full-text search engine that you can use to add search capabilities to your Internet or intranet websites. These capabilities can be integrated into your Apache Web Server environment through custom search forms and search result pages. These pages can be created from scratch or based on one of the included page templates.

This section introduces you to QuickFinder and its basic installation and configuration. However, for comprehensive information, see the OES Linux online documentation.

QuickFinder Capabilities

With Novell QuickFinder, you can

- Support searching multiple-language indexes from a single interface
- Host search services for multiple organizations
- Organize collections of related files from diverse sources as a single document

- Create custom search, print results, error and response messages and apply them to individual language searches or across all supported languages

- Gather customer metrics by reviewing searches to identify what your customers look for the most

- Improve employee productivity by helping them find information more quickly

Installing QuickFinder

Novell QuickFinder can be installed on a dedicated server using the Novell QuickFinder Server installation pattern or as an optional component during a custom OES Linux installation. QuickFinder can also be installed after the fact through YaST.

To install QuickFinder using YaST, complete the following steps:

1. Access YaST from a terminal using yast, or from a graphical environment using yast2 or the YaST launcher from the application menu.

2. Select the Network Services category in YaST. From within this category, locate and select the Novell QuickFinder module. This module will detect that the RPMs for QuickFinder are missing and ask if you want to install them. Select Continue to install the necessary packages.

3. At the conclusion of the software installation, SuSEconfig is executed to update the system configuration. When this completes, the configuration of the OES component will begin automatically.

4. At the Virtual Office Configuration screen, enter the required information (see Figure 15.5), and click Next.

   - *LUM Enable QuickFinder Admin User*—This option determines whether or not QuickFinder administration can be performed via an eDirectory user through LUM.

   - *QuickFinder Admin Name*—Enter the QuickFinder admin name in this field. If LUM redirection is enabled, enter the eDirectory administrator's credentials using fully qualified dot notation, for example, cn=admin.o=novell. Otherwise, enter the name of a local administration user (with no context).

   - *QuickFinder Admin Password*—Enter the password for the QuickFinder administrator.

■ *Add novlwww User to the Shadow Group*—For non-LUM-enabled users to access QuickFinder, the novlwww user must be added to the local shadow group. If only LUM-enabled users will be accessing QuickFinder, this option can be set to No.

FIGURE 15.5
QuickFinder Configuration options.

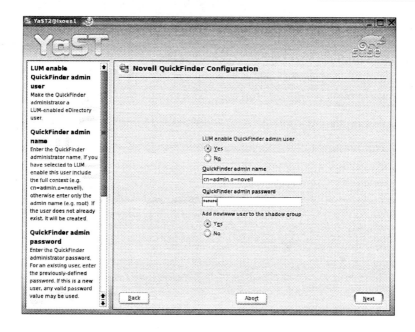

5. At the Virtual Office eDirectory Configuration screen, enter the required information, and click Next.

   ■ *Admin Name with Context*—Enter the eDirectory administrator's credentials using fully qualified dot notation, for example, `cn=admin.o=novell`.

   ■ *Admin Password*—Enter the password for the administrator user.

6. For QuickFinder to be active, select to restart Apache and Tomcat when prompted.

QuickFinder Basics

Before you get started creating and managing search sites, you should understand the basics of web searches. Web searches are driven by the idea of a *search site*. By definition, a search site is a collection of one or more indexes and their related configuration files. A typical search site consists of the following:

- *Indexes*—Indexes are at the heart of a search site. An index is an optimized binary file that contains keywords found in documents hosted on a web or file server. Indexes are used by QuickFinder to return search results to users.

NOTE

When you install QuickFinder, some of your server's content is automatically indexed and appears on the default search form as the "QuickFinder Server" and "DocRoot" indexes.

- *Log files*—A log file keeps a record of search statistics and performance of the search site.
- *Search and print templates*—These are templates that become populated with the results of a search and then are displayed to the user. Depending on which templates are used, the level of detail displayed in search and print results varies.
- *Scheduled events*—Index management, such as updating or regenerating, can be automated to occur at specific intervals using the Scheduling feature.
- *Themes*—A theme instantly adds a common look and feel to your search page, search and print results pages, and response and error message pages.

Testing QuickFinder

After QuickFinder has been installed and started, you can open the search page using your web browser and perform a search against the content that has been automatically indexed. To test Novell QuickFinder using the default search page, do the following:

1. Point your browser to the default search page at http://<*server DNS name of IP address*>/qfsearch/SearchServlet. Remember that the URL is case sensitive. For example:

http://prv-serv1.quills.com/qfsearch/SearchServlet

2. Type **Linux** in the search field and click Search.

The results of this search will be collected from the newly created QuickFinder index.

Working with QuickFinder

After installing QuickFinder, you can manage it through QuickFinder Server Manager. Open QuickFinder Server Manager by pointing your browser to the following URL: https://<*server DNS name or IP address*>/qfsearch/admin/. For example:

```
http://prv-serv1.quills.com/qfsearch/admin
```

This will open the Index Management page, as shown in Figure 15.6.

FIGURE 15.6
QuickFinder Server Manager interface.

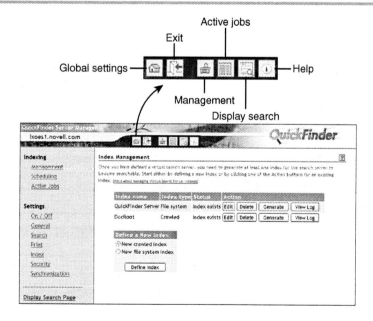

NOTE

You can set up access to QuickFinder Server Manager in iManager. Simply open QuickFinder Server Management in the Navigation frame and select Display QuickFinder Servers. In the Content frame, specify a name for the QuickFinder server you will manage, specify the appropriate QuickFinder URL, as described in the preceding example, and then click Add.

To access QuickFinder Server Manager, click Manage next to the QuickFinder server that you want to manage.

Four primary tasks are associated with configuring and managing QuickFinder:

- Creating a search site
- Creating and managing indexes
- Generating indexes
- Scheduling index events

Each of these is described in the following sections.

CREATING A SEARCH SITE

Using QuickFinder Server Manager, you can create and configure search sites, also called *virtual search servers*, and then begin adding indexes to them. To create a new search site, do the following:

1. Click Global Settings in the Header frame to open the Global Settings page, as shown in Figure 15.7.

FIGURE 15.7
Global Settings page in QuickFinder Server Manager.

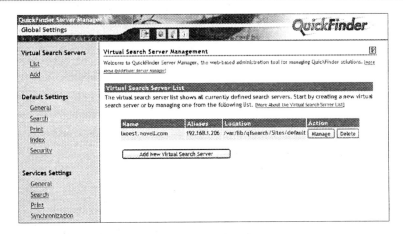

2. Open the Add Virtual Search Server page. There are three ways to do this: Click Add in the Header frame; select Add from the Navigation frame under the Virtual Search Server heading; or click Add New Virtual Search Server in the Content frame.

3. Provide the required information and click Add.

The following fields are provided on the Add page:

- *Name*—This field is required; you will specify a name for the new search site. This is typically the DNS or domain name of your server. When QuickFinder receives a query, it must determine which of the available search sites it should use to handle the request. There are two ways to do this:

    - Matching the domain name in the search query with a search site name in QuickFinder

    - Using the SITE=*searchsitename* query parameter to find matching search site names

- *Aliases*—Specify a secondary name for the search site. This is typically the IP address of your server. An alias name typically follows one of two conventions:

    - An IP address could be used either in the domain name portion of a URL or be included in a search query using the &site query parameter. Using an IP address in place of a domain name to select a search site works only in a hardware virtual server configuration where each search site has its own unique IP address. For more information on virtual web servers, see the discussion on Apache Web Server earlier in this chapter.

    - Any other numeric or textual value that can be passed as the value of the &site query parameter.

- *Location*—Specify the path to where you want the index and configuration files to be stored. If this field is left blank, QuickFinder will store the search site files in /var/lib/qfsearch/Sites/<*name*>, where <*name*> is the name you have assigned to this search site. The location can be set to any empty directory on the server where QuickFinder is installed, but not on other servers.

CREATING AND MANAGING INDEXES

QuickFinder supports two types of indexes:

- *Crawled*—Follows hypertext links until it reaches a dead end. QuickFinder can crawl one or more websites, specific areas of a website, or specific URLs, all the way down to specific filenames.

- *File system*—Indexes content on a file server. QuickFinder can index one or more paths on multiple volumes, including Storage Area Network (SAN) systems.

There are two forms you can use to create each type of index: the standard form and the advanced form. The standard form is discussed here. For information about the advanced form, see the OES online documentation.

QuickFinder can search across multiple indexes within a single search site, but cannot search across multiple search sites.

TIP

Searching a single index is generally faster than searching across multiple indexes.

To create a new crawled index, complete the following steps from QuickFinder Server Manager:

1. Access the Index Management page by selecting the Manage button beside the appropriate virtual server. If you only have one virtual server, the Index Management page is the default page seen when opening QuickFinder Server Manager.

2. In the Define a New Index box, select New Crawled Index and click Define Index.

3. In the Define Crawled Index screen, provide the required information and click Apply Settings.

   - *Index Name*—Specify a name for the new index. The name can be a word, phrase, or a numeric value. If you are going to have a large number of indexes, you should use a naming scheme so that you can manage your indexes effectively. Keep in mind that the index name will be visible to users, so you might want to choose a name that will mean something to them.

   - *URL of Website*—Specify the URL of the website you want to index. You can enter a URL by itself or include a path down to a specific file level. The standard index form includes two URL fields. Click Add More URLs to specify more than two URLs to be indexed.

To create a new file system index, complete the following steps in QuickFinder Server Manager:

1. Access the Index Management page by selecting the Manage button beside the appropriate virtual server. If you only have one virtual server, the Index Management page is the default page that you see when opening QuickFinder Server Manager.

2. In the Define a New Index box, select New File System Index and click Define Index.

3. In the Define File System Index screen, provide the required information and click Apply Settings.

   - *Index Name*—Specify a name for the new index. The name can be a word, phrase, or a numeric value. If you are going to have a large number of indexes, you should use a naming scheme so that you can manage your indexes effectively. Keep in mind that the index name will be visible to users, so you might want to choose a name that will mean something to them.

   - *Server Path to Be Indexed*—Specify the absolute path to the folder containing the information that you want indexed; for example, /marketing/collateral.

   - *Corresponding URL Prefix*—Specify the URL that should be used by the search results page to access the individual files. This corresponds to a document directory (Document Root) that has been defined on the web server. For more information on document directories, see the discussion on Apache Web Server in Chapter 14, "OES Foundations."

You can specify multiple paths for a single index by clicking Add More Paths.

GENERATING INDEXES

After you define an index, you must generate it before it can be used for searching. This is the actual process of examining website content or web server files to gather keywords, titles, and descriptions and to place them in the index file.

To generate a newly defined index, click Generate next to the specific index that you want to generate. This will open the Active Jobs screen, from which you will see the status of the current indexing jobs. If there is no current index job, the status page will read *No indexing jobs are currently running or defined*. To cancel the current indexing jobs, click Cancel in the Action column.

SCHEDULING INDEX EVENTS

QuickFinder can automatically update your indexes on specific dates and times by scheduling events. To configure an automatic generation event, complete the following steps in QuickFinder Server Manager:

1. Select Scheduling in the Navigation frame and click Add Event.

2. At the Schedule a New Event screen, provide the required information and click Apply Settings.

- *Dates, Days of Week, and Time*—Specify the month, days, days of the week, or time (in hours and minutes) when you want QuickFinder to run the event. You can use the Ctrl and Shift keys to select multiple dates and times.

- *Operation*—Select the type of operation you want performed on your indexes. Update will add any new content from the website or file system to the index file. Optimize will remove unnecessary content and make the index file smaller and faster. Regenerate replaces the existing index with a new one.

- *Perform Operations On*—Determine whether you want the chosen operation performed on all indexes (collections) in the search site or only on specified indexes. If you have large indexes, it might be best to create multiple events to update indexes at different times.

After the schedule is configured, the index will be automatically updated at the frequency specified in the schedule.

Managing QuickFinder

The Services settings give the QuickFinder administrator global control over the search services provided by Novell QuickFinder, including the capability to completely disable searching. These pages also control overall performance of the QuickFinder.

Services settings are available from the Global Settings page, as shown in Figure 15.8, organized under the Services Settings heading in the Navigation frame. There are four categories of services settings available for QuickFinder Server.

GENERAL

General service settings define error log and site list settings for all search sites. The General Service Settings page is shown in Figure 15.8.

FIGURE 15.8

The General Service Settings page in QuickFinder Server Manager.

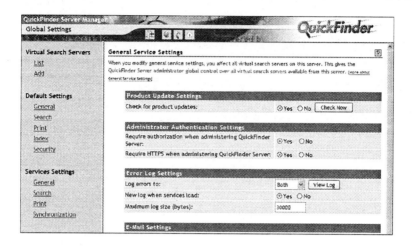

- *Product Update Settings*—In this section, you can arrange to automatically receive notifications of updates to QuickFinder software as they become available.

- *Administrator Authentication Settings*—In this section, you can enable/ disable authentication and secure communications for QuickFinder Server Manager.

- *Error Log Settings*—The following settings let you configure the error log in QuickFinder.

  - *Log Errors To*—Select where you want log results displayed. You can choose to log errors to a file, to the console, or both. Click the View Log button to see the error log directly from QuickFinder Server Manager.

  - *New Log When Services Load*—When set to Yes, this option starts a new log file each time you restart the QuickFinder.

  - *Maximum Log Size (Bytes)*—Limit the size of the log file to the size you specify (in bytes).

- *Email Settings*—These settings allow you to set up email notifications for errors that occur on QuickFinder.

  - *Enable Email Services*—Enables/disables email notifications for QuickFinder. Note that this is a global setting that affects all search sites configured in QuickFinder.

- *Outgoing SMTP Hostname*—Specify the DNS name of the outgoing SMTP mail server.

- *Outgoing SMTP Port #*—Specify the port to which the SMTP mail server is listening. Default—port 25.

- *Outgoing SMTP User ID (conditional)*—If the SMTP server requires authentication, specify a valid user ID for use by QuickFinder here.

- *Outgoing SMTP Password (Conditional)*—If the SMTP server requires authentication, provide the password associated with the user ID provided for use by QuickFinder.

- *Server Management Settings*—The following settings define some general characteristics of the QuickFinder:

  - *Maximum Number of Active Index Jobs*—Limits the number of indexing jobs that can run at the same time. Default is 5.

  - *Default Location of Virtual Search Servers*—Specifies the path where you want all search site files to be stored, including index and configuration files. Changing this setting won't move existing sites to a new location, but all new search sites will be placed here.

  - *Detect Manual Search Server Changes*—When set to Yes, this option directs QuickFinder to reload configuration files that are modified manually, instead of using QuickFinder Server Manager.

  - *Seconds Between Checking for Changes*—Specifies how often QuickFinder will look for manually modified configuration files, in seconds.

  - *Detect Template Changes*—When set to Yes, this option directs QuickFinder to automatically check for modifications to search, print, or error templates used by QuickFinder.

  - *Seconds Between Checking for Template Changes*—Specifies how often QuickFinder should reload search, print, results, and error templates, in seconds. Any changes to templates will be recognized within the time period specified here.

When you are done making changes, click Apply Settings.

SEARCH

The Search service settings let you turn search capabilities on or off and manage debugging and statistics settings. The Search service settings are shown in Figure 15.9.

FIGURE 15.9
The Search Service Settings page in QuickFinder Server Manager.

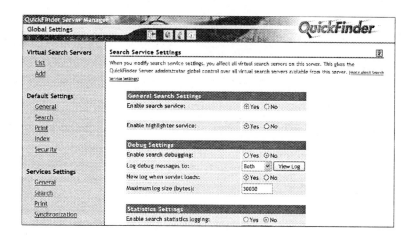

- *General Search Settings*—With these settings, you can enable/disable the primary search features of QuickFinder:

  - *Enable Search Service*—Enables search services for all search sites on the QuickFinder.

  - *Enable Highlighter Service*—This option configures QuickFinder to highlight instances of the search term or phrase within the searched documents.

- *Debug Settings*—With these settings, you can keep a log of all searches and query results going to all search sites. Typically, this option is used only when troubleshooting a problem with a search because the log file can grow very quickly.

  - *Enable Search Debugging*—Enables/disables debugging of searches.

  - *Log Debug Messages To*—Specifies whether debug messages should be logged to a file, to the server console, or both. Server console messages are immediately viewable from the View Log button found on the right of this setting.

  - *New Log When Servlet Loads*—Specifying Yes for this option will restart the debug file whenever QuickFinder is restarted.

  - *Maximum Log Size (Bytes)*—This setting specifies the size of the debug file, in bytes.

- *Statistics Settings*—Search statistics can provide you with information that can help you optimize QuickFinder over time to improve search performance.

  - *Enable Search Statistics Logging*—When set to Yes, this setting generates an updated log file containing statistics about searches performed against all search sites on your QuickFinder.

  - *Seconds Between Statistics Updates*—Specifies the time, in seconds, between updates of the statistics log file.

  - *Log Statistics To*—Specifies whether statistics log messages should be logged to a file, to the server console, or both. Server console messages are viewable from the Tomcat servlet container console screen.

  - *Maximum Log Size (Bytes)*—Specifies the size of the statistics log file, in bytes.

  - *New Log When Servlet Loads*—Specifying Yes will restart the statistics log file whenever QuickFinder is restarted.

  - *Log Error If Search Time Exceeds (Seconds)*—Specifies the timeout, in seconds, before QuickFinder should record the current search as exceeding the specified time limit on the statistics display.

When you are done making changes, click Apply Settings.

PRINT

This page manages Print services and has the same options and parameters described in the Search section. Click Apply Settings to save any changes you make to this page.

SYNCHRONIZATION

QuickFinder Synchronization enables you to manage multiple QuickFinder instances from a single administration interface. Changes made to one server are automatically replicated to the other servers in the cluster. You can also synchronize QuickFinder files across multiple QuickFinder instances, including generated indexes, configuration settings, and search results templates. For more information on using QuickFinder Synchronization, see the OES online documentation.

Managing Search Sites

The default site settings define characteristics for search sites that are created on QuickFinder. Changes to the parameters defined on these pages will be automatically applied to any new search sites that are created, unless overridden through the use of the Advanced Index Definition form.

In this way, you can manage your search sites by exception, rather than by having to define every setting for every site manually when it is created.

Default settings are available from the Global Settings page, as shown in Figure 15.10, organized under the Default Settings heading in the Navigation frame. There are five categories of default site settings, which are detailed in the following sections.

GENERAL

General settings enable you to manage query, response, and error log settings for all newly created search sites. The default general site settings are shown in Figure 15.10.

FIGURE 15.10
Default general settings in QuickFinder Server Manager.

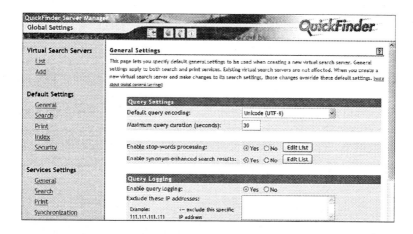

- *Query Settings*—This section enables you to configure general query parameters.

  - *Default Query Encoding*—Specifies an encoding that represents the character set encoding that most of your user queries will use. Default is UTF-8.

  - *Maximum Query Duration (Seconds)*—Specifies the maximum duration of any query, in seconds. Any query that reaches this limit will terminate whether or not the query has actually finished. Default is 30 seconds. This option helps you protect server resources from malicious rogue searches, which are intended to slow site performance by consuming server resources.

- *Enable Stop-Words Processing*—This option instructs QuickFinder to ignore insignificant search words (stop-words), such as articles, conjunctions, or prepositions. A list of common stop-words is configured by default, but you can modify the list by clicking Edit List.

- *Enable Synonym-Enhanced Search Results*—This option lets search users expand their search results to include synonyms of the original search terms. This is kind of like doing a thesaurus search that can help uncover related information using similar, but not identical, words to those being searched for. You can modify the synonym list by clicking Edit List.

- *Query Logging*—In this section you can configure a query log to track how QuickFinder is being used.

  - *Enable Query Logging*—Enables/disables query logging, which captures information about user queries, including total number of searches performed (for the current logging period), top 100 search terms, load statistics, and information about queries that resulted in a Not Found error message. You can use this information to optimize the configuration of your search service to improve performance.

  - *Exclude These IP Addresses*—Here you can specify those IP addresses to exclude from the query log. Separate each address by a space or hard return. This allows you to exclude internal addresses, for example, so you can focus your logs on external search requests.

  - *Log Period*—Specify the length of the log period. At the end of each log period, QuickFinder will start a new log file and automatically generate a report from the old log file.

  - *Email Log Reports*—Specify the email addresses where you want new log reports sent. Separate multiple addresses by a space or hard return. This option will not appear if email services are disabled on your QuickFinder Server. Email services configuration is available from the Global Settings page. Under Services Settings, select General and look for the Email Settings section.

  - *Available Log Reports*—This setting allows you to view previously generated log reports. To do so, select the report you want to view, then click View Report.

  - *Template to Use When Generating Reports*—QuickFinder provides a default log template, `ReportTemplate.html`, to format logs. You can replace the default template with one of your choosing by specifying the filename in this field. You can also specify `ExportTemplate.xml` if you want to export the log file to an external log-analyzing tool.

- *Response Settings*—This section enables you to configure a query log to track who is using QuickFinder.

  - *Default Encoding for Response Pages*—Specifies the encoding QuickFinder will use when responding to user queries with Search and Print Results templates, and Error and Response Messages templates. Default is Unicode (UTF-8).

  - *Refuse Queries If Potential Hits Exceed*—Specifies the maximum effective size of a search for QuickFinder. Use this field to cancel the processing of search results that might take a long time to complete because a large number of hits are being returned. Users should modify their queries in this case.

- *Error Log Settings*—This section configures QuickFinder's error log.

  - *Maximum Log Size (Bytes)*—Specifies the maximum size, in bytes, to which QuickFinder will allow the log file to grow. This protects your server's hard drive resources, particularly on a busy search server.

When you are done making changes, click Apply Settings.

SEARCH

Search default site settings let you turn search capabilities on or off and manage debugging and statistics settings. The Default search settings are shown in Figure 15.11.

FIGURE 15.11
Default search settings in QuickFinder Server Manager.

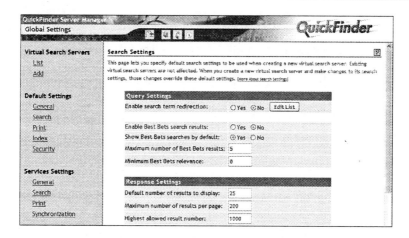

- *Query Settings*—These options enable you to configure some additional features to improve search performance and usability:
  - *Enable Search Term Redirection*—You can set up common search terms to go to a specific URL. For example, the term *programming* might take a user straight to your Developer website.
  - *Enable Best Bets Search Results*—Enables/disables Best Bets. *Best Bets* are common search destinations that can be displayed in addition to a user's specific results. They are generated from a special index just for that purpose.
  - *Show Best Bets Searches by Default*—Enables/disables showing Best Bets by default.
  - *Maximum Number of Best Bets Results*—Specifies the number of Best Bets results to display.
  - *Minimum Best Bets relevance*—You can set a minimum relevance value for Best Bets hits. Documents below this value will not be shown on the Best Bets display.
- *Response Settings*—These options configure the default format for replying to a search request.
  - *Default Number of Results to Display*—Specifies the number of search results that will be displayed on each search results page.
  - *Maximum Number of Results Per Page*—Sets a limit on the number of results allowed on any results page.
  - *Highest Allowed Result Number*—Specifies the maximum number of results that will be returned for any query.
  - *Enable Speller*—Enables/disables automatic spell checking on search terms.
  - *Spell Check If Total Hits Is Below*—Sets the spell checking threshold. QuickFinder's speller automatically detects common errors in users' search terms and suggests alternative spellings if a user query doesn't produce at least the number of hits specified in this field.
  - *Enable Search Terms Highlighter*—Specifies whether the search term highlighter is a default option for search sites configured on this QuickFinder.
- *Template Settings*—Sets basic information about the template used by QuickFinder.

- *Templates Directory*—Specifies the location of the QuickFinder templates files. The default path is `/var/lib/qfsearch/Templates`.

- *Default Encoding for Templates*—Specifies the character set in which your templates are written. This is a default value that will be used with templates that do not specify a specific encoding.

- *Default Search Page Template*—Specifies the name of the search page template file you want to use.

- *Default Search Results Template*—Specifies the name of the search results template file you want to use.

- *Default Highlighter Template*—Specifies the name of the highlighter template file you want to use.

- *Template to Use If No Results Returned*—Specifies the name of the template file to be used if no results are found.

- *Template to Use If Error Occurs*—Specifies the name of the template file to be used if there are errors while processing a query.

When you are done making changes, click Apply Settings.

PRINT

The default print settings let you manage templates for print results and parameters that affect result printing. The Print Settings page is shown in Figure 15.12.

FIGURE 15.12
Default Print Settings in QuickFinder Server Manager.

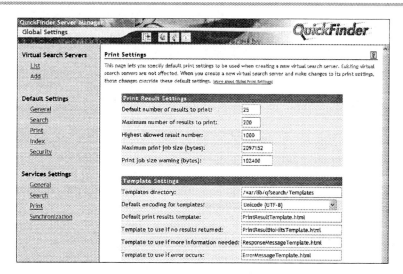

- *Print Result Settings*—These options let you configure some basic print settings for the QuickFinder environment:

  - *Default Number of Results to Print*—Specifies the number of print results that you want displayed on each print results page.

  - *Maximum Number of Results to Print*—Sets a limit on the number of results allowed on any results page.

  - *Highest Allowed Result Number*—Specifies the maximum number of results that will be returned for any query.

  - *Maximum Print Job Size (Bytes)*—Specifies the largest allowable print job size, in bytes. Any request for a print job larger than this value will receive an error message.

  - *Print Job Size Warning (Bytes)*—When a print job exceeds the specified size, in bytes, QuickFinder will send a warning message to the user via the `ResponseMessageTemplate.html` file. It then prompts the user to confirm the print job before continuing.

- *Template Settings*—These settings provide the same type of information described previously in the section on Search settings.

When you are done making changes, click Apply Settings.

INDEX

The index default site settings make the process of creating indexes easier by allowing you to configure common default settings. The Index default site settings are shown in Figure 15.13.

- *General Settings*—These options define the basic default features for indexes used by QuickFinder.

  - *Index Type*—Specifies the default index as either Crawled or File System.

  - *Obey Robots.txt Exclusions When Crawling*—Enable this option to have QuickFinder obey instructions in a Robots file. The `Robots.txt` file allows a website administrator to specify URLs that should not be indexed by a search engine.

  - *Crawl Dynamic URLs (URLs Containing '?')*—Enable this option if you want QuickFinder to crawl and index dynamically generated web pages as well as standard static web pages. Indexes are sometimes less effective with dynamic pages because the content can change at any time.

FIGURE 15.13
Default index settings in QuickFinder Server Manager.

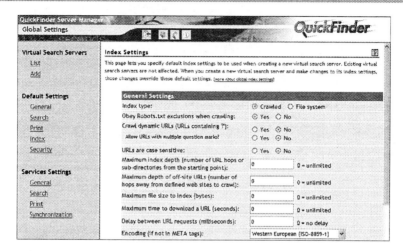

- *URLs Are Case Sensitive*—Check this box if you want QuickFinder to distinguish between URLs that are different only in character case. Leaving this box unchecked can help indexing duplicate information that comes from URLs that use different case but point to the same information.

- *Maximum Index Depth (Number of URL Hops or Sub-Directories from the Starting Point)*—Specifies the maximum number of hypertext links from the starting URL that QuickFinder will follow before it stops indexing.

- *Maximum Depth of Off-Site URLs (number of hops away from defined websites to crawl)*—When QuickFinder encounters an external link as it is indexing a website, this option allows you to specify the number of hops away from the original site to pursue before it stops indexing.

- *Maximum File Size to Index (Bytes)*—Specifies the largest file, in bytes, that QuickFinder will index.

- *Maximum Time to Download a URL (Seconds)*—Specifies the maximum time, in seconds, that QuickFinder will attempt to download a URL before it bypasses indexing of that URL.

- *Delay Between URL Requests (Milliseconds)*—Specifies the amount of time QuickFinder should pause between requests for URLs that it is trying to index.

- *Encoding (If Not in META Tags)*—Specifies the encoding to be used when indexing files that do not contain an encoding specification. Usually, HTML files will specify their encoding with a Content-Type META tag.

- *Synchronization Settings*—Enable this option if you want this index to be copied to other QuickFinder instances in the synchronization cluster.

- *Rights-Based Search Results*—These options let you restrict the ability to search sites with sensitive information. If users have rights to the restricted directory, they can perform a search against that data. If not, their request is denied.

  - *Authorization Checking*—To enable rights-based searches, select By Index and specify the file to be used in verifying user access. Make sure you assign the appropriate user rights to that file as only users with Read access to the file will be able to access the index.

  - *Unauthorized Hits Filtered By*—Specify how unauthorized search requests are handled. Selecting Engine performs the index search, but will prevent users from seeing any of the restricted results without first logging in. Selecting Template will force users to log in before the index search will be performed.

When you are done making changes, click Apply Settings.

SECURITY

Default security settings manage access to indexed content by requiring users to authenticate to a server before seeing rights-protected search results. The security default site settings are shown in Figure 15.14.

- *Rights-Based Search Results*—With these options, you can configure search results based on the rights granted to the user who is performing the search:

  - *Default Search Contexts*—Specify default context(s) for QuickFinder to search for user information. This way, users have to provide only their common name and not their fully qualified User ID.

  - *Check Authorization by Directory*—Enabling this option tells QuickFinder to speed up the authorization process by allowing a user who has rights to any file in a directory access to all files in that directory. This way, each file doesn't have to be authorized separately.

FIGURE 15.14
Default security settings in QuickFinder Server Manager.

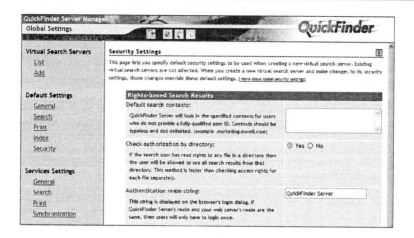

- *Authentication Realm String*—Defines the responsible authentication system accepted by QuickFinder. By default, QuickFinder will perform authentication itself, but you can set the Apache server authentication realm string in this field, so that users who authenticate to the local Apache Web Server won't have to authenticate again when using QuickFinder to search and access protected information.

- *Connection Settings*—These options provide additional security to web searches:

  - *Require HTTPS*—Select Yes if you want to protect usernames and passwords via SSL as they are sent across the network or Internet.

  - *Auto-Logout Time (Minutes)*—Specifies the amount of time, in minutes, that users can be idle before they are logged out of QuickFinder.

When you are done making changes, click Apply Settings.

Novell eGuide

Novell eGuide is a "white pages" application that provides a simple browser-based interface from which your employees can search through your LDAP directory (such as eDirectory) for all the people, places, and things they may need to locate.

eGuide may look like a standard address book, but it is completely platform- and application-independent. It can be accessed by any authorized user via a standard web browser.

You can use eGuide to search multiple LDAP data sources at the same time. This means that you can provide a unified view of data from disparate LDAP sources.

eGuide is also capable of launching secondary applications depending on the type of search a user runs. For example, when users find the people they are looking for, eGuide allows them to launch whatever type of communication fits their current needs—email, instant messaging, and even video conferencing.

Installing eGuide

Novell eGuide can be installed as an optional component during the OES Linux installation, or it can be installed after the fact through YaST.

To install eGuide using YaST, complete the following steps:

1. Access YaST from a terminal using yast, or from a graphical environment using yast2 or the YaST launcher from the application menu.

2. Select the Network Services category in YaST. From within this category, locate and select the eGuide module. This module will detect that the RPMs for eGuide are missing and ask if you want to install them. Select Continue to install the necessary packages.

3. At the conclusion of the software installation, SuSEconfig is executed to update the system configuration. When this completes, the configuration of the OES component will begin automatically.

4. At the eGuide LDAP Server Configuration screen, enter the following information and click Next:

   - *Local or Remote Directory Server*—Select the radio button that indicates whether eDirectory is running on the local server or a remote server.

   - *Directory Server Address*—If a remote eDirectory server is in use, enter the IP address for this server.

   - *Admin Name with Context*—Enter the eDirectory administrator's credentials using fully qualified dot notation, for example, cn=admin.o=novell.

   - *Admin Password*—Enter the password for the administrator user.

   - *Port Details*—If necessary, select this button to change the configured ports for the eDirectory server specified above. The default LDAP port for unencrypted communications is 389 and port 636 is used for SSL-encrypted communications.

5. For eGuide to be active, select to restart Apache and Tomcat when prompted.

When the installation is complete, you are ready to configure eGuide for your particular environment.

Configuring eGuide

Because eGuide is an LDAP client, it targets data and uses data from eDirectory and other LDAP-compliant data sources. To configure eGuide, you must identify the LDAP data source and specify how eGuide will access it. For more information on configuring LDAP with eDirectory, see Chapter 7, "Novell eDirectory Management."

There are three things you should know about your LDAP server configuration prior to configuring eGuide:

- *Does it support Anonymous bind?* Anonymous bind is an LDAP connection that does not contain a username or password. With eDirectory, an Anonymous bind provides access rights as `[Public]`. Because `[Public]` cannot browse object attributes, this is typically too restrictive for eGuide use. However, you can grant `[Public]` restricted attribute browse rights, suitable for the basic eGuide searches you want to allow in this case. For information on granting eDirectory rights, see Chapter 7.

WARNING

Granting rights to [Public] will, because of inheritance rules, grant those same rights to all eDirectory objects. This can have unintended consequences. A better solution is a Proxy user, described next.

- *Does it provide a Proxy user?* A Proxy user is a predefined user object, configured explicitly to provide the privileges required for an anonymous bind. With eDirectory, a Proxy user gives you the flexibility to offer an anonymous connection without potentially causing security problems by changing `[Public]`. For more information on configuring a Proxy user, see Chapter 7.

- *Does it use Transport Layer Security (TLS)?* You need to know how the LDAP server handles secure connections. eDirectory 8.7 uses TLS, an open-source Secure Socket Layer (SSL) implementation, to secure LDAP connections. For more information on configuring TLS with OES Linux, see Chapter 7. If the LDAP server is configured to use a secure connection, you must enable eGuide to also use a secure connection.

Beyond the LDAP information already noted, users can authenticate using their own eDirectory user object. In this case, each user views objects and attributes through eGuide based upon the effective rights associated with their user object. For more information on configuring and calculating effective rights in eDirectory, see Chapter 8, "Users and Network Security."

With this LDAP information in mind you can move forward with the configuration of eGuide.

Although eGuide is fully configured after an OES installation, it is a good idea to double-check the configuration options prior to allowing user access. To check several important configuration options, complete the following steps:

1. Open the eGuide Administration Utility by appending the eGuide path (/eGuide/admin/index.html) to the IP address or DNS name of the web server where eGuide was installed. For example:

   https://www.quills.com/eGuide/admin/index.html

2. From the Navigation frame, select LDAP Data Source under the Configuration heading. From this screen the default LDAP source can be configured, or a new LDAP source can be added to the eGuide configuration. Selecting Edit for the default data source will provide access to the following configuration items, as shown in Figure 15.15.

FIGURE 15.15
LDAP data source configuration in the eGuide Administration Utility.

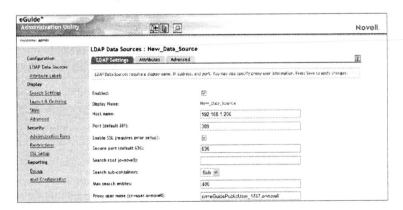

- *Enabled*—Determines whether or not the data source is available to eGuide.

- *Display Name*—Specifies a descriptive name for the LDAP server. The default LDAP source name cannot be changed.

- *Host name*—Specifies the DNS name, or IP address, of the LDAP server hosting the data source.

- *Port*—Specifies the port for LDAP communications. The default LDAP port is 389 and should work unless you have changed the LDAP port on your LDAP server for some reason.

- *Enable SSL*—Select Enable SSL to instruct eGuide to communicate with the LDAP server through a secure TLS connection.

- *Secure Port*—Specifies the port for secure LDAP communications. The default LDAP port is 636 and should work unless you have changed the port on your LDAP server for some reason.

NOTE

TLS imposes a significant performance impact. If eGuide and eDirectory are both running on servers in the same secure domain, you might consider disabling TLS to get better performance.

- *Search Root*—Contains the distinguished name of the container from which searching is allowed. If nothing is entered, the entire tree is searched.

- *Search Sub-Containers*—Determines whether a single level or the entire subtree is searched during eGuide operations.

- *Max Search Entries*—Determines the maximum number of search results returned with each query. This number should not be set higher than 1000.

- *Proxy User Name*—Specifies the eGuide proxy user name to be used for LDAP queries, for example: cn=user,ou=provo,o-quills. If the name is not entered, eGuide uses anonymous credentials (which are translated by eDirectory to be either [Public] rights or the rights assigned to an eDirectory LDAP proxy user).

- *Proxy Password*—Specifies the password for the Proxy user.

- *Authentication Group*—Enables the authentication based on user accounts stored within the directory. For Data Sources not in the Authentication Group, eGuide uses the default proxy credentials.

- *Authentication User Name*—Specifies the LDAP object name that eGuide should use when authenticating users to a Login server. This user must have Read rights to all distinguished names and to the attribute used as the user authentication key within eGuide.

- *Authentication Password*—Specifies the password for the Authentication user name.
- *Authentication Search Root*—Specify the location in the LDAP tree where eGuide should start looking to authenticate users attempting to use the eGuide service.

3. After making changes, click Save to complete the modifications.

When the initial configuration is complete, you can use the eGuide Administration Utility to further configure and customize eGuide. However, this advanced configuration is typically not required to begin to use eGuide. For more information on additional eGuide configuration, see the OES online documentation.

Using eGuide

After you've configured eGuide, accessing it to perform LDAP searches is simple. Open the eGuide search utility by appending "eGuide" to the IP address or DNS name of the web server where eGuide was installed. For example:

`https://www.quills.com/eGuide`

You will be required to authenticate using your regular eDirectory username and password. Upon successful authentication you will see the eGuide search page, as shown in Figure 15.16.

FIGURE 15.16
eGuide Search page.

From this page you can search for any user objects to which you have rights, as defined in eDirectory.

Additional OES Linux Web Services

OES Linux includes several other pieces to the web services puzzle, including MySQL, and scripting support through Perl and PHP. Although an in-depth discussion of these utilities is beyond the scope of this book, a brief introduction to these services and their capabilities is in order.

MySQL

MySQL is an open-source SQL (Structured Query Language) database program. It is easy to install and use, but offers exceptional power, security, and scalability. In fact, because of its small size and speed, it is an ideal platform for delivering database capabilities to your websites—and because it's an open-source application, and free with OES Linux, the potential return on investment (ROI) doesn't get much better.

MySQL runs on a wide variety of operating systems other than Linux, making it ideal for today's heterogeneous network environments. You don't have to learn different database systems just because you have different platforms. MySQL platforms include, in addition to Linux, NetWare, Microsoft Windows NT/2000, Sun Solaris, IBM AIX, FreeBSD, OS/2, and others.

MySQL can be installed during the OES Linux installation, or anytime thereafter through YaST.

Perl and PHP Scripting Support

Common Gateway Interface (CGI) scripting is the most common way for a web server to interact with users. It provides the capability to create dynamic content and increase the sophistication and functionality of your web pages.

In addition to the web application, scripting is also a valuable tool for automating network administrative functions and parsing and generating reports based on network activities. Because of this, Novell offers multiple scripting languages with OES Linux, with the goal of not making you learn yet another coding method in order to get your job done.

The most commonly recognized scripting languages are Perl (Practical Extraction and Report Language) and PHP (Hypertext Preprocessor).

Perl is an open-source language that was originally created specifically to process text. Because of this, it is particularly good at text parsing and report generation. It is also very good at web page generation and task automation.

PHP is a server-side HTML-embedded scripting language. It can be used to create dynamic web pages, collect form data, and receive cookie information. It can also be used for talking to other services through protocols such as IMAP, SNMP, and HTTP. PHP supports a wide range of web servers and databases, but is most commonly used with Apache Web Server and MySQL. This makes it a natural choice for the OES Linux Web services environment.

Both Perl and PHP support for Novell services offered with OES Linux is provided in the Novell Developer Kit (NDK) that is included with OES. For more information on the NDK, see the OES online documentation, and visit http://developer.novell.com/ndk.

PART V

Appendixes

The Most Essential Linux Commands

If you are new to the world of Linux, working on the command line can seem a daunting challenge. Although there is no substitute for a quality training course and in-depth personal practice and experimentation, sometimes simply finding the right command can be the difference between endless suffering and a quick solution to your problem.

To help ease your transition to the Linux world, this appendix has been compiled with some of the more common and important commands used at the terminal. Please keep in mind that this appendix is certainly not intended to provide every command you will likely need in your command-line work, but if you are struggling for that one important command, you may find this guide useful.

With that in mind, these commands have been organized in the following sections:

- Getting Help
- File Management
- Permissions and Identity
- Viewing Files
- Text Processing
- Finding Files and Text
- Regular Expressions
- Environmental Commands

- Working with Processes
- Troubleshooting Tools
- Compression Utilities
- Networking Utilities
- Working with Filesystems
- System Shutdown and Restart

NOTE

This appendix is intended only as an introduction to these utilities. For more information regarding each utility, see the respective man page using man *COMMAND.*

Getting Help

Perhaps the most important tools on the command line are those that you can use to get help. Table A.1 lists a few of these important tools.

TABLE A.1
Using Terminal-Based Help Systems

COMMAND	GENERAL USAGE	DESCRIPTION
apropos	apropos STRING	Searches the NAME field of all manual pages. Same as man -k [string].
info	info [OPTIONS] INFO_PAGE	Displays the information pages for the specified command.
man	man [OPTIONS] MANPAGE	Displays the manual pages for the specified command, configuration file, system call, and so on. Common options include -k [string] Searches NAME field of man pages for specified string
whatis	whatis KEYWORD	Displays the NAME field from the man page for the specified keyword.

File Management

File management tools include those used for navigation and general file and directory manipulation. Refer to Table A.2 for these commands.

TABLE A.2
Filesystem Navigation Commands

COMMAND	GENERAL USAGE	DESCRIPTION
cd	cd DIR	Changes directories.
cp	cp [OPTIONS] SOURCE DEST	Copies files or directories. Common options include -d Copy symbolic links -R Copy directories recursively
ln	ln [OPTIONS] SOURCE TARGET	Creates a link between two files. Common options include -s Create a symbolic, rather than hard, link
ls	ls [OPTIONS] FILE	Lists directory contents. Common options include -a Show all files, including hidden files starting with ".". -A Show almost all files—omit "." and ".." -d List directory entries rather than contents -l Display a long listing of contents, including file mode, ownership, and timestamp -R Perform a recursive listing
pwd	pwd	Prints the path of the current working directory.
mkdir	mkdir [OPTIONS] DIR	Creates the specified directory. Common options include -p Create parent directories if necessary
mv	mv SOURCE DEST	Moves files or directories from one location to another. Also used to rename individual files or directories.
rename	rename FROM TO FILES	Renames multiple files or directories. Example: rename .htm .html *.htm

TABLE A.2
Continued

COMMAND	GENERAL USAGE	DESCRIPTION
rm	rm [OPTIONS] FILE	Removes (deletes) files or directories. Common options include -i Prompt before deletion -r Delete contents of a directory recursively
rmdir	rmdir DIR	Removes empty directories.
touch	touch FILE	Creates an empty file.

Permissions and Identity

Your ability to manipulate files and directories at the command line is directly limited by your identity and the permissions available to that identity. Table A.3 lists commands that can be used to adjust file-level permissions, and commands used to temporarily change your identity.

TABLE A.3
Permissions and Identity Commands

COMMAND	GENERAL USAGE	DESCRIPTION
chgrp	chgrp GROUP FILE	Changes file and directory group ownership.
chmod	chmod [OPTIONS] MODE FILE	Changes access permissions on files and directories on native Linux filesystems.
chown	chown [OPTIONS] OWNER[:GROUP] FILE	Changes file and directory user and group ownership.
su	su [OPTIONS] USERNAME	Substitutes current user credentials with the specified user's identification. Common options include - Causes a complete login process to be performed using the new user identification
sux	sux [OPTIONS] USERNAME	Performs an su to the new user credentials, but also creates an Xauthority file necessary for accessing the local X server.

COMMAND	GENERAL USAGE	DESCRIPTION
		Common options include - Causes a complete login process to be performed using the new user identification
whoami	whoami	Displays current user identification.

Viewing Files

When working on the command line, you will most likely encounter plenty of opportunities for viewing log files, configuration files, or another other type of normal file. Table A.4 lists commands used for this purpose.

TABLE A.4
Commands Used to View Files

COMMAND	GENERAL USAGE	DESCRIPTION
cat	cat FILE	Concatenates files and displays output on standard out (typically the screen).
head	head [OPTIONS] FILE	Displays the first 10 lines of text from the specified file. Common options include -[N] Displays the first N number of lines
less	less FILE	Paging utility used to display text files.
more	more FILE	Paging utility used to display text files.
od	od [OPTIONS] FILE	Displays the specified file in octal mode. Common options include -h Hexadecimal display
strings	strings FILE	Prints text strings four characters long or longer from binary files.
tail	tail [OPTIONS] FILE	Displays the last 10 lines of text from the specified file. Common options include -[N] Displays the last N amount of lines -f Follows an active log file

Text Processing

Manipulating text files can be a time-consuming process if done manually. The commands in Table A.5 are commonly used to manipulate the contents of text files. These commands normally work by outputting the data to standard out (otherwise known as the screen), so to capture these changes, you normally redirect the output to another text file using the greater-than sign (>). For example:

```
sort /etc/passwd > /tmp/users.txt
```

TABLE A.5
Commands Commonly Used to Process Text Files

COMMAND	GENERAL USAGE	DESCRIPTION
expand	expand FILE	Converts tab characters to spaces in the specified file.
joe	joe FILE	Text-editing utility.
nl	nl FILE	Assigns line numbers and displays the specified file.
pr	pr [OPTIONS] FILE	Formats a text file for printing.
sort	sort FILE	Alphabetically sorts and displays the specified file.
unexpand	unexpand FILE	Converts spaces to tab characters in the specified file.
uniq	uniq FILE	Displays all unique lines in the specified file.
vi	vi FILE	Text-editing utility. Use vimtutor for an introduction to this utility.
wc	wc [OPTIONS] FILE	Returns the number of lines, words, and characters in the specified file.

Finding Files and Text

There are several methods for finding files and text within files from a terminal. Table A.6 contains the more common methods used.

TABLE A.6

Commands Used to Find Files and Text Within Files

COMMAND	GENERAL USAGE	DESCRIPTION
egrep	egrep [OPTIONS] PATTERN [FILE]	Searches the contexts of text files for the specified pattern. The pattern specified for egrep must be created using extended regular expressions. Common options include -i Ignore case for searches -r Recursive search for matching files For example: egrep (root|admin) /etc/* Syntax for extended regular expressions is available in Table A.8.
fgrep	fgrep [OPTIONS] PATTERN [FILE]	Searches the contexts of text files for the specified pattern. The pattern specified for fgrep will be interpreted literally and not translated as a regular expression. This allows for searching on such things as wildcard characters (*, ?). Common options include -i Ignore case for searches -r Recursive search for matching files For example: fgrep '*/15' /etc/crontab
find	find [PATH] EXPRESSION	Searches a directory structure for a specific file or files matching the specified expression. Common expression options include -name File name search -type File type search -uid File owner UID search For example: find /etc -name pass
grep	grep [OPTIONS] PATTERN [FILE]	Searches the contexts of text files for the specified pattern. The pattern specified for grep must be created using common regular expressions. Common options include -i Ignore case for searches -r Recursive search for matching files

TABLE A.6
Continued

COMMAND	GENERAL USAGE	DESCRIPTION
		For example: grep ^root /etc/* Syntax for common regular expressions is available in Table A.7.
locate	locate PATTERN	Searches the locatedb database for all instances of the specified pattern. Using locate is typically faster than find for filesystem-wide searches. However, unless updatedb is used to update the locatedb database, new files will not be contained in the database.
updatedb	updatedb	Scans the local filesystem and ensures that all filenames are contained in the locatedb database.
whereis	whereis NAME	Locates the binary, source code, and manual pages for the specified command.
which	which NAME	Searches your PATH for the specified command and returns the location of the first instance of that command.

Regular Expressions

Searching for text within files requires the use of regular expressions. Regular expressions can be either common regular expressions or extended regular expressions. An introduction to both types of expressions can be seen in Tables A.7 and A.8.

Not all utilities recognize both types of regular expressions, so be sure you are using the correct form for whatever utility you are using.

TABLE A.7

Common Regular Expressions

COMMAND	EXAMPLE	DESCRIPTION
.	**test.** matches `test1`, `test2`, `test3`	Matches any single character.
*	**test*** matches `test`, `testt`, `testtt`	Matches zero or more occurrences of the preceding character.
^	**^test** matches any line containing `test` as the first word	Matches the following characters if they are found at the beginning of a line.
$	**test$** matches any line containing `test` as the final word	Matches the preceding characters if they are found at the end of a line.
\	**test\$** matches `test$`	Used to escape metacharacters used in other regular expressions.
[...]	**test[1234]** matches `test1`, `test2`, `test3`, and `test4` **test[1-4]** also produces the same results	Matches one character in the specified range of possible characters.
[^...]	**test[^1234]** matches `test5`, `test6`, `test7`, and so on. **test[^1-4]** also produces the same results	Matches one character not found in the specified range of characters.

TABLE A.8

Extended Regular Expressions

COMMAND	EXAMPLE	DESCRIPTION
?	**test?** matches `tes`, `test`	Matches zero or one occurrences of the previous character.
+	**test+** matches `test`, `testt`, `testtt`	Matches one or more occurrences of the previous character.
{}	**test{2}** matches `testt` **test{1,4}** matches `test`, `testt`, `testtt`, `testttt`	Matches the specified number of occurrences of the previous character. Two numbers separated by a comma are used to specify a range of numbers.
(...|...)	**(From|Subject)** matches the word From or Subject. **Th(ey|eir)** matches the word They or Their.	Matches either of two sets of characters.

Environmental Commands

The environment of your terminal is based on a number of factors, such as what shell you are running, and what customizations you have performed. In-depth customization of your shell is quite complex, and entire books are devoted to the subject. Table A.9 lists a few of the common ways to adjust your working environment.

TABLE A.9
Environmental Commands

COMMAND	GENERAL USAGE	DESCRIPTION
alias	alias NAME=VALUE	Constructs an alias used to execute custom commands. (When no parameters are specified, current aliases are displayed.) For example: alias ll='ls -l'
echo	echo TEXT	Displays the line of text entered as a parameter. (Commonly used in shell scripts.)
env	env	Displays exported environment variables.
export	export VARIABLE	Exports the specified variable for use in subsequent subshells or command environments.
set	set	Displays environment variables and shell functions.
unset	unset VARIABLE	Removes an environment variable from memory.

Working with Processes

Interacting with user-level and system-level processes is an important aspect of administering Linux. Table A.10 identifies many of the tools used for this purpose.

TABLE A.10

Commands for Working with Processes

COMMAND	GENERAL USAGE	DESCRIPTION
`at`	`at TIME COMMAND`	Executes a one-time command at the specified time.
`bg`	`bg %JOB`	Sends the specified job number to the background. Note: Pressing Ctrl+Z will suspend the current foreground process. After the process has been suspended, it can be moved to the background using bg. To start a process in the background, append an ampersand (&) to the end of the command. For example: `updatedb &`

`crontab`	`crontab [OPTIONS] USERNAME`	Used to adjust or view a user's `crontab`. User `crontab`s contain commands scheduled for execution on a regular basis.
		Common options include
		`-e` Edit user's `crontab`
		`-l` List user's `crontab`

`fg`	`fg %JOB`	Brings the specified job number to the foreground.
`jobs`	`jobs`	Displays job numbers for all background processes.
`kill`	`kill [SIGNAL] PID`	Sends a `kill` signal to the specified process. Common `kill` signals are `SIGHUP (1)` Hang-up `SIGINT (2)` Interrupt `SIGTERM (15)` Terminate (default) `SIGKILL (9)` Absolute kill
`killall`	`killall [SIGNAL] PROCESS`	Sends the specified `kill` signal to all processes using the designated process name.
`nice`	`nice VALUE COMMAND`	Executes the specified command using a manually designated `nice` value. Possible `nice` values range from -20 to +19. The lower the value, the higher the process priority.

TABLE A.10
Continued

COMMAND	GENERAL USAGE	DESCRIPTION
nohup	nohup COMMAND	Executes the specified command in a no-hangup mode. This allows the process to continue execution after the initiating shell has been exited.
ps	ps [OPTIONS]	Displays information regarding running processes. Information displayed includes such things as the Process ID (PID), Parent Process ID (PPID), command line, and owner. Common options include -A All processes -f Full option listing
pstree	pstree	Displays running processes in a hierarchical format—including parent and child relationships.
renice	renice VALUE PID	Adjusts the nice value of a currently running process.
top	top	Displays statistical information regarding processes (memory allocation, priority, CPU utilization).

Troubleshooting Tools

Troubleshooting any operating system can involve a whole suite of specialized software. However, sometimes you just need a quick tool to report specific aspects of your computer. Table A.11 contains some of these utilities found in Linux environments.

TABLE A.11
Common Troubleshooting Tools

COMMAND	GENERAL USAGE	DESCRIPTION
dmesg	dmesg	Displays the kernel ring buffer.
free	free	Displays the amount of free and used memory on the system.
hwinfo	hwinfo	Queries and displays detected hardware.

COMMAND	GENERAL USAGE	DESCRIPTION
iostat	iostat [OPTIONS] INTERVAL COUNT	Displays CPU statistics and input/output statistics on block devices (hard disks). Common options include -d Print device utilization -t Print time for each report -x Print extended statistics
lsof	lsof [OPTIONS]	Lists currently open files. Common options include -b Find open files on the specified filesystem mount point
ltrace	ltrace [OPTIONS] COMMAND	Traces library calls made by a process. Common options include -c Count time and calls, and return a summary upon completion -p Used to attach to a running process
sitar	sitar	Comprehensive reporting tool used to generate a report documenting the entire running environment. The report file can be located in the /tmp/sitar-<SERVER-NAME> directory.
strace	strace [OPTIONS] COMMAND	Traces system calls and signals made by a process. Common options include -c Count time and calls, and return a summary upon completion -p Used to attach to a running process
uname	uname [OPTIONS]	Displays kernel version information.
vmstat	vmstat	Displays virtual memory statistics.

Compression Utilities

Compression utilities are a necessity in a Linux environment. Table A.12 contains a list of the main tools used in compression tasks.

TABLE A.12
Compression Utilities

COMMAND	GENERAL USAGE	DESCRIPTION
gzip	gzip FILE	Utility used to compress files. (Commonly used to compress tar archives.) Files compressed with gzip usually have a .gz extension.
gunzip	gunzip FILE.gz	Utility used to uncompress gzip files. (Same as gzip -d.)
bzip2	bzip2 FILE	Utility used to compress files. (Utilizes a different algorithm than gzip. Also used to compress tar archives.) Files compressed with bzip2 usually have a .bz2 extension.
bunzip2	bunzip2 FILE.bz2	Utility used to uncompress bzip2 files. (Same as bzip2 -d.)

Networking Utilities

Most networking utilities are somewhat standard across operating systems. Table A.13 contains the most commonly used Linux networking utilities.

TABLE A.13
Networking Utilities

COMMAND	GENERAL USAGE	DESCRIPTION
dig	dig HOST	Utility used to look up DNS information for the specified host.
ftp	ftp HOST	File Transfer Protocol client utility used to transfer files to and from FTP servers.
ifconfig	ifconfig [OPTIONS]	Utility used to display and configure network interface cards. Common options include -a Display all configured devices
ifdown	ifdown INTERFACE	Script used to stop the specified network interface card.

COMMAND	GENERAL USAGE	DESCRIPTION
ifup	ifup INTERFACE	Script used to start the specified network interface card.
netstat	netstat [OPTIONS]	Displays network statistics. Common options include -r Show routing table -n Do not resolve host names -s Display network statistics
ping	ping HOST	Utility used to test network connectivity using ICMP packets directed to the specified host.
route	route	Displays or modifies the current IP routing table.
ssh	ssh HOST	Secure shell client used to open a terminal session on a remote SSH server.
tar	tar [OPTIONS] FILE	Tape or disk archive utility used to combine multiple files into one single archive. Common options include -c Create new archive -t Test archive -x Extract archive contents -z Create archive using gzip compression -j Create archive using bzip2 compression
telnet	telnet HOST	Insecure method used to open a terminal session on a remote server.
traceroute	traceroute HOST	Utility used to test network connectivity and trace paths used to reach remote hosts.

Working with Filesystems

The majority of your filesystem-level tasks can be accomplished from directly within YaST. If necessary, these same tasks can be accomplished from the command line using the tools in Table A.14.

TABLE A.14
Commands Used to Create and Manage Filesystems

COMMAND	GENERAL USAGE	DESCRIPTION
df	df [OPTIONS]	Displays disk usage statistics for all mounted filesystems. Common options include -h Return output in human readable form
du	du [OPTIONS] [PATH]	Displays disk usage statistics for the specified path. Common options include -h Return output in human readable form -s Provide a summary of the specified directory
fdisk	fdisk DEVICE	Used to modify the partition table for fixed disks.
fsck	fsck [OPTIONS] PARTITION	Utility used to check and repair a Linux filesystem. This utility should be used with care and after ensuring that appropriate backup measures have been taken. Common options include -a Automatically repair the filesystem -r Interactively perform the repair operation -V Produce verbose output of the operation For information on advanced repair options for fsck, including filesystem-specific options, see man fsck.
fuser	fuser [OPTIONS] PATH	Used to identify users or processes currently using a specific filesystem. Common options include -u Display user ids
mkfs	mkfs [OPTIONS] PARTITION	Formats a partition with the specified filesystem type.
mount	mount [OPTIONS] DEVICE MOUNT_POINT	Associates the specified device with a directory in the root filesystem structure. This is used to gain access to hard disk partitions and physical devices such as CD-ROMs.

COMMAND	GENERAL USAGE	DESCRIPTION
		Common options include -t Filesystem type (ext2, reiserfs, iso9660, and so on) -o Filesystem-specific options (For information on filesystem-specific mount options, see man mount.)
umount	umount MOUNT_POINT	Unmounts the device currently mounted at the specified directory.

System Shutdown and Restart

Although it's not often necessary, you may find a reason to occasionally restart or shut down your server. Table A.15 contains these commands.

TABLE A.15
Commands for Changing the State of the System

COMMAND	GENERAL USAGE	DESCRIPTION
halt	halt	Shuts down the computer.
init	init [RUNLEVEL]	Changes the current runlevel to the specified runlevel. Possible runlevels are 0 System halt 1,S,s Single-user mode 2 Local multiuser, minimal networking 3 Full multiuser with networking 4 Not used 5 Full multiuser with networking and graphical environment 6 System reboot
reboot	reboot	Restarts the computer.
runlevel	runlevel	Displays previous and current runlevel. (If the previous runlevel is N, runlevel has not been switched since startup.)

TABLE A.15
Continued

COMMAND	GENERAL USAGE	DESCRIPTION
shutdown	shutdown [OPTIONS] time	Used to shut down or restart a Linux machine. Common options include -h Halt, or shut down computer -r Reboot computer For example: shutdown -h now

eDirectory Reference Materials

eDirectory is an extremely complex environment. Fortunately, it is largely self-sufficient. Most of the day-to-day tasks of maintaining and protecting directory data are handled automatically and transparently. Not only does eDirectory have many built-in integrity features, but it also employs several background processes that keep the directory environment stable and healthy.

eDirectory Background Processes

This section provides a look at the main background processes that do all the heavy lifting associated with eDirectory operations. These processes are

- Database initialization
- Flat cleaner
- Janitor
- Replica sync
- Replica purger
- Limber
- Backlinker
- Schema sync
- Time sync

When you use the various eDirectory monitoring and repair tools, of which some were discussed in Chapter 7, "Novell eDirectory Management," and more are discussed later in this appendix, these background processes and their effects are what you monitor and repair. For this reason, it's a good idea to know a little bit about what you are looking at.

Database Initialization

The Database Initialization (DB Init) background process is automatically initiated whenever the file system is mounted on the eDirectory server. It also executes whenever the eDirectory database is opened or when eDirectory is reloaded. DB Init is responsible for

- Verifying the usability of the eDirectory database files on this server

- Scheduling the running of other eDirectory background processes

- Initializing the various global variables and data structures used by eDirectory

- Opening the eDirectory database files for use by the version of eDirectory running on this server

DSTrace provides the capability to monitor the DB Init process directly.

Flat Cleaner

The Flat Cleaner background process is used to eliminate eDirectory variables and attributes that are no longer needed by the database. Flat Cleaner is responsible for

- Eliminating unused bindery and external reference (X-ref) objects and/or attributes.

- Making sure that each of the objects in a partition replica maintained on this server has a valid public key attribute.

- Eliminating X-ref obituaries that have been set as purgeable.

- Making sure that the Server objects in partition replicas hosted on this server have maintained accurate Status and Version attributes. The Server object maintains an attribute that specifies server status—up, down, initializing, and so on. It also keeps a record of the version of eDirectory running on that server.

Flat Cleaner can be indirectly monitored through the use of Check External References in DSRepair. DSTrace also provides the capability to monitor the Janitor process directly.

Janitor

As its name implies, the Janitor process is responsible for routine cleanup of the eDirectory environment. Janitor is responsible for

- Monitoring the value of the NCP status attribute maintained in the eDirectory Server object for this server.

- Keeping track of the [Root]-most partition replica on the server and the overall replica depth of the server. The [Root]-most partition is the partition root object highest in the tree (closest to [Root]). *Replica depth* describes how many levels down from [Root] the highest partition replica hosted by that server is.

- Executing the Flat Cleaner process at regular intervals.

- Optimizing the eDirectory database at regular intervals.

- Reporting synthetic time use by a partition replica on the server. Synthetic time occurs when a server clock set to a future time is reset to the correct time. Any eDirectory changes made while the clock was set at the future time will bear incorrect timestamps. This problem will self-correct as long as the gap between current and synthetic time is not too large.

- Making sure the inherited rights for each partition root object on this server are properly maintained.

Like Flat Cleaner, Janitor can be monitored indirectly by examining the Replica Ring repair options, Time Synchronization status, and Replica Synchronization status operations with DSRepair. DSTrace also provides the ability to monitor the Janitor process directly.

Replica Sync

The Replica Synchronization background process is responsible for two primary tasks:

- Distributing modifications to eDirectory objects contained within partition replicas maintained by the eDirectory server

- Receiving and processing partition operations involving partition replicas hosted by the eDirectory server

DSRepair can report the status of the replica synchronization process from a number of different perspectives:

- Synchronization status
- Synchronization status of all servers
- Synchronization status on the selected server

DSTrace also provides the ability to monitor the Replica Synchronization process directly.

Replica Purger

Replica Sync schedules the execution of the Replica Purger background process. It is responsible for

- Purging any unused objects and/or attributes that exist in eDirectory partition replicas hosted on this server
- Processing obituaries for objects maintained within partition replicas hosted on this server

DSTrace also provides the ability to monitor the Replica Purger process directly, commonly referred to as *Skulker*.

Limber

After questioning several sources, it is still unclear to me why this process is named Limber, so that will remain a mystery for now. However, naming issues aside, Limber is responsible for

- Making sure that the eDirectory referral information for this server is properly maintained in each partition hosted on this server.
- Making sure that the server hosting the Master replica of the partition in which the Server object for this server resides has the correct Relative Distinguished Name (RDN) for this server. The RDN identifies a target eDirectory object's context in relation to the context of the source eDirectory object. For example, the Admin object in O = Quills would receive the following RDN for CN = jharris.OU = Education.OU = Provo.O = Quills: jharris.Education.Provo. The O = Quills is assumed from the location of the Admin object itself.
- Making sure the server object in eDirectory correctly reflects the operating system version and network address in use on this server.
- Making sure the name of the eDirectory tree in which this server resides is correctly reported.

- Monitoring the external reference/DRL links between this server and the partition replica that holds this server's eDirectory Server object. This is done to make sure that the eDirectory server can be properly accessed via its eDirectory object.

- Making sure this server's identification information is correct.

Limber can be monitored indirectly through Check External Reference, Report Synchronization Status, and Replica Ring repair options in DSRepair. DSTrace also provides the ability to monitor Limber directly.

Backlinker

The Backlinker background process helps maintain referential integrity within the eDirectory environment. Backlinker is responsible for

- Making sure that all external references (X-refs) maintained by this server are still required.

- Making sure that each X-ref is properly backlinked to a server that hosts a partition replica that holds the eDirectory object specified in the X-ref.

- Eliminating X-refs that are no longer necessary. As part of doing this, the server hosting the partition replica that holds the referenced eDirectory object is notified of the elimination of the X-ref.

Backlinker can be monitored indirectly through Check External References in DSRepair. DSTrace also provides the ability to monitor Backlinker directly.

Schema Sync

The Schema Sync background process is responsible for synchronizing the schema updates received by this server with other eDirectory servers. DSTrace also provides the ability to monitor Schema Synchronization directly.

Time Sync

Although Time Sync is not an eDirectory process, it is necessary in order to perform some partition operations such as moves and merges. The underlying time sync mechanism is not important as long as the eDirectory servers are, in fact, synchronized. However, with OES Linux, time synchronization is normally achieved with the xntp daemon. Time Sync can be monitored directly through the Time Synchronization option in DSRepair.

DSTrace **with iMonitor**

Now that you have been introduced to the most common eDirectory processes, it's important that you know how to keep track of the health and general operation of those processes. To do this you can use iMonitor. iMonitor is presented in Chapter 5, "OES Management Tools," as one of the principal management tools for OES Linux. However, this section focuses on the iMonitor options for monitoring eDirectory processes and activities. Refer to Chapter 5 for information on iMonitor installation, general interface, and additional capabilities. For detailed feature information, see the OES Linux online documentation.

iMonitor is a web-based replacement for several of the console-based management utilities used with previous versions of NetWare, including DSBrowse, DSTrace, and DSDiag. Because the eDirectory processes discussed previously run on each eDirectory server, iMonitor provides a server-level view of eDirectory health as opposed to a tree-level view. You can view the health of processes running only on the server from which you are running iMonitor. To view another server, launch iMonitor from that server.

Prior to using DSTrace from iMonitor, you must configure the utility and specify the activity that you want to monitor. This is accomplished from the Trace Configuration page, shown in Figure B.1.

FIGURE B.1
Trace Configuration page in iMonitor.

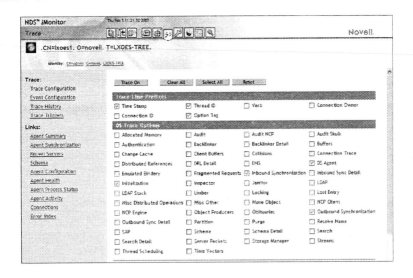

When you go into Trace Configuration, you will see four new links in the left navigation frame:

- *Trace Configuration*—This is the default view you will see when entering the Trace Configuration page. From this page, you can define the server-based eDirectory events and processes that you want to trace. The following configuration options are available from this page:

  - *Trace On/Off*—Enables/disables DSTrace monitoring. When DSTrace is enabled, you will see a Trace button (big lightning bolt) in iMonitor's header frame that you can use to view the active trace (see Figure B.2).

NOTE

DSTrace can increase CPU utilization significantly and reduce performance, so you should trace only when you are actively looking for something, and not as a standard practice.

  - *Update*—Applies new configuration options to an existing trace.
  - *Trace Line Prefixes*—These options let you specify what type of descriptive information to include with each trace line. These prefixes allow you to identify event sequence, group related messages together, and determine how long ago a problem occurred. This can be critical when analyzing DSTrace data, particularly historical trace data.
  - *DSTrace Options*—Specifies the eDirectory activities that you want to trace for this particular eDirectory server. In order to control the amount of data that you will have to sift through in DSTrace, it's best to restrict tracing to only those specific events that are of interest instead of tracing everything. Table B.1 provides a brief description of many of the common trace options.

- *Event Configuration*—This link provides a view similar to Trace Configuration, but it lets you select eDirectory events that you want to trace. eDirectory events include such things as adding/deleting objects, modifying attributes, and changing a password. The same configuration options described for Trace Configuration are available for Event Configuration, except that instead of listing DSTrace options, DS Events are listed.

- *Trace History*—From this page you can view a list of previous traces. A timestamp indicating the period of time during which the trace was gathered identifies each trace.

FIGURE B.2

Active DSTrace view in iMonitor.

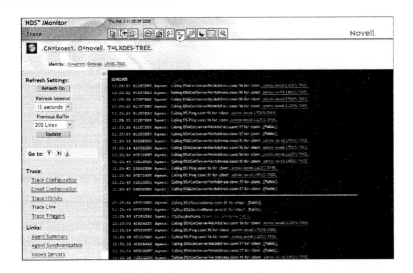

- *Trace Triggers*—This page lists some common DS Agent activities and identifies the DSTrace options that must be selected in order to trace that type of DS Agent activity. Selecting trigger options and clicking Submit will add those DSTrace options to the list of active DSTrace options, if they are not already active.

TABLE B.1

Common DSTrace Options

OPTION NAME	OPTION TAG	DESCRIPTION
Allocated Memory	ALOC	Trace messages related to allocation of memory for eDirectory processes.
Audit	AUMN	Trace messages related to the eDirectory audit process.
Audit NCP	AUNC	Trace Audit NCP (NetWare Core Protocol) events.
Audit Skulk	AUSK	Trace audit messages related to the replica sync process.
Authentication	AUTH	Trace messages related to eDirectory authentication events.

OPTION NAME	OPTION TAG	DESCRIPTION
Backlinker	BLNK	Trace messages related to the Backlink process.
Buffers	ABUF	Trace messages related to allocation of inbound and outbound packet buffers related to eDirectory requests.
Change Cache	CHNG	Trace messages related to the changing of the eDirectory memory cache.
Client Buffers	CBUF	Events related to memory buffers maintained for client connections.
Collisions	COLL	Trace messages related to the receipt of duplicate update packets. These duplicate packets usually occur on very busy networks.
DirXML	DMXL	Trace messages related to Identity Manager (DirXML).
DirXML Drivers	DVRS	Trace messages related to driver operations within Identity Manager (DirXML).
Distributed References	DRLK	Trace messages related to Distributed Reference Link operations.
DNS	DNSV	Trace messages related to Domain Name Service requests.
DS Agent	AREQ	Trace messages related to general eDirectory agent activities on this server.
Emulated Bindery	BEMU	Trace messages related to Bindery Emulation.
Fragmented Requests	FRAG	Trace messages related to the packet fragmenter that breaks up eDirectory messages for transmission in multiple packets.
HTTP Stack	HTTP	Trace messages related to the HTTP stack used by eDirectory.
Inbound Synchronization	SYNC	Trace messages related to incoming eDirectory synchronization requests.
Initialization	INIT	Trace messages related to the opening of the local eDirectory database.

TABLE B.1
Continued

OPTION NAME	OPTION TAG	DESCRIPTION
Inspector	INSP	Messages related to the Inspector process. Inspector is part of the Janitor that verifies the structural integrity of the eDirectory database.
Janitor	JNTR	Trace Janitor messages. The Janitor cleans up eDirectory by removing objects that are no longer needed.
LDAP	LDAP	Trace messages related to LDAP communications.
LDAP Stack	LSTK	Trace messages related to the memory stack associated with LDAP operations.
Limber	LMBR	Trace Limber messages. The Limber monitors connectivity between all replicas.
Locking	LOCK	Trace messages related to manipulation of the local eDirectory database locks.
Lost Entry	LOST	Trace messages related to obituaries, eDirectory attributes, and stream files.
Move Object	MOVE	Trace messages related to eDirectory object move operations.
NCP Engine	NCPE	Trace messages related to the NCP engine.
Obituaries	OBIT	Trace messages related to the eDirectory obituary, or object deletion, process.
Outbound Synchronization	SKLK	Trace messages related to background replica synchronization.
Partition	PART	Trace partition operations and messages.
Purge	PURG	Trace replica purger messages.
Resolve Name	RSLV	Trace messages related to eDirectory name resolution when traversing the eDirectory tree.
SAP	SADV	Trace messages related to the SAP protocol.

OPTION NAME	OPTION TAG	DESCRIPTION
Schema	SCMA	Trace schema modification and synchronization messages.
Server Packets	SPKT	Trace messages related to server packets.
Streams	STRM	Trace messages related to stream attributes in eDirectory.
Thread Scheduling	THRD	Trace messages related to the management of processor threads used with eDirectory.
Time Vectors	TVEC	Trace messages related to transitive vectors, which describe how caught up the replica is in the synchronization process.
Wanman	WANM	Trace messages related to WAN Traffic Manager.

Although the web-based DSTrace utility within iManager is the recommended method of monitoring eDirectory activity, there is also a command-line version of this utility called ndstrace. This utility is shown in Figure B.3.

FIGURE B.3
The ndstrace console-based utility.

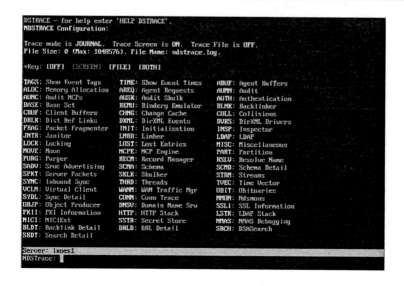

After starting the `ndstrace` utility, you are presented with an `NDSTrace:` prompt. From this prompt, `ndstrace` can be configured to display eDirectory events as they are occurring on the server. Some of the commonly monitored events are described in Table B.1. With the `ndstrace` utility, events are configured using the event tag as listed in the second column of Table B.1.

To enable or disable specific events within `ndstrace`, execute the following command from the utility command prompt:

```
ndstrace +/-[Option Tag]
```

Multiple options can also be specified on the `ndstrace` command line. For example, to enable Inbound Synchronization and disable Obituary messages, execute the following command:

```
ndstrace +SYNC -OBIT
```

For more information on using `ndstrace`, enter **help ndstrace** from the `ndstrace` command prompt, or see the `man` page for `ndstrace`.

Repairing eDirectory with DSRepair

Every database needs a tool for repairing inconsistencies when they occur. `DSRepair` has been serving in this capacity as long as eDirectory has existed. Even though Novell is shifting its focus toward web-based tools, `DSRepair` is still essential for working on your eDirectory on a day-to-day basis. `DSRepair` offers three main groups of features:

- Unattended full repair
- eDirectory monitor operations
- eDirectory repair operations

To load `DSRepair` on your OES Linux server, execute `ndsrepair` at the server console. This utility requires at least one startup switch to determine what operation will be performed. These startup switches can be confusing at first, but the `man` page and utility usage screen are available to help with command syntax. To access the `ndsrepair` utility usage screen, execute **ndsrepair** with the `--help` startup option, as shown in Figure B.4.

All `DSRepair` operations and results can be logged to a file for review. The default log file is `/var/nds/ndsrepair.log`. The `ndsrepair` utility also supports a startup option (-F) used for configuring the name and location of this log file.

The ndsrepair --help screen.

```
lxoes1:~ # ndsrepair —help
Repair utility for Novell eDirectory 8.6 - 8.7.3 v10550.86

ndsrepair - corrects problems in the NDS database
Usage: ndsrepair { -U | -E | -C | -P [-Ad] | -S [-Ad] | -N | -T | -J <entry_id> | —version}
[-F filename] [-A <yes/no>] [-O <yes/no>]
-U Unattended Full Repair option
-R Repair Local Database option
-E Report Synchronization Status option
-C Check External References option
-P Replica and Partition Operations option
-S Global Schema operations
-N Servers Known to this Database
-T Time Synchronization option
-J Repair Single Object
—version Print DSRepair Version Information

-A Append to the existing Log File
-O Log Output to file
-F Log Output to file 'fileName'

By default -A and -O options are set
Press ENTER to continue...
```

The following three sections describe the features available in each of the three main categories of DSRepair operations: Unattended Full Repair, eDirectory Monitor Operations, and eDirectory Repair Operations.

Unattended Full Repair (ndsrepair -U)

The Unattended Full Repair (UFR) is probably the most-used feature in DSRepair—although the huge database sizes now being supported by eDirectory might change that. UFR checks for and repairs most non-critical eDirectory errors in the eDirectory database files of a given server. UFR is activated by executing ndsrepair with a -U startup parameter.

The UFR performs seven primary operations each time it is run, none of which requires any intervention by the administrator. These operations are described in Table B.2. During some of these operations, the local database is locked. UFR builds a temporary set of local database files and runs the repair operations against those files. That way, if a serious problem develops, the original files are still intact. When these operations are complete, a UFR log file will be generated that outlines all the activities that have gone on, errors that were encountered, and other useful information in reviewing the state of your eDirectory environment.

TIP

Rebuilding the operational indexes used by eDirectory is possible only when the local database is locked. Given this, it is good to schedule a locked database repair on a regular basis, even in large eDirectory environments.

TABLE B.2

Operations Performed by Unattended Full Repair

OPERATION	LOCKED?	DESCRIPTION
Database structure and index check	Yes	Reviews the structure and format of database records and indexes. This ensures that no structural corruption has been introduced into the eDirectory environment at the database level.
Rebuild the entire database	Yes	This operation is used to resolve errors found during structure and index checks. It restores proper data structures and re-creates the eDirectory database and index files.
Perform tree structure check	Yes	Examines the links between database records to make sure that each child record has a valid parent. This helps ensure database consistency. Invalid records are marked so that they can be restored from another partition replica during the eDirectory replica synchronization process.
Repair all local replicas	Yes	This operation resolves eDirectory database inconsistencies by checking each object and attribute against schema definitions. It also checks the format of all internal data structures. This operation can also resolve inconsistencies found during the tree structure check by removing invalid records from the database. As a result, all child records linked through the invalid record are marked as orphans. These orphan records are not lost, but this process could potentially generate a large number of errors while the database is being rebuilt. Do not be overly alarmed. This is normal and the orphan objects will be reorganized automatically over the course of replica synchronization.

OPERATION	LOCKED?	DESCRIPTION
Check local references	Yes	Local references are pointers to other objects maintained in the eDirectory database on this server. This operation will evaluate the internal database pointers to make sure that they are pointing to the correct eDirectory objects. If invalid references are found, an error is reported in ndsrepair.log.
Repair network addresses	No	This operation checks server network addresses stored in eDirectory against the values maintained in local SAP or SLP tables to make sure that eDirectory still has accurate information. If a discrepancy is found, eDirectory is updated with the correct information.
Validate stream syntax files	Yes	Stream syntax files, such as login scripts, are stored in a special area of the eDirectory database. Validate stream syntax files checks to make sure that each stream syntax file is associated with a valid eDirectory object. If not, the stream syntax file is deleted.

WARNING

When the local database is locked, no changes are permitted while the operations execute. Some of these operations, when performed on very large eDirectory databases, will take an extended period of time to complete. When working with a large eDirectory database, it is best to schedule these types of operations carefully so as not to disrupt network operations.

DSRepair **Monitor Operations**

DSRepair offers several partition, replica, and server operations that are available to monitor the health of the eDirectory environment. These operations can be performed individually or as groups to help keep eDirectory stable and healthy.

Some of the DSRepair operations described in this section are available only when DSRepair is loaded in advanced mode. This is done by typing the following at the server console:

ndsrepair -P -Ad

The first category of operations can be loosely grouped into monitor operations that are designed to report eDirectory status and health. You will likely perform most of these tasks from iMonitor, but they are still available using the ndsrepair utility. Table B.3 describes the monitor operations available with ndsrepair.

TABLE B.3
DSRepair Monitor Operations

OPERATION	HOW TO ACCESS	DESCRIPTION
Report sync status	ndsrepair -E	Reports the sync status for every partition that hosts a replica on this server.
Report sync status of all servers	ndsrepair -P Select a partition number and then select Report Synchronization Status of all servers	Queries each server hosting a replica of the selected partition and reports the sync status of each replica.
Report sync status on selected server	ndsrepair -P Select a partition number and then select View Replica Ring Select a server number Select Report synchronization status on the selected server	Reports the sync status of the replica hosted by this server for the selected partition.
Report time synchronization	ndsrepair -T	Reports status of time synchronization.
Servers known to this database	ndsrepair -N	Queries the local database and compiles a list of servers known to this database.

DSRepair **Repair Operations**

Although monitoring the condition of the eDirectory database is important, it does little good if there are no tools for repairing inconsistencies when they occur. DSRepair offers several eDirectory repair operations. These repair operations can be organized into three categories:

- Database repair operations
- Partition and replica repair operations
- Global Schema operations
- Other repair operations

DATABASE REPAIR OPERATIONS

All database repair options are accessed using the Repair Local Database option (-R) startup switch with ndsrepair. In addition to that main startup switch, secondary switches may be used to enable or disable specific types of database rebuild operations. An example of using these secondary switches is as follows:

```
ndsrepair -R -t yes -i no
```

Each secondary option used with the -R repair option is explained in Table B.4.

TABLE B.4
DSRepair Database Repair Operations

OPERATION	SECONDARY NDSREPAIR SWITCH (WITH -R)	DESCRIPTION
Lock NDS database during repair	-l <yes/no>	Causes the database to be locked throughout the repair process. This will prevent access to eDirectory from clients, but may be necessary to resolve some database issues.
Use temporary NDS database during repair	-u <yes/no>	Causes the repair process to be performed on a temporary copy of the database. After successful completion of the repair, the new database is copied over the original.
Maintain original unrepaired database	-m <yes/no>	Causes the original database to be backed up prior to the repair.
Perform database structure and index check	-i <yes/no>	Reviews the structure and format of database records and indexes. This ensures that no structural corruption has been introduced into the eDirectory environment at the database level.

TABLE B.4
Continued

OPERATION	SECONDARY NDSREPAIR SWITCH (WITH –R)	DESCRIPTION
Reclaim database free space	-f <yes/no>	This operation searches for unused database records and deletes them to free up disk space.
Rebuild entire database	-d <yes/no>	This operation is used to resolve errors found during structure and index checks. It restores proper data structures and re-creates the eDirectory database and index files.
Perform Tree structure check	-t <yes/no>	Examines the links between database records to make sure that each child record has a valid parent. This helps ensure database consistency. Invalid records are marked so that they can be restored from another partition replica during the eDirectory replica synchronization process.
Rebuild operational schema	-o <yes/no>	This operation rebuilds the base schema classes and attributes needed by eDirectory for basic functionality.
Repair all local replicas	-r <yes/no>	This operation resolves eDirectory database inconsistencies by checking each object and attribute against schema definitions. It also checks the format of all internal data structures. Repairing all local replicas can also resolve inconsistencies found during the tree structure check by removing invalid records from the database. As a result, all child records linked through the invalid record are

OPERATION	SECONDARY NDSREPAIR SWITCH (WITH –R)	DESCRIPTION
		marked as orphans. These orphan records are not lost, but this process could potentially generate a large number of errors while the database is being rebuilt. Do not be overly alarmed. This is normal and the orphan objects will be reorganized automatically over the course of replica synchronization.
Validate stream files	-v <yes/no>	Stream syntax files, such as login scripts, are stored in a special area of the eDirectory database. Validate Stream Syntax Files checks to make sure that each stream syntax file is associated with a valid eDirectory object. If not, the stream syntax file is deleted.
Check local references	-c <yes/no>	Local references are pointers to other objects maintained in the eDirectory database on this file server. Check Local References evaluates the internal database pointers to make sure they are pointing to the correct eDirectory objects. If invalid references are found, an error is reported in ndsrepair.log.

NOTE

Executing ndsrepair –R will automatically cause the following options to be set to Yes: -i, -d, -t, -r, -v, and -c.

PARTITION AND REPLICA REPAIR

In addition to the database repair options, DSRepair offers partition and replica operations designed to keep the distributed eDirectory environment functioning properly. This changes the focus from the local database to the partition—

and all the replicas of that partition stored on servers across the network. To access these operations, execute ndsrepair -P, and then select the partition with which you want to work, as shown in Figure B.5.

FIGURE B.5
DSRepair replica and partition options.

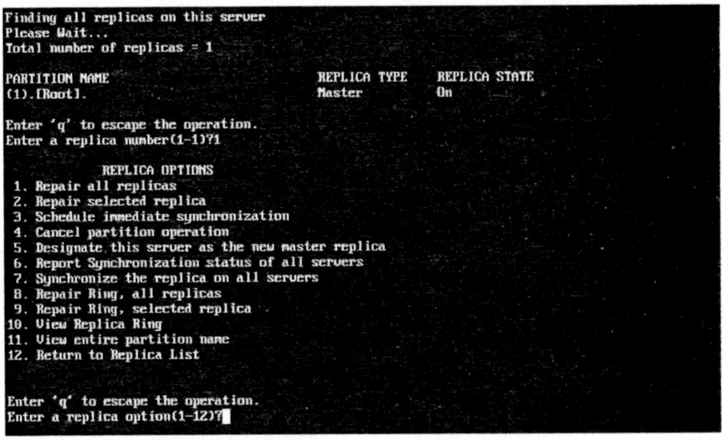

```
Finding all replicas on this server
Please Wait...
Total number of replicas = 1

PARTITION NAME                    REPLICA TYPE    REPLICA STATE
(1).[Root].                       Master          On

Enter 'q' to escape the operation.
Enter a replica number(1-1)?1

              REPLICA OPTIONS
 1. Repair all replicas
 2. Repair selected replica
 3. Schedule immediate synchronization
 4. Cancel partition operation
 5. Designate this server as the new master replica
 6. Report Synchronization status of all servers
 7. Synchronize the replica on all servers
 8. Repair Ring, all replicas
 9. Repair Ring, selected replica
10. View Replica Ring
11. View entire partition name
12. Return to Replica List

Enter 'q' to escape the operation.
Enter a replica option(1-12)?
```

Table B.5 describes the various partition and replica operations available.

TABLE B.5
DSRepair Partition and Replica Operations

OPERATION	DESCRIPTION
Repair ring – all replicas	Performs the replica ring repair operation for each replica ring in which this server participates.
Repair selected replica	Performs a replica repair on the selected replica only.
Schedule immediate synchronization	Initiates a replica synchronization cycle for each partition with a replica hosted on this server. This is useful for forcing the recognition of recent database changes.
Cancel partition operation	Causes the current partition operation (such as a move subtree) to be cancelled. Note: If the operation has progressed too far, it may not be possible to cancel the operation.

OPERATION	DESCRIPTION
Designate this server as new master replica	If the master replica of a given partition is lost due to hardware failure, this operation can be used to designate a new master in order for partition operations to function normally.
Report synchronization status of all servers	Reports the synchronization status for all servers that host a replica of this partition.
Synchronize the replica on all servers	Each server holding a replica of the selected partition is contacted and then a synchronization cycle is initiated.
Repair ring, all replicas	Performs a replica ring repair operation of all replicas on each server in the replica table.
Repair ring – selected replica	Performs a replica ring repair operation of the selected replica on each server in the replica table.
View replica ring	Displays all servers in the current partition replica ring.
View entire partition name	Displays the full distinguished name of the current partition.
Repair time stamps and declare a new epoch	**Advanced option visible with –Ad** Increments the epoch counter and timestamps all objects within the partition. Objects are then synchronized from the Master to all other replica servers.
Destroy the selected replica on this server	**Advanced option visible with –Ad** Removes the selected replica from the server. This option should only be used under the guidance of Novell Technical Support.
Delete unknown leaf objects	**Advanced option visible with –Ad** Deletes all objects in the replica that have an Unknown object class. Use this option only if the objects cannot be deleted through iManager.

Five other replica operations are available by doing the following:

1. Start ndsrepair using the –P startup parameter.
2. Start Select a replica and then choose View Replica Ring.
3. Start Select a server from the list.

These five operations are described in Table B.6.

TABLE B.6
DSRepair Replica Ring Operations

OPERATION	DESCRIPTION
Report synchronization status on the selected server	Reports the synchronization status of the selected partition's replica that is hosted on this server.
Synchronize the replica on the selected server	Causes the replica for the selected partition to begin a synchronization cycle.
Send all objects to every replica in the ring	The operation rebuilds every replica in the ring according to the objects found in this server's replica. Warning: Any changes made to other replicas that have not yet updated to this server will be lost.
Receive all objects from the master to this replica	This operation rebuilds the local replica from object information received from the master replica. Warning: Any changes made to this replica that have not yet updated to the master replica will be lost.
View entire servers name	Displays the distinguished eDirectory name for the specified server.

GLOBAL SCHEMA OPERATIONS

The schema in eDirectory is the set of rules that govern how objects are created and organized within an eDirectory tree. Though not normally necessary, ndsrepair has been provided with schema repair functionality should the local server become out of sync with other servers throughout the tree. To access these operations, start ndsrepair using the -S startup option. As schema operations can have consequences throughout the entire tree, authorization of an administrator is required to perform any of these functions.

Table B.7 describes the schema operations available with ndsrepair.

TABLE B.7
DSRepair Global Schema Operations

OPERATION	DESCRIPTION
Request schema from Master server	Requests the Master replica of the [Root] partition to synchronize schema to the local server.
Reset local schema	Resets the timestamps on the local schema and requests inbound schema synchronization. This operation is not permitted on the Master of [Root].
Post NetWare 5 schema update	Extends the schema for compatibility with Post-NetWare 5 schema changes. This option will only take effect on a server that holds a replica of the [Root] partition. This option should not be necessary on an OES server.
Optional schema enhancements	Extends the containment definitions of schema. This option will only take effect on a server that holds a replica of the [Root] partition. This option should not be necessary on an OES server.
Import schema from Tree	**Advanced option visible with –Ad** This option allows the import of schema from another eDirectory tree.
Declare a new epoch	**Advanced option visible with –Ad** This causes the Master of [Root] to update timestamps on schema and re-synchronize schema throughout the tree. This operation will cause a large amount of network traffic. Warning: If the Master of [Root] contains damaged or incorrect schema, this operation will propagate bad schema throughout the tree. This can cause extreme damage to the objects stored in the tree. This option should only be used under direct supervision of Novell Technical Support.

OTHER REPAIRS

Finally, there are four miscellaneous repair operations that are possible using the `ndsrepair` utility. Table B.8 describes these operations.

TABLE B.8
Other DSRepair Operations

OPERATION	HOW TO ACCESS	DESCRIPTION
Repair all network addresses	`ndsrepair -N` Select any server, and then select Repair all network addresses.	This operation checks server network addresses stored in all Root Partition objects in the tree against the values maintained in local SAP or SLP tables. If a discrepancy is found, eDirectory is updated with the correct information. If no corresponding SAP or SLP entry is found, DSRepair reports an error.
Repair selected server's network addresses	`ndsrepair -N` Select the desired server, and then select Repair selected server's network address.	Same as above, but only the Root Partition objects on the local server are checked.
Check external references	`ndsrepair -C`	External references are pointers to eDirectory objects not stored in partition replicas on this server. Check External References evaluates each reference to an external object to make sure that it is pointing to a valid eDirectory object. The external reference check also verifies the need for all obituaries maintained in the local database. An obituary is used to maintain database consistency while eDirectory is replicating changes such as object moves, deletes, or name changes. If a replica attempts

OPERATION	HOW TO ACCESS	DESCRIPTION
		to reference the changed object using old information because it has not received the replica sync yet, the obituary entry permits it to do so without generating an error. Once all replicas have synchronized with the new information, the Janitor process eliminates the obituary.
Repair single object	ndsrepair -J <EID>	Repairs a single object on the local server. This option requires the Entry ID (in hexadecimal format) of the object that is to be repaired. The Entry ID can be located using iMonitor.

By using the operations described in this section, you will be able to manage most noncatastrophic problems in your eDirectory environment.

DSRepair **Advanced Options**

In addition to the numerous functions described in the previous sections, DSRepair also has some advanced features that are hidden from normal use. These advanced features are enabled through switches when loading the ndsrepair utility. Table B.9 provides an overview of the advanced functionality available on each platform.

WARNING

The features described in this section can—and will—cause irreversible damage to your eDirectory tree if used improperly. These features should only be used only under the guidance of eDirectory professionals, such as the Novell Technical Services team, in order to resolve serious database issues. Always make a full backup of the eDirectory tree before using any of these features on a production tree. If you are going to use these features be sure you understand *all* the consequences before proceeding.

TABLE B.9
Advanced DSRepair Features

SWITCH	DESCRIPTION
-P -Ad	Loads ndsrepair with advanced Partition and Replica options available. After you select a partition, the following additional menu items will be available: Repair timestamps and declare a new epoch Destroy the selected replica on this server Delete unknown leaf objects This switch also allows the Designate This Server as the New Master Replica option to assign a Subordinate Reference as the new Master replica. Be careful!! If you select the View Replica Ring option and select a replica, you will see an additional option on that menu as well: Remove this server from the replica ring
-S -Ad	Loads ndsrepair with advanced schema operations. After entering the admin name and password, you are presented with the following additional menu items: Import schema from Tree Declare a new epoch
-R -Ad -OT	Causes all obituaries to be timestamped. This can resolve issues with obituaries not advancing due to prolonged server outages.
-R -Ad -XK2	Kill all eDirectory objects in this server's eDirectory database. This operation is used only to destroy a corrupt replica that cannot be removed in any other way.
-R -Ad -XK3	Kill all external references in this server's eDirectory database. This operation is used to destroy all external references in a nonfunctioning replica. If the references are the source of the problem, eDirectory can then re-create the references as needed.

These advanced options are seldom used because they are needed for only the most serious of cases. However, it is nice to know they exist when you get into a jam.

It is highly recommended that you work with these switches in a test environment and carefully study the ramifications of these radical operations. Sometimes the cure can be worse than the problem.

eDirectory Errors

There are a wide variety of error codes and conditions that can be reported in your Novell eDirectory environment. Specific information on each error is available in the Novell online documentation. You can also link to error code information from iMonitor by clicking an error from directly within the DSTrace screen. eDirectory error codes are usually displayed in decimal numbers.

NOTE

Because the eDirectory is designed as a loosely consistent database, temporary errors are normal. Don't be alarmed if temporary error conditions come and go as part of normal eDirectory operation. However, if errors persist for a significant period of time, you might need to take some action to resolve the problem.

eDirectory error codes can be categorized as shown in the following subsections.

eDirectory Agent Errors

These are the error codes with which you will typically work when tackling some eDirectory problem. They come in two ranges:

- −601 to −799
- −6001 or higher

The 6001 range is new to recent versions of eDirectory. These error codes identify errors originating in the eDirectory Agent running on your OES Linux server.

Operating System Errors

Certain eDirectory background processes or operations, such as network communications or time synchronization, require the use of functionality provided by the operating system on which eDirectory is running. These functions can return operating-system–specific error codes to eDirectory. These error codes are passed on to the eDirectory process or operation that initiated a request.

Generally, negative numbers identify all eDirectory-generated operating system errors, whereas positive numbers identify all other operating system errors:

- *−1 to −256*—eDirectory-generated operating system errors
- *1 to 255*—Operating system–generated errors

This is an esoteric distinction for your information only. During trouble-shooting, you should treat occurrences of operating system errors with the same number, whether negative or positive, as relating to the same event.

Client Errors

In some cases, an eDirectory server will function as a directory client in order to perform certain background processes or operations. This can result in client-specific error codes being returned to eDirectory background processes and operations. The eDirectory client that is built into ndsd generates these error codes. Client error codes fall in the range of −301 through −399.

Other eDirectory Errors

Some eDirectory background processes and operations require interaction with other daemons running on the OES Linux server. Examples of this include xntpd and the NCP Server. If any of these external processes encounter an error, that error can be passed on to ndsd. Errors in this category utilize codes ranging between −400 and −599.

Where to Go for More Information

Open Enterprise Server for Linux is a very large and complex product. It also includes a large number of services that many traditional Linux or NetWare administrators might not have seen before. Fortunately, Novell products are so popular and widely used that an entire support industry has developed around them. If you are looking for more information about Novell, Open Enterprise Server (for Linux or NetWare), or SUSE Linux, you're in luck. You can go to a variety of places for help.

This appendix points you toward sources of information that will help you:

- Dig further into Novell's vision and strategy
- Find more information on OES Linux configuration and troubleshooting
- Get more information on the new products and services offered with SUSE Linux Enterprise Server

General Novell Product Information

The main Novell information number, 1-800-NETWARE, is your inroad to all types of presales information about Novell or its products.

By calling this number, you can obtain information about Novell products, the locations of your nearest resellers, pricing information, and phone numbers for other Novell programs.

To access the online documentation for any current Novell product, visit Novell's online documentation site:

http://www.novell.com/documentation/

Novell on the Internet

A tremendous amount of information about Novell and SUSE products, both official and unofficial, is available on the Internet. Officially, you can obtain the latest information about Novell and SUSE from Novell's website. Novell also helps support several user forums that deal specifically with SLES, OES, or generally with networking and computers.

Novell's website is

www.novell.com

Novell user forums can be found at

support.novell.com/forums/

These user forums are not managed directly by Novell employees, but offer users access to a wide variety of information and files dealing with SUSE Linux, NetWare, and other Novell products, such as GroupWise. You can receive information such as technical advice from sysops (system operators) and other users, updated files and drivers, and the latest patches and workarounds for known problems in Novell products.

The Novell sites also provide a database of technical information from the Novell Technical Support division, as well as information about programs such as Novell Training classes and Novell Users International (NUI). You can also find marketing and sales information about the various products that Novell produces.

Novell Cool Solutions

Novell Cool Solutions is another way of hooking up with Novell's broad community of users. It offers product reviews, tips and tricks, and the opportunity to share knowledge with Novell users all over the world.

Information is organized by solution set and by product, and there is a lot to see. To check out Novell's Cool Solutions, visit the website:

http://www.novell.com/coolsolutions

Novell AppNotes

Novell's Research Department produces a monthly publication called *Novell AppNotes*. Each issue of AppNotes contains research reports and articles on a wide range of topics. The articles delve into topics such as network design, implementation, administration, and integration. AppNotes are available online:

http://developer.novell.com/research

Novell Connection

Novell Connection magazine is a bimonthly publication devoted to providing the latest and greatest strategy overviews, product reviews, and customer case studies. Novell Connection is written at a higher level than AppNotes, so it is ideal for helping you communicate IT messages to business executives.

Best of all, Novell Connection is available online free! To check out the latest edition of Novell Connection, or check out past issues, visit the website:

http://www.novell.com/connectionmagazine/

Novell Technical Support

If you encounter a problem with your network that you can't solve on your own, there are several places you can go for help:

- Try calling your reseller or consultant.
- Go online, and see if anyone in the online forums or Usenet forums knows about the problem or can offer a solution. The knowledge of the people in those forums is broad and deep. Don't hesitate to take advantage of it, and don't forget to return the favor if you know some tidbit that might help others.
- Call Novell technical support. You might want to reserve this as a last resort, simply because Novell technical support charges a fee for each service request (a service request can involve more than one phone call). The fee depends on the product for which you're requesting support.

When you call technical support, make sure you have all the necessary information ready, such as the versions of SUSE Linux or NetWare and any utility or application you're using, the type of hardware you're using, network or node addresses and hardware settings for any workstations or other machines being affected, and so on. You'll also need a major credit card if you don't already have a technical support contract.

Novell's technical support department also offers online information, technical bulletins, downloadable patches and drivers, and so on. They also offer the Novell Professional Resource Suite (NPRS). The NPRS is a collection of CDs, offered on a subscription basis, that includes the support knowledge base, product evaluation library, and other useful support tools to help you support your Novell environment and plan for the future.

To get in touch with Novell's technical support, or to find out more about Novell's technical support options, visit Novell's support website:

http://support.novell.com

To open a technical support incident call, call 1-800-858-4000.

Novell Ngage

Because of the complexity of many of the modern information solutions offered by Novell, it's not practical to assume that you are going to stay on top of every aspect of your modern network environment. To help you cope, and make the most of your investment in Novell solutions, Novell offers comprehensive, fee-based consulting services, marketed under the brand Novell Ngage, to help you with system planning and design, custom development, and comprehensive solution implementation.

For more information about Novell Ngage services, visit the Ngage website:

http://www.novell.com/ngage/

DeveloperNet: Novell's Developer Support

Developers who create applications designed to run on Linux or NetWare might qualify to join Novell's program for professional developers, called DeveloperNet. Subscription fees for joining DeveloperNet vary, depending on the subscription level and options you choose. If you are a developer, some of the benefits you can receive by joining DeveloperNet are

- Novell development CD-ROMs, which contain development tools you can use to create and test your applications in NetWare environments
- Special prereleases and early access releases of upcoming Novell products
- Special technical support geared specifically toward developers
- Discounts on various events, products, and Novell Press books

For more information, visit Novell's developer website:

http://developer.novell.com

You can also apply for membership or order an SDK by calling 1-800-REDWORD.

Novell Training Classes and Certification

If you are looking for a way to learn about Linux, NetWare, or any other Novell service or product, in a classroom setting, Novell Training offers a variety of options with hands-on labs and knowledgeable instructors. As a pioneer of IT training and certification, Novell has a broad range of training opportunities available. For the most current information on Novell Training courses, certifications and materials, visit the Novell Training website:

http://www.novell.com/training/

Novell classes are taught at more than a thousand Novell Training Service Partners (NTSPs) throughout the world. They are also taught at more than 100 NATPs (Novell Academic Training Partners), which are universities and colleges that teach these courses.

Certification courses offer an excellent way to get some direct, hands-on training in just a few days. Classes are also available in Computer-Based Training (CBT) form, in case you'd rather work through the material at your own pace, on your own workstation, than attend a class.

These classes also help prepare you if you want to become certified as a CNE, signifying that you are a Novell professional.

The Novell CNE program provides a way to ensure that networking professionals meet the necessary criteria to adequately install and manage NetWare networks. To achieve CNE status, you take a series of exams on different aspects of NetWare. In many cases, you might want to take the classes Novell offers through its NTSPs to prepare for the exams, but the classes aren't required.

The classes and exams you take depend somewhat on the level of certification you want to achieve. Although certain core exams are required for all levels, you can also take additional electives to achieve the certification and specialization you want.

The following levels of certification are available:

- *CNA (Certified Novell Administrator)*—This certification is the most basic level. It prepares you to manage your own NetWare network. It does not delve into the more complex and technical aspects of NetWare. If you are relatively new to NetWare, the class offered for this certification is highly recommended.

- *CNE (Certified Novell Engineer)*—This certification level ensures that you can adequately install, manage, and support NetWare networks. While pursuing your CNE certification, you "declare a major," meaning that you choose to specialize in a particular Novell product family. For example, you can become a NetWare 6 CNE or a GroupWise CNE. There are several exams (and corresponding classes) involved in achieving this level of certification.

- *Master CNE*—This certification level allows you to go beyond CNE certification. To get a Master CNE, you declare a "graduate major." You will delve deeper into the integration- and solution-oriented aspects of running a network than you would at the CNE level.

- *CNI (Certified Novell Instructor)*—CNIs are authorized to teach NetWare classes through NTSPs. The tests and classes specific to this level ensure that the individual taking them will be able to adequately teach others how to install and manage NetWare.

- *Certified Linux Professional*—This certification is geared toward IT experts interested in administrating SUSE Linux networks. This is a comprehensive course covering a wide range of Linux concepts. Obtaining this certification requires the successful completion of a hands-on scenario based exam.

- *Certified Linux Engineer*—This certification is an advanced certification for Linux administrators running Novell services under SUSE Linux. This certification requires the successful completion of a hands-on scenario based exam.

- *Certified Directory Engineer*—An elite Novell training program for IT experts using directory-enabled solutions.

- *Specialist Certificates*—These one-course, one-test certificates provide you with the solution-focused training you need to implement Novell products and solutions.

CNEs and Master CNEs qualify for membership in the Network Professional Association (NPA), which is explained later in this appendix.

Novell also offers extensive education courses and certifications based on SUSE Linux. These Linux-specific offerings are all outlined in Appendix A, "The Most Essential Linux Commands."

For more information about Novell Training certifications, classes, and programs, visit the website at

http://www.novell.com/training/

Numerous organizations also provide classes and seminars on Novell products. Some of these unauthorized classes are quite good. Others are probably of lower quality because Novell does not have any control over their course content or instructor qualifications. If you choose an unauthorized provider for your Novell classes, try to talk to others who have taken a class from the provider before, so you'll have a better idea of how good the class is.

Advanced Technical Training

In addition to standard Novell Training courses, Novell also offers highly technical and specialized seminars known as Advanced Technical Training (ATT). ATT is the most advanced training offered by Novell, and covers a wide range of advanced topics including support issues, in-depth architectural reviews, and advanced enterprise solutions. ATT is an excellent way to keep your skills, and those of your IT staff, in top form so that you are able to effectively support emerging technologies and complex network infrastructure solutions. For more information on ATT, visit the website:

http://www.novell.com/training/pep/att/def.html

Novell Users International

Novell Users International (NUI) is a nonprofit association for networking professionals. With more than 250 affiliated groups worldwide, NUI provides a forum for networking professionals to meet face to face, to learn from each other, to trade recommendations, or just to share war stories.

By joining the Novell user group in your area, you can build relationships and network with other Novell professionals in your area, attend regularly scheduled local user group meetings for training, and have access to regional NUI conferences, held in different major cities throughout the year. Best of all, there is usually little or no fee associated with joining an NUI user group.

For more information or to join an NUI user group, visit the NUI website:

http://www.nuinet.com

You can also call 1-800-228-4NUI.

Network Professional Association

If you've achieved, or are working toward, your CNE certification, you might want to join the Network Professional Association (NPA). The NPA is an organization for network computing professionals, including those who have certified as networking professionals in Novell, Microsoft, Cisco, and other manufacturers' products. Its goal is to keep its members current with the latest technology and information in the industry.

If you're a certified CNE, you can join the NPA as a full member. If you've started the certification process, but aren't finished yet, or if you are a CNA, you can join as an associate member (which gives you all the benefits of a full member except for the right to vote in the NPA's elections).

When you join the NPA, you can enjoy the following benefits:

- Local NPA chapters (more than a hundred worldwide) that hold regularly scheduled meetings that include presentations and hands-on demonstrations of the latest technology
- A subscription to *Network Professional Journal*
- Access to NPA Labs that contain up-to-date technology and software for hands-on experience
- Job postings
- NPA's own professional certification programs
- Discounts or free admission to major trade shows and conferences, including NPA's own conferences

For more information on the NPA, visit the website:

http://www.npanet.org

Index

D

I

J - K

O

P

S

YaST